At Full Speed

Hong Kong Cinema in a Borderless World

Esther C. M. Yau, Editor

University of Minnesota Press
Minneapolis   London

Copyright 2001 by the Regents of the University of Minnesota

The University of Minnesota Press gratefully acknowledges permission to reprint the following essays. An earlier and significantly different version of chapter 1, by Law Kar, appeared as "Hong Kong New Wave: Modernization amid Global/Local Counter Cultures," in *Hong Kong New Wave: Twenty Years After* (Hong Kong: Hong Kong Urban Council, Twenty-third Hong Kong International Film Festival, 1999), 44–50. Chapter 3, by David Bordwell, originally appeared as "Aesthetics in Action: Kung Fu, Gunplay, and Cinematic Expressivity," in *Fifty Years of Electric Shadows*, ed. Law Kar, Twenty-first Hong Kong International Film Festival (Hong Kong: Urban Council, 1997), 81–89; reprinted by permission of the Hong Kong International Film Festival and the Provisional Urban Council of Hong Kong. Chapter 8, by Elaine Yee-lin Ho, "Women on the Edges of Hong Kong Modernity: The Films of Ann Hui," originally appeared in *Spaces of Their Own: Women's Public Sphere in Transnational China*, edited by Mayfair Mei-hui Yang (Minneapolis: University of Minnesota Press, 1998), 162–87. Chapter 9, by Rey Chow, originally appeared as "A Souvenir of Love," in *Modern Chinese Literature* 7, no. 2 (Fall 1993): 59–78; reprinted with permission. An earlier version of chapter 11, by Gina Marchetti, originally appeared as "Transnational Cinema, Hybrid Identities, and the Films of Evans Chan," in *Postmodern Culture* 8, no. 2 (January 1998), at http://jefferson.village. virginia.edu/pmc/.

Published by the University of Minnesota Press
111 Third Avenue South, Suite 290
Minneapolis, MN 55401-2520
http://www.upress.umn.edu

Library of Congress Cataloging-in-Publication Data

At full speed : Hong Kong cinema in a borderless world / Esther C. M. Yau, editor.
    p.   cm.
    Includes bibliographical references and index.
  ISBN 0-8166-3234-0 (HC) —
  ISBN 0-8166-3235-9 (PB)
    1. Motion pictures—China—Hong Kong—History.   I. Yau, Ching-Mei Esther.
  PN1993.5.C4 A184   2001
  791.43′095125—dc21   00-011267

Printed in the United States of America on acid-free paper

The University of Minnesota is an equal-opportunity educator and employer.

12 11 10 09 08 07 06 05 04 03 02 01
10 9 8 7 6 5 4 3 2 1

Contents

Acknowledgments

Special thanks to Charles Wolfe, who suggested the project and guided it through its initial stages, and to David James and Marina Heung for their comments and encouragement. Visiting appointments at the University of California, Los Angeles, and the University of California, Irvine, in the year 1997–98 gave me the opportunity to work with colleagues and students who were both enthusiastic and rigorous, and I would like to thank especially Rhona Berenstein, Kyung-hyun Kim, Chungmoo Choi, Rey Chow, Anne Friedberg, Eric Rentschler, Robert Rosen, Vivian Sobchack, Nicholas Browne, and Teshome Gabriel. John Woo and Peter Chan were generous with their time and ideas when they visited my seminars at UCLA. The contributors literally made this volume possible. Law Kar and Li Cheuk-to always share with me their knowledge and rigorous criticisms of Hong Kong films. Alice Chan Chi of the Hong Kong International Film Festival Office facilitated the process of obtaining permissions to use published materials. Micah Kleit supervised the project while he was with the University of Minnesota Press, and Jennifer Moore saw it to completion with patience and wisdom. Robin A. Moir, Pauleen Ma, and Jennifer Peterson capably handled many details in the process.

I would like to dedicate the introductory chapter to the memory of Taiwan's Wang Jie-an, who shared his Marxist cultural criticism and idealism with me at UCLA in 1985. I am thankful for the love and friendship of Paul, Loretta, Hon-ming, Cecilia, Ying, and Peter.

Hong Kong Cinema in a Borderless World

Esther C. M. Yau

Globalization and Hong Kong Movies

Transactions across the terrain of a borderless world have become an economic prerogative in the new millennium. Increasingly, they shape the making of world styles in metropolitan centers. Along with migrant communities, media images, and imported music and arts, Hong Kong movies have become a highly visible component of changing world styles. The products of a world city and a colony lately transformed into China's Special Administrative Region, many Hong Kong movies circulate widely throughout the global cultural marketplace. Through video outlets, cable television, and digital networks, along with theatrical distribution and select festivals, these films have reached locations as distant and disparate as Calcutta, Boston, Berlin, London, New York, and Seoul. Their choreographed action scenes, melodramatic sentiments, poeticized violence, grotesque comic moments, and depressing yet erotic urban imagery furnish a unique cinematic experience for the audiences in these cities. In the cultural spaces already densely occupied by corporate advertising, television imagery, and American(ized) icons, Hong Kong movies and their stars have left some unusual imprints.

In the crossover decades of the twentieth century, exoticism and primitive passions, packaged by tourist images, nature shows, art films, and ethnic goods, have become commonplace or even old-fashioned antidotes for both the tensions and the blandness of modern everyday life. Increasingly, dangerous movements across space, transgressions of norms and good taste, and tweaked, nihilistic visions of the past and the present have become regular screen features to induce odd and new sensations in a young generation of image users. As a leader in this trend, Hong Kong movies deliver a wide range of sensations and an escapism that both stimulate and saturate the imagination by blasting apart a banal contemporary world with unruly talk, fast-paced images of danger, hysterical behavior, and excessive sentiments.   1

Playfully combining generic clichés with easy-to-read emotions and quite un-
thinkable circumstances that are meant to provoke spontaneous responses,
uncontrollable laughter, and bewilderment, the films communicate with
their audiences in a language of detached, borderless enjoyment even as they
make references to local events and conditions. Its high visibility in the
global cultural marketplace, however, has not shielded the Hong Kong film
industry from the local economic crisis or provided better conditions for its
filmmakers to improve on the qualities for which their films have been
known and loved by many for the past two decades.

Hong Kong cinema has made its statements in the global screen culture
with some of the most unbelievable and entertaining moments that have ever
appeared on film. In the midst of billion-dollar media industries, Hong Kong
movies are like small speedboats breaking the waves alongside a daunting
fleet of Hollywood *Titanics*, charging ahead on the basis of their irreverent
imagination, their unique mix of cultural references, and their reinvention of generic elements. Relatively free from obligations of national self-
representation and having for many years now adopted an apparently apolit-
ical stance with regard to the antagonisms between mainland China and
Taiwan, Hong Kong movies do not lock themselves within the old impasses
on issues of national culture. Their accessible language of film genres, drawn
abundantly from Hollywood's and Japan's examples, from old Cantonese
movies, and from popular fiction, frees the contemporary Hong Kong–
Chinese styles from the antiquated seriousness and parochialism found in
earlier works. Instead of displaying Chinese culture in depth, the movies
exude a modern, worldly sensibility that is at once part proletarian and
part bourgeois, both sentimental and rational, and fantasy oriented. This
quality has proven to be the key to their accessibility for many viewers who
are neither knowledgeable about nor interested in the tensions and the paradoxes of Hong Kong as a densely populated city of about 7 million residents;
at the same time, the films' light doses of "Chineseness" can be a panacea for
those seeking alternatives to Hollywood fare and for homesick overseas Asian
audiences. Circulating in the far-reaching networks already established by
immigrant businesses and economic diasporas, Hong Kong movies can appear provincial yet also Hollywood-like; they have become the cultural counterpart of the "cosmopolitan capitalist" undertakings that many Asians, especially ethnic Chinese entrepreneurs, have launched since the nineteenth
century (Hamilton 1999).

The global economy is a highly contested terrain, and the impact of
transnational capitalism continues to be debated around the poignant ques-

tion, "global village or global pillage?" (Jameson and Miyoshi 1998; Brecher and Costello 1998). Yet focusing on the village or the community as it is affected by transnational capital may miss an important point. Not only has the individual computer user become the target of Internet advertising and personal taste the basis for product marketing, but also the subjective realm is interfacing with information technology and mass media. Arjun Appadurai has identified imagination and media literacy as shaping migration and the formation of new ethnoscapes as people negotiate the uneven conditions created by global and regional flows of finance, technology, information, images, and ideas, both within and across national boundaries. Imagination in the era of globalization, moreover, adapts and processes images and forms that are already in circulation (Appadurai 1996). The subjective realm is increasingly articulated through technology and individual consumption, giving rise to the notion of an "economy of desire" (Jameson and Miyoshi 1998; Negri 1999). "When one speaks of globalization," Antonio Negri posits, "one really speaks of it in a double sense: *extensively*, as the global enlargement of the productive fabric through markets; and *intensively*, as the absorption of all social life within capitalist production" (Negri 1999, 83; emphasis in original). In the extensive sense, mobility and interchangeability are key terms for understanding the operations of productive forces and labor power that have been mobilized and absorbed by more-abstract forms of finance capital. In the intensive sense, culture, traditions, and innovation that were once considered "subjective" realms outside of capital are now reconstituted by an economy of desire. With consumption replacing production as the motor for market expansion, "affect" and "sentiment" have become economically viable terms in a postmodern conception of an economy of desire that revises the modernist notion of political economy (Negri 1999, 83–88).

Speed is of prime importance for global access. Cultural productions coming from the major metropolitan centers display an explicit self-consciousness of competitive time, as if they embody the notion that conquest of the vast marketplace can only be possible through fast production and instantaneous dispatches (King 1997; Knox and Taylor 1995). Speed is a particularly relevant concept in describing Hong Kong movies, as many of them follow a fast-paced rhythm in terms of shot length, dialogue duration, bodily movements, and use of multiple ellipses within scenes. Many of the films have been written, shot, and assembled within an extremely truncated time span — as short as seven days in the 1960s and an average of three to five months in the 1980s and 1990s. Almost as a rule, the genres that are successful at the box office become immediately fashionable, are widely imitated and spoofed by inferior quickies, and then, as soon as the genre or type has peaked and the market performance drops, fall out of favor. Individually and collectively, these films are temporal commodities, produced at full speed and consumed hastily, to a far greater degree than the lavish Hollywood product and the films of other national cinemas. The fetishization of speed in Hong Kong cinema anticipates what Paul Virilio calls "the instantaneity of ubiquity" or, simply, media presence in the era of immediate global access (Virilio 1991, 18). Local theatrical exhibitions also follow a tight screening schedule, with short intervals between shows. Even though the practice of skipping over parts of a film (*tou pian*) in order to shorten projection time is infrequent (and a protest against this practice appears in Allen Fong's *Ah Ying* [*Banbian Ren*] [1981]), theaters commonly turn up the full house lights even before the film credits appear so that the audience leaves quickly to make way for that of the next show. Without too much exaggeration, one could say that the speed of cultural production and consumption and the time inscribed in a Hong Kong film are generally in sync with the speed of investment, return, and financial trading that take place elsewhere, in many other world cities. In a rapid-fire manner, a city's forms of social life, along with its signs and stories, are turned into palpable commodities that are quickly consumed and forgotten. Faster individual consumption, however, can hardly catch up with the rate at which mass media overproduce and advance over private space and time. Not only the affect and sentiment themselves but also Negri's economy of desire are pressured to perform in a highly efficient manner. Riding on the winds of change, the mutations of commercial Hong Kong cinema since 1980 have foretold a new narrative of globalization: that of speed, or the emergence of a "permanent present" that paradoxically erases earlier notions of space and time and invites nostalgia. Indeed, Hong Kong movies are as much about this world city's paradoxes in a politically unusual and compressed time (that is, the 1997 handover) as they are about a technical culture's race for global economic opportunities and cultural capital. These movies equally anticipate and register the impact of a high-speed race for profit against the barriers of time and distance.

To consider Hong Kong cinema in terms of globalization is to consider Hollywood's domination over national cinema and to avoid making Hong Kong movies an adjunct to the grand narrative of Chinese cinema. This does not mean dismissing the presence of a greater China and Chinese culture in the films but, rather, recognizing the distance and the perspectives according to which contemporary Chinese entities are interpreted, dismissed, reworked, and reinvented by filmmakers and audiences. This would illuminate the power of images, stories, movie stars, and popular music in the global cultural economy. With speed and radical change in the subjective as major elements shaping a new global narrative, the history, economy, and symbolic aspects of Hong Kong's cultural productions in the 1980s and the 1990s both are and are not Hong Kong's own. Local cultural productions are not merely expressions of local identity and memory. Competing with Hollywood for Chinese audiences and for overseas markets, they are already a part of the media hegemonies, on the one hand, and they help generate other stories and memories in diverse instances of consumption, reading, and reinvention, on the other.

The basic considerations for Hong Kong cinema in the global and local contexts can be summarized in the following points: (1) Hong Kong films are produced in a city that was of immense geopolitical (or U.S.-Asian) significance both during and since the cold war years, and social orientation in this regional financial center has been consciously world oriented, profit driven, and time competitive; (2) Hollywood productions and American popular culture remain dominant, while Japanese popular culture has shaped the tastes of most adolescents; (3) Hong Kong's film productions depend on Taiwanese and Southeast Asian investment and distribution to balance their budgets and have had a hegemonic presence in these regions for many years without attending to these cultures; (4) the dependence on overseas audiences has contributed to the large number of action genres such as martial arts films and thrillers; (5) the films articulate a Hong Kong identity that is connected with and detached from both the Western world and the Chinese world, and they often refute the official "success" story while attempting to construct a native memory; (6) the commercial and art films engage the city's tensions and politics as Hong Kong negotiates and transacts with China and the rest of the world in order to stay competitive; and (7) renowned for their fast-paced rhythms, Hong Kong movies both anticipate and register the impact of speed in the era of immediate global access.

Cultural Androgyny, Piracy, and Flexible Identities

After Hollywood, Bombay, and a couple of others, Hong Kong has for several years been the world's fifth largest producer of commercial films. However, despite the volume of production, the survival of this film industry became a serious concern in the 1990s. Along with Cantonese music (or "Cantopop"), contemporary Hong Kong cinema, which speaks a Cantonese dialect, provides the sights and the sounds of this world city's popular self-expression.

The city's postwar generations, brought up in a milieu that encourages a laissez-faire economy and eclectic cultural tastes, are often less cognizant of the arts of traditional China than of the material cultures and popular trends coming from Japan, Taiwan, the United States, and Western Europe. In fact, many writers and filmmakers have begun thinking seriously about early Cantonese cinema, the city's history before World War II, and the counter-modern Chinese legends as a gesture of cultural introspection that motivates active remembering and rediscovery. Such a gesture, taken after years of exposure to an eclectic mix of Western trends and cultural fragments, signifies conscious efforts to reposition the films in a broad cultural setting. Even so, or perhaps as the result of this unique attempt simultaneously both to be by, of, and for Hong Kong and to reach out to worldwide audiences, many movies produced since the late 1970s appear extroverted, laced with multiple cultural references and engaged with expressive possibilities rather than the deep values of culture.

Paralleling the city's rapid transformations since the 1970s, Hong Kong cinema has become less and less the cultural offspring of Shanghai tastes and styles. A high-risk endeavor, filmmaking is an integral part of the city's vibrant, low-budget, competitive business environment—a stark contrast to the government-sponsored, artistically serious propaganda and art films of mainland China. Indeed, low-cost commercial feature film productions did so well that during the ten-year economic boom from the early 1980s to the early 1990s, they exerted a lot of pressure on the supposedly protected (i.e., closed) film market in the mainland. The smuggling of videos and even film prints (the latter being a topic rarely discussed in Chinese newspapers) made it possible for action movies, pornography, and blockbusters to reach far and wide, not only in the southern regions but all over mainland China. The titles that gave Zhang Yimou and Chen Kaige their reputations as world-class directors, such as *Raise the Red Lantern* [*Dahong Denglong Gao Gao Gua*] (1991) and *Farewell My Concubine* [*Bawang Bieji*] (1993), had little impact on Chinese audiences, and not simply because of censorship issues. Threatened by Hong Kong movies and American blockbusters in the form of videos and video compact discs (VCDs), the state-sponsored film studios in mainland China began to make films for mass entertainment, and many writers and directors began working on television dramas instead.

Conventional descriptions of Asian societies and their artifacts commonly present a picture in which Eastern and Western elements represent the mixing of traditional culture with modern values. Such a description has little value for the capital-intense aspects of contemporary film production and circulation in the global marketplace. Rey Chow's *Primitive Passions: Visuality, Sexuality, Ethnography, and Contemporary Chinese Cinema* (1994) examines more-complex intercultural issues by presenting selected mainland Chinese film directors of the 1980s and 1990s as cultural translators. These filmmakers use cinematographic technology, Orientalist icons, and visual strategies in full knowledge that their films are being viewed in a modern, intercultural context. Adapting the concepts of "film as ethnography" (Crawford and Turton 1992) and "autoethnography" (Pratt 1992) from anthropology and colonial studies, Chow notes that Chinese film directors should not be judged by the criteria of "authenticity" and "authentic cultural identity." Instead, the filmmakers have "ethnographized their own cultures" in the course of exhibiting them locally and overseas. Nationalist perspectives are suspect for collaborating with the nation-state, and intercultural self-writing is not constrained by obligations to be faithful to traditions and national cultures (Chow 1994).

In an era of immediate global access, disregard for boundaries is incarnate in the idea of a movie or a media product that appeals to local consumers for being unlike the local culture they inhabit while simultaneously presenting bits of palatable "native culture" to global audiences. Androgyny, which usually refers to gender ambiguity, names the instability coming from what Judith Butler calls the "citations" of gender norm to mime, exaggerate, and reverse the conventions. By theatricalizing emotion and politics, the performative mode recognizes, denaturalizes, and contests the norm's restrictive boundaries and hierarchies (Butler 1997). Androgyny as such can be an analogy for Hong Kong cinema, which uses wit, hyperbole, and sentiment rather than rage to position itself as a (post)colonial cinema that evaluates and counteracts the cultural regimes of both the British and the Chinese. Instead of holding on to a single identity tied to a small territory or replaying the norms of a bounded culture, the "culturally androgynous" film cites diverse idioms, repackages codes, and combines genres that are thought to be culturally, aesthetically, or cinematically incompatible. For this cinema, autoethnography has limited relevance in terms of addressing the citations and the performative model. In the 1980s and 1990s, hyperbole, parody, and reinvention became prevalent modes of creation to draw ideas and stylistic references from diverse sources. These modes help break down the notion of bounded cultures, so that the cultural entities that once appeared to be historically and geographically intact are often taken apart and reassembled. This process of "dis-integration" has contributed to the cultural androgyny of Hong Kong movies. This is not to dismiss the underside of reinvention or the rightful accusation that some film writers have simply copied ideas and done a poor job, nor does it overlook what reinventing tradition, culture, and even history in film could mean: shock, nostalgia, hilarity, and exhilaration, as well as massively regressive and mindless outcomes.

Citations and reinventions of cultural idioms unsettle notions of "authentic cultural identity." Furthermore, they make ethnicist or culturalist interpretations of Hong Kong films as unviable as autoethnography. The optic worlds of Hong Kong movies, filled with cultural references, spoofed media fragments, recycled clichés, unfamiliar idioms, and a mix of proletarian and bourgeois references, are not constrained by the desire to inform others about one's culture, nor are they simple representations of eclectic Hong Kong. Still, a refusal to act "authentically" and to comply with Orientalist assumptions has to take into account the double standard that modernism maintains when it comes to "authenticity": when Europe's artists reference the non-West, this gesture adds value to their work and their originality; but when non-Western artists reference Europe and the United States, their work is deemed derivative and inauthentic. In counteracting this double standard, it is not very useful to suggest that Chinese film directors are consciously "autoethnographic," as this term implicitly links film directors and the critic herself with "native informants" who are useful for their knowledge of indigenous cultures and intercultural translation but who do not take irreverent approaches or make unsafe citations. If commercial Hong Kong movies are shamelessly derivative and creatively irreverent at the same time, their culturally androgynous features are not just local, nor are they a cause for celebration; rather, they register the industry's pursuit of the global market, a pursuit that mirrors Hollywood's, whose "inauthentic" productions consolidate its screen hegemony.

The troubling phenomenon of piracy adds a new topic to the discussion of the global marketplace. Within a day or two following the world premiere of a Hollywood blockbuster such as *Titanic* or any Hong Kong action movie, inexpensive, sometimes poor-quality VCDs are available on the street for one-third to one-eighth of the price of a movie ticket. It is happening in the city of Hong Kong, in major mainland Chinese cities such as Shanghai and Beijing, and in small towns between Canton and Tibet. The speed of piracy far exceeds the regulated flow of copyrighted movies; the issue is tied to the nonexistence of a commercial distribution network as well as to the low cost of videos and VCDs. The violation of brand names points to the existence of a parallel or parasitic economy of reproduction and distribution. Ravi Sundaram's essay on electronic piracy in India indicates that violation of brand names is an act peculiar neither to Chinese opportunists nor to Asian societies alone, nor is it limited to movies — music compact discs (or MP3s), clothing, handbags, and other consumer goods are all objects of such activity (Sundaram 1999). Indeed, international antipiracy forces have continued to step up their collaborative, globally launched customs efforts since the late 1990s, and American studio executives, as much as Hong Kong's own, have kept their eyes on the "1-billion-customer China market." As both middle-class consumers living in suburbs and workers receiving less than a living wage pay for clones and pirated goods, cultural sovereignty simply loses out to transient entertainment commodities. National culture is distinctly an afterthought when audiences are indifferent to the quality productions that proudly exhibit their national cultures to the world; instead, they prefer imported or local cultural commodities that are inexpensive or even pirated copies, mass produced and globally available.

Piracy, which rides on the mainstream global economy and its expansive cultural property rights, is certainly disruptive of the assertion of identity. As mentioned above, movies that borrow, recycle, and remake existing materials, conventions, idioms, styles, and even images have increased in number. This is true in Hong Kong and in Hollywood productions of film sequels. None, however, would be considered pirated, since screenwriters, filmmakers, actors, and film crew add a certain amount of creative labor in the collaborations. The extreme pressures of time under which movies are made, however, frequently leads to the pilfering of popular ideas (or lesser-known ones) in the industry, turning the nationalist claims — captured by such phrases as "reflecting upon one's own culture" and "the integrity of national cinema" — into empty rhetoric. Piracy calls attention to the short life of commodity production and consumption that results from global overproduction. As unwelcome competition in the form of unauthorized reproduction, piracy is certainly one aspect of this rapid overproduction and consumption. Paradoxically, quite a few of Hong Kong's movie productions in the early 1990s thrived on borrowing, reinventing, and even plagiarizing, while the industry as a whole has suffered extreme setbacks because of aggressive piracy practices. The pirates and the users of pirated products, in Hong Kong as elsewhere, are not limited to any single social class, nor are people working in the music and film industries abstaining from using pirated products — especially when they are acquired during travel abroad.

In the realm of reinvention, filmmakers have turned out different versions of what one may call, for lack of a better term, experimental syncretism. The sword fights that bookend Wong Kar-wai's *Ashes of Time* [*Dongxie Xidu*]

(1994), for example, exemplify a unique movement-image sequence in high velocity with choreographed kinetic movements to create a heightened sense of spatial fluidity. Experimenting with cinematography (film speed, filters, lighting, and focus) and ways to visualize space and movement, Chris Doyle and Wong Kar-wai collaboratively assembled a different kind of cinematic visuality — one in which seductive images, erotic sensations, and electronic music combine to subtend the repeated motifs of loneliness, longing, and memory. Additionally, their works build upon the trend toward conscious employment of advertising concepts and artists trained in commercial design for filmmaking — a method pioneered in the early 1980s, notably by Cinema City Film Production Company. Elements of their style appear in other local feature film productions, television commercials, and subway station billboard designs; Wong made a Motorola commercial in 1997 featuring the popular singer and actress Faye Wong.

In many films, experimental syncretism is pursued with an irreverent playfulness that puts less emphasis on experimental cinematography and more on special effects and unexpected juxtapositions. A good film example is *A Chinese Ghost Story [Qiannu Youhun]* (1987), directed by Ching Siu-tung and produced by Tsui Hark. The film is highly conscious of genre conventions but at the same time keeps a close eye on style and exotic sensuousness. Art direction, special effects, kinetic choreography, and star personae all enjoy primary importance in the creative process. The film's juxtaposition of multiple references and temporalities combines a seventeenth-century literary classic by Pu Songling and comic book horror with ghost films from Japan — including Kenji Mizoguchi's *Ugetsu Monogatari* (1953) — and a Cantonese precedent, Li Han-hsiang's *The Enchanting Shadow [Qiannu Youhun]* (1960), from which *A Chinese Ghost Story* drew its Chinese title. Local critics at the 1989 Hong Kong International Film Festival commented on the film's hyperactive rhythm and packed special effects and likened it to a "[television] commercial" (Li 1989). One may add that the fantastic or ghostly dimension as rendered by special effects has benefited from George Lucas's *Star Wars* (1977) and Steven Spielberg's *Close Encounters of the Third Kind* (1977), just as its mood and visual imagery are inspired by King Hu's *wuxia* or swordplay film classics *The Dragon Gate Inn [Longmen Kezhan]* (1967) and *Legend of the Mountain [Shanzhong Chuanqi]* (1979). It is worth noting that both *The Dragon Gate Inn* and *Star Wars* were immensely profitable — the former broke all box office records in Taiwan, Hong Kong, Korea, and Southeast Asia, while the latter made huge profits in the world market and established new standards for special effects and Dolby sound. Entertaining and glamorous renderings and juxtapositions of popular-culture materials of the past and the present—eye-opening for local and overseas audiences alike—have replaced the low-budget look and "chop-socky" feel that most Westerners remember about the imitations of Bruce Lee films from the early 1970s. The linking of multinational advertising styles, classical ghost stories, heroic mythology, action stunts, the *wuxia* genre, and computer graphics exemplifies a creative move that disturbs the notion of homogeneous, linear modern time, even though the finished commodity may be said to resonate with the cultural logic of late capitalism (Yau 1997).

Like *A Chinese Ghost Story*, many Hong Kong films juxtapose divergent cultural materials to create crossovers between certain forms and mediums that were previously separate. Feature-length productions of the 1980s and 1990s have cited resources often associated with a national or cultural origin, such as contemporary Chinese martial arts novels, Japanese samurai pictures and comic books, American silent comedies and musicals, French crime thrillers, German auteurist works, and, not insignificantly, old Cantonese movies. Fragments of popular culture are eclectically displayed even when the films are intensely focused on local situations. The productions them-selves draw upon the creative labor of film-school graduates with a Western education and martial arts practitioners whose ideas and skills come from opera troupes and private masters or *sifus*. This interclass collaboration to deploy divergent cultural resources has produced a cinema that continues to enjoy a low cultural status at the same time that it is becoming a prominent representative of Hong Kong in the global marketplace.

Migrants and migration are an integral part of collaborative film work. Though Hong Kong's workers are predominantly ethnic Chinese, many were born outside of Hong Kong—in mainland China, Vietnam, Malaysia, Australia, or New Zealand—and have taken up temporary or long-term resi-dence in the city. These include the directors Zhang Che, King Hu, Ann Hui, Li Han-hsiang, Tsui Hark, and Wong Kar-wai; the actors Bruce Lee and Jackie Chan; the cinematographer Christopher Doyle; the composer Otomo Yoshihide; and the writers Ackbar Abbas, Roger Garcia, and Stephen Teo, among many others. Yim Ho's *The Day the Sun Turned Cold [Tianguo Nizi]* (1995) and Ann Hui's *Summer Snow [Nuren Sishi]* (1995), for example, were scored by Yoshihide, and Doyle has shot all of Wong Kar-wai's movies. In the case of coproductions, the films' credit sequence often reveals the extent to which film workers from other places have contributed to the finished product. Offscreen, domestic laborers from Thailand, Sri Lanka, and the Philippines, together with migrants from mainland China, continue to add change to the city's ethnoscape and the makeup of its local audiences. Likewise, filming in other Asian and overseas locations (such as Mexico and South Africa) has become an indispensable part of productions that seek difference in the face of an overbuilt metropolis. Not only are overseas locations popular in the films of Jackie Chan and Stanley Tong, but also many acclaimed art films use sites beyond the crowded city streets. The temples of Korea, the desolate villages of northern China, and the Iguaçú waterfall at the Argentina-Brazil border, for example, contribute significantly to the mise-en-scène of King Hu's *Raining in the Mountain [Kong Shan Ling Yu]* (1979), Yim Ho's *The Day the Sun Turned Cold*, and Wong Kar-wai's *Happy Together* (1997), while the boulevards of Paris and a park in Toronto become the background for action scenes in John Woo's *Once a Thief [Zongheng Sihai]* (1991) and Jackie Chan's *Rumble in the Bronx [Hongfan Chu]* (1995). Stereotypes of foreigners and superficial uses of cultural differences, however, also plague the latter films. Locally, the topographical characteristics of Central District on the island side, Mongkok on Kowloon peninsula, and Tuen Mun and the old Taipo Market in the "New Territories" are used to reinforce neighborhood identification in Wong Kar-wai's *Chungking Express [Chongqing Senlin]* (1994), Cha Chuen-yee's *Once Upon a Time in Triad Society [Wangjiao Zha Fit Ren]* (1996), Ann Hui's *Summer Snow* (1995), and Fruit Chan's *Little Cheung [Xilu Xiang]* (1999).

With experimental syncretism, citation and irreverent remaking of cultural materials, mixed locations, and cross-cultural collaborations, these films proffer a space-time in which Hong Kong appears in many versions. In these culturally androgynous worlds, "Hong Kong" is an unstable symbolic construct making affiliations, both conventional and unexpected, with the many signs and stories circulating in mass-mediated cultures. The anthropologist Aihwa Ong discerns a "flexible identity" in the city's economic migrants, who fashion themselves to thrive despite discriminatory and dislocating circumstances (Ong 1993; 1999). Such a notion of flexible identity can be adapted to a discussion of the cinematic constructs that continue to evolve and mutate, not just alongside Hong Kong's local history and politics, but also with trends and idioms coming from elsewhere. This does not mean that filmmakers and critics have abandoned notions of realism, history, and lived experiences in gauging the social significance of films at a particular historical juncture. Rather, flexibility and syncretism are two prevailing modes by which the complex and unexpected turns of history and politics throughout the 1990s were staged on film and which in turn shaped mass audiences' (self-)understanding of Hong Kong identity.

Perspectives on Hong Kong Cinema

A special section of the June 1988 issue of *Film Comment* was dedicated to celebrating contemporary Hong Kong cinema as a refreshing form of guilt-less pleasure for the jaded critic and viewer. Evoking early Hollywood films and their innocence, David Kehr notes that the kinetics in Jackie Chan's films are reminiscent of those of Fred Astaire, Buster Keaton, and Harold Lloyd (Kehr 1988, 38–40), while David Edelstein writes, "At their best, Hong Kong directors churn out the most delirious and astounding fantasy se-quences in world cinema" (Edelstein 1988, 48). As American critics intro-duced the names of John Woo, Chow Yun-fat, Jackie Chan, Tsui Hark, and Sammo Hung in the descriptive accounts that drew attention to films such as *Project A, Part II [A Jihua, Xuji]* (1987) and *Peking Opera Blues [Daoma Dan]* (1986), they assured their readers that Hong Kong movies appealed to Western audiences through their "exuberant storytelling," impossible acro-batics, and downright fun. These critics promoted an image of Hong Kong cinema that was unpretentious, unself-conscious, and always easily acces-sible. Their description said much about the critics' nostalgia for innocent entertainment, as the movies of one world city (Hong Kong) cured the jaded sensibilities of cinema dominated by another world city (Los Angeles– Hollywood). Not all critics were fans, however, and many shunned these low-budget images and their violent, "eye-popping effects" associated with "comic book aesthetics"—a protest that echoed the disapproval of many Hong Kong critics (Dannen 1995, 32). Both nostalgia and disapproval are part of cross-cultural consumption, and American critics writing on these films confirm David Howes's suggestion that "the West is no less caught up in the processes of hybridization or creolization than anywhere else" (Howes 1996). This is true in production terms as well—not only action choreogra-phers such as Yuen Wo-ping and his crew, but also the directors and stars of action movies, including John Woo, Ronnie Yu, Chow Yun-fat, and Jet Li, have been hired by Hollywood, which has been absorbing "foreign" talents and labor (from England, Germany, Australia, and Canada, in particular) since the silent era. Hollywood's readiness to integrate Hong Kong action choreography into the American commercial mainstream has resulted in movies such as *Mortal Kombat* (1995), *Lethal Weapon 4* (1997), and *The Matrix* (1999)(Ansen 1996).

The Hong Kong movie fan culture that emerged during the 1980s was active in seeking innocent fun in many ways. Sustained by special programs and festivals in art theaters, fan magazines, video outlets, and, later, Web sites, a broad spectrum of fan interest finds a variety of channels for declaring their love of the movies and exchanging forthright opinions. The desire for fun drives the search for non- or counter-mainstream entities. Fan interests cover a wide range: star worship and gossip; martial arts interests; popular music crazes; movie trivia, including trading jokes on horrendous subtitles; and so on. Fanzines and independent magazines such as *Asian Cult Cinema* (originally *Asian Trash Cinema*) and *Giant Robot* motivate readers to seek out lesser-known titles and actors. Media corporations were also quick to create spinoffs of cult interests. The editors of the book *Sex and Zen and a Bullet in the Head*, for example, tell the reader that the Hong Kong movies "kick ass," deliver "fertile mayhem," and induce an "over-the-top euphoria" (Hammond and Wilkins 1996, 12–13). The Internet, which offers a great deal of information on this subject, has become the most convenient marketplace for distributors and buyers of Hong Kong movies to find each other. Web pages and electronic mail are now the major "para-sites" where personal comments on any and all aspects of the movies can circulate among users in different corners of the world. These sites make Hong Kong movies "hot" for new audiences even long after the films are made and the local industry has experienced repeated box office failures.

Counteracting the pleasure-seeking gestures of nostalgic fans, Stokes and Hoover's *City on Fire* (1999) provides a critical discussion of Hong Kong's political economy. The authors undertake a classical Marxist reading of the industrial practices, work conditions, and issues of class and labor they find embedded in the films' narratives. Discussions of films persistently remind readers that these are the products of a capitalist cinema and exhibit the class politics and social contradictions of a city whose inhabitants are constantly pressured to seek maximum profit and pleasure. "If screen action and comedy allow film audiences to displace their anxieties, such diversion cannot eliminate the social inequities that the free market engenders, nor prevent the inevitable economic crises that laissez faire policies cannot effectively manage" (Stokes and Hoover 1999, 304). With respect to the city and its vicissitudes in the 1990s, the authors argue that Hong Kong cinema is a "'crisis cinema,' at once paralleling, producing, and reflecting the identity, legitimacy, and sovereignty predicament of the people themselves" (Stokes and Hoover 1999, 304). As it captures and produces the chaotic and highly conflicting scenarios of the late colonial years, this crisis cinema not only epitomizes the "cultural logic of late capitalism," as Stokes and Hoover suggest, it also poses questions about vision and comprehension regarding the complexities of late-colonial capitalism.

The Dis/Appearing City

> It's a new world out there. Seems like Hong Kong has become a baby overnight.
> — *THE LONGEST SUMMER* (FRUIT CHAN, 1998)

During the months of May and June of 1989, public demonstrations, student hunger strikes, and the state violence in Beijing's Tiananmen Square, telecast over the Cable News Network (CNN) and reported on most national news hours, became the most absorbing and shocking spectacles on television screens in all corners of the world. These events also marked the most direct and important experience for nearly everyone in Hong Kong. According to the Sino-British Joint Declaration signed in 1984, Hong Kong would cease to be a British colony on 1 July 1997, and the mainland Chinese government would exercise sovereignty over the city from then on. Sharing a collective wish to seek a democratic future for themselves that they never had before, more than one-fourth of Hong Kong's residents participated in massive local rallies, donated generously to the cause, and watched the news closely, while many visited Tiananmen Square, started soul searching, and began to take Chinese history very seriously. China's modernization policy in the 1980s had drawn many to business opportunities, but the divide between Hong Kong and the mainland was immense, both cognitively and emotionally. Then, like everyone else, citizens of Hong Kong had their hopes dashed when the state began to go on the offensive and the student democracy movement was crushed. Within a few months, fear motivated everyone to seize any remaining opportunities to accomplish everything before the year 1997: these few years saw an increased demand for overseas passports and assets, a real-estate boom, reinvigorated interest in Hong Kong's history, a sudden respect for local writers and artists, the birth of a tabloid newspaper, and strategically, a rush on the part of the late-colonial government to establish district representation and political parties. Everything developed quickly and all at once. In this frenzied atmosphere of rapid accomplishments,

Hong Kong entered an unprecedented era: it became a glittering boom town with a deadline. This metropolis of rapid prosperity and high anxiety immediately attracted transnational corporations seeking a foothold in the mainland Chinese market; likewise, writers eagerly took note of the end of one colonial era and the beginning of another.

Not surprisingly, Hong Kong also became a handful of clichés. Intertwined with the legacies of empire and the workings of transnational capitalism, Ackbar Abbas notes, the city became a special tourist attraction and the subject of exotic tales. In other words, it enticed and challenged the imagination of writers and filmmakers. In *Hong Kong: Culture and the Politics of Disappearance* (1997), Ackbar Abbas writes that blindness is epidemic when it comes to the cultural space of Hong Kong. A number of descriptions recycle clichés about the city as an economic success, the "Pearl of the Orient," and a cultural desert. Bringing orthodox ideas of the colony with them, many suffer from a "reverse hallucination": they are unable to see what is there. Even those writers who celebrate Hong Kong's marginal and indigenous characteristics simply end up reiterating a center-periphery relationship that is part of the colonial imaginary. In short, the clichés kept both overseas and local writers trapped within a "pathology of presence"; they seemed to have forgotten how elusive the space of representation could always be.

Relating to Hong Kong was nothing less than an obsession with the vanishing city. This was true for Abbas as much as for those who were making or acquiring historical souvenirs. Nostalgia was widespread when local residents and travelers began in the 1980s to revive memories of earlier days by collecting items and paraphernalia from the past, though such objects and styles had by then almost totally disappeared from the lived spaces of the hyperurbanized city. The paradox of hallucination and reverse hallucination, or seeing something that was not there and not seeing what was there, sustained and intensified the "culture of disappearance," according to Abbas. Alert and reflective, exceptional film directors and literary writers such as Wong Kar-wai, Stanley Kwan, Clara Law, Ye Si (also known as Leung Ping-kwan), and Xi Xi have used images, poetry, and fiction to evoke this unique culture of disappearance and to capture their responses to a reality that constantly outpaces conventional awareness (Abbas 1997, 26–35).

For many who followed the worldwide reportage on China in June 1989, Hong Kong became a question and an unfinished story. The interrogative refrain accompanying the images broadcast on CNN of tanks and dying students—"What will happen to Hong Kong in 1997?"—indicated in no uncertain terms that the city's future was tied to a larger Chinese spectacle and a set of concerns and political agendas beyond the postcolony itself. In the minds of many television viewers, Hong Kong, instead of being an elusive cultural space, was simply dropping out of the comfort zone and becoming another of the world's potential disaster areas. In an American televisual setting in which the refrain was uttered by news anchors, however, this potential disaster was external to the normalcy of American capitalist temporality, marked by Dow Jones reports, AT&T commercials, sports programs, and soap operas.

It may sound a little far-fetched to suggest that the interest in Hong Kong as a last colonial site/sight was a secret longing for disaster—a dramatic news sequel to the Tiananmen Square episodes. Yet, it is true that memories of CNN's images of rolling tanks were on the minds of many as they posed the same questions to everyone from Hong Kong that they met. More often than not they were rhetorical questions reflecting negative views of the Communists that were learned during the cold war—views reinforced, to be sure, by the behavior of the Chinese army and the political leaders themselves. Eight years later, when more than 5,000 journalists flew to Hong Kong to report on the 1997 handover, they kept the question alive and reminded the audience that the uneventful ceremony and public rituals that they were seeing had everything to do with state violence and with China's future. This was the one story that they told, and many worked hard to interpret the bland footage of the People's Liberation Army crossing the border in trucks, while others found the cagelike living conditions in old buildings to make horrific but desirable stories when political dramas failed to materialize. Once again, professional and amateur reporters found themselves surrounded by staged clichés and in turn recycled them. The official ceremonies in which the transition from British to Chinese rule took place were complete with flags, uniformed soldiers, political celebrities, singers, dancing children, and journalists. The photogenic Victoria Harbor and its skyline, together with the new wing of the Hong Kong Convention Center, built expressly for the official ceremony, provided a unifying background to a singular narrative of Hong Kong falling into Communist hands. Hong Kong, to borrow Paul Virilio's words, was translated into a luminous surface before it vanished from the global television screen.

The disappearing city is, after all, a condensation and reduction of its many stories and facets into short-lived spectacles, and as such, it is a phenomenon of global media reports and technoculture. As many in Hong Kong have discovered in the years since 1997, the city flourishes or founders on the basis of hypermobile capital, financial products, and media attention, its vicissitudes bound to the cycles of transnational capital and their stories—now told by distant journalists and national leaders rather than fully embedded in regional economies and national allegories. In *The Lost Dimension* (1991), Paul Virilio announces the age of "tele-conquest," in which one's sense of the world is defined by numerical, unstable images of bits and pixels and by the digital sensitization of television and computer screens. The screens' "lumino-centrism" replaces the Quattrocentro's order of the visible and topology as an analytical approach to the city's geometric reference points. In place of the analogical, stable image of static nature, the electron announces an "aesthetics of disappearance" (Virilio 1991, 30). Virilio's suggestive and prophetic thesis delineates a landscape strangely devoid of humans. Virilio was quite right. Many stories about the changes that are still taking place in Hong Kong have become globally accessible, thanks to television and the Internet. Laptops, mobile phones, and dot-coms are transforming the city's space and time. In an effort to stay on the map of global capital, the Hong Kong Special Administrative Region government competed with Shanghai and won the bid for a Disney World to be built near its new airport and a Silicon Harbor on the Hong Kong island.

Still, a new round of human stories has just begun to unfold alongside politically, economically, and technologically driven changes. Its postnostalgic character began in the figure of a Chinese British soldier turned deliveryman at the end of Fruit Chan's *The Longest Summer* [*Qunian Yanhua Tebie Duo*] (1998), shot during and after the 1997 handover. Ambitious experiments in digital effects and explosions in Andrew Lau's *The Stormriders* [*Feng Yun Xiongba Tianxia*] (1998) and Benny Chan's *Gen-X Cops* [*Tejing Xin Renlei*] (1998) appeal to a young audience. Johnnie To's *Running Out of Time* [*An Zhan*] (1999) and *The Mission* [*Qiang Huo*] (1999) continue to add psychological complexity and stylistic redefinition to the crime and triad film genre. Patrick Yau's *Expect the Unexpected* [*Feichang Turan*] (1999) tightens the grip of death in the thriller, and the film's economic crisis takes on a murderous tone and a horror setting in Ringo Lam's *Victim* [*Mu Lu Xiong Guang*] (1999). Ann Hui's *Ordinary Heroes* [*Qianyan Wanyu*] (1999) revisits tical movement of the 1980s led by an Italian priest who has legend. Going beyond nostalgia and political anxiety, reduc- taking stock of a changing ethnoscape, Fruit Chan's *Little* and Yu Lik-wai's *Love Will Tear Us Apart* [*Tianshang Ren-* ger around old neighborhoods where longtime residents rants from mainland China live side by side, and Lawrence ts a disturbing and realistic picture of messed-up juvenile lives using amateur actresses who partly play themselves in *Spacked Out* [*Wuren Jiashi*] (2000). Wong Kar-wai and Chris Doyle continue to find new ways to visualize an old story of suppressed desire in the 1960s in Wong's *In the Mood for Love* [*Huayang Nianhua*] (2000), featuring Maggie Cheung and Tony Leung, for which Leung won the Best Actor award at the Cannes Festival.

The critical acclaim that has followed several years of bad business suggests that Hong Kong cinema continues to weather economic cycles and crises. It seems that filmmakers are gathering momentum once again by building on and refining what has been achieved since 1980. Will the many hidden stories of the city get told on screen? Will diverse approaches and alternative perspectives find better opportunities to make their imprints as a result? Will popular memories be buried by massive information and entertainment packages? Will infantile reactions gain popularity over critical insights? Writings about Hong Kong films, as much as the films themselves, are about the circulation of hybrid cultural discourse in a world that is presumably without borders. In the midst of media saturation, they must reinvent a fantasyscape by engaging the politics of the present to connect experiences of a globalized modernity across boundaries.

Transcultural Readings

The essays in this anthology are organized into three sections. In the first section, Law Kar and Hector Rodriguez map the terrain of Hong Kong's New Wave cinema. Law's essay gives a comprehensive overview of New Wave directors and their works on television and in film. Social activism in the late 1960s, the rise of television in the 1970s, and the phenomena of cine clubs and publications are important arenas from which the postwar generation, along with their modern expressions, emerged. Cantonese films were transformed into a cultural space where Western mass culture and local concerns could be juxtaposed. The cosmopolitan outlook of the filmmakers and critics constitutes an important aspect by which New Wave discourse defined itself, according to Rodriguez. In his essay, which delineates Hong Kong's film culture field, he carefully examines the cultural activities and debates that produced the "Hong Kong New Wave." Several concerns that surface in this analysis of a critical community and its New Wave discourse are those of film as art, of an ethical concept of authorship, of the film auteur's social responsibility regarding Hong Kong, and of cinematic realism as a preferred mode of cinematic representation that reflects artistic and ethical commitment to a local community. The New Wave cinema as a constitutive moment was reaffirmed about two decades later, when the film industry was plagued by low box office returns, lack of quality productions, and piracy. In 1999, the Hong Kong International Film Festival commemorated New Wave cinema and invited audiences to rediscover the historical identity of their city's film culture (Law 1999). Subsequent developments have confirmed the collaborative search and affirmation of local identity that both Law's and Rodriguez's essays acknowledge.

In the second section, four essays address the transcultural meanings of Hong Kong action cinema. David Bordwell dissects the typical action sequence and brings in discussions of Sergei Eisenstein and traditional Chinese opera to elaborate on the theoretical aspects of its "expressive amplification" of movement. The action film's stylistic strategies and tactics are examined in detail through the specifics of shot composition, framing, choreography, kinetic movement, and editing pattern. As an exemplary exercise in comparative formal analysis, Bordwell's essay corrects many impression-based comparisons of Hollywood and Hong Kong movies and provides the terms of analytic dialogue regarding film action sequences. Action movies are frequently consumed in the transnational context as cult films. Jinsoo An explores the lure of melodramatic sentiments and stylistic exuberance for the cult fans of John Woo's films *The Killer* [*Diexue Shuangxiong*] (1989) and *A Better Tomorrow* [*Yingxiong Bense*] (*Part I* [1986] and *Part II* [1987]). A focused analysis of the former gives rise to a discussion of consumers' indifference to textual and cultural coherence when their visual and generic reading capacities are already primed by diverse media texts. An's analysis of the shifts in meaning of *The Killer* for young male followers in the United States and in Korea suggests that the notions of "camp" and "cult" readings are crucial in cross-cultural consumption.

The increasing homogenization of Hong Kong action movies as they cater to the global marketplace can be counterproductive for ambitious stars and directors such as Jackie Chan and Stanley Tong. Steve Fore hints at such a possibility as he maps the shifts in the screen personae of Jackie Chan from his early *kungfu* comedies, which kept a nice balance between tradition and modernity, to his recently packaged products, which showcase a "faux-global identity" that has been likened to that of the movies' James Bond. The changes indicate an ongoing "disembedding" and restructuring process, and martial arts, as a potent symbol of cultural China once embodied in Bruce Lee's films, has become increasingly diluted. The essay argues that there are telling analogies between the changes in the martial arts genre since the

1970s and the social ideologies of Hong Kong as a global city. While recent Jackie Chan films still feature meticulously choreographed martial arts sequences and highly creative acts of physical skill, Fore finds them less interesting and unique than Chan's early *kungfu* comedies, with their parodies of styles, verbal comedy built around puns, anachronisms, and slapstick routines, of which *Drunken Master II [Zui Quan II]* (1990) is only reminiscent.

Among New Wave filmmakers, Tsui Hark, with his turn toward commercial filmmaking, has been seen as instrumental in the uses of special-effects technology and the subsequent visual appeal of new Hong Kong cinema. From *Peking Opera Blues* (1986) to *The Blade [Dao]* (1997), Tsui has taken an unconstrained and stylized approach to swordplay films (*wuxia pian*), turning them into allegories. Stephen Teo and Bhaskar Sarkar are both drawn to the cultural meanings of Tsui's films. Teo considers Tsui a pioneer of Hong Kong's postmodern cinema who has constructed an inclusive, multicultural Chinese world. Tsui's films both deconstruct and reconstruct Orientalist myths and icons, rework swordplay conventions such as heroism and justice, and challenge the idea of a "rational national style." Teo suggests that the impetus for Tsui's work comes from the director's own sense of Chinese otherness. Overseas audiences are drawn to his gender-bending, cross-dressing characters, which have given the director a cult reputation and which, Teo suggests, may be attributed to the inclusive world depicted in his films.

The incoherent moments in Tsui Hark's swordplay films, Bhaskar Sarkar posits, are the allegorical "hysterical texts" of Hong Kong cinema. Adapting Fredric Jameson's notion of "cognitive mapping" to the discussion of a hypermodern Asia, Sarkar notes that generic films are allegorical expressions of extensive spatial transformation and intensive dislocation in which masses of people find their lived experience constantly slipping beyond their comprehension. The excessive traits displayed by the swordplay films of the 1990s—with their breathless pace, dizzying energy, askew angles, spectacular special effects, and cross-dressing, gender-bending performances—are expressions of anxiety over emerging structures and new economic realities and political alignments. The incomplete, often facetious and provisional nature of the allegories plays out a Baudrillardian implosion that, Sarkar argues, is not deleterious but that questions the concept of the nation even as the allegories reflect the impossibility of mapping an accelerated reality. It is in this regard that successful martial arts films have "transnational Asian" significance.

A New Wave director who by 1998 had completed television dramas, educational and propagandistic dramas, and fourteen feature films, Ann

Hui remains active as one of only a few women directors and producers in Hong Kong cinema. Elaine Yee-lin Ho argues that Hui's social discourse on modernity has particular significance for women, even though the director consistently denies any interest in womanist or feminist issues herself. Ho performs critical analyses of four films that are taken from the director's early and later periods: *The Secret [Feng Jie]* (1979), *Princess Fragrance [Xiang-xiang Gongzhu]* (1987), *Song of the Exile [Ketu Qiuhen]* (1990), and *Summer Snow* (1995). By examining the films' narrative discourse and cultural meanings, Ho identifies women's agency and voices that depart from the dominant version of Hong Kong's Westernized, technologized modernity. Her essay also provides a much-needed discussion of women in Cantonese cinema by contrasting stereotypical females who comply with Chinese patriarchy and colonial authority with progressive women characters who do not; she points out that since the retreat of left-wing cinema in the 1970s the latter have largely disappeared from the screen. In terms of romantic relationships, Ann Hui's films are not unlike many mainstream works featuring complicit women shaped within the bourgeois paradigm. Even so, Ho finds in these films certain voices, scenes, and rituals that mark the edges of Hong Kong's colonial and patriarchal institutions. Particular women protagonists, Ho argues, have gone beyond serving the function of focalizing cultural contestation to become agents who disrupt the patriarchal institutions as they enact complex transactions with modernity.

In a rapidly developing environment, the disintegration of fixed locales alters people's relations to the past, and strong feelings of nostalgia are both provoked and absorbed by consumer culture. The third section of this book begins with two essays that explore the cultural significance of nostalgia in the art film and the entertainment movie. Rey Chow's essay "A Souvenir of Love" undertakes a meticulous analysis of Stanley Kwan's exquisite nostalgia film *Rouge [Yanzhi Kou]* (1988) and offers a fresh interpretation of nostalgia as a (re)collection of objects, which are compressed forms of time. According to Chow, elements such as the film's rich colors and erotic images, as well as the female ghost's excessive capacity for faithfulness in love, make up a romantic ethnography involving fantasy and fiction. Rather than expressing a desire to return to a simpler past or revealing the social hardships of the past, through nostalgia film a materially affluent society conjures up a tragic but beautiful mythic community.

Many films ride the wave of nostalgia in addressing local audiences, which represent a broader social cross-section than do art cinema audiences and critics. Linda Chiu-han Lai identifies the films that cite and re-encode popular Cantonese and Mandarin film conventions. In Peter Chan's *He Ain't*

Heavy, He's My Father! [Xin Nanxiong Nandi] (1993), Derek Yee's *C'est la vie, mon cheri [Buliao Qing]* (1993), and Clifton Ko's *I Will Wait for You [Niannian you Jinri]* (1994), Lai finds nostalgia intertwined with a sense of local community and faith in modern progress. Stephen Chow's nonsense comedies, which are directed against norms of social propriety and hence against what is being upheld in the official public domain, privilege local viewers with their wordplay, Cantonese slang, folk and burlesque humor, mischievous characters, and obsession with oral pleasures. In films such as *Fight Back to School [Taoxue Wei Long]* (1992), *Justice, My Foot [Shensi Guan]* (1992), *From Beijing with Love [Guochan Ling Ling Qi]* (1994), and *Forbidden City Cop [Danei Mitan Ling Ling Fa]* (1996), Lai identifies a "rhetoric of subversion." While they give voice to subterranean, everyday local culture and practices, the nostalgic film and nonsense comedy also turn the former into material for mass consumption. Collective memories of history and everyday experiences are intertwined with the history of popular culture — with the idioms and icons of old television programs, forgotten or half-forgotten movies, headline news items, old songs, and popular music.

The politics of transcultural spaces is an urgent topic that replaces identity and nationality in the discussion of consciously translocal films. Three essays consider the meaning of multiple border-crossings in a floating, fluid world. Gina Marchetti looks at Evans Chan's *To Liv(e) [Fushi Lianchu]* (1991) and *Crossings [Cuoai]* (1994) as palimpsests of modern(ist), postcolonial, diasporic, postsocialist, postmodern, and global elements. These works, by a New York–based director whose life straddles the United States and Hong Kong and whose films bridge the international art film–melodrama–commercial cinema illustrate the difficulty of and the need for a transcultural approach. Chan's characters are transcultural, with the recurrent Eurasian female in both films signifying an intellectual and a personal ear for voices that have a marginal presence in mainstream cinema. In Marchetti's view, intimate moments between displaced female characters in Chan's films invite the spectator to contemplate the personal dimension of the political concerns of 1997.

Kwai-cheung Lo traces films that create a "trans-subjectivity" and further deconstruct familiar notions of home and local community. Lo reminds us that Hong Kong localism is always open to a capitalist narrative and the claim of Westernization. Stanley Kwan's *Full Moon in New York [Ren Zai Niuyue]* (1989), Ann Hui's *Song of the Exile* (1990), Mabel Cheung's *An Autumn's Tale [Qiutian De Tonghua]* (1987), and Clara Law's *Farewell China [Ai Zai Biexiang de Jijie]* (1990) all rethink local subjectivity from overseas locations, displaying even more ambivalence regarding Hong Kong local and foreign.

In Lo's view, the local as transnational Chinese and as a reconfigured space of national deterritorialization is well exemplified in Peter Chan's *Comrades, Almost a Love Story [Tianmimi]* and its diegetic uses of the late Teresa Tang's sentimental popular songs. This film and others by Peter Chan and the director Lee Chi-ngai are among Hong Kong's low-budget, transcultural productions, which try to survive by taking on characteristics of globalist American cinema. Eventually, they provide a different perspective for looking at home as a fantasy and an image that is already creolized.

Desexualized and heterosexual diasporas still carry the ideological baggage of the nation-state. Despite the deconstruction of home, only a few films provide instances for considering the global meaning of sexual intimacies that take place outside of the private bedroom and heteronormative assumptions. Marc Siegel undertakes a queer reading of Wong Kar-wai's *Happy Together* by going beyond the director's and cinematographer's dis/articulation of the film's homosexual elements. Building on the insights of Lauren Berlant, Michael Warner, and Guy Hocquenghem, Siegel notes that *Happy Together* depicts a sexual relationship between two men, nighttime cruising in public locations, and the fleeting connections between characters in public spaces. The film's explicit references to the details of a sexual ghetto dovetail in an abattoir scene that affirms the materiality of flesh at a moment of emotional suffering, resonating with a scene in Rainer Werner Fassbinder's transsexual story *In a Year of Thirteen Moons* (1978). The public world of belonging and transformation, or the translocal "sexual ghetto," as Siegel calls it, is a queer world in which intimacies between its travelers bear no necessary relationship to domestic space or to the nation. Furthermore, the transcultural meanings of a Hong Kong film are not restricted to what its critical acclaims mean for the image or identity of Hong Kong — and *Happy Together* is the first local Hong Kong film to win a Cannes Festival Golden Palm award. But it is the global, gay/queer, and sexualized context, not the issues of national identity, that has endowed the film with significance.

The contributors to this anthology have answered the fascinating imagination of Hong Kong films with their own enthusiastic and insightful readings. As intercultural spectators and critics, they have just begun to address selective aspects of this cinema and the related cultural phenomena of local and even transcultural relevance. Insofar as many Hong Kong films do not fit easily into the sets of criteria that are still commonly used to valorize national cinema, Chinese culture, Hollywood standards, and modernist achievements, they continue to challenge critics and scholars to consider carefully the comparative terms that would address late-twentieth- and early-twenty-first-century productions circulating within and outside a world that is increasingly borderless, yet troubled by new faces of dislocation. The current range of concepts and cultural theories that the contributors have brought to bear on their readings represents some of the most exciting work currently being done in Asian film studies. Their juxtaposition of terms and methods taken from fields outside Hong Kong cinema and cinema studies strikes an interesting parallel undertaking to the flexible affiliations that Hong Kong films have made: both films and readings have articulated themselves with diverse references, original citations of cultural idioms, and reinvention of concepts.

The study of Hong Kong cinema within the global culture remains incomplete. Research on local and overseas distribution and consumption of cinema has become a complex task as film is increasingly consumed in the form of videos, VCDs, and DVDs (digital video discs). Reception studies of Hong Kong films (or films in general) in the urban and rural sites of Southeast Asia, India, South America, Africa, and Eastern Europe, for example, are barely available and dependent on the migration of scholars and on English translations. Much collaborative work needs to be done when it comes to examining the intersections of local and translocal contexts. A recent discussion of Bruce Lee and *kungfu* movies in socialist Tanzania in the 1970s, for example, offers rare information and illuminating insights (Joseph 1999). Transnational studies of cinema remain a challenge when a high percentage of scholars and critics live and work in the major cities in Asia-Pacific, North America, and Western Europe.

The future of Hong Kong cinema is an unfinished story filled with paradoxes and elusive moments. The global popularity of Hong Kong cinema, according to some, is a grassroots phenomenon rather than the result of expensive publicity efforts. While this can be a reason for celebration, a large body of Cantonese films remains inaccessible and unknown to both local and overseas audiences. Movie fans are unlikely to obtain a very broad intercultural experience if they focus solely on action cinema and male-centered worlds that reinforce mainstream masculinist interests. Current film reviews and commentaries that build on such an interest have yet to excavate inventively the less publicized aspects of Cantonese films and their mundane, esoteric, womanist, queer, and communitarian moments and voices (like those in alternative films and video, for that matter). Despite the films' improved status in the global marketplace, the conditions for feature film productions in Hong Kong deteriorated throughout the 1990s. This industry crisis contrasted strongly with the high visibility of notable Hong Kong directors and actors who are now working in Hollywood (such as John Woo, Stanley Tong, Sammo Hung, Chow Yun-fat, and Jet Li). With low box office returns in Hong Kong and nearby regions, creative personnel looked for work at mainland Chinese television stations, among other places, putting their skills and approaches to use in products not stamped with the name of Hong Kong. Meanwhile, however, Hollywood's distribution arm has established an even stronger basis in Hong Kong as well as other major Asian cities with U.S.-owned multiplex theater chains as well as Blockbuster video stores. The same is true for Disney: in November 1999, the Special Administrative Region government approved the building of a Disney theme park with a planned investment, from taxes, of HK$22.4 billion.

In the area of publication and archiving, book-length studies in the English language, such as Stephen Teo's *Hong Kong Cinema: The Extra Dimensions* (1997), Lisa Odham Stokes and Michael Hoover's *City On Fire: Hong Kong Cinema* (1999), and David Bordwell's *Planet Hong Kong: Popular Cinema and the Art of Entertainment* (2000), are invaluable additions to the study of this cinema overseas. The Hong Kong Film Archive, building upon the Hong Kong International Film Festival's exhibition and publications efforts, has begun the painstaking work of retrieving old Cantonese films and film-related materials from Chinatown theaters and film lovers all over the world. Thus far, three filmographies of earlier films have been published (see bibliography). The collection of documents and materials of a cinema that had its earliest productions in 1909 has become an important part of salvaging a disappearing past, even as its future seems rather uncertain. Fredric Jameson and Masao Miyoshi once noted that globalization needs to be understood as marking a space of tension rather than a stabilized field (Jameson and Miyoshi 1998, xvi). From Hong Kong cinema and in the city's media spaces, many captivating stories and paradoxes continue to unfold that are unmistakably local and personal. Hong Kong's filmmakers and cultural workers have visualized some of these stories and paradoxes in their own ways, and there is hope that, together with an expanded critical community, they will not only map the past and the present of one cinema, but also reinvigorate imaginative alternatives in the midst of media saturation, ethnic tensions, and corporate technologies.

Works Cited

Abbas, Ackbar. 1997. *Hong Kong: Culture and the Politics of Disappearance*. Minneapolis: University of Minnesota Press.
Ansen, David. 1996. "Chinese Takeout." *Newsweek*, 19 February, 66–68.

Appadurai, Arjun. 1996. *Modernity at Large: Cultural Dimensions of Globalization.* Minneapolis: University of Minnesota Press.

Bordwell, David. 2000. *Planet Hong Kong: Popular Cinema and the Art of Entertainment.* Cambridge, Mass.: Harvard University Press.

Brecher, Jeremy, and Tim Costello. 1998. *Global Village or Global Pillage: Economic Constructions from the Bottom Up.* Boston: South End Press.

Butler, Judith. 1997. "Critically Queer." In *Playing With Fire: Queer Politics, Queer Theories*, ed. Shane Phelan, 11–29. New York: Routledge.

Chow, Rey. 1995. *Primitive Passions: Visuality, Sexuality, Ethnography, and Contemporary Chinese Cinema.* New York: Columbia University Press.

Crawford, Peter Ian, and David Turton, eds. 1992. *Film as Ethnography.* Manchester and New York: Manchester University Press.

Dannen, Fredric. 1995. "Hong Kong Babylon." *New Yorker*, 7 August, 30–38.

Dannen, Fredric, and Barry Long. 1997. *Hong Kong Babylon: An Insider's Guide to the Hollywood of the East.* New York: Hyperion.

Edelstein, David. 1988. "Eastern Haunts." *Film Comment* (June): 48–51.

Hamilton, Gary G., ed. 1999. *Cosmopolitan Capitalists: Hong Kong and the Chinese Diaspora at the End of the Twentieth Century.* Seattle: University of Washington Press, 1999.

Hammond, Stefan, and Mike Wilkins. 1996. *Sex and Zen and a Bullet in the Head: The Essential Guide to Hong Kong's Mind-Bending Films.* New York: Fireside.

Howes, David, ed. 1996. *Cross-Cultural Consumption: Global Markets, Local Realities.* London and New York: Routledge.

Hui, Desmond. 1996. "The Architecture of Necessity: On City Form and Space in Hong Kong." In *The Metropolis: Visual Research into Contemporary Hong Kong, 1990–1996*, ed. Sylvia S. Y. Ng. Hong Kong: Photo Pictorial Publishers and Hong Kong Arts Center.

Jameson, Fredric, and Masao Miyoshi, eds. 1998. *The Cultures of Globalization.* Durham, N.C.: Duke University Press.

Joseph, May. 1999. "Kung Fu Cinema and Frugality." In *Nomadic Identities: The Performance of Citizenship*, 49–68. Minneapolis: University of Minnesota Press.

Kapur, Geeta. 1997. "Globalization and Culture." *Third Text* 39 (summer): 21–38.

Kehr, Dave. 1988. "Chan Can Do." *Film Comment* (June): 38–41.

King, Anthony D. 1997. *Culture, Globalization, and the World-System: Contemporary Conditions for the Representation of Identity.* Minneapolis: University of Minnesota Press.

Knox, Paul L., and Peter J. Taylor. 1995. *World Cities in a World-System.* Cambridge and New York: Cambridge University Press.

Li, Cheuk-to, ed. 1989. *Phantoms of the Hong Kong Cinema.* Thirteenth Hong Kong International Film Festival. Hong Kong: Urban Council.

Lii, Ding-tzann. 1998. "A Colonized Empire: Reflections on the Expansion of Hong Kong Films in Asian Countries." In *Trajectories: Inter-Asia Cultural Studies*, ed. Kuan-hsing Chen, 122–41. New York: Routledge.

Negri, Antonio. 1999. "Value and Affect." Translated by Michael Hardt. *boundary 2* 26, no. 2 (summer 1999): 77–88.

Ong, Aihwa. 1993. "On the Edge of Empire: Flexible Citizenship among Chinese in Diaspora." *Positions: East Asia Cultures Critique* 1, no. 3: 745–48.

————. 1999. *Flexible Citizenship: The Cultural Logics of Transnationality*. Durham, N.C.: Duke University Press.

Pratt, Mary Louise. 1992. *Imperial Eyes: Travel Writing and Transculturation*. New York: Routledge.

Stokes, Lisa Odham, and Michael Hoover. 1999. *City on Fire: Hong Kong Cinema*. London and New York: Verso.

Sundaram, Ravi. 1999. "Recycling Modernity: Pirate Electronic Cultures in India." *Third Text* 47 (summer): 59–65.

Teo, Stephen. 1997. *Hong Kong Cinema: The Extra Dimensions*. London: British Film Institute.

Virilio, Paul. 1991. *The Lost Dimension*. Translated by Daniel Moshenberg. New York: Autonomedia.

Wilson, Rob, and Wimal Dissanayake, eds. 1996. *Global/Local: Cultural Production and the Transnational Imaginary*. Durham, N.C.: Duke University Press.

Yau, Esther. 1997. "Ecology and Late Colonial Hong Kong Cinema: Imaginations in Time." In *Fifty Years of Electric Shadows*, ed. Law Kar, 107–13. Twenty-first Hong Kong International Film Festival. Hong Kong: Urban Council.

Part I

Hong Kong's
New Wave Cinema

CHAPTER ONE

An Overview of Hong Kong's New Wave Cinema

Law Kar

In the early 1980s, some young directors and screenwriters who came to film through television began to address the city's tensions in several Hong Kong films that conveyed a strong sense of the city's contemporary rhythms. Beginning in 1979, the impact of these young people on Hong Kong's Cantonese cinema was powerful. Young critics used a borrowed label and began debating the existence of a New Wave cinema in Hong Kong. There was no doubt that the films and their makers were forging a new cinema at the time. Even though this new cinema has changed its contours, the directors associated with it, such as Tsui Hark and Ann Hui, have continued to play a significant role in its subsequent development. To the extent that the New Wave filmmakers helped turn Cantonese cinema into a modern cultural entity with a cosmopolitan outlook, their contribution bears further discussion and analysis.

This chapter offers a short, comprehensive account of the key aspects of Hong Kong's New Wave cinema. My discussion will situate the emergence of Hong Kong's New Wave cinema in the social and the political context of the 1960s and the 1970s and identify certain connections between local politics and the world of counterculture. In addition to the changes in Cantonese cinema, the rise of television and the appearance of cine clubs and experimental filmmaking are instrumental as well. Readers will be introduced to films and television programs that will expand their understanding of the New Wave cinema beyond the better-known titles and their directors.

Political Activism and Counterculture

The major events and movements of the 1960s can be seen in hindsight to have been manifesting the global aspects of modern political and popular culture. The Vietnam War and the student and worker unrest in Eastern and Western Europe crossed national boundaries and left their mark on Hong

Kong, especially on cultural workers and university students, whose outlook was greatly influenced by international events and trends. Together with the Cultural Revolution, these events outside of Hong Kong marked the decade as a particularly politicized one. In the years following the city riots in 1967, social and political uprisings fueled a local antiestablishment counterculture, including an antiwar movement. In a development that was new for Hong Kong, workers, college students, intellectuals, and young social workers organized themselves into social pressure groups.

The colonial government suppressed political activism throughout the 1950s and 1960s, thus sowing the seeds of discontent and defiance of the establishment. In May 1967, an industrial dispute in Kowloon sparked unprecedented city riots, which were supported by leftists whose loyalty lay with the Cultural Revolution in mainland China. Even though overt political confrontations ended as the result of severe suppressions, anticolonial sentiment did not subside. Within a few years, many social pressure groups were partaking in demonstrations and fighting for rights and social justice. The issues became very specific and locally oriented. One notable episode was the 1971 Diaoyutai Movement, which protested Japanese intrusions (with the consent of the United States) into what was regarded as the sovereign Chinese fishing zone surrounding the Diaoyu Islands (known to the Japanese as the Senkaku Islands). The demonstrations culminated in violent confrontations between demonstrators and what was then called the Royal Hong Kong Police Force. In seeking theoretical support for their actions, intellectuals and college students looked to Chinese Marxism and the theory of the New Left. The following year teachers, students, and social workers participated in citywide demonstrations protesting official discrimination against the Chinese language. They petitioned the colonial government to legalize use of the Chinese language, along with English, in all government documents. This movement once again signaled the collective assertion of a strong anticolonial, prolocal identity. During the same era, many young people became interested in popular culture, including rock music imported from England and films from Europe and Hollywood; for some, their politicized interest in local affairs and their love of Western popular culture were inseparable.

Political activism did not directly change mainstream cinema, which was still dominated by studio productions and genre films. The Shaw Brothers studio, for example, continued to produce such genre films as swordplay, *kungfu*, comedy, horror, and sexploitation. New energies for film culture, nevertheless, were inspired by social activism. A new critical community emerged with cine clubs, publications, and experimental filmmaking. None of these cultural activities were funded by either private enterprise or the government; instead, they emerged in the invisible margins on the basis of some young people's passions. This youthful counterculture detested commercialism and in this respect was very different from the youth culture of the 1990s, which merged well with Hong Kong's increasing affluence and the pervasiveness of commodity culture.

Precursors: Three Filmmakers Who Modernized Cantonese Films

In the mid-1960s, Hong Kong cinema was dominated by studio productions and two major film genres: the Cantonese "youth" films and the Mandarin *wuxia pian* (swordplay movies). The "youth" films featured the movie stars Chan Po-chu and Josephine Siao, who sang, danced, and frolicked in the out-of-doors. Their youthful screen images (which were markedly different from their image in the swordplay films) were the creations of the film directors Chan Wun and Wong Yiu, who capitalized on Chan and Siao's popularity among young moviegoers, as well as on the fashionable trends inspired by American popular culture, particularly the Beach Boys. The "youth" movies remained popular for about three years, but because of their low budgets and limited distribution, they were eventually overcome by the more durable *wuxia pian*, a martial arts genre produced by the Shaw Brothers studio. The Shaw Brothers at the time introduced innovations into their productions with bigger budgets and new talent, and their efforts ushered in a spectacular era of new martial arts cinema in which they dominated the market.

At this time, Cantonese films were struggling for survival in a competitive market with rivals ranging from local Mandarin productions to imported movies from Japan and Hollywood. The Cantonese film industry had its "golden age" back in the early 1950s, when the Zhonglian Company, the famous cooperative of filmmakers and performers, produced some excellent family melodramas with compelling social content. By the 1960s, the Cantonese film industry, with its quickly made, low-budget productions, was in financial crisis. It was at this point that three filmmakers — Chor Yuen, Lung Kong, and Shu Shuen — began to attempt something new by integrating contemporary elements into local productions.

Chor Yuen is the son of the famous Cantonese family melodrama actor Cheung Wood-yau. In 1968 Chor Yuen founded the New Films Company, a cooperative of filmmakers and performers whose manifesto read: "We unite in the struggle to find a new way for Cantonese films to advance toward higher goals." It was an ambitious move, in the spirit of the Zhonglian Company of the 1950s. Chor himself directed the company's first two features in 1969, tackling urban unease in far greater depth than had ever been done up till then. His *Joys and Sorrows of Youth [Lengnuan Qingchun]* (1969), starring Tsang Kong, Nam Hung, Tina Ti, and Lydia Shum, depicted youth gangs, murder, drug traffic, and rape in a university. The film, shot in color for wide screen, responded to increasing youthful restlessness in Hong Kong by playing on young people's feelings of repression and their hatred of the bourgeoisie. It took pointers from such Hollywood films as *Rebel without a Cause* (1955) (as in the scene of the game of "chicken") and *West Side Story* (1961) (in scenes of knife fights between rival youth gangs). One can identify in this film the genre mixing, accelerated rhythms, and ideological inconsistencies that would later become Hong Kong films' most notable characteristics. A year before, Chor had completed *Winter Love [Dong Lien]* (1968), starring Patrick Tse, Josephine Siao, and Lung Kong. It had a nonlinear narrative and used monologue and flashback to interweave reality and memory in a manner truly rare for contemporary Cantonese cinema. The technique in some scenes is reminiscent of Alain Resnais's *Hiroshima, Mon Amour* (1959).

Lung Kong, a versatile director who sometimes acted in his own films, responded to film theory and practice in a more systematic way. Theoretically, he was fascinated by the Soviet montage school and the writings of Lev Kuleshov (especially the latter's *Fundamentals of Film Directing*). He wrote his own screenplays, was meticulous about the details in each scene, and attended to the rhythms created by montage editing. In *Story of a Discharged Prisoner [Yingxiong Bense]* (1967), starring Patrick Tse, he created a scene, inspired by the use of space and montage editing in the well-known "Odessa steps" sequence in Sergei Eisenstein's *Battleship Potemkin* (1925), in which a physically handicapped person was beaten by some gangsters. He was also interested in the more subtle visual style of European films, experimenting with handheld cameras and emphasizing acting and dialogue. Like Chor, Lung dramatized the problems in a changing urban society, but he had a more consistent and explicit socially critical perspective and thus was known also as a "conscience" filmmaker. *Prisoner* was Lung's "remake" of Ralph Nelson's *Once a Thief* (1965), a French-American coproduction. Nineteen years later, this film would itself be remade by John Woo as *A Better Tomorrow [Yingxiong Bense]* (1986).[1]

Lung continued his new approach with *Teddy Girls [Feinu Zhengzhuan]* (1969), in which he also starred, along with Josephine Siao, Sit Kar-yin, and

Lydia Shum. *Teddy Girls* is an unflinching look at the consequences of youth alienation, exemplified by the internal struggles of a girls' reform school. In the final scenes, a group of "teddy girls" (rebellious young women), having escaped from the reform school, seek revenge against boyfriends or parents who have hurt or neglected them in the past. The film climaxes in a bloody struggle between the girls, headed by Josephine Siao, and their uncaring foster father, played by Lung himself. *Teddy Girls* was one of the first Cantonese films to use graphic violence in a modern setting to make a moral point.

Lung's *Yesterday, Today, and Tomorrow [Zuotian Jintian Mingtian]*, made in 1968, was shocking for its apocalyptic vision of a plague-torn Hong Kong. The screenplay was based on the writer Xi Xi's adaptation of Albert Camus's *The Plague*. Lung changed it further to make the plague a metaphor for the May 1967 riots. This "local" conflict, triggered by an industrial dispute in a plastic flower factory in San Po Kong, Kowloon, soon mushroomed into a general strike throughout the territory, accompanied by terrorist activities and bomb attacks that resulted in heavy casualties. The 1967 riots were part of the leftist-organized protests against the colonial administration — turmoil that endured for five months in the ominous shadow of China's Cultural Revolution. Censors banned Lung's film, which compared communism to the plague, for two years, until a heavily cut version, allegedly prepared after the film had been seen and commented upon by the New China News Agency, was released in December 1970. All of the film's censored outtakes were destroyed before its citywide release.

Shu Shuen's short film career began after she had completed her film education in California. With financial support from a Chinese merchant, Paul D. Lee, she made her seminal debut film, *The Arch [Dong Furen]* (1970), with preproduction assistance from Lung Kong. This extraordinary film was shot by Subrata Mitra, who was the Indian director Satyajit Ray's main cinematographer.

The Arch was the first Hong Kong film to gain international recognition. It was presented at Cannes, Locarno, San Francisco, and several other film festivals and won plaudits from admirers as diverse as Henry Miller, Karel Reisz, and Josef von Sternberg. A quote from Miller praising the "poetry, the fantasy, the quietude, the blissful stillness and the simple human touch" confirms the Orientalist appeal of the film. This attention predated that which was later won by the director King Hu and the *kungfu* star Bruce Lee. Indeed, *The Arch* is arguably the first Chinese film to depict, in a very subtle and moving manner, a woman's inner emotional life (that of a widow and her sexual desire). It evokes classical Chinese poetry and paintings with a slowly paced Oriental eroticism. Yet, the film was clearly filtered through a modern temperament, as if Chinese folklore were being retold from an existential point of view.

Shu Shuen's second feature, *China Behind [Zaijian Zhongguo]* (1974), is a technically daring work. Shot in Taiwan with the support of the Kuomintang government and some experimental filmmakers, *China Behind* uses China's Cultural Revolution (which was entering its final phase at the time) as the background for a strong human drama. It tells a story of four mainland students who are driven by the Cultural Revolution to flee to Hong Kong as illegal immigrants and are subsequently stunned by Hong Kong's unbridled capitalism. China's much-feared Gang of Four was then in power, and the film was banned on the grounds that it would "damage good relations with other territories" or "contribute to possible breaches of peace" with Hong Kong's great neighbor. For unknown reasons, it was not released in Taiwan either. The film was screened at a French film festival, and it was not until the late 1980s that its significance was fully recognized.

Between 1967 and 1971, these three directors and their remarkable efforts lit a beacon for a modern cinema to come, even though they could not stem the immediate decline of Cantonese cinema at the time. In 1972 no Cantonese films were produced, and the Cantonese cinema sank into an eighteen-month coma. Chor Yuen was absorbed by Shaw Brothers Studio as a contract director, while Lung Kong retained his independent spirit to continue exploring new genres and techniques in controversial films such as *The Call Girls [Yingzhao Nulang]* (1973) and *Hiroshima 28 [Guangdao Erba]* (1974). After making more-conventional films for about three years, Lung quit the business in 1977, reemerging briefly as the producer of Patrick Tam's *Love Massacre [Ai Sha]* (1981). Shu Shuen's third feature film, *Sup Sap Bup Dup [Shisan Buda]* (1975), was an unconventional satire on the local residents' passion for gambling. It was a surrealistic work, aptly described by one critic as a "scatterbrained collection of short comedic sketches." After her fourth feature, *Hong Kong Tycoon [Baofa Wu]* (1979), failed, Shu Shuen quit filmmaking. Despite her outstanding work, Shu remained a somewhat mysterious figure, especially regarding her artistic background. Still, she left other traces on the as-yet-unformed New Wave directors by founding and liberally sponsoring a new film magazine, *Close Up Film Review*, in 1976. It drew together such young writers as Li Kok-chung, Law Wai-ming, Shu Kei, Cheung Kam-moon, Leung Noong-kong, Kam Ping-hing, and Cheuk Pak-tong. In 1979, when the magazine stopped publication, many of Shu's

Figure 1.
China Behind (1974).
Daring work on China's
Cultural Revolution,
shot in Taiwan, by
director Tang Shuxuan.

Figure 2.
Hiroshima 28 (1974).
Controversial film by
"conscience director"
Lung Kong.

collaborators founded *Film Biweekly*, the first magazine to promote and monitor New Wave cinema, which emerged that same year.

The Shaping of a New Film Culture

Publications and Cine Clubs

During the chilliest years of the cold war (from the late 1940s to the early 1960s), Hong Kong media was the battleground of the conservative Right (with pro-Nationalist and pro-American forces) and the conservative Left (with pro–orthodox Communist forces). From the mid-1960s onward, the beginnings of a "new Left" coming from global countercultural movements began to influence young critics and their film and literary writings in Hong Kong. In the early 1970s, more than 200 independent magazines came onto the scene, all of them published by volunteer organizations and private groups to pursue interests in social criticism, literary criticism, and creative writing. Magazines like the *Tabloid* and *New Sensibility* focused on cultural and social criticism, and the *'70s Biweekly*, a radical "new Marxist" magazine for students and workers, covered topics directly linked to Chinese politics. Other popular magazines such as *Youth Garden Weekly* ran regular discussions on cinema, espousing a leftist view that commercial films from the West were "polluting" local culture, while the *Hong Kong Youth Weekly* accepted Western culture as a liberating force and introduced Western films and popular music. From 1963 onward, the *Chinese Student Weekly*, under the editorship of Law Kar and Ada Luk, carried a regular film page and printed film criticism and other writings by authors such as Sek Kei, Xi Xi, Dai Tin, Kam Ping-hing, Shu Ming, Ng Ho, Yong Fan, Ng Chun-ming, Fong Yuen, Lin Nien-tung, Chan Yum, Do Do, and Ku Chong-ng, and, later, Shu Kei, Patrick Tam, Wong Chi, Leung Noong-kong, Freddie Wong, and Liang Hai-chiang. These and other publications provided a battle-ground of ideas, venues for information on popular culture, and a practice ground for a critical community of film critics and scholars.

Shu Shuen's *Close Up Film Review* in 1979 became *Close Up Weekly*, but it folded quickly. Its writers and other young critics came together and launched the influential *Film Biweekly* in 1979. *Film Biweekly* soon became the city's major film magazine espousing the "new Hong Kong cinema." This focus had much to do with the fact that some of the editors and writers were also television writers and actors. Shu Kei, for example, wrote screenplays for Ann Hui, Yim Ho, and Patrick Tam; Law Wai-ming wrote for Allen Fong and Ann Hui; and Lee Kwok-chung acted in the television films of Yim Ho and Ann Hui. In the mid-1980s, *Film Biweekly* (later known as *City Entertainment*) sustained artistic and critical interests in national cinemas and in Hong Kong's New Wave films and filmmakers.

Cine club activities began in the early 1960s as part of the youth culture. Until then, there were no venues for the screening of student, art, or experimental films. The first major film club, Studio One Film Society of Hong Kong, was formed in 1962, the year city hall opened on Hong Kong island. The organizers were western expatriates and local enthusiasts who were particularly keen on European art films. Even though they showed no interest in Hong Kong films and their programs were published in English, these art films provided a rare alternative viewing experience at the time. Studio One's membership peaked in the late 1970s with over 3,000 people, but it folded in the mid-1980s.

Between 1967 and 1968, local, nonexpatriate film buffs launched the College Cine Club (Dai Ying Hui) in Kowloon. Its core members were the writers and editors of both *College Life* and *Chinese Student Weekly*. The club's activities were more or less coextensive with the *Chinese Student Weekly's* topics on auteur theory, Taiwanese modernism, and contemporary trends in Western poetry, theater, and literature.[2] It was during this time that film buffs and young critics happily "discovered" Hollywood's auteurs, as well as those from Europe and Japan. Prominent "B" features from Hollywood and Japan, as well as experimental cinema from both Europe and Taiwan,[3] became more widely known.

Experimental Films

From the late 1960s on, film club activities became increasingly popular among university students, who organized screenings and discussions. Some young critics joined the College Cine Club to make their own 8-millimeter and 16-millimeter shorts. Between 1968 and 1971, when it folded, the College Cine Club ran three exhibitions of local experimental films made by core members and friends. In 1974 Kam Ping-hing, who would later teach college-level film courses, founded the Phoenix Cine Club, which worked with the government's Urban Council to present short film exhibitions. This club was active until the mid-1980s, and its members, including Wong Ka-wah, Freddie Wong, Jimmy Choi Kam-chun, and Lambert Yam, have helped nourish more experimental filmmakers.

The Film Guard Association (Film Guard) was formed in 1972 and used the *Chinese Student Weekly* as a forum to express views on cinema. Among its core members were Cheung Kin, Liang Hai-chiang, Wong Kin-yip, Lee Yiu-ming, Mok Tai-chi, and Cheung Wai-nam. A year later, the Hong Kong Federation of Students organized the territory's first Experimental Film Contest. Alex Cheung, Freddie Wong, and Ng Yu-sum (John Woo) all won prizes with their short films. From 1974 to 1976, Film Guard organized annual screenings of experimental short films, which received some funding from the government's Urban Council. In 1976, Film Guard presented a ten-year retrospective of local experimental films. Appearing in its catalog were Ann Hui, Patrick Tam, Alex Cheung, Lau Shing-hon, Eddie Ling-ching Fong, Allen Fong, Wellington Fung, Terry Tong, Poon Man-kit, Apple Pak-huen Kwan, David Hoi-lum King, George Chan, William Cheung, and Ng Yu-sum (John Woo). All of these people became prominent filmmakers in the 1970s and 1980s. In 1977 the Phoenix Cine Club joined Film Guard to organize the new Hong Kong Independent Short Film Competition, which took experimental film exhibition into a new era.

The Television Connection

Without television as the training ground, there would not have been a New Wave cinema in Hong Kong. Selina Chow, a television producer, should be credited with much of the development of quality television drama (among other programs) and turning a commercial television station into a rigorous training school—a "Shaolin temple"—for emerging filmmakers.

There were three television stations in Hong Kong, two private (TVB and RTV, which became ATV after 1982) and one public (RTHK). All of them

produced their own programs for the local market with their own studio fa-
cilities and production personnel. In this regard, the television stations in
Hong Kong are different from those in England or Germany, as they do not
sponsor feature films for theatrical release. But the television stations became
an important training ground for young scriptwriters, directors, and producers who ended up being the creative core group for Hong Kong's new cinema, and they formed what amounted to television's New Wave. The main
members of this group include both those who received their film or art
education overseas and those who were self-taught.

In 1975 Selina Chow began moving away from popular variety shows to
head the programming and production departments of Television Broadcasting Limited (TVB). She introduced half-hour drama series shot on
16-millimeter film. Patrick Tam, Chow's anchor director, who later became
known for his New Wave films, won a bronze award at the New York International Film and Television Festival for *Superstars [Qunxing Pu]* with the
"Wang Chuanru" episode (1975). A year later, encouraged by the success of
the series *Superstars, Seven Women [Qi Nuxing]* and *Wonderfun [Qiqu Lu]*,
Chow set up a film unit, which attracted young graduates such as Ann Hui,
Dennis Yu, Yim Ho, Agnes Ng, Ben Lam, Lau Shing-hon, Cheuk Pak-tong,
Hilda Chan, Kirk Wong, and Patrick Tam, all of whom had returned to Hong
Kong after studying abroad. Directors, writers, and cinematographers in-
cluding Law Kar, Lee Pui-kuen, Alex Cheung, Ng Ho, Josephine Ho, Joyce
Chan, Shu Kei, David Chung, and Bill Wong also worked for this film unit.
The television films were usually shot within ten working days and edited in
four days, with a budget that ranged from 10 to 20 percent of that of an aver-
age feature film. But the unit's regularity and the enormous creative freedom
it offered enabled several directors, including Patrick Tam, Ann Hui, and
Alex Cheung, to launch their careers on the silver screen a few years later.
Patrick Tam, a talented director, developed a feel for good cinema and completed many film episodes under the film unit. His best television work includes *Seven Women*, especially the "Miu Kam-fung" episode (inspired by
Jean-Luc Godard's *Two or Three Things I Know about Her* [1967] and *A Married Woman* [1964]) and the "Murder Thy Father" and "Double Murder"
episodes (thrillers in the styles of Alfred Hitchcock and Roman Polanski);
Social Worker [Bei Dou Xing] (the eleventh episode); and the "Four Moods"
episode in the *CID* series. All of these works are comparable, if not superior,
to Tam's later works in cinema (which include *The Sword, Love Massacre,*
and *Nomad*).

The impressive works of Ann Hui also began with television. The "Ah

Sze" episode of the *Social Worker* series in 1977 was an intimate study of a poor immigrant from mainland China who was forced to surrender her body, but not her dignity, to a Hong Kong pimp. In 1977 and 1978 Hui directed six beautifully executed episodes for a new ICAC series that dramatized the issues of corruption and the culture and complexity of bribery. These series were sponsored by the then-new official body, the Independent Commission Against Corruption (ICAC). Hui immediately followed up with three excellent episodes made for RTHK's *Below the Lion Rock [Shizi Shanxia]* series. The "Boy from Vietnam" episode, scripted by Wong Chi and Shu Kei, explored the life of boat people arriving from Vietnam; "The Bridge" exposed the politics behind the government demolition of a bridge in a slum; and "The Road" portrayed three female drug addicts from the lower class. Hui's New Wave feature films, *The Secret, The Story of Woo Viet,* and *Boat People,* all bear traces of her 16-millimeter television films.

Tam and Hui are strict and uncompromising directors. Tam's highly controversial television film *Seven Women* made explosive comments on sex and complacency and punctured prevailing middle-class values in a way that invited the wrath of moralists and tested the outer limits of censorship. His third feature, *Nomad [Liehuo Qingchun]* (1982), criticized Japan's economic and cultural invasion of Hong Kong. Similarly, two of Hui's six *ICAC* episodes ("The Investigation" and "Real Men") were banned for their uncompromising attacks on police and civil servants. "The Bridge," an episode that Hui directed for *Below the Lion Rock,* exposed the inefficiency and bureaucracy of the Housing Department, the Social Welfare Department, and the Royal Hong Kong Police.

Alex Cheung, who did not quite make the "New Wave director" list, developed superb technical skills in his television work, especially in the TVB's *CID* series. These include seamless and dynamic action sequences, the use of dramatic suspense, and exploration of the human dimension in well-defined characters of the lower classes. Cheung was the first director to experiment with terror, speedy car chases, choreographed gunfights, and more realistic use of explosives on the screen. His *Cops and Robbers* (1979) and *Man on the Brink* (1981) are cinematic extensions of his *CID* episodes, including "The Trio" and "The Car Thief" in the *Taxi Driver* series and "The Occult" in the *Interpol* series.

Radio-Television Hong Kong (RTHK) turned out to be another training ground for local filmmakers. RTHK is a government station with a propagandistic mission: to produce programs that address social problems as seen through the eyes of the ordinary person and to provide solutions from the

Figure 3.
The Bridge (Ann Hui, 1978). An episode in the television series *Below the Lion Rock* condemns the government's indifference to slum residents.

government's point of view. From 1975 onward, the government liberalized its culture and media policies. Cheung Man-yee, whose work was the public service–sector counterpart to Selina Chow's commercial productions, supervised the *Below the Lion Rock* series and became the administrative head of its television production wing. Cheung turned the series into a Shaolin temple as well, giving opportunities to the young Allen Fong, Wong Chi, Lo Chi-keung, Lam Tak-luk, Lillian Bik-wah Li, John Law, Yim Wai, David King, Calvin Wong, Rachel Zen, and Lawrence Ah-Mon. Under Cheung, RTHK introduced the celebrated series *When We Were Young* and nourished the talents of Rachel Zen, who combined anger at social injustice with docudrama and melodrama to give voice to the underprivileged. The television films *Songs of Yuen Chau Chai [Yuanzhouzai Zhige]* and *Wild Child [Ye Haizi]* confirmed Allen Fong as a brilliant filmmaker who used a documentary style combined with a poetic rendering of realism.

Rediffusion Television (RTV), the precursor of today's Asian Television (ATV), experienced a high point between 1976 and 1978. Johnny Mak, the producer and director of two hour-long series, *Ten Sensational Cases [Shida Qian]* and *Ten Assassinations [Shida Cike]*, turned RTV's fortunes around. The sensational hit episodes in *Operation Manhunt [Da Zhangfu]* and *Operation Manhunt II [Xin Da Zhangfu]* revealed a particularly violent and honest picture (by that era's television standards) of the city's underworld, and its use of exaggeration was dramatically successful. RTV's *Operation*

Manhunt series was generally more realistic and far less sentimental than TVB's *CID* series; the three-hour "Bar Girl" episode directed by Mak was regarded as the best in the series. As a producer, Mak ushered in new directorial talents, including David Lai, Michael Mak, and Manfred Wong, as well as the script supervisor Siu Yeuk-yuen. These men joined the Johnny Mak Production Company upon Mak's departure from RTV.

The year 1978 saw some stormy changes in Hong Kong television. Selina Chow left TVB at the end of 1977, taking several able administrators and filmmakers with her in order to join the newly formed CTV (City Television). The group included Tsui Hark, Patrick Tam, Ringo Lam, Stephen Shin, Eddie Fong, Annette Shum, Hilda Chan, Shu Kei, Joyce Chan, Kam Ping-hing, Lee Dun, Tam Ning, and Chan Fong. It was an immediate shot in the arm for CTV, especially during Chow's ten-month tenure, which boasted Tsui Hark's outstanding work in the cinematic *Gold Dagger Romance [Jin-dao Qingxia]* series that launched Tsui's career. In late August 1978, however, CTV collapsed financially. The creative honeymoon with television ended abruptly, and the directors moved on.

Essentially, television provided a stepping-stone for most young directors, and by the end of 1979 the film industry was witnessing a surge of creative energy. Tsui Hark worked with the Seasonal Film Corporation to direct *The Butterfly Murders*; Stephen Shin turned in *Affairs [Yuanjia]* (1979) for the Great Wall Production Company; and Golden Harvest recruited Patrick Tam for *The Sword [Ming Jian]* (1980). The scriptwriters Kam Ping-hing, Joyce Chan, Chan Fong, Shu Kei, and Szeto Cheuk-hon turned to the cinema, as did the cinematographers David Chung and Bill Wong. Clifford Choi made his directorial debut with *Encore* (1980), followed by *Teenage Dreamers [Lingmeng Kele]* (1982); both were youth films depicting the lives and dreams of teenage students. Dennis Yu brought his administrative and producing skills to commercial films including *See-Bar* (1980), *The Beasts* (1980), and *The Imp [Xiong Bang]* (1981). Selina Chow, who left CTV, codirected her only feature film, *No Big Deal* (1979), a teen comedy, with Leong Po-chih.

It would be fair to say that the film directors were innovators of the system who were very conscious of their audience. Their bold and inventive work for television had created a New Wave. When they moved on to filmmaking, they brought television virtues to cinema, including location filming with simple equipment, efficiency in working with tight schedules and lower costs, and a sense of realism that gave the city of Hong Kong a starring role in their works.

The Hong Kong New Wave

In late 1979 new films began to appear that gave the audience a rare sense of experiencing contemporary Hong Kong onscreen. These films, which differed from the era's dominant *kungfu* and comedy genres, used techniques that demonstrated their directors' understanding of well-known contemporary Western and Japanese films. Local critics named the phenomenon the "new Hong Kong cinema"[4] or, simply, New Wave. Yet, there was no uniformity among the New Wave films, and the commercial turn of its directors took place within such a short time after they gained their reputations as New Wave directors that the phenomenon was still the subject of considerable debate.

Some signs of change appeared around the mid-1970s. In 1973, John Woo made a low-budget feature, *Farewell Buddy [Guo Ke]*, as a conventional *kungfu* movie, but the film failed to find a distributor. On the strength of that effort, however, Golden Harvest hired Woo as a director and released his film as *The Young Dragons [Tiehan Rouqing]* (1975). Alex Kwok-ming Cheung, who had moved into television after winning a prize in the Hong Kong Experimental Film Contest of 1973, attempted to expand an experimental short into a full-length film but failed to obtain adequate backing. Then, in 1976, the television director Leong Po-chih and the actress Josephine Siao (the latter had just completed her film education in America) codirected their first feature, *Jumping Ash [Tiao Hui]*, which was financed by Bang Bang, an independent film company. Its scriptwriter, Philip Chan, who would become a prominent filmmaker, was still a member of the Royal Hong Kong Police at the time. *Jumping Ash* had the third highest box office revenues of 1976, HK$3.87 million, after Steven Spielberg's *Jaws* (which grossed HK$5.51 million), and was regarded by some as the first actual feature exhibiting the New Wave spirit.

In 1978 two reputable television directors, Dennis Yu and Yim Ho, joined Ronnie Yu and Philip Chan to form Film Force Productions. The company's first feature, *Extras [Ke-li-fei]* (1978), was also financed by Bang Bang. *Extras* is an unusual tragicomedy detailing the forlorn existence of a film extra, who stands for the little man exploited and abandoned by society, represented here by the film industry itself. The film's director, Yim Ho, added the unlikely elements of pathos and sympathy for the plight of these workers to a style of Cantonese comedy then in vogue. It did moderately well at the box office and was ranked as the second best film of the year, earning fourteen votes from a panel of twenty-eight young critics, some of whom had worked for the film magazines *Close Up* and *Film Biweekly*; twelve of these critics who voted for *Extras* in the Chinese film category also voted for Woody Allen's *Annie Hall* and Steven Spielberg's *Close Encounters of the Third Kind* in the foreign film category, which won twenty-one votes and eighteen votes, respectively.

Even before Yim Ho's *Extras* won critical acclaim, Yim and seven other television directors caught the critics' attention. In 1978 a short article in *Close Up* titled "Hong Kong Cinema New Wave: Revolutionaries That Challenge Tradition?" linked these young people with the possibility of change. Critics showed great excitement in 1979 when four films appeared that confirmed their notion of the New Wave: Ann Hui's *The Secret [Feng Jie]*, Tsui Hark's *The Butterfly Murders [Die Bian]*, Alex Cheung's *Cops and Robbers [Dian Zhi Bing Bing]*, and Peter Yung Wai-chun's *The System [Xing Gui]*. All four, however, were box office failures.

A long list of exciting films appeared in the early 1980s. The year 1980 brought Dennis Yu's *See-bar [Shi Ba]* and *The Beasts [Shan Gou]*, Lau Shing-hon's *House of the Lute [Yuhuo Fenqin]*, Clifford Choi Kai-kwong's *Encore [He Cai]*, Patrick Tam's swordplay film *The Sword*, Yim Ho's *The Happenings [Ye Che]*, Selina Chow and Leong Po-chih's *No Big Deal [Youni Woni]*, and Ann Hui's second feature, *The Spooky Bunch [Zhuang Dao Zheng]*, as well as two films by Tsui Hark, *We Are Going to Eat You [Diyu Women]* and *Dangerous Encounter—1st Kind [Diyi Leixing Weixian]*. Notable titles of 1981–83 include Patrick Tam's *Love Massacre* (1981), Alex Cheung's *Man on the Brink [Bianxuan Ren]* (1981), Ann Hui's *The Story of Woo Viet [Huyue De Gushi]* (1981) and *Boat People [Toubin Nuhai]* (1982), and Allen Fong's *Father and Son [Fuzhi Qing]* (1981) and *Ah Ying [Banbian Ren]* (1983).

The New Wave phenomenon aroused heated debate among several critics. Responses were polarized. Law Wai-ming, for example, praised the New Wave directors for films that were based on Hong Kong's contemporary life. Roger Garcia did not think that a new cinema existed because the films simply repackaged and restated conventions of Hong Kong cinema, and postwar Hong Kong cinema had been influenced by the West. Li Cheuk-to pointed out that the critics longed for a new vision and a new aesthetic horizon. Other critics pointed out the excessive violence in some of these films and to their failure to break away from the dominant ideology or to "question cinema's own form of expression" and "explore the relationship between con-

徐 陳
演導 飾為
克 家
蓀
破天荒携手

馮愛慈 武術指導
陳少玲 程小東
客串主演 攝影
特別邀請五路明星 鍾志文
史提夫勒沙 燈光
林 榮

車保羅・龍天生
施瑞華・胡大為
葉德嫻・溫燦華
陳華南・麥大成
楊又祥・朱承彩
余頭允・余慕蓮
周國基・曹廣慶
馮潤泉・馮苦漢
盧家智・區樹湛
布魯士白龍
姬約翰・古美嬌

第一類型危險
Dangerous Encounter ~ 1st Kind

羅 林 區 呂
烈 珍 瑞 良
奇 奇 強 偉
領銜主演 領銜主演

監製 馮永發
影藝電影有限公司
Fotocine Film Production Limited
創業百萬鉅製

Figure 4.
*Dangerous Encounter—
1st Kind* (Tsui Hark,
1980). A metaphor
for social chaos and
discontent.

sciousness and expression of meaning and activity." But there was no new aesthetic landscape. Thus, the new films, when compared to those of the French New Wave, neither were aesthetically new, nor did they open new doors to cinema. The common denominators among their creators were youth, energy, and ambition. The early 1980s provided timely opportunities for these directors to break into the industry to realize their first films, altering the visual landscape of Hong Kong cinema. Still, the term New Wave is not inappropriate if by this one refers to the use of innovative techniques, an urban sensibility, interest in new visual styles, and more personal means of expression. There were also technical improvements, including improved dubbing and sound effects, more-serious attention to music, and more-flexible camera techniques. These changes represented a modernization of film language and techniques that was gradually adopted by the industry.

The innovations did not come from a complete rupture with the past or from self-reflexivity. Instead, old genres were freshened up with new approaches. Tsui Hark's *Butterfly Murders*, for example, was not a "contemporary" film, but it reconstructed a dominant old genre in the light of Japanese *manga* and new science-fiction techniques that were inspired by contemporary Hollywood. In the film *We Are Going to Eat You* (1980), Tsui added horror elements, à la Hollywood's zombie films, to an otherwise "typical" *kungfu* plot that was, in fact, Tsui's metaphorical projection of the Cultural Revolution.

Ann Hui's *The Secret* reworked the crime-of-passion murder mystery by incorporating a ghost story into it. There are layered flashbacks and shifting narrative perspectives that culminate in a climatic unveiling of gory details by a madman that finally solve a double murder. In her freewheeling comedy *The Spooky Bunch* (1980), Hui further experimented with shifting points of view and mixed genres — comedy, horror, thriller, and *kungfu*.

Patrick Tam's *The Sword* invests the standard swordplay film (*wuxia pian*) with the precision treatment of a Jean-Pierre Melville film in terms of its mise-en-scène, editing, and contrasts between sound and silence and between static and dynamic images. Tam's *Love Massacre* (1981), which was inspired by a real case in San Francisco, concerns a serial killer of college girls. An off-the-wall film starring Brigitte Ching-hsia Lin, *Love Massacre* was a conscious homage to Jean-Luc Godard, with its experiments in color and settings that externalized the killer's emotions. Tam's next film, *Nomad* (1982), confirmed him as a formalist very much concerned with film language, sometimes at the cost of content.

Yim Ho's *The Happenings* follows a group of troublemaking teenagers in the course of one night. Independently produced, it adopted the rhythm and reality of a documentary as it accompanied the youths (using a cast of unknowns) plunging deeper and deeper into trouble, culminating in violence and a killing.

Lau Shing-hon's low-budget *House of the Lute* was financed by the director himself and was similarly independent in spirit. This offbeat tragedy sets the eternal triangle, involving a young woman, her paralyzed husband, and a handsome young laborer (suggesting D. H. Lawrence's 1928 novel *Lady Chatterley's Lover*). The story takes place inside a big old house with a traditional Chinese interior. Although it was bold in its depiction of sexual politics and its critique of traditional mores, criticism fell on its low production values.

In both *Father and Son* (1981) and *Ah Ying* (1983), Allen Fong revived an old Cantonese staple, the family drama. *Father and Son* was imbued with a spirit of Italian neorealism, which was unusual for Hong Kong films of the 1970s. It is direct and touching in its memory of the 1950s up to the 1970s as recalled by a son whose father dies at the beginning of the film. *Ah Ying* uses cinema verité to depict the dreams of the two main characters, a plain-looking young fish vendor and her drama teacher, each of whom "enlightens" the other.

Two additional productions directed by Alex Cheung are worth mentioning. Cheung's feature debut, *Cops and Robbers* (1979), did nothing new with

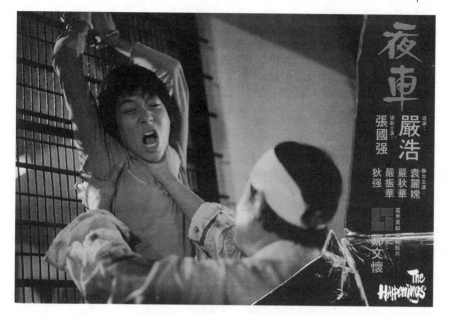

Figure 5.
Young people plunged
deep into trouble in
The Happenings
(Yim Ho, 1980).

the modern crime thriller, but he did transplant it into a contemporary Hong Kong setting by featuring a cat-and-mouse chase by the Royal Hong Kong Police of a psychotic serial killer. The quick pace and clean-cut narrative greatly appealed to the film's young audiences. Cheung's next film, *Man on the Brink* (1981), is a kind of vigilante film set in a new, lower-middle-class housing estate. It successfully combines sensational human drama and excellent action scenes in a compelling mixture that drew mixed reactions from the critics. Although in *Man on the Brink* he adhered to the standard conventions of melodrama, Cheung remains one of Hong Kong's most successful crime-action directors, John Woo notwithstanding.

In 1980 Peter Wai-chun Yung, a veteran documentary director, made his first fiction feature, *The System*. A story about a paid drug informer living in double jeopardy of possible betrayal by the police and death at the hands of the drug runners he betrays, Yung's film, for which he did much in-depth research, presented some uncomfortable truths. The film was drastically re-edited before its release. Tsui Hark also confronted the censors with *Dangerous Encounter—1st Kind* (1980), a metaphor for the social chaos and discontent of 1960s and 1970s Hong Kong. It initially focused on four youngsters who rebel against the colonial government by planting bombs; when this version was banned, Tsui reshot the film with a new story line in which a group of tough U.S. mercenaries smuggle machine guns and other weapons into Hong Kong to engage in illegal arms trading. They exploit a group of local youngsters, whom they then try to liquidate one by one. Apart from its extreme violence, the film was uniquely nihilistic in approach and politically subversive in its depiction of "foreign forces" destroying the common people.

New Wave films are Cantonese films that emerged at a time when traditional Cantonese cinema had already disappeared and when Mandarin cinema—*kungfu* and *wuxia pian*—had become sterile. As major studios (the Shaw Brothers and Golden Harvest) searched for new talent for their productions, expanded opportunities awaited young filmmakers, especially those who had completed their directorial apprenticeships in television.

Concluding Remarks

Even if there was no "new aesthetic landscape," the term "Hong Kong New Wave" was still appropriate for the new techniques, daring sensibility, and new genres (and generic mixes) that young television directors and filmmakers brought to Hong Kong cinema. The new arrivals sought innovative visual styles and more personal means of expression, which necessitated technical improvements. Improved dubbing and sound effects, more-serious attention to film music, and more-flexible uses of the movie camera helped modernize Cantonese cinema.

Many filmmakers tried to maintain the relative creative freedom they had enjoyed while working in television. But these attempts could not be sustained over several feature films, and most directors had to learn to please the market. Not everyone was happy about the transition, and few were able to preserve strong personal visions in their commercial undertakings.

As members of the postwar generation, the New Wave directors had a broader social vision than their older colleagues. Some consciously sought cross-cultural subjects and settings for their stories; many were sensitive to the changing urban environment and to contemporary social and political issues. Tsui Hark's *Dangerous Encounter—1st Kind*, Patrick Tam's *Love Massacre* and *Nomad*, Ann Hui's *Story of Woo Viet* and *Boat People*, Yim Ho's *The Happenings* and *Homecoming*, and Kirk Wong's *The Club* and *Health Warning* all brought something different into the system. Through their collective efforts, the films reflect upon such subjects as the emptiness of a commodity-oriented society, the struggles of young people coming from working-class backgrounds, and the cultural and economic domination of foreigners in the city. Location shooting, away from the stuffy studios, added a great sense of realism to the films and laid the tracks for what may be argued as Hong Kong cinema's "Second Wave." The New Wave films made Hong Kong itself a star.

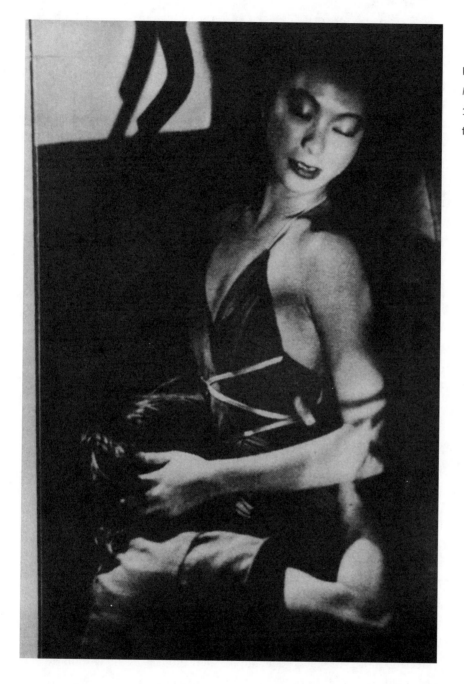

Figure 6.
Nomad (Patrick Tam,
1982) displays bold
formalist concerns.

Notes

This essay has been adapted by the editor and Law Kar from his "Hong Kong New Wave: Modernization Amid Global/Local Counter Cultures," in *Hong Kong New Wave: Twenty Years After* (Hong Kong Urban Council: The Twenty-third Hong Kong International Film Festival, 1999), 44–50.

1   A web of sentiment connects Woo's films from 1986 on with movies he had loved in the 1960s. For example, he remade Lung's *Story of a Discharged Prisoner* as *A Better Tomorrow*, keeping the same Chinese title. Soon afterward, he used "Once a Thief" as the *English* title of a caper movie starring Chow Yun-Fat, Cherie Chung and Leslie Cheung (the film was inspired by a French movie, *Les Aventuriers*, starring Alain Delon). Chow's persona in *A Better Tomorrow* and *The Killer* may have been modeled in part on Delon's work for director Jean-Pierre Melville. Moreover, the Chinese title of Woo's *Bullet in the Head* was the same as that of *Once a Thief*.

2   Taiwanese modernism was influenced by modern French literature such as that of Jean-Paul Sartre, Jean Genet, Alain Robbe-Grillet, Eugene Ionesco, and Marguerite Duras, and other famous works by modern European poets, dramatists, and novelists were widely translated into Chinese. Also, abstract painting was much admired and practiced by Taiwanese artists. This trend was subsequently introduced to Hong Kong in the 1960s and became very popular among the young artists and intellectuals there.

3   *Theatre Quarterly*, published in Taipei, organized Taiwan's first-ever experimental film exhibitions in 1964 and 1965, arousing keen local interest. When two prominent exhibitors, Chiu Kang-chien and Wong Hua-chin, later came to Hong Kong as scriptwriters for Shaw Brothers, they were simultaneously involved in experimental film activities in Hong Kong.

4   [It did not co-opt the term from the earlier French "New Wave" since the term signified "New Waves" for other aspects of Hong Kong culture—Ed.]

CHAPTER TWO

The Emergence of the Hong Kong New Wave

Hector Rodriguez

Writing in the Hong Kong periodical *Film Biweekly* in October 1979, the editor, Law Wai-ming, heralded "the beginning of a new era" in local cinema, an artistic revolution presumably ushered in by the films of the young directors Tsui Hark, Ronnie Yu, Alex Cheung, Ann Hui, and Patrick Tam. This rhetoric of rupture and transformation crystallized around the concept of a "Hong Kong New Wave"; Law described the emerging filmmakers as "a collective symbol of all that is new in the industry," whose presence marked the birth of a genuine art cinema movement.[1] Employing similar terms, many Hong Kong film critics shaped the "Hong Kong New Wave" as a category of classification, description, evaluation, and debate.

My argument reconstructs the avatars of the idea of a "Hong Kong New Wave" by examining its emergence as an object of critical discussion. This essay is not an exercise in aesthetic appreciation but a sociological analysis of the role that a vocabulary of aesthetic appreciation has played in the institution of film criticism and (sometimes) the self-understanding of filmmakers. The discourse of the New Wave principally arose within a critical community that had already developed a network of protocols, commitments, concepts, and institutions in the late 1960s and 1970s. I describe this sociohistorical background as a "film culture field."

My aim is to command an overview of the cultural arena where intellectuals and artists worked to define and defend various criteria of cultural legitimacy, to discuss and refine their shared identity, to play out their emotional investment in the idea of culture, to elaborate and address their implied audience, and to establish their moral and aesthetic authority. The result of these efforts was a practice of criticism and a set of enduring public institutions where that practice could unfold. At stake in these activities were the mission of the film critic, the relationship between culture and society, and the identity of Hong Kong itself.

Cognitive Praxis

It is convenient to begin by characterizing in general terms the concept of a "cultural field," which in my account includes several components: (1) an institutional system of formal organizations and informal circles that may, but need not, contain codified membership requirements and internal hierarchies; (2) a set of values and commitments directed toward shared identities, intellectual traditions, and patterns of emotional investment in common concerns; (3) a network of shared topics and practical protocols ranging from fixed norms to indeterminate rules of thumb; (4) a collective memory constituted not only by early efforts at creating the field but also by "great achievements" or "golden periods" in its later evolution; and (5) a way of relating to other social institutions and groups that provide material support and inspiration for, or enter into conflict with, members of the field. The self-identity of a field frequently constitutes an external social phenomenon as an other. Characteristically not an imaginary or purely discursive construction but a real entity (an institution, organization, doctrine, way of life, person or type of person, etc.), the other is excluded from membership in the field and often also provides a target for the group's ambivalence, hostility, contempt, hatred, competition, enmity, mistrust, or fear.

The concept of a field therefore comprises institutional, emotional, ethical, and cognitive backgrounds. In his contribution to this anthology, Law Kar has outlined the institutional system of the film culture field in Hong Kong. It includes film pages in cultural magazines (*Chinese Student Weekly*); columns in daily newspapers (*Ming Pao Daily, New Life Evening News,* and the *Hong Kong Standard,* among others); screen journals and magazines (*Close Up Film Review* and *Film Biweekly*); film forums and student organizations biased toward auteur and avant-garde cinema (the College Cine Club, the Film Guard Association, and the Phoenix Cine Club); humanities programs in tertiary education institutions (the Chinese University of Hong Kong, the Hong Kong Baptist College, and, more recently, the Hong Kong Academy for the Performing Arts); film and drama courses in independent organizations (the Film Culture Centre and the Hong Kong Arts Centre); events like the Independent Short Film Competition and the Hong Kong International Film Festival; and, especially, the annual publications and retrospectives of the Hong Kong International Film Festival. These public spheres often interacted with one another. Many of the critics who had collaborated in *Close Up* throughout the 1970s also joined the newly established

Film Biweekly when the former folded in 1979. Articles by members of associations like the College Cine Club and Film Guard also appeared in the *Chinese Student Weekly,* whose contributors would often also write for *Film Biweekly,* occupy important roles (such as editors and programmers) in the International Film Festival, enroll in film and communication departments in institutions of higher education, and write regular columns for newspapers. Thus, the institutional nexus of the film culture field comprised an interlocking network of public spheres where critics and aspiring filmmakers came together as a community with a shared interest in film as art.[2]

An implication of the concept of a cultural field is that its discourses and institutions cannot be wholly characterized in isolation from each other. The film culture field was a total context of activities, organizations, and interests that interlocked with, and ramified into, the explicit concepts of the critical community. This interconnectedness between ideas and institutions can be brought out by describing the Hong Kong film culture field as a process of detaching criticism from the institutions of the commercial cinema, and its critical methods and vocabularies were integral to this institutional process. Contributors to the *Chinese Student Weekly* often saw themselves as representatives of something like an ideal of "pure culture," not bound by the profit imperative. Instead of gossip columns, semifictional hagiographies of famous stars, and glossy promotionals of upcoming films, critics produced in-depth analyses, personal reminiscences, translations of foreign articles, and discussion forums on new films, auteurs, and local industry trends. The self-conscious goal of cultural autonomy from market imperatives underpinned the activities of members of the field. Frequently recounted and sometimes idealized, these protracted early efforts to consolidate film culture institutions, initially conducted with no government assistance, became part of the critical community's institutional memory and buttressed its cultural seriousness and dedication. Recollection was a crucial element in the process of collective identity formation. Thus, the 1960s have been retrospectively spoken of as a "golden age" in Hong Kong film criticism, presumably characterized by the sheer energy, intelligence, and independence of its practitioners. Critics often remember how *Film Biweekly* consistently published academic, independent, and professional reviews rather than "publicity blurbs."[3] The film culture field generated its own institutional memory to sustain its members' shared identity.

The self-understanding of the critical community was thus bound up with its cultivated autonomy from dominant institutions of economic power. Their defense of the integrity and autonomy of art, their putative seriousness of purpose and indifference to the pursuit of profit or popular approval, defined the film culture field in ways that reflected pervasive hostility, or at least ambivalence, toward its other: the cinematic marketplace. Critics thus invoked the idea of film as art to request government support for festivals and screen education activities and to promote the idea of film culture among aspiring filmmakers. The film cultural field was a "cognitive praxis," by which I mean the activity of borrowing, elaborating, refining, modifying, testing out, disseminating, and otherwise putting into practice a framework of ideas.[4]

Art Cinema

The idea of art cinema was a constitutive assumption of the film culture field. Interpretation and evaluation were intimately connected, in the sense that evaluation gave the point to interpretation while interpretation was a condition of (informed) evaluation.[5] The task of interpreting a film was connected to the task of assessing its value as a work of art. Inspired by the *politique des auteurs*, film criticism often became a practice of canonization and dismissal. The *Monthly Magazine* of the College Cine Club, for instance, established a system whereby individual critics would rate films on a four-point system, while the *Chinese Student Weekly* elaborated annual ten-best lists that were in turn debated in the pages of daily newspapers. This was a highly self-conscious movement in the field of criticism whose aim was to establish a canon of great foreign and Chinese directors that demanded or deserved authorial interpretation, an approach that drew extensively on European and North American models, which were sometimes modified and criticized. The praxis of screen criticism was characterized by a tendency to reflect on the values and protocols of criticism itself. Film theory was, at least during its formative stages, a species of metacriticism. The principles of auteur theory and film art were consciously imported and debated in the *Chinese Student Weekly* and the College Cine Club's *Monthly Magazine*, which contained frequent references to art cinema auteurs like Federico Fellini or Michelangelo Antonioni and critics like Andrew Sarris or V. F. Perkins.

In many critical writings, the figure of the author as an expressive agent remained an important principle of interpretation. The ideal of the filmmaker as a creative personality depended on not only aesthetic but also ethical criteria. In addition to praising the formal and thematic inventiveness of individual auteurs, film critics also demanded personal courage, independence, and integrity from local directors. In this sense, the category of the film au-teur mirrored that of the film critic: Law Kar has retrospectively character-ized the critical community that emerged in the 1960s as a group marked by great sincerity and independence.[6] The ideal of the art cinema author and that of the art cinema critic were conceived in homologous terms that com-bined aesthetic and ethical interests. One may speak of a general movement in the field of criticism whose aim was not simply to erect a canon of great foreign directors but also to establish the artistic values of Chinese directors by erecting a corpus of canonical filmmakers and film texts that in their view demanded or deserved authorial interpretation. A powerful example of this auteurist framework was the critical reception of the Hong Kong filmmaker Tang Shuxuan, whose films throughout the late 1960s and early 1970s dis-played the kind of intelligence and independence admired by younger re-viewers. Herself a former critic who worked to forge a film culture in Hong Kong inspired by art cinema paradigms, Tang exemplified a widely shared aspiration for an alternative film practice. Her critical review *Close Up* had upheld ideals of artistic independence and personal expression in the 1970s, and she made her films under a concept of cinema as art, employing self-conscious thematic, stylistic, and narrative innovations that critics then ex-tracted and commented on.

Tang's corpus was the subject of two intelligent analyses by the critics Law Kar and Lau Shing-hon. The former concentrated exclusively on her first film, *The Arch [Dong Furen]* (1970), while the latter provided a more comprehensive evaluation of her overall career. To consider the rhetorical strategies and assumptions behind these two essays is to study how the idea of the author functioned as a source of identity and legitimacy for the emerging film culture field in Hong Kong. First of all, the two critics cele-brated Tang's independence from commercial concerns. Law Kar described Tang Shuxuan as a "bold" director whose project did not take "commercial factors into consideration," thus mounting a "challenge" to the dominant practices of the industry: *The Arch* was "a revolution, in spirit if not in prac-tice."[7] Lau constructed a similar image of the filmmaker as a pioneering fighter for the creation of a genuine film culture. While the Hong Kong cinema of the 1970s was dominated by martial arts films, Lau argued, Tang Shuxuan's "courageous" films explored political and existential questions.[8] Aesthetic criteria once again ramified into ethical ones: the artistic quality of the films was assumed to be inseparable from the personal courage and in-dependence of their director.

Second, both essays extracted a set of consistent themes that pervaded the

director's work and testified to the seriousness of her art. The two interpretations were remarkably similar and implicitly or explicitly echoed the director's own statements: while Law Kar described Tang's first film as an illus-
tration of "the existential proposition that people should be responsible for
their own actions and decisions," Lau emphasized "the helplessness of the
individual under pressure from the system" and the difficulty of making a
meaningful and effective choice.[9] Both critics also noted the presence of
Freudian sexual symbols and existentialist themes in Tang's work, thus establishing the filmmaker's importance by drawing on familiar elements of high-
brow European literature.[10] At the same time, Law Kar also praised *The Arch*
for incorporating "subtle metaphors and ambiguous juxtapositions of scenery and emotions" that combined "the spirit of classical Chinese painting
and poetry with a modernism enlightened by contemporary philosophy."[11]
Thus Tang's concerns intersected with an important preoccupation of such
Hong Kong film theorists and filmmakers of this generation as Lin Niantong:
the way that cinematic representation can keep faith with distinctly Chinese
aesthetic traditions within a modernist framework influenced by international art cinema themes.

Third, the essays praised not only Tang's thematic contents but also her
exploration of style and narrative form. In line with the interpretive protocols
of art cinema explication, Law Kar argued that *The Arch* "breaks away from
the traditional confines of dramatic action and plot, and centres on the psychological conflicts of the characters."[12] And although Lau found the self-
conscious technique of *The Arch* excessive and distracting, he praised the
more accomplished use of "surreal" images and sounds in her second film,
China Behind, thus organizing her authorial career as a development from
initial exploration to full artistic maturity. Every film was framed as a stage
in the evolution of a creative personality.

Finally, both Law Kar and Lau Shing-hon organized their accounts partly
in order to foreground and defend the contribution of art cinema institutions to the development of a Hong Kong film culture. Law explicitly noted
that both the *Chinese Student Weekly* and the seminal Taiwan magazine
Influence defended Tang's work against the pressures from the industry, thus
working to create a heroic image of the critical community of which he remains a pivotal figure.[13] The figure of Tang Shuxuan furnished material for
a reaffirmation of the film culture field in its independence from industrial
pressures, thus affirming the kinship between the auteur and the critical
community. Law's emphasis on the foresight of local critics also contributed
to the institutional memory of the achievements of the film culture field. In

a similar vein, Lau Shing-hon appropriated Tang Shuxuan as an ancestor of the Hong Kong New Wave, using her films to valorize the efforts of a later generation of film culture workers. The history of Hong Kong cinema was thus retrospectively rewritten from the standpoint of the new directors: "If [Tang Shuxuan] had made her appearance ten years later, joining forces with the younger generation of filmmakers, her chances of making it commercially would have been much better. Her debut was made before her time."[14]

The general paradigm of auteur cinema interpretation mobilized by Law Kar and Lau Shing-hon offered the critical community important advantages: it furnished a fruitful interpretive approach that relied on the figure of the director as an organizing principle of textual meaning; it provided a set of moral and aesthetic norms, such as originality and independence, that underlay the daily business of reviewing films as well as the longer essays written for scholarly journals and film festival booklets; it fostered an awareness of film history by encouraging critics to identify individual filmmakers of previous generations as independent artists who anticipated the New Wave by departing from commercial expectations; and finally, art cinema's struggle against mere commerce helped to alert critics to the uneasy institutional relationship between film culture and capitalism. The critic Gu Er noted that "film-making in Hong Kong today is business first with films as the commodity," thus creating a situation wherein some filmmakers "are only interested in the box-office" while "others are more concerned with the quality of the films and feel more responsibility towards the audience."[15] This emphasis on "responsibility" shows how an ethical definition of authorship underpinned critical descriptions of Hong Kong's commercial industry.

Reflectionism

In defining its antagonistic, or at best ambivalent, relationship to commercial culture, critical discourses sometimes decried the lack of cultural cosmopolitanism among local filmmakers and the moviegoing public, whose overwhelming interest in commercial entertainment putatively precluded the rise of a genuine art cinema movement. The birth of the Hong Kong International Film Festival in 1977 has to be viewed, at least in part, against the twofold background of an image of the city as a cultural desert and a self-definition of critics as cultural connoisseurs with a pedagogic mission. Writing in 1981, Law Wai-ming asserted that the festival was "established primarily to afford the local audience the opportunity to acquaint itself with cultural developments overseas" and to compensate for the absence of a "climate more conducive to the development of film culture" in Hong Kong.[16] Cultural cosmopolitanism often became a criterion measured against which local moviegoers were found wanting. Sek Kei similarly described Hong Kong as "an extremely commercialized and opportunistic city in which the cinema is regarded purely as an entertainment medium"; in his view, Hong Kong society "lacks a knack for analysis in depth."[17]

The central categories of art cinema (sincerity, independence, originality, and cultural leadership) were thus connected to an ambivalent image of the people of Hong Kong as cinema consumers. This image was constructed from the institutional standpoint of a critical community with an interest in the idea of art. The critics defined their own social mission by producing a description of the population of Hong Kong as indifferent to the idea of culture. In 1965, Liu Fang described the contribution of the *Chinese Student Weekly* film critics as a pedagogic practice of "enhancing the audience's standards of aesthetic appreciation" through continuing endeavors of film analysis and explication.[18] The "guidance" of viewers became an important project for the new critics, whose societal function required the presence of an implied audience in need of cultural leadership.

Members of the film culture field also addressed the relationship between the cinema and society, for several additional reasons. First of all, interpretation was sometimes regarded as a practice of contextualization. To grasp the meaning of a film seems to require a reconstruction of the cultural and social environment out of which that film emerged, or against which it reacted. Secondly, the organizational needs of the members of the critical community demanded a more thorough and realistic assessment of their societal environment. As early as 1965, Law Kar was urging fellow film writers to take note of the practical possibilities and constraints available in the Hong Kong environment before setting out to promote art cinema.[19] The practical goal of creating an institutional space for the production and appreciation of cinematic art gave point to the study of Hong Kong society.

The third reason for the Hong Kong critics' sociological bent was more overtly political: the ivory tower apoliticism of an art-for-art's-sake approach, it was sometimes felt, would banefully divert intellectuals from more urgent societal and political problems. The sense that the selective curriculum fostered by the colonial education system deprived Hong Kong of a genuine historical awareness of its own past, coupled with the growth of a distinct local identity in the 1960s and 1970s, supplied a cognitive background that encouraged Hong Kong cultural critics to demand a realist cinema. I propose the term "normative realism" to describe the conviction that filmmakers ought to depict their social and historical reality. Law Kar, for instance, complained that the dominant cinema of the 1960s was made in the Mandarin dialect by exiled mainlanders detached from Hong Kong life.[20] Critical discourses often used normative realism to denounce the commercial cinema for failing to portray characters and situations that were explicitly *of* Hong Kong and to furnish insights about its society and history. Sek Kei, for instance, described the "social psychology" of the Hong Kong cinema as a practice of "collective hypnotism" based on "standard formulas" that "pander to a mass commercial market in an effort to entertain," indulging in "the artificial and make-believe" rather than producing a "realistic objective study" of society.[21] The point was not only that local filmmakers failed to convey historical information or to show and analyze important facts of economic and political life, but that they cultivated a general attitude of indifference to history. This understanding of Hong Kong commercial cinema pervaded a study by Leung Noong-kong that identified a putative "collective tendency" or "collective consciousness" among Hong Kong commercial filmmakers. Their work "neither aims to remind us of our specific past (i.e., the various historical factors), nor does it strive to present us with our specific present, not to mention inducing reflection on the city's future."[22]

The critics' sense of social responsibility stemmed from a sense of urgency regarding the recovery of the territory's forgotten history and promotion among the public of the capacity for sociological and political reflection on their own present situation. The task at hand was to analyze the relationship between film and society, with a critical interest in unmasking the ahistorical commercialism of Hong Kong cinema. The project of promoting art cinema ramified into a practice of cultural critique. Critics not only described the local cinema's putative evasion of history but also sought to explain it; and they (sometimes) did so by appealing to a reflectionist framework. Reflectionism is an interpretive approach that accounts for the presence of stylistic, narrative, and thematic devices by reference to societal processes, structures, and events. Some critics argued that Hong Kong cinema's putative flight from social reality was determined by the colonial administration and its dominant political culture. The stringent censorship regulations imposed by the government, Sek Kei observed, discourage local filmmakers from accurately depicting the territory's social conflicts, a situation rooted in the fact that the Hong Kong people are "not truly the masters of their city."[23] At the same time, the "provincial" traditionalism of the local cinema functioned "to offer a colonized people a link with their past" and to project an "anti-Western" sentiment.[24] Another widespread variation on this reflectionist framework argued that all or most recent Hong Kong films were explicitly or implicitly about the 1997 reversion to Chinese rule.

Reflectionism is the other side of the coin of normative realism. Although these two categories do not logically entail one another, many scholars who uphold the one often also, and for similar reasons, uphold the other. It is easy to understand why: since the cinema is (presumably) always determined by society, any film that fails to illuminate its social context remains blind to its own process of construction. A nonrealistic film is a blind symptom of its own social determinants that fails to offer genuine insight into them. The assumption that the cinema reflects society places cultural producers under the obligation to portray that society as accurately and honestly as possible. Thus reflectionism sometimes gave point to normative realism.

The film historian Ng Ho, for instance, mobilized both normative realist and reflectionist paradigms in asserting that "Chinese History has died in Hong Kong Cinema."[25] He contended that the colony's films contained so many errors of historical fact as to symptomatically reveal a collective "historical amnesia." This lack of historical awareness presumably reflects two social realities. First of all, the colonial administration's education policy undermined the students' awareness of contemporary Chinese history, in line with dominant economic and political interests. Secondly, Ng Ho invoked Fredric Jameson's familiar theory of postmodernism to suggest that Hong Kong's flight into an imaginary, nostalgic past was fostered by the worldwide expansion of the commodity form. This application of the ideas in Jameson's essay is crude and uncritical; but it is in any case important not to overemphasize the influence of postmodern theory on Hong Kong critics. Jameson's symptomatic interpretation of postmodernity as the "cultural logic" of late capitalism was, I think, chosen because it provided something like a sophisticated reflectionist model. This theory obviously fit in well with the sociological orientation that the Hong Kong critical community had already developed prior to their acquaintance with postmodern theory. A Jamesonian approach could therefore be readily accommodated within a preexisting critical interest in reflectionism. At the same time, the incorporation of poststructural and neo-Marxian paradigms also functioned as markers of intellectual authority for the critics, as they addressed a growing scholarly readership with an avid interest in the latest theoretical trends of the West.

In addition to providing a sociological explanation for the local film industry's lack of historical awareness, the reflectionist framework also functioned to promote a perception of the cinema as a source of historical documentation about Hong Kong society. The Twelfth Hong Kong International

Film Festival marked a milestone in this vision of film history as "changes in Hong Kong society through cinema." The commercial cinema of Hong Kong was regarded as a mirror of its audience's mass psychology. Although this presupposition is not shared by every critic and scholar, Sek Kei looked to popular culture as a site where the ethos of the general population, the "social psychology" of Hong Kong, finds its clearest expression, where the discourses of the film culture field have been at the forefront of a growing scholarly interest in redeeming Hong Kong history. Theoretical interest in writing a local history was entwined with a practical interest in showing and preserving local films. Introducing the aims of that year's festival, its coordinator, Li Cheuk-to, forcefully underscored the "contributions of our filmmakers towards our local culture and history" and asserted that "without a local history, there is no local culture."[26] I would use the term "disappearing history thesis" to denote what Sek Kei has described as "the common perception that a vital part of [Hong Kong's historical] legacy may vanish."[27]

New Wave

The development of the film culture field as an institutional, ethical, and aesthetic system during the 1960s and 1970s paved the way for the emergence of the category of the Hong Kong New Wave in several ways. The institutions of the field furnished a domain where aspiring filmmakers and critics conversed with one another, directly or through the mediation of the printed word. The idea of film culture included an aspiration to create a fruitful dialogue between theory and practice, such that theoretical insight could guide and inform creative efforts. Filmmakers such as Allen Fong, Tsui Hark, Patrick Tam, and John Woo had participated in the cine club movement, sometimes collaborated with critical publications, invoked art-cinema conventions in their films, and were ready to dialogue with the critical community.

Members of this critical community often described the New Wave by drawing on a range of concepts or tropes developed in the film culture field. The first trope was an ethical conception of authorship. In a 1979 *Film Biweekly* editorial, for instance, Law Wai-ming described the figure of the "new Hong Kong director" in terms of an ideal of the personality that combined aesthetics and ethics. In line with protocols of art cinema interpretation, the new directors were partly characterized and differentiated from previous generations, and from the mainstream industry as a whole, by reference to ethical criteria: they were not only "intellectually capable of expressing themselves in a serious artistic way," but also worked to "keep their integrity and ethical sense, and their individuality." New directors presumably asserted their individuality by seeking out new themes, new narrative methods, and a new mise-en-scène. Thus Law Wai-ming defined the new cinema in terms of a struggle between the individual and the collective: "originality is a matter of personal experience" and courage, a definition in conflict with the "basic principle of commercial cinema," which "subordinates individuality to popular taste." [28]

Second, critical descriptions of the New Wave retained the ambivalent image of the commercial film industry as the other of the film culture field. Leung Noong-kong, for instance, argued in 1979 that the Hong Kong film industry reproduces "proven formulas with as little variation as possible." [29] The notion of a "static" commercial cinema provided a rhetorical strategy for highlighting the difference between the new generation and the dominant cinema. At the same time, many critics assumed that it was not practically feasible for young filmmakers to break away completely from "commercialism." The main task of the new directors, then, was to employ existing commercial genres while adapting them to their individual concerns in accordance with the criteria of originality and seriousness. The presupposition that the ideal auteur kept faith with the aspiration of the film culture field even within the constraints of a commercial film industry not only provided a yardstick for critical evaluation and analysis, but also determined the aspirations and self-justifications of some filmmakers. Patrick Tam's debut film *The Sword [Ming Jian]* (1980), for instance, transformed the generic conventions of the *wuxia pian* (swordplay film) by reframing the epic figure of the heroic swordsman as a passive or self-destructive character. This interest in generic variation was also informed by the work of European auteurs like Roman Polanski (*Dance of the Vampires, Chinatown*) who had self-consciously transformed existing commercial genres. Tsui Hark described the making of his own debut film *The Butterfly Murders [Die Bian]* (1979) as a solution to the aesthetic problem of how to depart "from the orthodox martial arts world as expounded in the novels of Ku Lung and Chin Yung" in order to "strike a new path." [30] He achieved this aim by introducing anachronistic elements from other genres, including science fiction, the detective thriller, and the James Bond–type spy film.

A third trope highlighted the filmmakers' unprecedentedly cosmopolitan (international or modern) orientation. Critics and directors often appealed to exemplary models from European or North American film or theory in reviews, interviews, and allusions in individual films. Ann Hui has troped Alain Resnais in *Starry Is the Night [Jinye Xingguang Canlan]* (1988) and Roman

Polanski in *The Spooky Bunch [Zhuang Dao Zheng]* (1980). This international outlook did not preclude an interest in locating distinctly Chinese aesthetic forms. Noel Burch's *To the Distant Observer*, for instance, influenced Patrick Tam's search for a specifically Chinese or "Oriental" cinematic language in his early work. A related critical discourse on the New Wave, sometimes underpinned by Marxist theory, urged directors to step back from and reflect on their cultural and political presuppositions so as to attain greater clarity about the social implications of their work. The rhetoric of cosmopolitanism incorporated a demand for self-reflexivity. In an important 1981 *Film Biweekly* essay titled "Notes on the New Cinema," Evans Chan criticized Allen Fong's *Father and Son [Fuzi Qing]* (1981) for failing to take a reflective distance from its own bourgeois and patriarchal assumptions.[31] Chan's point was that the director's implicit, although well-intentioned, traditionalism led to a sentimental nostalgia that detracted from the film's emotional expressiveness and aesthetic power. The implication was, of course, that New Wave directors have a duty to stand back from taken-for-granted presuppositions and thematize their own ideological and cultural horizons.

Fourth, normative realism provided a criterion by which to demarcate the new Hong Kong cinema from the old. Sek Kei praised New Wave films for incorporating urban settings and exploring historical and social changes, thus producing "a sense of belonging to Hong Kong itself."[32] Wider social factors, particularly changes in government censorship and the future transition to Chinese sovereignty, presumably encouraged directors like Ann Hui to capture a "local Hong Kong flavor." This historical consciousness became a central criterion of membership in the New Wave. Speaking with hindsight, Evans Chan recently observed that Ann Hui's *The Secret [Feng Jie]* (1979) "showed my generation that Hong Kong had a past, even a haunted past" and therefore marked an important stage in the process of constituting an evolving Hong Kong identity: the film, together with the work of Allen Fong and others, "recognized the validity" of a distinctly Hong Kong experience.[33]

According to the standard description, then, the New Wave combined a cosmopolitan understanding of film form influenced by world cinema models with a realist commitment to the specificity of a local identity. This standpoint, of course, mirrored the similarly twofold self-understanding of film critics as cultural connoisseurs of world culture and redeemers of Hong Kong history. New Wave directors have sometimes also explicitly framed their own work as a record of local history. Thus *Father and Son*, which its director described as the "autobiography" of his own generation, contained references to the Shep Kip Mei fire of 1953.[34] Art cinema criteria

Figure 1.
Hong Kong had a
haunted past in *The
Secret* (Ann Hui, 1979).

of verisimilitude and sincerity frequently undergird Allen Fong's interest in depicting a history that has been suppressed from commercial cinema, and in celebrating those everyday activities and experiences that have been treated as nonevents by the commercial film industry. The director has himself evoked the vanishing history trope through the voice of a fictional character: a drama teacher and aspiring filmmaker in his *Ah Ying [Banbian Ren]* (1982) asserts that he wants "to make a film that reflects our time. Otherwise, nobody will ever know that we existed." This historical intent underlies Fong's use of actual locations and nonprofessional actors to depict a local history on the verge of disappearance. While this prevalent concern with history echoed critical efforts to define and capture a "Hong Kong experience," the work of self-conscious directors such as Allen Fong or Ann Hui in turn helped to encourage critics of this generation to continue analyzing and collecting their local history.

Periodization and Nostalgia

For a critical community to describe a film as an example of the new cinema, or to name a filmmaker as a new director, was to confer on the film the status of a candidate for aesthetic appreciation, or to ordain its maker a serious artist, and to encourage further work in the same direction. The critic's role also contained the self-proclaimed authority to deny or withdraw status, which has been exercised as frequently as that of bestowing it. The most dramatic way of denying status or withdrawing a commendation was to argue that the Hong Kong New Wave never existed. In June 1981, *Film Biweekly* published a round-table discussion between the young critics Roger Garcia, Jerry Liu, and Li Cheuk-to. Its surprising title, "Re-Evaluating the New Cinema," suggests that the nature of the Hong Kong New Wave, its very existence as a movement, had already become problematic less than two years after its inception. In one of the more extreme formulations, Garcia asserted that "perhaps there is no such a thing as a Hong Kong New Wave."[35] Critics sometimes used the very ideal of artistic originality, which had initially helped to define the New Wave, against those selfsame new directors by stressing their failure to break away from the traditions of Hong Kong commercialism.

The initial expectations aroused by the work of the New Wave have often given way to widespread disappointment with its eventual evolution. In 1991, Sek Kei symptomatically wrote that the New Wave had "not gone deep enough into arts, politics, and society" and had thus fallen into a trap of "superficiality and confusion."[36] Some critics chose to blame the filmmakers themselves, or the putative commercial orientation of Hong Kong audiences, or the lack of public funding, but the consensus had nonetheless been reached that the moment of the New Wave, if it ever existed, had in any case come to an end. These discourses project a sense that the relative autonomy of film scholarship and criticism from market pressures did not correspond to the creation of a similarly autonomous context of film production and dissemination, creating a mismatch between the demands of a critical community with an interest in art and the economic constraints of filmmaking institutions. The tension between art and commerce has remained a central trope of Hong Kong film criticism. In retrospect, the movement's pioneering years, variously understood to comprise the television apprenticeship of the mid-1970s or the early cinema work around 1979, sometimes became an object of nostalgia and idealization, a romantic "golden age" of local cinema when critics and filmmakers came together as a community, a film culture field, whose shared aspirations and potentials have yet to be fulfilled.

Notes

This essay could not have been written without the generosity of Evans Chan, Law Kar, and Linda Chiu-han Lai.

1 Law Wai-ming, "Tre editoriali sul 'Nuovo Cinema,'" in *Cinemasia*, ed. Marco Müller (Pesaro: Mostra Internazionale del Nuovo Cinema/Marsilio Editori,

1983), 154. Originally published as "Bainjishi Baogao," *Dianying Shuangzhoukan [Film Biweekly]* 20 (October 1979): ii.

2   For some reminiscences of the period, see *Fifty Years of Electric Shadows: Report of Conference on Hong Kong Cinema* (Hong Kong: Urban Council, 1997), 65–68.

3   Ibid., 66. Law Kar, "Luo Ga Huishouhua Dianying" ["Law Kar Looks Back on the Cinema"], *Boyi Yuekan* 14 (15 October 1988): 133.

4   Ron Eyerman and Andrew Jamison, *Social Movements: A Cognitive Approach* (Cambridge: Polity Press, 1991).

5   Cf. David Bordwell, *Making Meaning* (Cambridge: Harvard University Press, 1989), 43–52.

6   Law Kar, "Luo Ga Huishouhua Dianying," 133.

7   Law Kar, "The Significance of *The Arch*," in *A Comparative Study of Post-War Mandarin and Cantonese Cinema: The Films of Zhu Shilin, Qin Jian, and Other Directors* (Hong Kong: Urban Council, 1983), 163.

8   Lau Shing-hon, "Su Shuen: The Lone-Rider in Hong Kong Cinema in the 1970s," in *A Study of Hong Kong Cinema in the Seventies* (Hong Kong: Urban Council, 1984), 109.

9   Lau, 108; Law Kar, "The Significance of *The Arch*," 165.

10 Lau, 106; Law Kar, "The Significance of *The Arch*," 166.

11 Law Kar, "The Significance of *The Arch*," 164.

12 Ibid., 164.

13 Ibid., 163.

14 Lau, 106.

15 Gu Er, "Li Chenfeng," in *Cantonese Cinema Retrospective (1950–1959)* (Hong Kong: Urban Council, 1971), 71.

16 Law Wai-ming, *The Fifth International Hong Kong Film Festival* (Hong Kong: Urban Council, 1981), 4.

17 Sek Kei, "Achievement and Crisis: Hongkong Cinema in the 80s," in *Hong Kong Cinema in the Eighties* (Hong Kong: Urban Council, 1991), 58.

18 Liu Fang, "Dianying Piping de Lichang Wenti" ["The Problem of Standpoint in Film Criticism"], *Xinsheng Wanbao [New Live Evening News]*, 7 May 1965.

19 Law Kar, "Dui Xian Jieduan Xianggang Yingping de Jidian Yijian" ["A Few Points on the Present Style of Film Criticism in Hong Kong"], *Xinsheng Wanbao*, 7 May 1965.

20 Law Kar, "Luo Ga Huishouhua Dianying," 133.

21 Sek Kei, "The Social Psychology of Hongkong Cinema," in *Changes in Hong Kong Society through Cinema* (Hong Kong: Urban Council, 1988), 15.

22 Leung Noong-kong, "Notes on the Hong Kong Cinema," in *The Hong Kong Contemporary Cinema* (Hong Kong: Urban Council, 1982), 13.

23 Sek, "The Social Psychology of Hongkong Cinema," 19.

24 Sek Kei, "The Extraordinary History of the Cantonese Cinema," *Cantonese Cinema Retrospective (1950–1959)* (Hong Kong: Urban Council, 1971), 36.

25 Ng Ho, "Imbecility of History in Hong Kong Cinema," in *A Perspective of Chinese Cinemas of the 90's* (Taipei: Taipei Golden Horse Film Festival, 1994), 70.

26 Li Cheuk-to, introduction to *Changes in Hong Kong Society through Cinema* (Hong Kong: Urban Council, 1988), 9.

27 Sek, "Achievement and Crisis: Hongkong Cinema in the 80s," 53.

28 Law Wai-ming, "Tre editoriali sul 'Nuovo Cinema,'" 155.

29 Leung Noong-kong, "Towards a New Wave in the Hong Kong Cinema," in *Hong Kong Cinema '79* (Hong Kong: Urban Council, 1979). Roger Garcia argued in a similar vein that the commercial structure of Hong Kong film production encourages a reliance on "rigid" conventions and codes and theatrical emphasis on dramatic content over form. Roger Garcia, "The Static Image," in *The Hong Kong Contemporary Cinema* (Hong Kong: Urban Council, 1982), 6.

30 *The Fourth International Film Festival* (Hong Kong: Urban Council, 1980), 173.

31 Evans Chan, "Bununian — 'Xin Dianying' Biji" ["Notes on the New Cinema"], in *Xianggang Dianying Fengmao [The Style and Features of Hong Kong Cinema]*, ed. Peggy Chiao (Taibei: Shibao Chuban, 1987), 47.

32 Sek, "Achievement and Crisis: Hongkong Cinema in the 80s," 53.

33 Personal conversation with the author, 1998.

34 Olivier Assayas, "Du bon usage de la télévision: Entretien avec Allen Fong," *Cahiers du cinéma* 360–361 (September 1984): 109.

35 Li, "Chongxin Jiantian 'Xin Dianying,'" 368.

36 Sek, "Achievement and Crisis: Hongkong Cinema in the 80s," 58.

Part II

In Action

Entertainment, Aesthetics,
and Reinventions

CHAPTER THREE

Aesthetics in Action: *Kungfu,* Gunplay, and Cinematic Expressivity

David Bordwell

In 1996 a major American publisher issued *Sex and Zen and a Bullet in the Head,* a guide to what the authors consider the most headbanging, let-'er-rip filmmaking on the planet. "Gone are the flying pigtails and contrived fist-thuds of your father's favorite chopsockies," the blurb on the back tells us. *Sex and Zen and a Bullet in the Head* is a hilarious read, and the peppy plot synopses play up the films as seedy, sexy, bloody, and nutty. But the authors' introduction warns that "film school polemics," dosed with "pointy-headed, white-wine-and-baked-brie philosophizing," cannot adequately describe the "scalding propulsion" of these movies.[1]

These barbs strike me like a flurry of ninja throwing stars. I am old enough to be the father of the young fans, and my love for martial arts films goes back to the 1974 double bill of *Fist of Fury [Jingwu Men]* and *Five Fingers of Death* (also known as *King Boxer [Tianxia Diyi Quan]*) in the Majestic Theatre in Madison, Wisconsin. Even worse, I am a film studies professor. I do not drink white wine or eat baked brie, but I do spend time trying to figure out what makes movies work. I find myself asking questions. How, for instance, is it possible for Hong Kong action movies to trigger such unbridled passions? How are they put together? How do they exploit the film medium? What is the craft behind them? After you walk out of the best Hong Kong action movies you are charged up, you feel that you can do anything. How can mere movies create such feelings?

This pointy-headed essay explores some answers to these questions. The itinerary will take us through contemporary Hollywood, with side trips to some technicalities of film style and some detours into the writings of that older fan of Asian action, Sergei Eisenstein. I will also try to show that if we want to understand these movies as well as enjoy them, it turns out that film-school polemics can actually help.

During the 1980s the action picture — the cop movie, the crime thriller, the adventure film, the space opera, the movie of chase and combat — 73 became one of the dominant Hollywood genres. Often such films won places on the top ten box office grossers list, while the home video boom assured an almost endless stream of less prestigious product. The genre extended stylistic strategies that had been evident in films such as *Goldfinger* (1964), *Bonnie and Clyde* (1967), *Bullitt* (1968), *The Wild Bunch* (1969), *Butch Cassidy and the Sundance Kid* (1969), and *The French Connection* (1971). By the time the action revival emerged in *Road Warrior* (1981), *Raiders of the Lost Ark* (1981), *48 Hours* (1982), and other films, directors could draw upon a range of conventional techniques.

Consider a sequence in Richard Donner's *Lethal Weapon* (1987). In the climactic chase, Mel Gibson has escaped from Gary Busey's torture chamber and now pursues him through the night streets of Los Angeles. Busey seizes a passing car, and Gibson sprints through traffic after him. From an overpass, Gibson fires at Busey's car. The engine bursts into flames and Busey smashes into a telephone pole. As Gibson approaches, Busey commandeers another car just as Gibson is struck by a passing cab.

Donner handles this situation in ways typical of Hollywood action sequences. The cutting is rapid, creating an average shot length of two and a half seconds. No one will make an action picture in long takes, of course, but Donner, like most of his Hollywood peers, creates a fairly jerky rhythm by cutting after a movement has begun and before it is completed, even when the second shot shows an entirely different action. For instance, when Gibson leaves Danny Glover behind at a lamppost, Glover starts to leave the shot. But Donner does not give him what editors call a "clean" exit; the next shot interrupts Glover in the middle of his movement. "The axiom of action cutting," claims the film editor Richard Marks, "is, never complete an action. Always leave it incomplete so it keeps the forward momentum of the sequence."[2] Moreover, two-thirds of Donner's shots contain some camera movement (panning, reframing, tracking, craning down, and the like). And Gibson is virtually never in repose. Except when he stops to fire at Busey's getaway car, he races down streets across lanes of traffic, even leaping up onto cars parked by the curb.

This scene seems to me characteristic of the Hollywood approach in trying to produce an overwhelming but loose and sketchy *impression* of physical activity. There is, for instance, no effort to dramatize the fact that Gibson's run through traffic is dangerous. Although he runs through traffic, he never comes close to any moving vehicle. Donner's long lenses, in lessening apparent distances between Gibson and the background traffic, merely suggest that he might eventually be in danger. There is a moment early on when it seems that a car might strike him from behind, but Donner cuts away to Busey, and when we return to Gibson later, the car has disappeared. True, at the scene's climax Gibson is hit by a car, but now Donner has recourse to the well-established device of what V. I. Pudovkin called "constructive editing." [3] No overall view establishes that Gibson is at risk. Instead we get ten quick shots of slowing taxicab wheels, the driver's startled face, and then shots of Gibson (actually a stunt man) already rolling around on the hood of the car he is flung off. The crucial action of the car hitting the Gibson character is completely omitted.

Hong Kong fans rightly object to such bogus action, but we can generalize from their annoyance. The sequence gives us the idea: we understand that the car strikes Gibson, but the collision is not directly delineated, and thus the scene has no wallop. In substituting an editing ellipsis for a more direct presentation, this passage exemplifies a broader strategy. Put generally, the actor's performance is minimized and other cinematic techniques compensate for it. The rapid cutting, constant camera movement, and dramatic music and sound effects must labor to generate an excitement that is not primed by the concrete event taking place before the lens.

Stunts and special effects likewise deemphasize the actor's performance. Donner gives pride of place to the sparks struck by bullets and above all to a series of auto stunts. Busey skids around corners, drives the wrong way on a one-way street, and steers a flaming car into a telephone pole, actions that are dwelt upon in extreme long shots. In fact, Donner favors medium long shots, long shots, and even extreme long shots throughout the sequence. He thus assures himself that the action is broadly covered; but it sets the action, however spectacular, at a considerable distance. Donner offers us few close-ups of characters, giving Busey and Gibson one quick reaction shot apiece; most of the close-ups show parts of the pockmarked car. Moreover, the line of movement is constantly broken by impediments (parked cars that Gibson must hop over) and countermovements (traffic passing to and fro), so the shots register as fairly cluttered.

The sequence is, then, physically unspecific in two respects. First, the concreteness of the individual actions is sacrificed to a broad sense that something dynamic is going on. Second, instead of conveying a specific expressive quality — Gibson's risky but tenacious pursuit, Busey's desperation in the face of impending capture — the nervous busyness of the style creates a relatively undifferentiated visceral arousal. We understand that Gibson is in danger, but we do not have any reason to sense it. The result is a diffuse feeling of general excitement.

Admittedly, this nervous style can be considered somewhat realistic, in that such a chase in real-life traffic would create graceless, helter-skelter movement. And even the interruptive cutting and occasional jerky camera movement can be justified as plausibly reflecting the messiness of extreme action in the world we know. But there is a cost as well. Michael Bay, director of *The Rock*, explains how he shot inserts for the chase through San Francisco:

> I film actors driving in these scenes from a dolly a few feet in front of
> a stationary car. I do whip pans and whip zooms and violently shake
> the camera, trying to make the whole screen rumble. Used in
> snippets, it looks as if the actors are driving ferociously.[4]

The director seeks to suggest the ferocity of the action solely through camerawork. But when only the screen rumbles, we carry away just an impression of a violent chase. And the actor has almost nothing to do, since the cinematography is carrying the emotional jolt of the movements.

During the 1980s there emerged two broad approaches to creating this rough sense of incessant movement. The busy, sketchy approach typified by *Lethal Weapon* can be found as well in the *Beverly Hills Cop* series, *Die Hard 2* (1990), and *Heat* (1995). The jerkiness of this style reaches a kind of apogee in *The Rock*'s Humvee chase, with its 1.2-second average shot length and the spasmodic camerawork of which Bay is so proud. Here the aim is to create the impression that everything is in frantic motion. People lurch about, vehicles smash up, the handheld camera wobbles, and cuts fracture every instant of action into a barrage of brief, sometimes barely legible images.

Admittedly, a more poised and clean-line approach also emerged during the 1980s. It relies on wide-angle compositions, more complex staging, and somewhat more legible shot design. This style is in evidence in the Indiana Jones series, as well as in *Aliens* (1986), the original *Die Hard* (1988), *The Fugitive* (1993), and *Speed* (1994). Still, these films remain committed to the belief that an action scene must move, and move incessantly. All other things being equal, the goal is constant and continual activity.

This overall strategy and the specific stylistic devices that fulfill it have been enormously influential on action pictures around the world. But there are significant differences, and these are, I submit, one source of the intuitive sense that something original is going on in the Hong Kong action cinema.

In Law Man's cop thriller *Hearty Response* [*Yi Gai Yun Tian*] (1986), a police officer (Chow Yun-fat) breaks into a tattoo parlor. There he finds that a young woman (Joey Wong) has been tattooed and raped by her former boy-friend. The tattooist leaps out the window and Chow gives chase, followed quickly by Joey, who has grabbed a gun. As Chow searches the streets, the tattooist tries to run him down by smashing a car through a fence. But Joey catches up with him and fires, wounding him just before she is struck by a car. Still, she runs on, chasing the rapist into a nightclub. When Chow discovers the two, a gunfight ensues. Chow blocks a bullet meant for Joey; she then advances on the tattooist and, sobbing with nervous rage, fires bullet after bullet into his body.

This climactic sequence is virtually identical in length to the *Lethal Weapon* chase, but it offers instructive stylistic contrasts.[5] A serious Hong Kong fan will note immediately Law Man's much more vivid handling of the car accident. After wounding her rapist with her first bullet, Joey starts to run across the street toward him. Cut to a shot taken from the front seat of a car bearing down on her. The image creates an immediate and concrete sense of danger that mere glimpses of tires and a driver's expression cannot summon up: the shot shows the car about to hit her. Cut to a reverse angle, with the car approaching the camera and going into a skid as she continues across the street. The car sideswipes her and knocks her out of the frame. In a still closer view, she hits the sidewalk and rolls bumpily across the pavement to the right. Cut to a tight, brief shot of the skidding car smashing into another car. The last shot shows her still rolling, now to the left, before she slaps down her hands to stop herself. She pauses briefly to gather strength before rising to pursue her quarry.

Of course, the *Hearty Response* action was faked in the sense that a stunt man (in wig and miniskirt) took the impact and the fall. Nonetheless, the kinetic impact of the action is much stronger than in *Lethal Weapon*. This is because we register in a straightforward way the impending collision and the sickening thud of the car against body. The controlled execution of the act was put at the center of the mise-en-scène, and other film techniques were devoted to presenting it vividly. Each shot has the schematic clarity of a cartoon panel, and the lighting renders everything in bold relief. No telephoto lens creates a safe illusion of risk; no elliptical editing gets by with fragments of action. The final crash of the car into another vehicle is extremely modest by Hollywood standards, and it is given only one shot, as if we needed only to see where it ended up and to feel again the vehicle's deadly momentum. In five shots adding up to six seconds, a range of film techniques has been used to put the emphasis squarely on the sheer physical and emotional force of the action.

Naturally, we must remember that U.S. studio executives were probably more squeamish about showing a body ricocheting off a car than the Hong Kong censor was. And certainly the low budget of *Hearty Response* forces Law Man to create his thrills cheaply. But these factors reveal only that Law Man, like other directors, has turned the opportunities and constraints of his filmmaking situation to artistic advantage. Moreover, we might expect a low-budget production to have plenty of recourse to shortcuts like Pudovkin's constructive editing. Here the big-budget picture, eager to protect its star and its audience's sensibilities, embraces the cheaper and more roundabout solution, while the exploitation picture gives us the event more vividly.

Much the same could be said of the tattooist's attack on Chow Yun-fat, a nine-second barrage of trim medium long shots and close-ups in which Chow dodges a car and then saves a boy from being run down. As in the collision with Joey Wong, Chow's split-second avoidance of the car relies on artifice, but not the sort that, as André Bazin puts it, turns an actual event into something imaginary. Someone, if not Chow, very nearly gets smashed.

My key point is not that Hong Kong films employ death-defying stunts; that is not news. What is important is that the stunts are staged, shot, and cut for readability. In the auto's lunges at Chow, the rapidity of our uptake starts from the smoothness and cogency of the physical action that is shown. The entire *Hearty Response* sequence is even more quickly cut than the passage from *Lethal Weapon*, with an average shot length of about one and a half seconds; but it does not look as skittish. This is because the shots tend to be readable at a glance — fairly close, simply composed, and displaying only one or two trajectories of movement. And, significantly, Law Man uses half as many moving camera shots as Donner does, thereby making it all the more important for the action in front of the lens to engage our attention.

The lesson of this comparison is quite general. If Hollywood movies sketch a pervasive but often inexact sense of physical action, the Hong Kong norm aims to maximize the action's legibility. From the 1960s swordplay films and 1970s *kungfu* movies to the cop movies and revived *wuxia pian* of the 1980s and 1990s, this filmmaking tradition has put the graceful body at the center of its mise-en-scène. In order to follow the plot, one must be constantly apprised of the actor's behavior, down to minute changes of posture, stance, or regard. Like Soviet films of the 1920s, which took their inspiration from the precise gymnastics of popular theater, Hong Kong cinema has emphasized the concreteness and clarity of each gesture. Doubtless, traditions of martial arts and Peking opera — cultural factors quite different from those governing Hollywood style — have been central to this aesthetic, but I am not competent to trace out lines of influence here. I want to concentrate on some principles of film style governing action sequences.

How to achieve such gestural clarity on film? Several important tactics are on view in your father's prototypical *kungfu* film of the 1970s or early 1980s.[6] Most obviously, the director must provide an unobstructed view of the action. The bare stretch of earth that provides the arena for so many *kungfu* duels, though often the sign of a skimpy budget, has the virtue of making salient every instant of the fight. By contrast to Bay's efforts to make his screen rumble, Hong Kong cinematography seeks not to hide the action. The baseline is the long shot or medium long shot, with closer views serving to enlarge details or offer breathing space between stretches of combat.

At times, of course, difficult or impossible physical feats may be faked by means of the "Kuleshov effect," as when cutaways cover tremendous leaps or dexterous juggling. But again, the presentation of these feats will be diagrammatically clear. To take a typical instance: In Chu Yuan's 1972 film *The Killer* (also known as *Sacred Knives of Vengeance [Da Sha Shou]*), some thugs invade the hero's room. He is concealed in the rafters watching them. A low-angle shot shows him leaping down, and as he passes out of the lower frame edge he comes down into a long shot of the group of men. Some space has been reserved in the center of the frame for him, and as soon as he hits the floor he springs up (thanks, presumably, to a mini-trampoline) and plunges head first through a window, already visible in the rear of the set. Cut to a new angle of him diving through the window, somersaulting over the porch, and landing in the courtyard, ready to face more gang members, all conveniently spread out to create a vacant spot for him to occupy. The staging cooperates with the cutting to make each leap and landing maximally evident.

Similarly, key factors of manual combat — the demeanor of each fighter, and especially the exact distance between them — must be depicted unambiguously. Cinematography enters not as a substitute for the physical feat but as an enhancer of it, as when zooms show a detail of the fight or when slow motion allows us to examine an action that would otherwise pass too quickly.

Within the martial artist's performance, clarity can be achieved not only through the precision of the movement but also by an effort to focus the entire body's energy in each gesture. Eisenstein can help us understand the latter tactic a bit better. He believed that every movement activates the entire body, and so in theater and film one must "sell" each action by exaggerating the body's role in forming it. Eisenstein imagines how one might inject kinetic expressivity into a line of dialogue like "But there are two," with the actor showing two upraised fingers on the final word.

> How much the persuasiveness of the phrase itself will be strengthened, the expressiveness of the intonation, if on the first words, you make a recoil movement with the body while raising the elbow, and then with an energetic movement you throw the torso and the hand with the extended fingers forward. Furthermore, the braking of the wrist will be so strongly directed that the wrist will vibrate (like a metronome).[7]

This sort of stylized clarity, verging on cartoon movement, is quite different from the more subdued performance style characteristic of contemporary Hollywood acting, which tends to emphasize the face rather than the entire body. When called upon to create gestures, today's American actor produces something approximate, perhaps more realistic but also less sharply defined than the Eisenstein ideal. At the end of our *Lethal Weapon* scene, when Gibson gets up after the taxicab accident, he starts to spar with the driver before dropping his guard and half-sweeping his hands up and down in a mixture of dismissiveness and apology. The gestures are tentative and incomplete, insufficiently articulated.

By contrast, in the Hong Kong action sequence actors leap, twist, and scramble with an energetic explicitness that reveals a dynamic of forces at work on the entire body. No one just falls down. In *Hearty Response* Joey Wong hits the ground sideways in a vigorous roll that testifies to the pitch and impetus of the launching force. Or the actor may land with a splat, arms and legs splayed wide, or on his neck or spine, creating the very picture of an awkward, painful fall. By exploiting all the actor's limbs, the Hong Kong action film can present the specifics of each action with diagrammatic clarity.

This tendency is aided by the actor's ability to build the performance out of fast, crisp gestures. The Hong Kong performer has recourse to something like Eisenstein's idea of recoil. For the actor's key movements are often *separated* by noticeable points of stasis. We might describe this as the pause-burst-pause pattern. A punch lands, and there is a pause; it misses, and the extended arm is held poised, if only for a fraction of a second. The hero leaps and lands, resting in place briefly. The tattooist in *Hearty Response* glances back to see Joey gaining on him; instead of glancing over his shoulder, as he might in a Hollywood film, he runs frantically, stops, swivels his head, registers Joey's pursuit, swivels his head again, and then pounds downstairs into the nightclub. A pause often enframes each instant of action, giving it a discrete, vivid identity. The result is a kind of physics of combat and pursuit: out of quiescence rises a short, sharp action, which ceases as energy is switched off and stored for the next action. A parallel strategy rules the overall scene of fight or pursuit: moments of near-absolute stillness alternate with bursts of smooth, rapid-fire activity.

Somewhat like meter in music, the pause-burst-pause pattern creates a regular and recognizable pulse. Any one piece of combat can realize this accentual pattern in different rhythms and tempos. Some action choreographers sustain the pauses by dwelling on blocks and parries, achieving remarkable comic effects in such films as Yuen Wo-ping's *Snake in the Eagle's Shadow* [*Shexing Diaoshou*] (1978) and *Dance of the Drunken Mantis* [*Nan Bei Jui Quan*] (1979). Sammo Hung and Jackie Chan seek a faster pace, so they allow only a split second of pause between the lightning punches and kicks. Both artists enhance this presto tempo with fast-motion cinematography.

A beautiful example of a more measured rhythm occurs early in Lau Karleong's *Legendary Weapons of China* [*Shibaban Wuyi*] (1982). In an inn, two guests, each bent on assassinating a swordsman, unknowingly converge in a storeroom above his room. Their attempts to stab through the floorboards to his bed are played out in rhyming thrusts and dodges, each conveyed in a shot with its own pause-burst-pause rhythm. When the swordsman eludes them, the two assassins begin to fight each other. In one shot the young man flings a dart at the woman; in the reverse shot she dodges away and the dart plinks into a grain sack beside her. (Beat.) A closer view of her shows her staring at the dart. (Beat.) Then she flings a claw-headed weapon. Reverse angle: he ducks and it clatters against a rake. A new angle shows the rake in the foreground, out of focus. (Beat.) Then the rake falls abruptly backward as she yanks on the cable attached to the weapon. In the next shot, the rake continues to fall and strikes the young man. (Beat.) Now the young man lies in the foreground under the rake while the young woman crouches in the background. (Beat.) She glances down through the floorboards to see if anyone below has heard. (Beat.) Throughout, the scene manifests a perceptible pulse in the pause-burst-pause pattern.

For a parallel instance from a recent *policier* we need look no further than John Woo's *The Killer* [*Diexue Shuangxiong*] (1989). The famous gun-to-gun confrontation between Chow Yun-fat and Danny Lee depends on briskly alternating the swift movements of each one's pistol hand with long periods of immobility (Figure 1). Less obvious is the way in which the final shootout of *Bodyguard from Beijing [Zhongnanhai Baobiao]* (1994) employs the crisp rhythm laid down at the very start of the film. Jet Li is being addressed by his superior officer. In one shot Li is sitting calmly (pause; Figure 2), but at the cut his head is *already* popping up across the lower frame edge (burst; Figure 3) to stop smartly before his superior (pause; Figure 4).

A director can squeeze the pause-burst-pause pattern into glances and small gestures within confined spaces. In the climactic fight of *Bodyguard from Beijing*, the villain's gang has invaded the heroine's living room, and Li must fight them in the dark. At the beginning of one passage, Li twists and rolls into view before his face rises abruptly into close-up (burst), immediately freezing warily (pause; Figure 5). Looking down, he sees a sneaker poking out from behind a pillar (Figure 6). (Beat.) Li's pistol snaps abruptly into the shot and fires (Figure 7). (Beat.) In a reverse angle, we see Li from a low angle as the opponent drops down into the foreground (Figure 8). Li's pistol snaps up and fires again (Figure 9) and his victim is hurled out of the frame (Figure 10). The metronomic fall and rise of the gun arm suggest a robotic efficiency appropriate to the killer-automaton Li plays.

Very likely the martial arts tradition, with its repertory of forms and combinations, cultivated a belief that combat involved a balance between poised stillness and swift attack or defense. Possibly this tendency was reinforced by the long pauses and outbursts of violence to be found in Sergio Leone's influential westerns. And perhaps the technique owes something to the Peking opera tradition of *liang hsiang* ("displaying"), which presents a frozen pose assumed for an instant after an acrobatic feat. (Significantly, Asian theater was also an important source of Eisenstein's theory of expressive movement: the instantaneous shift from action to pose is akin to the "transitionless acting" he found in kabuki.[8])

The pause-burst-pause pattern is not visible in every Hong Kong action film, but it seems to occur so rarely in Hollywood action films that we can treat it as an important mark of difference. In *Lethal Weapon* the continual, often lumbering movements of the actors do not isolate discrete gestures on this moment-by-moment basis. Similarly, all the storyboarders in the world cannot give *Indiana Jones and the Temple of Doom* (1984) a visual pulse on celluloid. The opening fight scene in the Shanghai nightclub is at once over- and underwrought because its compositions and cutting impose a rhythm on haphazard runs and dives, while the film's protracted climax, showing Jones in a mine tunnel grappling with a *thuggee* on a conveyor belt, presents a vague, achingly slow tussle. In Hollywood, too often when a fight scene is fast, it is not clear, and when it is clear, it looks laborious.

Figure 1

Figure 2

Figure 3

Figure 4

Figure 5

Figure 6

Figure 7

Figure 8

Figure 9

Figure 10

So when fans praise a Woo or Ringo Lam sequence for its "continuous action," I am suggesting a slight correction. It is Hollywood that relies on continuous hustle, and the sequence often suffers from it. One source of a Hong Kong sequence's power is a clarity born of discontinuity, of lightning switches between quick, precise gestures and punctuating poses. This staccato performance tactic gives a fistfight or gun battle or martial arts bout a visual snap almost completely lacking in the American action picture.

The vividness of Hong Kong action depends on more than visual intelligibility. There is as well what we can call the *expressive amplification* of action. At bottom, this tactic pushes beyond Western norms of restraint and plausibility — bypassing that appeal to realism that makes the typical Western action scene comparatively diffuse in its stylistic organization and emotional appeal. Like a good caricature, the Hong Kong action sequence selects and exaggerates for a precise effect. The Hong Kong action sequence arrests us not because it mimics normal behavior but because it felicitously magnifies the most emotion-arousing features of pursuit or combat. The stylization of Eisenstein's "But there are two" line not only clarifies the gesture and the meaning; it also provides expressive thrust and provokes a distinct response in the audience. A Hong Kong punch or tumble or agonized death may seem cartoonish to viewers who do not recognize that in this tradition every movement gains its proper impact from being "sold" in Eisenstein's sense. Expressive amplification is one major way in which the Hong Kong film, as the fans like to say, goes over the top.

I call this tendency *expressive* amplification because it seeks to characterize each chase or fight quite emotionally. A given sequence will vividly exemplify power, elegance, vengeful fury, awkwardness, indefatigability, or some combination of such qualities. In our *Hearty Response* sequence, Joey Wong's performance is defined by her frantic, quavering desperation mixed with a reckless impulse for vengeance. This informs her every action — firing at the tattooist, scrambling up from the pavement, crumpling under his blows in the nightclub, and finally advancing, pistol trembling, on her trapped attacker. In addition, a scene can articulate contrasting expressive qualities, building emotion by their alternation. In Woo's *Killer*, the gangsters who have invaded John's apartment die in grotesque poses of slow-motion agony while in separate shots he cruises serenely through the haze.

A Hollywood action scene may occasionally display such expressive qualities, but it tends not to be as sharply delineated on a moment-by-moment basis. In our *Lethal Weapon* case, we know that Mel Gibson is furious, but although he races along the pavement urgently, nothing else in his demeanor evokes the rage his character is presumably feeling. And Donner supplies no close-ups comparable to those that specify the emotional flow in *Hearty Response*.

Nor does much emphasis fall upon the sheer physical effort Gibson invests; unlike Hong Kong characters, he never gets so winded he must collapse in tears. A performer like Jackie Chan creates an extended suite of postures and facial gymnastics just in order to exhibit the strain of executing a stunt. This can be played for laughs, as Chan frequently does when, after fiercely delivering a blow, he half-turns to hide his smarting hand. In *Fong Sai-Yuk [Fang Shiyu]* (1993), after a ferocious barrage of blows to the villain, our hero steps back, scrunches up his face, and suddenly flaps his arms frantically, creating an unmistakable picture of shooting, stinging pain. For such reasons, the expressive characterization of the action may well mix in recognition of the physical harm it involves. The hair-raising stunts of Jackie Chan, Sammo Hung, Yuen Biao, and many other adepts modify the action's dominant expressive quality — say, resourcefulness or tenacity — by reminding us how easily the hero might be hurt.

I call this tendency expressive *amplification* because the emotional qualities are not presented laconically; the filmic handling magnifies them. Thus, the actor may exaggerate the gesture to underlie its expressive quality, as Jet Li does in the *Fong Sai-Yuk* instance. Or the expressive quality may be amplified through ensemble playing, the exchange and rhyming of gestures among the performers. This was of course a staple of the 1970s martial arts film. Later in the decade, the comic *kungfu* movies turned each combat episode into a distinctive, almost dancelike symmetry of action and reaction. The same tendency was developed in the heroic gunplay movies of the 1980s.

The synchronized running, leaping, and diving of Waise Lee and his partner in the incendiary climax of *The Big Heat* (1988) add up virtually to a circus act. By American standards, many Hong Kong films (of all genres) look broadly played, perhaps seeming closer to silent film conventions than to those of post-Method Hollywood. But I suggest that this is part of a distinct aesthetic, in which expressive amplification is central to the performance of actor and ensemble.

The Hong Kong cinema goes beyond the performance and uses other film techniques to amplify the expressive dimensions of the action. Consider, for instance, the much-maligned zoom shots of the 1970s *kungfu* films. The rapid zoom itself often manifests the pause-burst-pause pattern found at the level of the performance, as pose-strike-pose can be underscored by static framing–fast zoom–static framing. Moreover, the zoom often intensifies the expressive qualities of the bodies' postures and movements. Although 1980s action films tend to avoid the zoom, the technique illustrates the tendency of the Hong Kong tradition to take a commonplace stylistic device and exploit it to make the action larger than life.

Editing also offers a rich array of tactics for amplifying the action, and here the 1980s action picture owes an even larger debt to the martial arts picture. Editing can, as in the hero's leap and bounce in *Sacred Knives of Vengeance*, create a smooth continuity of action, tracing out the geometry of the body's trajectory. Cuts can mark the pause-burst-pause pattern in a variety of ways. The rapid action may start at the end of one shot, continue across one or more shots, and halt in a final shot. Or the pause-burst-pause pattern may be confined to a single shot, and a series of shots may play the actions off against one another. Right before the moment I have already discussed in *Legendary Weapons of China*, the assassins hop abruptly apart, each one assigned a separate shot and a path that mirrors that of the other.

The expressive force of running, jumping, punching, or kicking can also be strengthened by overlapping editing. Repeating a portion of the movement at the cut is common in the Hollywood action picture, often in order to fake stunts like Mel Gibson's roll across the taxicab hood. In Hong Kong, however, overlapping serves to clarify key gestures by distending the time they take onscreen. Indeed, Hong Kong directors often unabashedly repeat entire actions. The most famous examples are Jackie Chan's instant-replay stunts, such as the fall from the clock in *Project A [A Jihua]* (1983), the slide down the post in the climactic mall fight in *Police Story [Jingcha Gushi]* (1985), and his leap from a motorcycle to a pallet dangling from a crane in *Armour of God II [Feiying Jihua]* (1991). Another example is Conan Lee's appalling plunge from a lamppost in *Tiger on the Beat II [Laohu Chugeng II]*

(1989). One way to make an action transparently evident is simply to run it again, but this means of clarification is not available to the Hollywood film-maker, bound by conventions of a certain kind of realism.

Repetitive cutting to bring out a movement's trajectory is similar to the expansion of an action by slow motion, and of course this has long been a favored resource of 1970s and 1980s filmmaking. For the Hong Kong action film, slow motion can intensify the fury or effort or danger of a blow while also stressing its grace. Similarly, fast-motion cinematography can emphasize the precision and timing of the kicks, punches, and parries. Tsui Hark's and John Woo's willingness to intercut shots displaying *different* rates of slow motion to the stuttering pause-burst-pause printing one finds in Wong Kar-wai's work probably owes a debt to the tradition of amplifying an action's emotional overtones by playing with speed of motion.

Like the zoom, the soundtrack of the martial arts movie has had its share of bad press. Westerners are often put off by the impossibly loud, absolutely uniform whacks, smacks, whooshes, and air-smiting thuds to be heard in film after film. Yet these can be understood as conventional signals that a blow has landed or missed. The sounds, that is, clarify the action on a moment-by-moment basis. (I am especially fond of the rustle of fabric or invisible wings, which announces that someone has taken flight.) Just as important, these implausible noises give the action an extra expressive force, like the crash of cymbals during combat scenes in Peking opera.

The action scene, then, can draw on a wide range of cinematic techniques that underscore and magnify the performers' movement. But this profusion presents a new problem. For if every blow or block is bracketed by pauses, if every kick or punch emits the same thud, if variable-speed photography and printing constantly clarify and accentuate a gesture—then how can there be any gradation of emphasis? How can the decisive punch stand out from all the hundreds of other blows that might look and sound exactly the same? Directors soon developed a *multi-accentual* system enabling them to single out certain pieces of action. The performance, filmed in long shot or broken into closer views, along with a normalized level of sound effects, yields a baseline over which certain techniques can be layered to highlight a particularly intense moment. In the *kungfu* film, a key action can be presented as, say, a stupendous piece of acrobatics, treated in super-slow motion accompanied by a piercing cry from the attacker and a throbbing, high-reverberation thwack on the soundtrack.

More recent action films exploit the same multi-accentual system. In *Hard-Boiled [Lashou Shentan]* (1992), during the massive gun battle in the hospital, Tony Chiu-wai Leung accidentally shoots a fellow policeman. How to distinguish this crucial moment from the dozens of other gunblasts that have preceded it? As Leung hears an elevator open offscreen right, he whirls and fires, and the multi-accentual system comes into play. In an instant, the shot slips into step-printed slow motion, the camera pans right and moves in on the victim, the natural sound drops out, and we hear the spectral tinkling and roiling of synthesizer music. The camera swings back to Leung, who halts abruptly. The camera holds on him as Chow Yun-fat steps toward him from behind and pushes him into the elevator. Woo refuses one obvious accentual cue, a cut to a closer view of the victim, evidently because that would disrupt the very long tracking shot that has followed Leung and Chow through a maze of corridors and will stay with them in the elevator and through the firefight on the next floor. And step printing by itself would not distinguish movement from other stretches of slow motion in the shot. Woo chooses to laminate several received techniques together to intensify this pitiful accident. By combining cues for expressive qualities, the filmmaker can, as it were, underscore an action doubly or trebly.

I do not mean to suggest that clarifying and amplifying physical movement is just a matter of conveying important information to the viewer. These processes do that, but they also aim at a piercing arousal of the spectator's senses and emotions. Clearly many Hong Kong filmmakers aim, as Yuen Wo-ping puts it, to make the viewer "*feel* the blow."[9] Not only must the action be legible and expressively amplified; it must be *communicated*, as energy is communicated from one body to another; it must be stamped on the spectator's senses. And this is what Hollywood fights, falls, and car crashes so often fail to do. We *watch* them, sometimes with keen interest and anticipation, but we seldom *feel* them because all the resources of performance, filming, and editing are not focused upon transmitting the sensory and emotional expenditure of energy that propels the scene from instant to instant.

All this is, once more, far closer to the tradition of Sergei Eisenstein than of Steven Spielberg. Throughout his career Eisenstein, always a man of the theater, emphasized that expressive movement was the core of cinematic mise-en-scène. First the filmmaker had to discover concrete actions an actor could be trained to execute in simplified and stylized form. Then the filmmaker had to devise ways of framing (*mise-en-cadre*) and editing (montage) that would sharpen the expressive movements and make them more dynamic. And at key moments these techniques could complement, double, and intensify one another in a massive assault on the spectator's senses.

If the effort was successful, the force of the movement and its onscreen presentation would stir in the viewer's body a palpable echo of the actor's gesture. "It is precisely expressive movement built on an organically correct foundation, that is solely capable of evoking this emotion in the spectator, who in turn reflexively repeats in weakened form the entire system of the actor's movements; as a result of the produced movements, the spectator's incipient muscular tensions are released in the desired emotion."[10] Since for Eisenstein affective qualities were no more than the result of agitation of the nervous system, expressive movement could give a viewer a uniquely exhilarating experience, at once physical and emotive. He dreamed of an ecstatic cinema, one that carried spectators away, tearing them "out of stasis" and arousing a rapt, electric apprehension of sheerly pictorial and auditory momentum.[11] The delirious kinetic exhilaration we find in Hong Kong cinema seem designed to elicit just such a response.

It is not the whole story, of course. Part of our pleasure is created by an appreciation of innovation — imaginative variations on formulas, unexpected uses of familiar schemas. Consider the device of one fighter tossing the gun to another. Woo uses the gesture to suggest the rituals of courtly honor when the opponents of *A Better Tomorrow II* [*Yingxiong Bense Xuji*] (1987) exchange pistols. In *Pom Pom and Hot Hot* [*Shenqiangshou Yu Gali Ji*] (1992), however, it becomes a manic gag; two cops caught in a firefight must share the same automatic and flip it back and forth, always just in time to dispatch an attacker.

And certainly part of our pleasure comes from the film's display of skill for its own sake. In any art, we enjoy the virtuoso's mastery of craft, the way she or he sets up difficult problems and solves them with easy brilliance. Later in our specimen sequence from *Bodyguard from Beijing*, Jet Li is fighting the main villain around, behind, and on top of a kitchen counter. Earlier Yuen Kwai has conveyed the pause-burst-pause visual pulse by coordinating cutting with performance, but now he manifests it within a single flashy shot. To prevent his adversary from reaching water, Li cracks a towel like a whip, snapping the swiveling faucet sharply from side to side before our eyes (Figures 11–12).

Nonetheless, at the base of these more "knowing" pleasures remains the sheer kinetic transport offered by doings that are felicitous, functional, and laden with infectious emotion. These actions are the opposite of brute force. They rivet our attention because they are clearer and more expressive and expansive than ordinary running or jumping or arm swinging. Hollywood offers an all-purpose blanket "excitement." Directors try to turn graceless stars into action heroes by hurling them into a loud, vague bustle. Hong Kong action genres at their best offer balletic performers carrying out concrete,

Figure 11

Figure 12

intelligible physical tasks. Each gesture is honed to a fine edge and carries specific expressive qualities, standing out by virtue of a visual design stripped of clutter, amplified by the resources of film technique.

What I have proposed are only hypotheses; probably they need recasting and nuancing.[12] There are other questions to be asked as well. Are there not distinct stylistic trends in this tradition? What more specific lines of influence can we trace out—not just within Chinese traditions and between Hong Kong and Hollywood, but also between Hong Kong and Japan? (The Zatoichi and Lone Wolf and Cub films, for instance, achieve a more sober, attenuated, and grotesque expressivity, and this resurfaces, it seems to me, in the films of Kitano Takeshi.) And how much theoretical merit is there in Eisenstein's account of the spectator who repeats, in less forceful form, the muscular rhythms apprehended on the screen? Approaching Hong Kong action movies as an "ecstatic cinema" may help us understand why so many of them infect even film professors, heavy with middle age and polemics if not baked brie, with the delusion that they can vault, grave and unflappable, over the cars parked outside the theater.

Notes

1 Stefan Hammond and Mike Wilkins, *Sex and Zen and a Bullet in the Head: The Essential Guide to Hong Kong's Mind-Bending Films* (New York: Fireside Books, 1996), 11.

2 Quoted in Vincent LoBrutto, *Selected Takes: Film Editors on Editing* (New York: Praeger, 1991), 181.

3 Indeed, Pudovkin's example is an automobile accident, broken into several shots to give the impression of the event. See V. I. Pudovkin, *Film Technique and Film Acting*, trans. Ivor Montagu (New York: Grove, 1960), 95–100.

4 Quoted in Eric Rudolph, "*The Rock* Offers No Escape," *American Cinematographer* 77, no. 6 (June 1996): 64–73.

5 I do not mean to argue that *Hearty Response* is a masterpiece or even a particularly good movie, only that it is fairly typical in its stylistic strategies.

6 For excellent discussions of the martial arts film as a genre, see A *Study of the Hong Kong Martial Arts Film* (Hong Kong: Urban Council, 1980), particularly Sek Kei's fine overview, "The Development of 'Martial Arts' in Hong Kong Cinema," 27–38.

7 Sergei Eisenstein and Sergei Tretyakov, "Expressive Movement," in *Meyerhold, Eisenstein, and Biomechanics: Actor Training in Revolutionary Russia*, ed. Alma Law and Mel Gordon (Jefferson, N.C.: McFarland, 1996), 189.

8 Sergei Eisenstein, "Beyond the Shot," in *Selected Works*, vol. 1, *Writings, 1922–34*, ed. and trans. Richard Taylor (London: British Film Institute, 1988), 148. See also "An Unexpected Juncture," ibid., 115–22, and "To the Magician of the Pear Orchard," in *Selected Works*, vol. 3, *Writings, 1934–47*, ed. Richard Taylor, trans. William Powell (London: British Film Institute, 1988), 56–67.

9 Interview by author with Yuen Woo-ping, 23 November 1996.

10 Eisenstein and Tretyakov, 187.

11 I discuss this aspect of Eisenstein's theory, as well as his conception of how mise-en-scène and other techniques can create the effect of ecstasy, in *The Cinema of Eisenstein* (Cambridge, Mass.: Harvard University Press, 1993), chapters 3–5.

12 I try to refine these arguments in chapter 7 of *Planet Hong Kong: Popular Cinema and the Art of Entertainment* (Cambridge, Mass.: Harvard University Press, 2000).

CHAPTER FOUR

The Killer: Cult Film and Transcultural (Mis)Reading

Jinsoo An

I regard The Killer *as a romantic poem.* —JOHN WOO

It [The Killer] *is the theater of the ridiculous.* —JAMI BERNARD, NEW YORK POST

Those of us who love Hong Kong action cinema think of the lousy subtitling as one of the incidental pleasures of the genre. When Chow Yun-fat voices his suspicions of a drug smuggler's underwear in Tiger on the Beat, *and it comes out as "I suspect her bra also contains cock," you can't really be irritated by it. (emphasis in original)*
—A READER'S RESPONSE TO "LOUSY SUBTITLING," SIGHT AND SOUND

Critical attention to John Woo's Hong Kong action films in the West has engendered inquiries about the relationship between his exuberant cinematic style and the social anxiety driven by the historical situation of Hong Kong.[1] According to some views, these films are preoccupied with the rapidly changing geopolitics of Hong Kong and its uncertain future after the 1997 takeover. Such contextual readings locate Woo's action films ambiguously in the tropes of national cinema, which are concerned particularly with the ways in which the social anxiety attendant on impending takeover is configured in crisis and apocalyptic visions. By reading the films in close relation to their sociopolitical settings, critics have rescued the cinema of John Woo from the pejorative descriptions of exploitation action flicks or cult movies.

Yet, Woo's Hong Kong action films consistently occupy the center stage of cult cinema in the United States. More specifically, his 1989 film *The Killer* [*Diexue Shuangxiong*] has become one of the most celebrated cult films in recent years.[2] To overlook the cult phenomenon of the film, it seems to me, is to leave out too many questions about the film's unique textual system and the cultural space that popular Hong Kong films occupy in the United States. In this essay, I examine *The Killer* primarily in the critical terms of the cult film phenomenon. This means that the film will be discussed, in the most literal sense, as foreign film. Consequently, my attention lies in the practice of transcultural readings of the cult film experience and what this reception indicates with respect to the exchange of films between Hong Kong and the United States.[3] I argue that *The Killer*'s particular reception mode and formal features are of certain theoretical importance for inquiries into film culture in the transcultural age, for the film's enduring cult following not only illustrates the existence of an expanding space for popular Asian cinema in America, it also poses questions regarding the relationship between the practice of cultural misreading and the increasing dissemination of Hong Kong film images in the West. Later in this essay, I will expand my inquiry beyond cult film in the United States by examining the film's different reception and meanings in Asian transcultural settings, specifically in Korea. How Woo's films have been understood by Korean viewers, and how those viewers have engaged them, will inform a dynamic transcultural reading practice that is significantly different from the American mode.

As Ella Shohat and Robert Stam point out, global media exchange can no longer be explained using a strict binary model of the First World as a sender of culture and the Third World as its recipient. The inquiry must come to terms with a contemporary media condition where global mass culture and local indigenous culture tend to coexist and interact in complex ways.[4] The phenomenal cult status of *The Killer* is unique within this context of transnational exchange precisely because it illustrates a pattern distinct from the previously conceived norm. I am not suggesting here that the film testifies to a reversal of the old model of cultural exchange; this does not simply represent the emergence of non-Western local culture in the domain of global mass culture controlled by the West.[5] Unequal terms of cultural exchange do exist between the two poles, and its political economy cannot simply be ignored in celebration of cultural globalization. Yet, the expanding sphere of popular Hong Kong films in the United States illustrates the process whereby foreign cultural artifacts bring special meaning and pertinence to local consumers living in a global mass culture. Repetitive engagement with the foreign film text, thus, indicates a persistent and active effort to seek a particular viewing pleasure not available in conventional American films, a practice that signals a certain limitation of the cultural hegemony maintained by the Hollywood machine. Crucial here is a specific mode of transcultural appropriation that operates in reading (or misreading) this foreign text. By inserting a popular Hong Kong genre film into the canon of cult films, I intend to advance the debate on contemporary cult film, which until now has largely been studied in terms of intracultural phenomena, that is, focused mostly on the cultural value and textual meaning from within.

In order to discuss *The Killer* in terms of cult film, I would first like to delineate its categorical boundaries.[6] This slippery journalistic term derives from a sociological phenomenon: cult film experience refers to the feverish

Figure 1.
The Killer (John Woo,
1999) became a
celebrated cult film
in the 1990s.

worshiping of privileged film by the fans, who share exclusive knowledge of it. However, this sociological account is often too broad to mark a visible boundary of cult film. Descriptions such as "it's a cult film if it has a devoted fan following" tend to be so indiscriminate in the numbers and kinds of films included that the term itself runs the risk of losing its specificity. Recently, more rigorous scholarship has modified the territory of cult film by adding the deviant and overtly disruptive nature of the film's subject into the discussion. The cultural role of cult film, namely the relationship between film text and audience, has been central to theory on cult film.[7]

Transgression, or the violation of boundaries, is one of the most important features of cult films. Whether it is a boundary of time, style, genre, cultural convention, or aesthetic evaluation, cult films demonstrate volatile energy for crossing the constraints of these established boundaries. According to Bruce Kawin, classic cult films such as *Casablanca* (1942) provide their worshipers with a sense of deep nostalgia for the glamour of stars who transcend temporal constraints. Meanwhile, midnight movies like *The Rocky Horror Picture Show* (1975) form a subcultural terrain where urban teenagers' desire to resist mainstream conformity is expressed in a participatory viewing practice.[8] In any case, as Telotte notes, this irrational worshiping is tied to the gestural act of transgression, which is concerned particularly with crossing formal or cultural boundaries. That is, cult film serves an arena of transgression after which one safely returns home but with the feeling of transgression intact.[9]

In the case of *The Killer*, then, the questions we must ask are: What kind of formal and cultural boundaries does *The Killer* transgress and violate in becoming an object of popular worship in the United States? What ends do the film's unique formal and stylistic elements serve in the production of this peculiar pleasure? How does this transgressive pleasure differ from that available from other types of cult films? And, finally, what does this pleasurable effect tell us about the location of Hong Kong cinema in contemporary film culture in the United States? To answer these questions, I begin my analysis with the film's formal design and textual effect. This approach affords a view of the film's textual system, which is distinct from the system of other Euro-American cult texts. Furthermore, it will further understanding of the popularity in the West of Hong Kong action films, of which *The Killer* is a prime example.[10] These formal features are thus understood here as a vehicle for conceptualizing the film's distinctive aesthetics that is rooted in different cultural sensibilities and viewing patterns. In addition, the film's peculiar hybrid characteristics, especially in terms of genre and style, will enable us to discern its engagement with the popular American cinema. Such a textual system, derived from stylistic exuberance and spectacular excess, aims to project and articulate the world according to emotional truth and overt moral certitude.[11]

First, a synopsis of the film is in order. Jeff (Chow Yun-fat), a professional assassin, accidentally blinds Jenny (Sally Yeh), a singer, during a shoot-out at a nightclub. Guilt-ridden, Jeff decides to follow the advice of his friend Sydney (Chu Kong) for one last job to procure the resources needed for an operation to restore Jenny's sight. This last assassination unveils the betrayal of the mob that hired him, and Jeff is chased by both the mob and Inspector Lee (Danny Lee), a chase that for the inspector has become an obsession. The two men develop a friendship, and they end up forming a partnership in the final shoot-out against the mob gunmen. In the end, Jeff and his loyal friend Sydney die, and Jenny is left blind. Lee shoots the mob boss and weeps over the loss of his friend Jeff.

The Killer is a troubling text to evaluate by a single critical and aesthetic standard. It strives to achieve success through such crafted elements as gunfight scenes (with "1,000 bullets"), gross "sentimentality," a theme of male bonding, and a code of honor, all enmeshed within the generic framework of the gangster or action film. The term "troubling text" requires further explanation. I am using it here to describe a text that falls short of achieving the high degree of verisimilitude required for dramatic film. According to Aristotle, drama must avoid "implausible possibilities" in favor of "plausible impossibilities" in order to increase the credibility of dramatic situations.[12] This naturalization of events in drama has been carried over to classical Hollywood cinema as the primary rule of dramaturgy and filmic expression. The Hollywood mode structures film events within the tropes of the law of cause and effect, motivation-driven characters, clear configuration of space and time, and lucid resolution.[13] The aesthetic effect of this mode of filmmaking is an illusory and psychologically plausible representation of phenomenal world. Hollywood's genre films essentially operate within these prerogatives of the dominant film mode, although their repetitive semantic and syntactic features familiarize viewers with thematic and stylistic modification. In the case of action film, which has become a privileged genre of contemporary Hollywood, success depends on the effective conversion of implausible situations and actions into believable narrative components.

In contrast, the dramaturgy of *The Killer* is built on the oscillation between plausible impossibilities and implausible possibilities. John Woo sets up the film's generic framework by introducing familiar character types and motivations. Initially, such character types and their interactions work well within the generic conventions. The characters of the lone assassin, the injured woman, and the conflicted cop are fully developed from the beginning. They are, however, often oddly combined with implausible and chance-ridden circumstances, which produce an inept dramatic effect.[14] One such instance is the beach sequence. After successfully carrying out his assassination, Jeff tries to leave the scene on a boat but is chased by Inspector Lee. Jeff safely lands his boat on a quiet beach and hides himself among some children, who are playing games. His plan for a quiet escape fails, however, as the hired guns are waiting at the beach to kill him. A violent shoot-out takes place between Jeff and the mob, and a girl on the beach is caught in the crossfire and fatally wounded. The protagonist defeats the mob and quickly takes the girl to a nearby hospital. In this sequence, the motif of the innocent girl in danger emphasizes Jeff's high moral stand, which echoes the killer's kindness and courage in helping the blinded singer. Although this dramatic event serves to underscore the killer's physical and moral superiority, the manner in which the sequence unfolds far exceeds the realistic convention that had previously set the terms for the film's narrative development. Jeff's urgent need to escape extreme danger is entirely displaced here by his overtly moral endeavor to save the innocent child. Melodramatic moral occult suddenly enters into the picture, transforming the hero into a vital agent of a moral universe.[15]

The use of a church setting with a statue of the Virgin Mary follows the similar pattern of overt authorial intent and melodramatic effect. The mythic dimension of the hero's struggle, displayed through a Catholic icon in an excessively crude and self-conscious manner, is amplified by the burst of grandiose classical music that accompanies the destruction of the statue of the Virgin. These apparent stylistic excesses allow viewers to recognize the discrepancy between the filmmaker's lofty artistic intention and the peculiarly jarring dramatic effect. In short, the film contains a series of obtrusive and hyperbolic images that often disengage viewers from the narrative absorption and remind them of the very performance of genre film.

The inappropriate shift in tone also moves the audience away from the envelopment of the diegetic world.[16] The gunfight on the beach, which amplifies Jeff's heroics, abruptly cuts to a car chase with a rough shift in nondiegetic music. In another instance, Sydney is beaten repeatedly and gruesomely by his evil boss, Weng, yet he stands up in a dignified manner to fix his necktie as if nothing had happened to him, stating, "Even being a dog, I have to fix myself." The theatricality of acting here displaces the seemingly naturalistic performance in prior scenes. Later on, Jeff's mercy killing of Sydney in the church is an explosion of anger and passion for vengeance that provides Jeff with the moral justification he needs for his act. Yet the tone of the scene soon shifts to the joy and excitement of fraternization between Jeff and Lee in action. These disconcerting transitions of tone and character portrayals enable viewers to see the rough edges in otherwise highly skillful filmmaking.[17]

I have used several examples here to convey how the film's narrative decisively digresses from the conventional realistic mode of American filmmaking. Each of these instances of excess and rupture articulates the moral polarity of the world's vice and the virtuousness of the protagonist(s). The film repeatedly emphasizes, in hyperbolic terms, the emotional and moral soundness of the protagonist's struggle and virtue. It clearly engages the melodramatic mode, a mode of representation different from the realistic mode of present-day Hollywood cinema. Instead of accounting for the characters' actions in psychological causes and motives, the film is more preoccupied with what Linda Williams calls the "retrieval and staging of innocence" and virtues.[18] What is clear from these observations is that passionate melodramatic pathos has returned through excessive violence, figuring the protagonists as the moral authority in a hostile and brutal environment.

The cinematic excess of graphic violence is the locus of the film's principal energy and attraction. Kristin Thompson's theory of cinematic excess provides critical terms for conceptualizing this distinctive filmic effect. According to Thompson, cinematic excess occurs as the materiality of images functions beyond the purpose of narrative progression. Narrative film is ba-

Figure 2.
The return of passionate melodramatic pathos in *The Killer*.

sically the site of tension between narrative logic and the materiality of images that often transgresses intended meanings. Reading cinematic excess in cine-formalist terms, Thompson defines excess that "implies a gap or lag in motivation" as "counter-narrative" and "counter-unity."[19] She attributes value to obtrusive and "strange" works like *Ivan the Terrible* (1944), as they make the audience aware of "the structure," rather than the narrative, of the film.[20]

The strong images and forced motifs in *The Killer* certainly function beyond the narrative purpose. The recognition of these excessive elements, however, does not simply encourage intellectual contemplation, as Thompson contends. Unlike *Ivan the Terrible*, where the slow progression of the narrative forces viewers to observe or reflect on the "materiality" of the images, the rapid kinetic images in *The Killer* do not call for meditation as such. Instead, Woo's masterful manipulation of spatiotemporality through a continuous sequence of shootings in confined space shows the characteristics of exhibitionism and theatrical display often associated with what Tom Gunning calls "the cinema of attractions." According to him, the cinema of attractions refers to the early cinema in which an exciting spectacle itself is the central feature stimulating spectator attention. Unlike narrative film, with its voyeuristic nature, the cinema of attractions is an exhibitionist cinema.[21] Woo's experiment with formal properties such as slow motion, overlapping, and shot repetition often exceeds the narrative requirement, calling attention to the film's presentational and exhibitionistic features. Instead of contemplative engagement, Woo's cinematic excess aims at a certain psychological impact on viewers through the elaborate choreographed violence.

In terms of generic affiliation, *The Killer* transgresses a boundary of the action-film genre. Its sentimentality suggests a melodramatic mode of representation operating parallel to the kinetic and sensational world of the action film. According to Julian Stringer, Woo's *A Better Tomorrow [Yingxiong Bense]* (1986) and *The Killer* present a configuration of masculinity different from the Hollywood mode in that the demarcation between the male action ("doing") genre and the female ("suffering") genre collapses in these films. The male protagonists in both films engage simultaneously in "doing," that is, in violent action and heroism, and in "suffering"—loss, sadness, and melancholy.[22] The jarring dramatic effects I have mentioned owe a great deal to odd generic features of the "male melodrama of doing and suffering."[23] In this context, excessive violence is a transferred figuration of the melodrama's intention to express that which is unutterable in realistic convention. Given that melodrama of excess is rare in the contemporary Hollywood filmmaking scene, the suffering yet morally authoritative male protagonists in Woo's films come to be viewed as a kind of new, odd, and fascinating cinematic representation: something that waits to be "discovered" by American audiences.[24]

When *The Killer* was released in the United States, film critics largely failed to understand this dynamic of generic hybridity and charged that the film displayed sentimentality and emotional excess. But these affective features, which had been unavailable in the Western cinematic tradition, are precisely the lure of Hong Kong action cult films. Contrary to film critics, cult followers of these film texts find that the melodramatic ordeal and tragic fate of the male protagonists broadly speak for, in Telotte's term, their "deepfelt and perhaps unacknowledged desire."[25] Cult audiences have been able to grip the "structure of feeling" of the text, which, beneath its incoherence and ricketiness, is truthful, sincere, and moving.

The melodramatic dimension of *The Killer* described above helps to explain how the film's campiness is registered and maintained. According to Barbara Klinger, the generic conventions of film melodramas are especially subject to mass camp appropriation.[26] Mass camp views and evaluates old objects from contemporary realist standards and makes fun of its artifices and anachronism.[27] In the case of classical Hollywood melodrama, Klinger notes, the subject matter and socially pertinent theme look decidedly outdated in a contemporary context because of the changed social circumstances. More importantly, the genre's expressive conventions such as intensified dramatic conflicts and emotional affect fail to register once-serious meanings to contemporary viewers.[28]

Although Klinger's study focuses exclusively on Hollywood melodramas, her observations on the deterioration of generic integrity by mass camp can be applied to *The Killer*. Here the degradation of textual coherence appears in terms of both temporal and cultural difference. The present cultural condition of mass camp, as led by increasing mass production and dissemination of media texts, affects the ways in which the modern viewer perceives and understands film texts from other cultures. In *The Killer*, the melodramatic expression is a dominant narrative articulation in many crucial sequences. Yet, it is an outdated mode of expression that has long been swayed by a more realistic mode of representation in America. Simultaneously, the film is also a chic contemporary action genre film filled with sophisticated action sequences, far surpassing the artistry of conventional Hollywood action films. Thus, the film registers dual generic features. On the one hand, its affective design has some ties to the visible representational mode of the past, that is, melodrama. On the other hand, its dynamic configuration of kinetic activities suggests new possibilities and directions for the burgeoning contemporary genre. It is old *and* new. *The Killer*, in other words, is an accessible action film that looks decidedly foreign, with its prominent melodramatic subtext of male suffering. This dual tendency, this odd combination, is the essential fabric of *The Killer*'s cult universe.

In addition, *The Killer*'s textual oddity is circumscribed by the major shift in representational mode and viewing pattern in the United States. Besides discussing camp, critics also describe the postmodern crisis of representation, which set the stage for the formation of contemporary cult films like *The Killer*. Defining the emergence of camp sensibility as occurring after the era of modernism and locating camp objects in opposition to serious high art, Susan Sontag suggests that the discovery of old, vulgar, and foreign objects is a consequence of modernism in crisis, that is, the exhaustion of the ability of a pristine style to represent current conditions.[29] Her emphasis on the sensory experience of style over interpretive meaning, therefore, signals a postmodern spectatorship that is evidenced in its ultimate form in campy cult film. Interest in the text is disengaged and fragmented, and little attention is paid to historical and social meanings. Klinger similarly notes how the proliferation of media texts and images created an environment conducive to camp readings. She writes, "[T]he postwar explosion in media recycling . . . encouraged a campy perspective on classic Hollywood films by creating an audience schooled in convention and primed by parodies to discover the inherent artifice of the more 'naive' products of film industry."[30]

Under these changed viewing conditions and in the audience's relationship to the film text, most films are being watched by their audiences as "private, domesticated performances or spectacular backgrounds to public lives."[31] In this view, any film can become a cult film through the "adoption" of the audience.[32] What these essays elucidate is the expansion of the cult film's territory, conditioned by a proliferation of film texts and, consequently, a loss of the images' indexical representational power. More than thematic features of transgression, contemporary cult films such as *The Killer* emerge from a pervasive lack of interest in textual coherence and serious thematics.

Having discussed the factors that formed the cult phenomenon of *The Killer* in the United States, I now turn to a popular film exchange in an inter-Asian context. In particular, the way *The Killer* and other Hong Kong action films achieved success in the South Korea of the late 1980s illustrates a distinctive pattern of cultural dialogue and appropriations. In order to understand the dynamics between Hong Kong action films and film reception in Korea, one needs to go back to 1987, when *A Better Tomorrow* was first shown to Korean viewers. This flagship film neither received critical attention nor achieved commercial success when it was first released in Korea.[33] Consequently, it went to "mini-theaters."[34] In this marginal film exhibition arena, the film rapidly gained unusual popularity among local audiences. Ching Siu-tung's *A Chinese Ghost Story [Qiannu Youhun]* (1987) followed a similar trajectory of cult following in Korea: the film did not do well initially but was accepted by the same audiences upon repeated viewing. This quiet cult film phenomenon has largely been ignored by the mainstream media. Yet, the growing interest in cult film has transformed Korean film culture in subsequent years, particularly in the area of fan culture, where Hong Kong film stars like Chow Yun-fat and Joey Wong became symbols of masculine and feminine ideals, respectively. This scattered cult following entered into mainstream culture in following years, and *A Better Tomorrow II [Yingxiong Bense Xuji]* became the ninth largest box office draw in the following year.[35] The trend continued in 1989 as *The Killer* and Wong Jing's *Casino Raiders [Zhizhuan Wuxiang]* (1989) took the seventh and eighth places in the year's box office receipts, respectively.[36]

A Better Tomorrow's atypical success proved the formidable presence of marginal film culture in Korea, along with an audience that appropriates the text's appeal and values on its own terms through an act of "discovery." Unlike major urban theaters, where young females comprise the majority of the audience, the mini-theater audience is composed mainly of teenaged males. Such an audience composition significantly affects the programming of the mini-theaters, which regularly offer action genre double features or soft-core erotic flicks. Thus, the success of Hong Kong films like *The Killer* owed much to the established marginal film culture, where spectacles of action and eroticism were preferred to coherent and serious drama. In addition, the promulgation of video contributed significantly to the development of intense and repeated film viewing.[37] Demand for both new and old films increased greatly with video rentals, and the flood of Hong Kong action films filled the gap effectively. Video rentals also promoted individual viewing, where a viewer feels empowered for being able to have instant control of filmic images for selective viewing.

The term "cult film" requires some retooling when one examines Korean film culture, where it has a different set of implications and followed a different trajectory of development. After first entering cultural discourse in South Korea during the late 1980s, it was widely embraced by film buffs and journalists alike. The term "cult film" in South Korea usually refers to a group of Western "midnight movies" that generally feature grotesque themes and a peculiar style and formal design. Rather than being an indigenous subcultural phenomenon, "cult film" is understood more in terms of genre.[38] Such titles as David Lynch's *Eraserhead* (1978) and *Blue Velvet* (1986) and Alexandro Jodorowsky's *El Topo* (1971) appear regularly on the list, while popular Hong Kong films rarely appear on the same list, despite their cultish followings. This is because Hong Kong films have a long-established, solid generic and (trans)national identity of their own and do not blend easily with other kinds of genre or national cinema. Despite this categorical difference, I argue that the Korean mass interest in cult film and the spectacular success of Hong Kong films are historically linked cultural phenomena. That is, the atypical success of Hong Kong films, more specifically Woo's films, and the growing demand for cult film share some common ground that are shaped and developed by complex industrial, social, and cultural factors in Korea.

The success of *The Killer* in South Korea owed a great deal, to be sure, to the textual appeal and ingenuity of Woo's filmmaking. Woo's films, starting with *A Better Tomorrow*, signaled what to Korean viewers seemed to be a new departure in Hong Kong cinema. Korean journalists and critics discovered something very different in new Hong Kong gangster and action films and coined the term "Hong Kong noir" to conceptualize the peculiarly pessimistic energy and allegorical implications.[39] The films' success also depended upon the translatability of their common themes, such as loyalty and male bonding, which were very accessible to Korean viewers, especially a male audience. This is partly owing to the fact that virtues such as loyalty are still powerful social mores in the Confucian tradition in South Korea. Furthermore, Korean subtitles conveyed the subtleties of the films' original dialogues more faithfully than English ones, shielding the films from the accidental and campy misreadings that are central to cult pleasure in the United States.

There are, however, more important social factors that played a significant role in shaping the growth of Hong Kong cinema into the Korean film vocabulary. As I mentioned above, in the 1980s Korea saw drastic changes in film exhibition; the number of mini-theaters and video rentals increased rapidly, and there was a greater diversification of film preferences and exhibition practices. In 1987 the Korean government, pressured by U.S. government agencies, passed a law that opened the film sector up to more imports. Since the new film law allowed foreign film companies to produce and directly distribute films in Korea, the new legislation met with fierce resistance from the local film industry. The industry launched a popular campaign to protect Korean films from the aggressive cultural imperialism of the United States; it included mass demonstrations and boycotts of directly distributed foreign (mainly American) films. Theaters that showed these films were subject to fierce criticism and attack, which culminated in paint being thrown at the screen and snakes (!) and tear gas being released into the auditorium.[40] This contentious situation also promoted an urgent need to reform and restructure the existing film industry in the areas of production, distribution, and exhibition. The biggest beneficiaries of the new law during these years of struggle for Korean cinema were, however, Hong Kong films. Because of hostility toward the cultural aggression of Hollywood and the high price of its products, many film importers in Korea turned their interest toward Hong Kong films, which already had a reputation for wide appeal. Concurrently, the unrecognized cult following of Chow and other Hong Kong film stars began to translate into box office receipts. Thus, the number of Hong Kong film imports increased strikingly during this period, from four films in 1986 to ninety-eight in 1990, close to the number of Hollywood pictures.[41]

Central also to these films' success was the image of new masculinity that Hong Kong film stars, and Chow Yun-fat in particular, embodied. As I noted, films like *The Killer* did not generate camp appeal, but were understood in Korea as more earnest texts on masculinity. This is closely linked to the translatability of a new paradigm of Hong Kong masculinity within a Korean cultural context. The masculine ideals these films articulate hardly seem radical to Korean viewers. The notions of honor, loyalty, and male bonding are very common in masculine discourses in Korea. What these films offered, however, was a refashioning and reaffirmation of the masculine ideals with which much of the Korean male audience felt a deep affinity. Historically, the wave of Hong Kong action films thus coincided with radical changes in the structure of Korean society during and after the 1988 Seoul Olympic Games. In the midst of proliferating discourses on globalization and the formation of a new national identity lies social anxiety over how contemporary demands might be combined with old values. In this context, the Hong Kong action film's reiteration of traditional masculine values and melodramatic pathos provided an arena of fantasy where the Korean male subject was able to come to imaginary terms with these pressing anxieties.

The films' success subsequently brought Chow Yun-fat's masculine star image into the spotlight in Korea. On the one hand, Chow's manners and dress were widely imitated by the young Koreans. Popular journalism called this cult following the "Chow Yun-fat syndrome." For his fans, Chow represented the new man, invincible and honorable. Unlike Chow's star persona in the United States—that of a "cool" professional assassin—his star image evolved from that of a professional gunman to a more benign and friendly figure as more of his films came to be shown in Korea. This evolved masculine image then provided a vehicle for him to appear in product advertisements on Korean television. Chow Yun-fat (and Joey Wong) appeared in a soft drink commercial, while Leslie Cheung was in an advertisement for a chocolate bar. These commercials highlighted the amiable and friendly personae of these stars and helped boost product sales immensely.[42]

The increasing presence of Hong Kong film stars in Korean society also brought cultural anxiety, however. In particular, there were critical concerns over the impact of Hong Kong movies on Korean society.[43] On the dark side of the spectrum, a group of young criminals, whose brutal killings shook Korea in 1994, confessed that they took their inspiration from the life styles of Hong Kong action heroes.[44] In particular, one Hong Kong film, Wong Jing's *Casino Raiders* (1989) inspired the name of a gangster group, *chijonpa* (taken from "Ji Juen" [zhi zhuan], the first two characters of the title of *Casino Raiders* [*Zhi Zhuan Wo Xiang*], and provided a model for a gangster lifestyle. The theme of loyalty to one's friends was taken to a disturbing extreme in this case as a weapon to strengthen one's will for brutal crime and class vendetta. While the code of honor and loyalty in Hong Kong films revived the already prevalent masculine discourse of *ŭiri* ("loyalty") in Korean society, it spoke differently to those who are deeply disenfranchised from society. For those in the lowest social strata, these films testified that being loyal to close associates is the only viable survival option in a hostile environment.

Hong Kong movie stars' cult followings also raised questions about the terms of masculinity that were increasingly defined by Hong Kong models. In particular, an idealized masculinity strongly associated with Hong Kong movie stars such as Chow Yun-fat, Leslie Cheung, and Andy Lau was viewed as problematic. It was under these anxiety-ridden circumstances that Im Kwon-taek, a renowned Korean filmmaker, directed a commercial gangster film, *The General's Son [Chang'gun-ŭi Adŭl]* (1988), in an endeavor to articulate a distinct and authentic Korean masculinity.[45] The film quickly became the biggest blockbuster of 1990, setting the model for Korean gangster films in subsequent years. Im noted later that the flood of Hong Kong action films propelled him to revive the Korean masculine image onscreen.[46] This production shows how deeply Hong Kong action films and their masculine ideals engage with the discourse of Korean masculinity and cultural production. Korean audiences embraced a new configuration of masculine ideals that Hong Kong action films offered; yet, Hong Kong films' increasing visibility also produced anxiety over the boundaries of Korean cultural identity. While the production of *The General's Son* was an attempt to distinguish the popular cinema of Korea from Hong Kong cinema, it demonstrates the degree to which the former was influenced by the latter.

A specific set of formal, narratological, generic, extratextual, and cultural factors constitutes the cult phenomenon of *The Killer*. Its cult film aesthetics derive from particular cinematic excesses and implausibilities situated within a cultural misreading. As demonstrated above, *The Killer*'s narrative construction reveals numerous implausible turnarounds. In the United States, the film's ambiguities or organic imperfections place it in the category of camp, but this camp reading is different from the conventional ridiculing of old objects. This mass camp involves cultural distance and generic (un)familiarity. In terms of generic association, the film is a hybrid, that is, a combination of male melodrama and action film, which further complicates the viewer's perception of it. Instead of being a historical artifact that has lost its relevance to history, the film becomes culturally sanitized so that it is "outrageous" and "ridiculous." Additionally, the postmodern crisis of representation and increasing privatization of cultural artifacts has encouraged this practice of "pleasurable misreading."

Hong Kong film's immense popularity in Korea shows a different pattern of cultural exchange, however. Articulation of the affective economy works more seriously here, preventing any possibility of camp readings. Instead, the code of masculine ideals and virtues found their proper translation in a Korean context. More importantly, the expanding space for Hong Kong films in Korea resulted from various contextual factors such as changing modes of film exhibition and the introduction of new media. The phenomenon also coincides with immense anxiety caused by the cultural aggression of the United States. Consequently, Hong Kong films offered that which Korean cinema was unable to provide during this historical juncture: an imaginary and imaginative space of (male) fantasy where traditional virtues appear to be a viable option for coping with rapidly changing circumstances. Thus, while for viewers in the United States *The Killer* seems to be a fresh new film with curious and odd components, for Korean viewers it projects a deeply moving tragic vision of the world and heroic struggle.

Changing film viewing practices both in the United States and Korea have created ghettoized film viewing communities that valorize the performance of non-Hollywood texts. Audiences relate their deep-seated desire and fulfillment to the outrageousness of the performing text. Paradoxically, the cult film connotes a liberating interpretive practice where the audience constructs its own meanings regardless of the intended textual effects. This also signifies the deterioration of textual authority and serious thematic. Yet, the space that the cult film *The Killer* carved out for itself illustrates how a non-Western film text can resist being aggressively appropriated by the hegemonic West. In the case of Korea, this film facilitated the debate on the question of national cultural identity. In this way, *The Killer* occupies a smooth and fluid cultural space for Korean viewers and as such provides an alternative imaginary landscape to the hegemonic Hollywood model. Still, the overt valorization raises the question of the cultural boundaries of contemporary Korea. Meanings are always distorted and misread in cult films; yet, there is also a profound sense of distance between our projected reading, conditioned by various contextual factors, and the performance of the foreign text. The reason for feverish worship of such films may lie in this odd textual integrity, a complex aura that brings us together in shared pleasure despite (or because of) distance and differences.

Notes

1 See Chiao Hsiung-ping, "The Distinct Taiwanese and Hong Kong Cinema," in *Perspectives on Chinese Cinema*, ed. Chris Berry (London: British Film Institute, 1991), 155–65; Li Cheuk-to, "The Return of the Father: Hong Kong New Wave and Its Chinese Context," in *New Chinese Cinemas: Forms, Identities, Politics*, ed. Nick Browne et al. (Cambridge and New York: Cambridge University Press,

1994), 160–79; Tony Williams, "To Live and Die in Hong Kong," *CineAction* 36 (1995): 42–52, and "Space, Place, and Spectacle: The Crisis Cinema of John Woo," *Cinema Journal* 36, no. 2 (winter 1997): 67–84.

2 The film has also been an inspiration for a new generation of filmmakers in the United States. Quentin Tarantino and Robert Rodriguez, who acknowledge Woo's influence on their films, have refashioned the genre of the action film in recent years.

3 For the stylistic and thematic peculiarity of cult films, Timothy Corrigan uses the metaphor of foreign film to characterize the strange film-viewing experience. Viewing cult film is, according to Corrigan, an experience equivalent to traveling and souvenir gathering. These activities secure a sense of ownership and pleasure over the objects while leaving the sense of their foreignness intact. Corrigan, "Film and the Culture of the Cult," in *The Cult Film Experience: Beyond All Reason*, ed. J. P. Telotte (Austin: University of Texas Press, 1991), 26–37.

4 Ella Shohat and Robert Stam, "From the Imperial Family to the Transnational Imaginary: Media Spectatorship in the Age of Globalization," in *Global/Local: Cultural Production and the Transnational Imaginary*, ed. Rob Wilson and Wimal Dissanayake (Durham, N.C.: Duke University Press, 1996), 149.

5 It should be noted that Hong Kong has historically been among the most productive film meccas in world cinema. Its cinema has enjoyed formidable popularity, reaching audiences in Asian countries and often surpassing that of Hollywood films. See Li Cheuk-to, "Popular Cinema in Hong Kong," in *The Oxford History of World Cinema*, ed. Geoffrey Nowell-Smith (Oxford: Oxford University Press, 1996), 704–11.

6 The most useful book on cult film is Telotte, *The Cult Film Experience*, cited in note 3 above. My understanding of cult film is deeply indebted to a number of essays in this anthology.

7 The first three essays in Telotte, *The Cult Film Experience*, lay out this central issue clearly. J. P. Telotte, "Beyond All Reason: The Nature of the Cult," 5–17; Bruce Kawin, "After Midnight," 18–25; and Timothy Corrigan, "Film and the Culture of the Cult," 26–37.

8 Bruce Kawin employs the terms "inadvertent" and "programmatic" to describe these two kinds of cult films. The former appeals to viewers through the maintaining of conservative values, while the latter generates disruptive and subversive ideological voices. Kawin, 19.

9 Telotte, "Beyond All Reason."

10 The success of *The Killer* should not, therefore, be understood as an isolated phenomenon. Popular Hong Kong cinema has long enjoyed a cult following in the United States, although the scale of such popularity often remained localized — in neighborhood community theaters and some art houses. The valorization of *The Killer* illustrates largely a continuing and burgeoning fascination for popular Hong Kong cinema.

11 Bruce Kawin fully articulates the concept of "exuberance" in cult film. According to Kawin, programmatic cult film, i.e., midnight movies, strategically disrupts mainstream ideology through the mode of exuberance. Instead of political awareness, these texts provide "intense pleasure" and make direct statements through stylistic and generic containment. Kawin, 19.

12 Aristotle, *Poetics*, trans. Gerald F. Else (Ann Arbor: University of Michigan Press, 1994), 71.

13 David Bordwell, *Narration in the Fiction Film* (Madison: University of Wisconsin Press, 1985), 156–204.

14 In this regard, I disagree with Tony Rayns, who characterizes the film as having "an almost flawless thriller plot (no holes, no glaring implausibilities, no hard-to-take coincidence)." Although the film is economically executed with energetic momentum, it is not difficult to recognize rough transitions and tonal shifts in the film. The film's originality and ingenuity, with which Rayns seems to be preoccupied, should not deter us from observing its jarring formal effects. Rayns, "The Killer," *Monthly Film Bulletin* 57, no. 680 (September 1990): 260–61.

15 The notion of "moral occult" is derived from Peter Brooks, *Melodramatic Imagination: Balzac, Henry James, Melodrama, and the Mode of Excess* (New Haven: Yale University Press, 1976), 20–21. The "moral occult" refers to "the domain of spiritual forces and imperatives that is not clearly visible within reality, but which they believe to be operative here, and which demands to be uncovered, registered, and articulated."

16 I am indebted to Maitland McDonagh's insight on the film's tonal inconsistency and hyperbolic style. McDonagh, "Action Painter: John Woo," *Film Comment* 29, no. 5 (September–October 1993): 46–49.

17 An odd and pleasurable misreading of *The Killer* comes in part from an accidental extratextual element: lousy subtitles. Prepared in speedy postproduction, English subtitles in Hong Kong films often lack the emotional subtleties and nuances of the original Chinese language and distract viewers from the film's diegesis. (See the third epigraph to this essay.) This crude communication tool intensifies the sense of sentimentalism already heightened by jarring textual elaboration.

18 Linda Williams, "Melodrama Revised," in *Refiguring American Film Genres*, ed. Nick Browne (Berkeley: University of California Press, 1998), 42.

19 Kristin Thompson, "The Concept of Cinematic Excess," in *Narrative, Apparatus, Ideology: A Film Theory Reader*, ed. Philip Rosen (New York: Columbia University Press, 1986), 134.

20 Ibid., 130.

21 Tom Gunning, "The Cinema of Attractions: Early Film, Its Spectator and the Avant-Garde," in *Early Cinema: Space, Frame, Narrative*, ed. Thomas Elsaesser, with Adam Barker (London: British Film Institute, 1990), 56–62.

22 Julian Stringer, "'Your Tender Smiles Give Me Strength': Paradigms of Masculinity in John Woo's *A Better Tomorrow* and *The Killer*," *Screen* 38, no. 1 (spring 1997): 30.

23 I borrowed this term from Julian Stringer, ibid.

24 Telotte argues that this pattern of "discovery on the part of the audience" often disguises the transgressive dimension of cult film. It also signals the audience's power over film text. Telotte, "Beyond All Reason," 15.

25 Ibid.

26 Barbara Klinger, *Melodrama and Meaning: History, Culture, and the Films of Douglas Sirk* (Bloomington: Indiana University Press, 1994), 132–56.

27 Andrew Ross articulates this appropriation as redefinition: "The camp effect, then, is created not simply by a change in the mode of cultural production (and

the contradictions attendant on that change), but rather when the products . . . of a much earlier mode of production, which has lost its power to produce and dominate cultural meaning, becomes available, in the present, for redefinition according to contemporary codes of taste." Ross, "Uses of Camp," in *Camp Grounds: Style and Homosexuality*, ed. David Bergman (Amherst: University of Massachusetts Press, 1993), 58.

28 Klinger, 143.

29 Susan Sontag, "Notes on Camp," in *Against Interpretation*, 2nd ed. (New York: Anchor Books–Doubleday, 1986), 275–92.

30 Klinger, 139.

31 Timothy Corrigan, *Cinema without Walls: Movies and Culture after Vietnam* (New Brunswick, N.J.: Rutgers University Press, 1991), 80.

32 Ibid., 81.

33 The box office records show no sign of popularity, and it was not included in the top-ten-grossing foreign films lists. Ching Siu-tung's *Chinese Ghost Story* (1987), which later became another cult film, had a similar performance upon its initial release. See 1988 *Annual Film Report* [1988dopan Hanguk Yŏnghwa Yŏn'gam] (Seoul: Korean Film Commission, 1988), 45.

34 "Mini-theaters" [sogŭkchang] refer to small, third-rate movie houses, in the truest sense, in Korea. They are located in the outskirts of major cities and provincial towns and have a seating capacity of 200. Their programs are always in double feature. These theaters burgeoned throughout the 1980s; by 1987 their numbers surpassed those of regular first- or second-rate theaters in every major city in Korea. See 1988 *Annual Film Report*, 46.

35 1989 *Annual Film Report* (Seoul: Korean Film Commission, 1989), 46.

36 1990 *Annual Film Report* (Seoul: Korean Film Commission, 1990), 44.

37 Ku Hoe-young points out the importance of video media and mini-theaters to the formation of cult film in Korea. See his *Two or Three Facts You Want to Know about Movies* [Yŏnghwa-e Taehayŏ Algoshipŭn Handugaji Kŏtdŭl] (Seoul: Hanul, 1991), 237.

38 For a critique of the term "cult film," see Chung Jae-hyung, "New Dependency on Western Culture, or Critique on the Fashion of Cult Film," [Saeroun Sŏgumunhwa Chongsok Hogŭn Yuhaeng Pipan] *Korean Film Critiques* [Yŏnghwa P'yŏngnon] 6 (1994): 57–60.

39 "Hong Kong Noir: Apocalyptic Film Genre from Postmodern City of Hong Kong," [Posŭtŭ'modŏn Toshi Hong Kong-ŭi Segimaljŏk Changnu] *Roadshow* [Korean monthly film magazine] (June 1989): 117; Ku Hoe-young, "Hong Kong Noir: Heroic Tales of Fin-de-Siecle," [Hong Kong Nŭwarŭ, Segimal-ŭi Yŏng'ungdam] in *Two or Three Facts You Want to Know about Movies*, 203–4.

40 1990 *Annual Film Report* (Seoul: Korean Film Commission, 1990), 47.

41 This growth is particularly revealing when compared to the number of U.S. films shown in Korea. For instance, in 1989, the number of American imports exceeded those of Hong Kong by only two.

42 Chow Yun-Fat's appearance in a soft drink commercial, in particular, increased the sales of the product by six times. See *Roadshow* [Korean monthly film magazine] (August 1990): 254.

43 See the debate on the increasing visibility of Hong Kong movie stars in Korea, "Hong Kong Movie Stars in Korea: Import or Invasion?" [Hong Kong Sŭta Han'guk Sangnyuk, Chinch'ulinga Chŏmnyŏng'inga] *Roadshow* [Korean monthly film magazine] (August 1989): 254–55.

44 *Joong Ang Ilbo [Korean Central Daily]*, (21 September 1994).

45 *The General's Son* is based on the true story of Kim Du-han, a legendary gangster and fighter. The film focuses on his rite of passage and struggle against the Japanese *yakuza* during the colonial period.

46 During the 1960s, Im made a number of gangster action films. *The General's Son* was for him, in many ways, a return to a familiar genre. The film's success led to the production of two sequels, both directed by Im.

CHAPTER FIVE

Life Imitates Entertainment:
Home and Dislocation in the Films of Jackie Chan

Steve Fore

Especially in the 1980s and 1990s, Hong Kong filmmakers have been high-profile participants in the trend toward what Ackbar Abbas describes as a "new localism" in the territory that "investigates the dislocations of the local, where the local is something unstable that mutates right in front of our eyes."[1] The films of directors such as John Woo, Clara Law, Tsui Hark, Ann Hui, Wong Kar-wai, and others have been recognized by Chinese and Western critics alike as genre-based articulations of the parameters of this new localism. More recently, though, a handful of Hong Kong directors (including Woo, Tsui, Ringo Lam, Kirk Wong, Stanley Tong, and Peter Chan) have become sojourners in the creative hills and valleys of the Hollywood movie industry. This is in part because of uncertainty over the future of the Hong Kong film business, and in part because Hollywood represents today, as it has for several decades, the brass ring of global entertainment cinema.

In this essay, I will concentrate on the career trajectory of the Hong Kong action and martial arts star Jackie Chan, who for twenty years has been a top box office draw not only in Hong Kong but also in much of the rest of Southeast and East Asia. Since 1995 Chan also has achieved a measure of success in the United States with the release of several of his recent films, including *Rumble in the Bronx* [*Hongfan Chu*], *Supercop* [*Jingcha Gushi III: Chaoji Jingcha*], *First Strike* [*Jingcha Gushi IV: Jiandan Renwu*], *Operation Condor* [*Feiying Zhihua*], and *Mr. Nice Guy* [*Yige Haoren*].[2] These films, produced through Chan's production company and distributed in Asia by the Hong Kong–based Golden Harvest (which has handled all of Chan's movies since 1980),[3] cumulatively have grossed approximately U.S.$90 million in U.S. theatrical release alone (excluding other release windows such as home video and pay television). In the era of the global mega-blockbuster, this is not an especially impressive figure, but each of these films had already achieved profitability prior to its U.S. release thanks to revenues generated in markets where Chan's star status was already established. For Chan and his business partners, these U.S. sales represent the critical and commercial vindication of a long-term effort to sell Chan's films and Chan's style to U.S. audiences. More recently, Chan has successfully ascended to the next rung of success Hollywood style by starring in *Rush Hour* (1998), his first commercially successful American-made film.[4]

It needs to be emphasized, in other words, that unlike the other Hong Kong filmmakers who have achieved or are aspiring to success in the United States, Chan initially broke into that market not by making movies in Hollywood but with films that were produced within the context of the Hong Kong movie industry. Chan's motivations in seeking new markets and a new creative climate, like those of other such filmmakers, are both voluntary and involuntary. As sojourners from Hong Kong, a territory undergoing significant political and social transformation, Chan and the others occupy a cultural space between the involuntary migrations of political and economic refugees and the voluntary cross-border travels of expatriate professionals employed by transnational corporations (and the filmmakers have more in common with the latter than the former). To date, though, Chan has maintained a greater degree of control over his creative and fiscal destiny than have Hong Kong's other diasporic directors;[5] he has remained a more identifiably "local" filmmaker, and the production environment of his movies has ensured that they have continued to articulate — at least to a degree — an identifiably "local" sensibility (although I will argue that this characteristic has diminished noticeably in his most recent films).

I will look here at some of the cinematic and social contexts of Chan's career in order to provide some observations on the thematic and industrial implications of a particular spatial division in his films between those shot in Hong Kong or "greater China" and those shot in locations that are tangibly nonlocal (from the faux New York of *Rumble in the Bronx* to the Malaysian sequences of *Supercop* to the Australian and Russian settings of *First Strike*). With regard to the former, I believe that Chan's longstanding popularity in Hong Kong is partly a product of his ability to build a screen and public persona on a network of traditional Chinese and, more narrowly, Cantonese values and character traits, many of which have been reconfigured, updated, and transformed in the context of Hong Kong's polyglot cultural and social setting.[6] As for the latter, his inclination to shoot more and more often in overseas locales may be more usefully correlated, I think, with marketplace considerations (for example, Chan increasingly has targeted his films for a regional and now global market in ways that parallel, to an extent, the James Bond franchise) than with explorations of the Chinese diasporic experience

(although fitful and unsystematic narrative and thematic gestures in this direction are present in his films). I argue that over the past two decades (and
at an accelerating pace in recent years), Chan's persona, which in his early
films drew almost exclusively on a core of cultural meanings and experiences
characteristic of the Hong Kong ecumene, has become progressively more
diffuse and less emphatically tied to a specific cultural space. This is in keeping with the logic of the corporate version of "global culture," which is always
directed toward the establishing of a maximally rationalized worldwide consumer market for a particular range of goods and services originating primarily in First World contexts (though not exclusively — movement in the opposite direction is increasingly possible, as Chan's recent marketing success
in the United States indicates). The creation of global culture in turn involves a process Anthony Giddens calls "disembedding," by which he means
"the 'lifting out' of social relations from local contexts of interaction and their
restructuring across indefinite spans of time-space."[7] As the geographical and
marketing radius of Chan's films has expanded, then, the cultural meanings
attached to his persona have become progressively more disembedded, lifted
out of these "local contexts of interaction" and "restructured" to meet the demands of a new set of economic circumstances. To begin unpacking this notion, I will consider first some of the contradictory ideas about "national
identity" that are circulating in the world today, some of which are at odds
with current patterns of social, cultural, and economic experience and interaction for many people.

The Symbolic Politics of the National, or, Lee versus Chan

In recent years, a prominent debate among China scholars has involved the
idea of "cultural China," a universalizing assertion of pride and unity that ostensibly connects all people of Chinese ethnicity all over the world. The
terms of this debate have focused in part on the practical and philosophical
viability of this idea, given the worldwide dispersal of ethnically Chinese
peoples, the sheer numbers involved, and the divergent life experiences of
people residing in different Chinese communities (in addition to the populations of the People's Republic of China, Hong Kong, Taiwan, and Singapore, there are approximately 36 million overseas Chinese).[8] A prominent recent test of the symbolic status of cultural China was the flare-up in the
summer and fall of 1996 of a longstanding territorial dispute over the Diaoyu
Islands (known in Japan as the Senkaku Islands), a group of barren and un-
inhabitable islands that lie in an area of the Pacific Ocean triangulated by

Japan, Taiwan, and mainland China. As in other flare-ups, the most recent Diaoyu controversy set Japan primarily against the People's Republic of China and Taiwan, but also against Hong Kong and (ostensibly) all overseas Chinese.

The modern version of the Diaoyu controversy dates back to the late 1960s and early 1970s and has been characterized by long periods of inactivity and public invisibility punctuated by periodic flashes of rhetorically loud and passionately nationalistic posturing on all sides. A small group of right-wing Japanese activists deliberately provoked this particular confrontation by erecting a small, teetering lighthouse on one of the islands. This action was intended at least as much to embarrass the Japanese government, which the rightists perceive as insufficiently aggressive in pursuit of Japan's alleged international interests, as to challenge Chinese interests. In any case, the emblematic erection of this modest structure on a Diaoyu crag achieved the result desired by the Japanese rightists — it triggered large-scale anti-Japanese, pro-Chinese demonstrations and protests in Hong Kong and Taiwan and in Chinese communities in North America. These rallies culminated in September 1996 in two heavily publicized boat journeys by Hong Kong–based activists to the Diaoyus in order to plant on the islands the flags of both the People's Republic of China *and* Taiwan. While the second of these crusades was ultimately successful, the earlier one resulted in the tragic drowning of one longtime Diaoyu activist and the near drowning of three other members of the group. One of the survivors, who was rescued by the Japanese coast guard and subsequently transported to a hospital in Japan, stated in an interview by the press during his recuperation that he wanted "to return to Hong Kong wearing either traditional Chinese dress . . . or a Bruce Lee T-shirt."[9]

I find this juxtaposition of Chinese feudal culture and Hong Kong popular culture suggestive, as is the implied view that Bruce Lee (who has been dead since 1973) is the most potent Hong Kong–specific symbol of cultural China and of a particular version of the Chinese nation and Chinese nationalism. That is, it is suggestive that the activist hit upon Lee as a symbol rather than Jackie Chan, who is as big a star in Hong Kong as Lee ever was and who by now can claim the status of a living Hong Kong institution. While he spends little time in the territory these days (he has a home in Australia and since the success of *Rush Hour* has been spending more time in the United States as well), in Hong Kong Chan endows university scholarships and contributes to many other philanthropic causes, is regularly photographed posing with government officials at various ceremonial functions, has substantial business and real estate investments in the territory, and is

handsomely paid to appear in local and regional advertisements for consumer goods. His winning grin is featured in television spots produced by the
Hong Kong Tourist Association.

But there is, I think, a popular perception in Hong Kong that Jackie Chan
(who works within the same commercial, entertainment-based movie industry that made Bruce Lee a wealthy man twenty-five years earlier) does not
stand for something more than "mere entertainment." It is easier for many
people to see Bruce Lee as a more expressive, more aggressive, and more
fundamentally "serious" symbol of Hong Kong identity and of an uncritical
brand of Chinese nationalism that could be more appealing to a Diaoyu activist. Part of this difference in perception is the result of the decision by
Chan and his mentors at the outset of the successful phase of his career
to construct for Chan a screen identity calculatedly different from Lee's.
In contrast to Lee's comparatively somber persona as the defender of a
nostalgia-infused cultural China, Chan's onscreen character emphasized an
unassuming, self-effacing comedy more attuned to his particular strengths as
a performer. Part of the difference is the product of Lee's early death, which
forever freezes him as a romantic myth defined largely by the three films he
made in Hong Kong immediately before he died and by the parts of his bi-
ography that show him as a Chinese sojourner to the United States returning
to his homeland and achieving great popular and commercial success. But
this perceptual gap is also due, I think, to the differences between the cultural and economic contexts of the early 1970s and the late 1990s. As commercial entertainers, Lee was and Chan is sensitive to the kind of screen
character to whom audiences are most likely to respond favorably, and they
share as well the entertainer's interest in maintaining from project to project
a consistency in narrative content, thematic emphasis, and overall emotional
tone. The key point here is that these factors are in important ways differently
inflected today than they were thirty years ago.

Stephen Teo has argued that the three Hong Kong films Bruce Lee completed in the early 1970s—*The Big Boss* [*Tang Shan Daxiong*] (1971), *Fist of
Fury* [*Jingwu Men*] (1972), and *Way of the Dragon* [*Meng Long Guo Jiang*]
(1972)—were expressions of ethnic pride in the idea of "Chineseness," a
universalized "quest to make the Chinese character a dignified, respected and
honoured one."[10] This quest is subsumed in each film within the personal,
individualized quest of Lee's character. The perceived need for this revitaliza-
tion of the Chinese national identity draws on the legacy of China's humiliation and partial subjugation by foreign powers in the nineteenth and twentieth centuries. In this sense, Lee's films may be seen as an unusual offshoot

within a commercial cinema form of the anti-imperialist, anticolonial cinema of the 1960s and 1970s produced elsewhere in the Third World.[11] And indeed, in each of these films Lee's character is pitted against a medley of foreigners in scenes of unarmed combat, in which Lee demonstrates the superiority of his revisionist Chinese martial arts (itself a hybrid of indigenous and foreign styles) over Western and Japanese varieties of fighting.

It seems likely that some Hong Kong and Taiwanese movie viewers in the early 1970s may have noticed and responded positively to Lee's nationalist message, but as products of Hong Kong's very commercial film industry, his films also provided audiences in Hong Kong, Taiwan, and the rest of the world with alternative modes of engagement—the dynamic choreography of the martial arts sequences, the pleasure in seeing Lee's classic working-class underdog character pound the stuffing out of an ethnically and racially mixed bag of villains and authority figures.[12] More importantly, though, Lee's version of Chinese nationalism was built on a combination of cultural mythologies and an essentialist vision of Chineseness and the Chinese nation. The timeless, ahistorical Chinese national culture endorsed by Lee provided viewers who chose to connect with it what Benedict Anderson describes as "the image of their communion."[13] That is, as Anderson and many other writers have pointed out in recent years, the nation is a constructed entity, a product of discourse, of ongoing discussions and debates over what constitutes the "nation" and "national culture"—its construction is an ongoing process rather than a static, timeless entity. And while the official and popular rhetoric of the nation typically promotes the idea that the founding of a nation represents the harmonious coming together of people sharing common bonds of culture, ethnicity, and/or values, the truth is, as Stuart Hall says, that "modern nations are all cultural hybrids,"[14] and that a

> national culture has never been simply a point of allegiance,
> bonding and symbolic identification. It is also a structure of cultural
> power. . . . Most modern nations consist of disparate cultures which
> were only unified by a lengthy process of violent conquest—that is,
> by the forcible suppression of cultural difference. . . . These violent
> beginnings which stand at the origins of modern nations have first to
> be "forgotten" before allegiance to a more unified, homogeneous
> national identity could begin to be forged.[15]

This antiessentialist perspective correlates with China's historical origins, as Allen Chun points out:

Figure 1.
Way of the Dragon
(Bruce Lee, 1972)
as an expression of
ethnic pride.

The Chinese may attribute their ethnic unity to the Han, but, in fact, the peoples consolidated by the Han empire were certainly not ethnically homogeneous. . . . [T]he centripetal unity emanating from this civilizing center was something that in predynastic times actually united different polities occupied by diverse peoples who had inherently different languages, beliefs, and practices — in short, different ethnic cultures.[16]

That is, the inadequacy of the essentialist imagining of the nation by Bruce Lee and Diaoyu activists (among others, including the public-relations arms of virtually all nation-states) is becoming clearer to more and more people everywhere in the world, primarily because the everyday experience of more and more people tends to foreground diversity, difference, and heterogeneity rather than unity, similarity, and homogeneity.[17] This transformation has been conceptually associated with processes of cultural and economic globalization, usefully summarized by Anthony McGrew as

the multiplicity of linkages and interconnections that transcend the nation-states (and by implication the societies) which make up the modern world system. It defines a process through which events, decisions, and activities in one part of the world can come to have significant consequences for individuals and communities in quite distant parts of the globe.[18]

Several theorists of economic globalization have pointed out that this is not a recent phenomenon; rather, it is an "intensification" of tendencies inherent within the capitalist condition (for instance, within the economic realm, attempting to maximize the efficiency with which goods and services are moved across time and space, i.e., attempting to extend markets through space as much as possible). With the development of new modes of communication and transportation, this goal has become more achievable than ever before, and it is significant for my purposes that David Harvey and other theorists of globalization date the beginning of the phenomenon's current phase from the economic slump of the early 1970s, which affected capitalist economies all over the world and greatly stimulated their ongoing desire to maximize operational efficiency and the size of target markets.[19]

In short, Bruce Lee died on the cusp of what has been revealed to be a major (though still incomplete) transformation and reorganization of economic, political, and cultural conditions all over the world. As a resident of and worker in Hong Kong, he was situated at one of the storm centers of these changes; his death cut short his development as a filmmaker and as an expressive builder of cinematic worlds. Insofar as Jackie Chan has inherited Lee's mantle as the most prominent and successful maker of Hong Kong martial arts films, I am also arguing that Chan is the premiere Hong Kong action filmmaker of the era of globalization.[20] But what exactly does that mean? This, for starters: in order to become culturally and economically disembedded, one first has to be embedded.

Chan's Context

Hong Kong's industrial takeoff in the 1950s was stimulated by a combination of the post-1949 influx of refugees from the mainland (many of whom arrived in the territory with useful skills and entrepreneurial experience) and the related embargo on Chinese trade by most of the capitalist West, which at the time destroyed Hong Kong's entrepôt status and generated an immediate need to develop a new economic base.[21] The territory's subsequent industrialization was built initially on the production of inexpensive, relatively low quality manufactured goods designated primarily for export to the West; a second phase of industrialization involved moving into the assembly of bet-

ter quality, more upmarket goods.[22] By the early 1970s, Hong Kong's economy was much stronger, but the industrial sector was already beginning to
decline, a process that speeded up as the People's Republic of China began
to open up with the beginning of the reform era in the late 1970s.[23] Over the
last quarter century, the manufacturing economic base has been supplanted
to a considerable extent by a service economy,[24] a transformation approximately mirroring that of other postwar industrialized economies and coin-
ciding with the intensification, modification, and expansion of preexisting
tendencies within the framework of a globalizing capitalism.

From the late 1940s through the 1970s, there was also a substantial shift in
the dynamics of Hong Kong society and culture, including popular culture.
The post-1949 refugees (the majority of whom came from southern China)
brought with them a framework of values developed in circumstances rather
different from those of Hong Kong's more urban and heterogeneous environment. As Leung writes:

> Popular culture in Hong Kong in the decade or so after the end of the
> Second World War bore the characteristics of the traditions preserved
> by the refugees from China who then made up a substantial portion
> of the territory's population. Coming mostly from rural, pre-modern
> parts of the mainland, these refugees were disposed to resort to their
> traditional rural values in coping with urban life in Westernized
> Hong Kong. In addition, there was also a minority of refugees who
> came from Shanghai, then China's industrial and cultural centre,
> and they brought with them, apart from capital and entrepreneurship,
> a taste for that city's popular culture. Throughout the 1950s, Hong
> Kong's popular culture was very much the continuation of the
> cultural heritage of these two groups of new arrivals.[25]

Leung suggests that the economic and social pressures of the time on the recent arrivals in this city of immigrants encouraged the production of movies
with an unusually therapeutic agenda. Many films reassured viewers of the
continuing viability and strength of traditional Confucian values, either by
setting stories in nostalgic versions of China's past, or in versions of Hong
Kong's present where unworldly but virtuous protagonists triumphed over
forces of duplicity and confusion characteristic of modern urban life.

Within this social and cultural environment, the remarkably resilient post-
1949 series of films featuring the character Wong Fei-hung are quite
significant. Wong (1847–1924) was a real historical figure from Guangdong

province (which immediately adjoins Hong Kong)—a martial arts master, purveyor of traditional Chinese medicine, and all-around Confucian role model who was something of a regional celebrity during his lifetime. Subsequently, his name and increasingly fictionalized accounts of his exploits were preserved in folktales and, increasingly, in popular-culture forms such as novels serialized in Hong Kong newspapers.[26] The transition of the character to film in postwar Hong Kong was natural enough, given the long history of martial arts movie production in the territory. Hector Rodriguez argues that the subsequent Wong film series was a specifically Cantonese popular cultural expression that combined a progressive use of cinematic technique (in pursuit of a heightened verisimilitude within the martial arts genre and in the representation of China's historical past) and political attitudes (an exploration of the Chinese experience with modernity) with a reverence for Confucian tradition.[27] The Wong films proved enormously popular in Hong Kong, especially in the 1950s; twenty-five feature-length installments were made in 1956 alone, and by the time the first Wong cycle wound down in 1970, there were seventy-six titles.[28] All but two of these films starred the actor Kwan Tak-hing in the title role (who resurrected Master Wong for a 1970s television series, as well as a few subsequent movie cameos). Kwan was himself a native of Guangzhou, a former Cantonese opera star, and a martial arts expert in his own right. His casting was fortuitous, as Kwan's performances and impeccably virtuous presence on- and offscreen became crystallized in the popular imagination as the personification of Wong Fei-hung. Although Kwan appeared in more than 130 films during his lifetime (he died in 1996 at the age of ninety), he became so identified with this character that it became almost impossible to cast him in any other role.[29]

Wong Fei-hung came to represent in Hong Kong popular culture of the 1950s a potent and resilient symbol of Confucian virtue and Cantonese tradition in the midst of a rapidly evolving urban society, a source of comfort and stability in the face of accelerating social and cultural changes. Ever since the end of the Kwan Tak-hing era of Wong films in 1970, the character has been revived periodically (most successfully in the series of films produced by Tsui Hark in the 1990s and known collectively in English as *Once Upon a Time in China [Huang Feihong]*, which itself spawned a new cycle of Wong films by other filmmakers), but not without undergoing some serious revision.[30] Master Wong, it seems, has yielded to the pressure of new times, and Jackie Chan has been a part of that revisionist process.

By the early 1970s, Hong Kong society was in many ways very different from the rickety refugee haven it had been twenty years earlier. For one thing, the population of the territory was getting younger, with significantly fewer people having direct experience of the struggles of the immediate post-1949 era (Law Kar notes that as early as the 1961 census, "out of a population of over 3 million, more than 1,200,000 were youths below 15 years of age"[31]). The first year in which the Hong Kong–born segment of the population topped 50 percent of the total was 1966, and by 1971 that figure was 57.2 percent.[32] This younger, more localized population was also better educated and relatively more affluent, in general could "be expected to differ from the class of manual labourers in lifestyle, attitudes, and social aspirations," and did "not share the refugee experience and mentality of the older generations."[33] As James Kung and Zhang Yueai have put it, "this period can be seen therefore as a transition (for the population) from village to city and the replacing of a refugee experience by urban living."[34]

These changing demographics had major ramifications for the Hong Kong movie industry: new genres and story formulas developed, especially as Hollywood movies became more popular in the territory. For instance, there was a cycle of imitation James Bond movies in the mid-1960s (including several featuring female secret agents skilled at hand-to-hand combat[35]), as well as a late-1960s series of youth-culture films that ranged from serious analyses of juvenile delinquency to the Hong Kong equivalent of beach party flicks.[36] These newly imported genres were transformed in interesting ways in the context of Hong Kong popular culture, while at the same time established local genres, including the martial arts film, were also refurbished and streamlined. This was also an era of fiscal combat between Cantonese and Mandarin films for dominance of the local movie business, and as Sek Kei points out, the Mandarin production companies temporarily won the day in significant part because of the innovative swordfight and *kungfu* movies made by Zhang Che and others, which provided a revisionist, hypermasculine version of the Chinese male hero figure.[37] By the beginning of the 1970s, martial arts films, which had been somewhat less popular for much of the previous decade, were once again a dominant genre.

However, these movies, like the rest of Hong Kong culture, were feeling the strain of changing values and beliefs, and the martial arts genre of the 1970s eventually developed two rough subdivisions. The first of these included films focusing on the proper display and demonstration of specific martial arts styles, superimposed on narratives based around revenge and/or a quest to become a "supreme" champion in the world of martial arts. These films emphasized either an unambiguously communicated adherence to traditional values or a somewhat cynical, jaded view of tradition. The second variation came to be described as "*kungfu* comedy." This subgenre consisted of movies that took martial arts seriously to an extent but were not above providing parodies of styles, entirely fabricated styles, and sly commentaries on the traditional belief systems inscribed within the martial arts legacy. There were also slapstick routines, gross-out jokes, and verbal comedy built around puns, anachronisms, and miscellaneous references that ran the gamut of degrees of crudity.[38] While these films were set in China's past and had antecedents in traditions of street acrobatics, martial arts scenes from Peking opera performances, and stage adaptations of Monkey King stories,[39] the comedic variation on the martial arts genre especially marked the transformation of Hong Kong from a colonial backwater to a rapidly modernizing and fast-paced urban capitalist society. Filmmakers accomplished this by implicitly embracing a value system that, contrary to the martial arts tradition, emphasized a combination of pragmatism, cynicism, personal ambition, rebelliousness, ruthlessness, acquisitiveness, and quick-wittedness. Ng Ho describes the typical protagonist of these comedies as a *young* man (younger than most previous martial arts heroes),

> a bright but hopelessly lazy kid, who lacks both the staying power needed for martial arts training and respect for his *sifu* [teacher]. He may, indeed, try to cheat his *sifu*. Often after suffering a defeat, he will muster the perseverance to train in the martial arts more seriously, and will eventually reach the point where he surpasses the skills of his *sifu*. . . . He adapts himself easily to his environment and circumstances. . . . After his ultimate victory, he has no interest in furthering himself in the martial arts world; he prefers to go on living from day to day, aimlessly.[40]

That is, this was a martial arts "hero" that much of Hong Kong's younger generation could relate to far more easily, because this was a generation less connected to Chinese tradition or to China itself than their elders and increasingly connected to Western renditions of urban industrial society and to the emerging translation of modern urbanism within the Hong Kong context.

While there were significant predecessors (including the cracks in Bruce Lee's straight-faced armor in *Way of the Dragon*), the *kungfu* comedy hit its stride as a reliably commercial subgenre in the mid-1970s in films directed by Karl Maka, Sammo Hung, Wu Ma, and others. Jackie Chan entered the picture in a big way in 1978 with the smashing success of two movies directed by Yuen Wo-ping, *Snake in the Eagle's Shadow* [*Shexing Diaoshou*] and *Drunken Master* [*Zui Quan*].

Chan's Embedding

Chan was a product—though not necessarily a very typical one—of Hong Kong's turbulent post-1949 era. Born in the territory in 1954 (his given name in pinyin is Chen Gangsheng) to parents who had recently emigrated from Shandong province, he moved to Australia with his family at the age of six and returned to Hong Kong a year later under a ten-year contract to study Peking opera at the Zhongguo Xiju Xueyuan (China Drama Academy). This was less an educational opportunity than an economic decision by his parents, who were very poor; sending their son away to "school" (which included little or no formal education in the conventional sense) both relieved them of the burden of another hungry mouth and assured them that he at least would be housed and fed. His lengthy apprenticeship was difficult,[41] but in conjunction with his innate aptitudes, it provided him with an excellent foundation in martial arts, tumbling, and acrobatics, as well as an eventual avenue of entry into Hong Kong's movie industry.[42] One point needs to be emphasized here, though. The situation Chan grew up in was unusual in that there was an enforced split in his acculturating influences: as a child and teenager, he was exposed both to the tradition-bound experience of the opera school and, when he ventured outside its gates, to the industrial, urban, and increasingly cosmopolitan (but still colonial) Hong Kong that was aspiring to the status of a global economic power.

Chan appeared in a few films as a child, and after leaving the drama academy he initially took small acting roles and worked as a martial arts "body double" for featured performers who were incapable of performing their own stunts (for instance, he had the privilege of being pummeled by Bruce Lee in *Enter the Dragon*). By 1973 he had worked his way up to the more prestigious position of martial arts instructor and director, and in 1976 was signed by the Lo Wei Film Company,[43] for which he starred in a series of depressingly ordinary *kungfu* films over the next two-plus years. In most of his film appearances, he played a conventionally upright and stern-visaged martial arts hero. Chan's big break came when Lo Wei loaned him to Ng See-yuen's more innovative Seasonal Films, where he starred in *Snake in the Eagle's Shadow* and *Drunken Master*, both directed by the gifted Yuen Wo-ping, the scion of a martial arts–steeped family who at the time was helping to kick the *kungfu* comedy subgenre into high gear.[44]

It was these films (and the subsequent *Fearless Hyena [Xiao Quan Guai-zhao]* and *Young Master [Shidi Chuma]*, both of which Chan directed as well as starred in) that established him as a major star in Hong Kong, Taiwan,

Japan, and much of Southeast Asia. By the early 1980s Chan had developed
a large audience in what Joseph Straubhaar has described as a situation of
cultural proximity — that is, his movies may have been especially appealing
to local Hong Kong audiences, but they also had a regionally based attraction
based on historical connections between Chinese culture and other East
Asian cultures.[45]

It was in this period, too, that Chan crystallized the screen persona that he
has maintained for two decades now. The structure, characterizations, and
plot lines of Chan's early *kungfu* comedies are more than a little similar to
each other and follow many threads of the formula used in some previous examples of the subgenre. Our young protagonist, a basically decent and virtuous but at times devious and mischievous individual with little apparent ambition, is a halfhearted martial arts student until a crisis befalls his family or
dojo. At this point he is apprenticed to a colorful elderly *sifu*, who does not
look very strong or agile but proves to be more than a match for his younger,
bigger opponents. The young hero, now somewhat more committed to the
discipline of learning martial arts skills, undergoes a lengthy training process
(during which the film's narrative all but grinds to a halt), rendered as a se-
quential spectacle of painful-looking but comedy-inflected exercises (in
which the still fundamentally indolent protagonist looks for ways to trick the
sifu in order to avoid hard work), agility tests, and what are most accurately
classified as beatings. Before, during, and after the scenes of training, there is

Figure 3.
Hong Kong's colonial
hierarchy in *Project A,
Part II* (Jackie Chan,
1987).

an ongoing series of increasingly elaborate fight sequences, culminating in a lengthy climactic *mano a mano* that pits the young hero against the primary villain, who is impossibly evil and an expert martial artist himself. After a see-saw battle that features much less comedy (concentrating instead on the intricacies of martial arts choreography and on a comparison of the opponents' styles, strength, and endurance) that may occupy more than fifteen minutes of screen time, the protagonist is ultimately victorious. At that point the film typically ends, usually without the young hero's announcing his moral reformation and unflinching commitment to the world of martial arts, and sometimes with a final throwaway gag that seems to send up altogether any ethical lesson that might have been suggested previously. In *Young Master,* for instance, Chan's character, after taking a severe beating at first, wins the final combat righteously enough, but in a brief comic coda is paraded through town wrapped from head to toe in bandages while broadly mugging in the direction of the camera.

Significantly, in *Drunken Master* (which follows this narrative blueprint closely), Chan played a young version of Wong Fei-hung, whose onscreen presence previously had been all but monopolized by Kwan Tak-hing's nimble but increasingly elderly paragon of virtue and experience. This was not the first revisionist Wong, however; the first young version appeared in Liu

Chia-liang's *Challenge of the Masters* [*Lu Acai yu Huang Feihong*] (1976), in which the character is figured as a reverential mirror of his older self.[46] But Yuen and Chan were the first filmmakers to run the Wong persona through the *kungfu* comedy formula, and what they came up with in this film (and earlier in *Snake in the Eagle's Shadow*) was the mildly rebellious (but ultimately decent), immature (but quick to gain from experience), and wonderfully athletic screen character Chan inhabited in the liftoff phase of his career. Writing of Yuen Wo-ping's comedies, Roger Garcia suggests that "the comic emphasis of his films . . . offers irreverent, but not subversive, readings of well-established and famous characters—a crucial factor in the popularity of the films since they allow audiences to laugh without really feeling that tradition is being threatened."[47]

Chan was the key element in establishing this thematic duality. His early persona was itself a balancing act between the dual manifestations of tradition and modernity in Hong Kong, between the traditional association of personal virtue with traits of selflessness, loyalty, and empathy and the urban jungle's survivalist emphasis on pragmatism and self-interest.[48] In *Drunken Master*, Chan's young Wong is initially portrayed as something of a trial for his very tradition-steeped father, but when his father's *dojo* is threatened by an unscrupulous businessman (and after an overconfident Fei-hung has been humiliated in combat by the businessman's hired thug), the son veers only slightly from the straight and narrow for the remainder of the film. He ultimately saves his father's school (earning the respect of his father and his *sifu*) and avenges his earlier beating. Even then, however, he does so through the successful use of the drunken boxing style, which is both historically inauthentic and suspiciously current in connotations—Ng Ho likens it to "contemporary pop dance styles"[49]—and Chan's Wong takes an unseemly pleasure in lurching about in drunken, comically graceful abandon.

Chan's Disembedding

Since these early successes, Chan's screen persona has evolved in some interesting ways. By continuing to negotiate the terrain between Chinese tradition and Hong Kong modernity, he has continued to make films that are especially attuned to local and regional audiences, though such considerations have diminished consideration in his most recent projects (which I will discuss below). In his later roles, Chan is still enormously likable, in part because he remains emotionally and physically vulnerable. He is also winningly resourceful and determined, and a physical dynamo. After his early success playing a mildly rebellious youth in films set clearly in the past, he began to take on a preponderance of contemporary roles and has moved from tweaking adult authority figures to playing them (or at least someone with an identifiable career): a cop in several films; a member of the Hong Kong colonial coast guard in the *Project A [A Jihua]* films; an orchestra conductor *and* an auto mechanic/race driver in a dual role in *Twin Dragons [Shuanglong Hui]*; an Indiana Jones–style adventurer in the *Armor of God [Long Xiong Hu Di]* films; a lawyer in *Dragons Forever [Fei Long Mengjiang]*; and even a Martin Yan–style television chef in *Mr. Nice Guy*. This onscreen maturation process has moved Chan's screen persona almost entirely away from the more wily and irresponsible kid he once played, and it has established a new context for his martial arts prowess and feats of daring: these are no longer part of a rite of passage, but the acts of a grown man confident in his abilities (but still utterly modest about them).

As he has grown older, in addition to meticulously choreographed martial arts sequences (which, with the exception of a few projects, have diminished in frequency and duration over the years) and highly creative acts of physical skill (a recurrent bit of business has Chan scaling walls twice his height by *running* up and over them), Chan's films have come to regularly include one or two showpiece stunts. These are undeniably spectacular: in *Project A* (1983), for instance, he tumbles from a clock tower about sixty feet down to an uncushioned landing on a hard dirt surface, his fall broken only by two flimsy awnings; in *Police Story* (1985), Chan slides several stories down a live electrical wire, popping dozens of light bulbs in his descent, and crash-lands through plate glass; in *Police Story III: Supercop* (1992), he dangles from a rope ladder attached to a helicopter as it swoops and dives over downtown Kuala Lumpur; and in *First Strike* (1996), he again incorporates a helicopter into a stunt by taking a running leap off the edge of a sheer cliff and catching himself on the runners of a hovering chopper. The payoff shot of these stunts is always filmed in a single take (to confirm their authenticity) and with multiple cameras. The resulting action is edited into the finished film in a rapid sequence of the same action shot from three or four different perspectives (highly reminiscent of the sailor smashing the dishes in *Battleship Potemkin*). In almost all of his films since *Project A*, Chan has ended his films with the credits scrolling over outtakes from the film we have just watched. In these outtakes, actors breaking down in laughter over blown lines alternate with shots of carefully arranged stunts and martial arts moves going badly wrong. The audience looks on with a combination of amusement, enlightenment, and mild horror as Chan, his co-stars, and various stunt people take frightening-looking falls, absorb hard punches to the face, or are plastered with large inanimate objects — they crumple in pain, and sometimes we see them being rushed away on a stretcher. This reflexive cinema verité actually adds to Chan's mystique as "the action hero who does all of his own stunts" (as the tag line for the U.S. release of *Rumble in the Bronx* put it), confirms his status as a "human-sized" superstar, and reminds his fans and competitors that he is the hardest-working man in show business.[50]

And as such, Jackie Chan is also a commodity, and the monetary and spatial expansion of his success since the late 1970s has gradually changed the geographic and cultural connotations of his films, especially since he negotiated and signed his most recent U.S. distribution deals. Although he has appeared in numerous movies set outside Hong Kong since 1980, until recently his public persona was strongly connected with Hong Kong as a specific, local cultural space. That is, his onscreen character was, again, defined significantly within the tension created by its oscillation between tradition and modernity in the context of present-day Hong Kong. This tension has tangibly lessened as Chan and his management team have developed a marketing strategy that takes him well beyond the culturally proximate East Asian region and, especially, into North America.

Chan's films and his screen persona have become an increasingly vivid example of Giddens's process of disembedding. While the majority of his films have been set in Hong Kong, several Chan films have taken him to locations such as Malaysia, Thailand, a South Pacific island, North Africa, the United States, and Spain, but in most of these earlier situations the narrative has turned at least in part on Chan's status as a displaced Hong Konger. Five of his last six films have been set entirely or, in the case of *Thunderbolt [Pili Huo]* (1995), mostly overseas (and mostly outside of Asia),[51] but in these films Chan's Hong Kong identity has been progressively less central. This seems to be a result of the strategy through which he is being sold as what David Morley and Kevin Robins call a "global product" packaged for "a new 'cosmopolitan' marketplace," one that uses cultural difference as just another marketing tool.[52] And as Morley and Robins suggest, this is a typical part of the global strategy of transnational corporations, which usually acknowledge these days that many products need to be modified in order to meet local tastes. But these modifications are "combined with the search for opportunities to sell [substantially the same product] to similar segments throughout the globe" and, as a result of the flows of people and culture associated with globalization, target "consumers on the basis of demography and habits rather than on the basis of geographical proximity."[53] In these circumstances (from Benetton's unthreateningly multicultural fashion ads to "world music" on the order of Deep Forest's New Age combinations of synthesizer schmaltz and pygmy chanting), difference is not ignored but foregrounded, though typically only within carefully regulated parameters; these products usually provide only a superficial (and implicitly Western) tourist's gaze at unfamiliar peoples, places, and beliefs.

The notion of global cinema, of course, has long been identified with the Hollywood industry, and as Hollywood has become increasingly dependent on revenues generated outside North America,[54] the controlling strategy for domestic success and worldwide domination alike since the 1970s has involved a reliance on the production of blockbuster movies with "presold" elements, including the presence of particular stars, tie-ins with other pop culture icons, status as a sequel, and a reliance on tested story formulas and genres (primarily action films and broad comedies).[55] That is, the global marketing of movies historically has involved the movement of product from a location within the so-called economic "core" (i.e., Hollywood) to everywhere else, including other "core" nations as well as those that have been part of the world's economic "periphery."

This situation has undergone some modification in recent years. As part of a reconfigured "mediascape" flowing in a direction opposite that of the long-established norm—from the international movie business's historical periphery into the core—Jackie Chan and the other creators of his most recent films have adopted narrative and marketing strategies that nonetheless parallel those of Hollywood. As I said earlier, these films seem most analogous to those of the James Bond franchise, which continue to be based around a core of ersatz "Englishness" while always including plenty of highly exoticized (and often quite ethnocentric or racist) renderings of locales thousands of miles from Whitehall. At the same time, as Tony Bennett and Janet Woollacott have suggested, Bond films over the years have become progressively Americanized, based on the premises that a high degree of Englishness was less attractive in the U.S. market specifically, and that making Bond films look and feel more like other Hollywood action spectaculars also increased their box office potential in the global market.[56]

Coming from a historically contrasting cultural and economic direction, Chan's films have become Bondlike in their reliance on placing Chan in exotic locations that provide plenty of lovely scenery *and* tend to obscure notions of cultural specificity. For example, in *First Strike* (the most overtly Bondian of these recent films), we see Jackie (who is identified in the film as a Hong Kong cop) cavorting in the snow in Russia and playing with a koala bear in his Australian hotel room; and *Mr. Nice Guy* is set entirely in Australia, with numerous postcard shots of natural settings and local architecture. In the latter film, which was also the first Chan project scripted and shot in English,[57] the closest Chan comes to having an identity beyond the one he wears on his face is when he refers to himself as "the Chinese guy." Within this evolved production protocol, then, concrete intimations of a place-specific identity are to be deemphasized in favor of an amorphous, disembedded, faux-global identity. And, as mentioned earlier, these recent films also deemphasize elaborate martial arts set pieces in favor of the use of stunts and props (a giant earthmover in *Mr. Nice Guy*, a leap from a parking garage roof to a narrow balcony in *Rumble in the Bronx*), which are less culturally specific forms of cinematic spectacle.

But even now, there are brief segments in these films that seem to reconnect Chan with aspects of Hong Kong culture, and sometimes the effect can be jarring for his new audiences. In *Rumble in the Bronx*, his breakthrough U.S. release, he plays a very recent arrival in New York City, although the storyline mostly steers clear of explorations of cultural dislocation and homesickness — Chan's character is perplexed by the situations in which he finds himself, but in ways that are almost indistinguishable from those seen in his Hong Kong–set films. Still, even in *Rumble*, there is a scene in which Chan lectures a group of previously vicious bikers (after having administered them a sound thrashing) about their socially irresponsible behavior, at which point they instantly convert to the path of virtue. This moral lesson almost seems lifted from a Kwan Tak-hing film, and both times I saw the film in the United States with largely non-Asian audiences, it caused a wave of laughter. And even the Bond-inflected *First Strike* includes a scene in which Chan uses dishonorably devious means to gain access to the bedside of a dying (Chinese) man. Chan then informs the man that the man's son is an international criminal. He is clearly ashamed of his moral compromise here, and his redemption becomes a plot thread within the film.

In any case, Jackie Chan's global strategy is continuing to move forward. He has signed with the William Morris Agency in hopes of getting a parallel U.S.-based career (acting only, at least for now) off the ground, a strategy that bore its first fruits with the sleeper success of *Rush Hour*. Chan has agreed to star in a sequel to that film and is presently shooting another Hollywood film called *Shanghai Noon*, in which (according to the Internet Movie Database) he "plays a Chinese man who travels to the Wild West to rescue a kidnapped princess." He continues to negotiate distribution deals for the films produced through his own company; in March 1997, for instance, New Line bought

Figure 4.
Mr. Nice Guy (Jackie
Chan, 1997).

the worldwide distribution rights for *Mr. Nice Guy* outside Asia from Golden
Harvest for U.S.$6 million.[58] At the same time, Chan has maintained ties
with his base market by signing a new contract with Golden Harvest (also in
March 1997) to make four movies (to be budgeted at U.S.$10–25 million)
over the next two to three years; *Who Am I? [Woshi Shei]* and *Gorgeous* are
the first two of these releases. This is a nonexclusive deal, meaning that Chan

and Golden Harvest are anticipating bids for distribution rights to these films in the United States and elsewhere. Chan may well have struck this deal in part out of loyalty to Golden Harvest and his Asian fans, but for a globe-hopping design professional[59] it also makes practical sense. Working through the Hong Kong–based company, he has autonomy over his productions, and the kinds of increasingly costly action spectaculars Chan is making these days can be filmed more economically outside of the United States, and with a mostly Chinese creative team. In any case, in Hong Kong, where his career began, Chan is still a major star, but instead of the young rebel he first hit it big with, he has become modernity's Kwan Tak-hing. These days, he is an institution, a role model, and a visible symbol of Hong Kong culture and of Hong Kong's materialist dreams — even as Chan has set up residence in Australia and is seldom seen in the territory. He is now comfortably ensconced as an "elder brother," if not a father figure, within Hong Kong's movie culture, a member of the older generation.

Ironically, though, one of Chan's best movies of the 1990s is *Drunken Master II* [*Jui Quan II*] (1994), a sequel to one of the early *kungfu* comedies that launched him to stardom and the first film he had made with a period setting in several years. In the film, Chan once again plays a young Wong Fei-hung who is clever and mildly rebellious, but also, in the last analysis, moral and respectful of tradition. He has no *sifu* in this film, perhaps out of deference to his real age (although he still looks young enough onscreen). Instead, the internal conflict involves Chan's relationship with his very traditional father (played by Ti Lung, who made his name in Zhang Che sword-fight films in the late 1960s and early 1970s and is actually only a few years older than Chan), the melodrama of which is leavened by an excellent comic performance by Anita Mui (actually several years younger than Chan) as Wong Fei-hung's stepmother. The martial arts sequences in the film are both funny and breathtakingly complex — Chan seems to have thrown himself into the creation of these scenes as a means of showing his fans, his rivals within the industry, and himself that when called upon he can still deliver the pure goods, without relying on car chases and the like. And, significantly, there is also an external conflict in *Drunken Master II* involving the plundering of Chinese national treasures by the British and other Western powers, which have employed the services of several quisling Chinese toughs willing to betray the Chinese nation and its heritage and to brutally exploit Chinese citizens, all for their own personal gain. What marks this film most as an older filmmaker's perspective on Wong Fei-hung and what he represents is the implicit support for the notion of a cultural China, a plea for the patriotic unity of Chinese people everywhere. This is at odds with Chan's late-1970s incarnation of Wong, which seemed to question, if not cast aside, some aspects of Chinese tradition in favor of a persona that was more attuned to the needs and desires of a younger, faster-moving, and more polyglot society that was and is Chinese, but not in the same way that the People's Republic of China or Taiwan is. *Drunken Master II* is a contradictory film in that it is simultaneously Chan's last unambiguously "local" film to date (in terms of the geographical setting and the incorporation of somewhat culturally specific values and narrative threads) and implicitly a denial of the Hong Kong identity "movement" of the past decade and a half. Be that as it may, within the logic of the international film business, this particular movie does not seem to be a comfortable fit with the strategy of repositioning Jackie Chan as a global product. The North American distribution rights for *Drunken Master II* were among those acquired by Miramax, but so far no release date has been announced, apparently because the film is considered "too local" and therefore a tough sell. It will be interesting to see if Chan continues to identify himself as a Hong Kong filmmaker and star, or whether he will ultimately re-embed himself professionally and culturally as a transnationalized cinematic icon. It does seem symptomatic that his 1998 Lunar New Year release (shot in South Africa) was entitled *Who Am I?*

Notes

1   Ackbar Abbas, *Hong Kong: Culture and the Politics of Disappearance* (Minneapolis: University of Minnesota Press, 1997), 28.

2   *Rumble, First Strike,* and *Mr. Nice Guy* were distributed in the U.S. by New Line, while *Supercop* and *Operation Condor* were part of a package of slightly older Chan films acquired for U.S. distribution by Miramax.

3   For additional discussion of Golden Harvest, see Steve Fore, "Golden Harvest Films and the Hong Kong Movie Industry in the Realm of Globalization," *Velvet Light Trap* 34 (1994): 40–58.

4   *Rush Hour* was shot on a modest budget of $35 million and grossed more than $140 million in theatrical release. It has also been very popular in the home video market. As spectacular as these numbers are, this was not Chan's first attempt to break into the U.S. market. In the early 1980s, he made two commercially and critically unsuccessful films directed by Hollywood hacks and had small roles in the two *Cannonball Run* films.

5   See the discussion of John Woo's Hollywood travails in Jillian Sandell, "Reinventing Masculinity: The Spectacle of Male Intimacy in the Films of John Woo," *Film Quarterly* 49, no. 4 (summer 1996): 23–34.

6   I have discussed this idea previously in "Jackie Chan and the Cultural Dynamics of Global Entertainment," in Sheldon Hsiao-peng Lu, *Trans/National Chinese Cinema* (Honolulu: University of Hawaii Press, 1997), 239–62.

7   Anthony Giddens, *The Consequences of Modernity* (Stanford: Stanford University Press, 1990), 21.

8 An influential discussion of the idea of "cultural China" may be found in Tu Wei-ming, "Cultural China: The Periphery as the Center," in *The Living Tree: The Changing Meaning of Being Chinese Today*, ed. Tu Wei-ming (Stanford: Stanford University Press, 1994), 1–34. For an articulate critique of the notion, see Allen Chun, "Fuck Chineseness: On the Ambiguities of Ethnicity as Cultural Identity," *boundary 2* 23, no. 2 (1996): 111–38.

9 Gren Manuel, "Recovering Protester Requests Battle Dress for HK Return," *South China Morning Post*, 29 September 1996.

10 Stephen Teo, "The True Way of the Dragon: The Films of Bruce Lee," in *Overseas Chinese Figures in Cinema*, ed. Law Kar and Stephen Teo (Hong Kong: Urban Council, 1992), 70. See also the discussion of Lee's persona and career in Stephen Teo, *Hong Kong Cinema: The Extra Dimensions* (London: BFI, 1997), 111–21.

11 And in another sense, Lee's films are decidedly dissimilar, in that their focus is antiforeign in a very direct, nonanalytical way; themes common to revolutionary cinema of the time (e.g., considerations of neocolonialism, the historical framework of imperialism and colonialism, and the structure of indigenous authoritarian regimes) are not addressed at all.

12 Tony Rayns, "Bruce Lee and Other Stories," in *A Study of Hong Kong Cinema in the Seventies*, ed. Li Cheuk-to, Michael Lam, and Leong Mo-ling (Hong Kong: Urban Council, 1984), 27.

13 Benedict Anderson, *Imagined Communities* (London: Verso, 1983), 15.

14 Stuart Hall, "The Question of Cultural Identity," in *Modernity: An Introduction to Modern Societies*, ed. Stuart Hall et al. (Cambridge, Mass.: Blackwell, 1996), 617.

15 Hall, 616.

16 Chun, 112–13.

17 The new nationalisms and manufactured ethnocentrisms of the world we live in now show mainly that some people prefer to cling to simpler, more reassuring versions of the world.

18 Anthony McGrew, "A Global Society?" in Hall et al., *Modernity*, 470.

19 David Harvey, *The Condition of Postmodernity* (Oxford: Basil Blackwell, 1989).

20 Ackbar Abbas provides a somewhat parallel argument in *Hong Kong: Culture and the Politics of Disappearance*, 29–31.

21 Benjamin K. P. Leung, *Perspectives on Hong Kong Society* (Hong Kong: Oxford University Press, 1996), 4–5.

22 Leung, 5–6.

23 Since then, many Hong Kong manufacturing operations have migrated to the mainland in search of cheaper labor and fewer environmental regulations.

24 See the discussion and tables in chapter 1 of Leung.

25 Leung, 64.

26 Yu Wo-man, "The Prodigious Cinema of Huang Fei-Hong: An Introduction," in *A Study of the Hong Kong Martial Arts Film*, ed. Lau Shing-hon (Hong Kong: Urban Council, 1980), 79.

27. Hector Rodriguez, "Hong Kong Popular Culture as an Interpretive Arena: The Huang Feihong Film Series," *Screen* 38, no. 1 (Spring 1997): 1–24.

28 Data provided in *Wong Fei-hung: The Invincible Master* (Hong Kong: Urban Council, 1995).

29 Yu Mo-Wan and Yung Ling-Man, eds., "Biographical Notes," in Lau, *A Study of the Hong Kong Martial Arts Film*, 175.

30 Tsui Hark's series, which began in 1991, is the most commercially successful and thematically cohesive of the revisionist Wongs. Five sequels to the original have been produced, with the most recent installment appearing in 1997. Four of the six have starred Jet Li as Master Wong; the other two featured the underrated Zhou Wenzhou. The popularity of Tsui's Wong films successfully, if temporarily, revived the moribund period martial-arts genre in Hong Kong, and—as is typical of the industry—generated a flurry of imitative or parodic Wong projects by other filmmakers.

31 Law Kar, introduction to *The Restless Breed: Cantonese Stars of the Sixties*, ed. Law Kar and Stephen Teo (Hong Kong: Urban Council, 1996), 10.

32 Bruce Campbell Robinson, "Hong Kong Film: The Cultural Dragon Faces Reunification" (master's thesis, University of Texas, 1995), 142. Robinson places the current proportion of Hong Kong–born residents at 70 percent.

33 Leung, 12.

34 James Kung and Zhang Yueai, "Hong Kong Cinema and Television in the 1970s: A Perspective," in Li, Lam, and Leong, *A Study of Hong Kong Cinema in the Seventies*, 15.

35 Sam Ho, "Licensed to Kick Men: The Jane Bond Films," in Law and Teo, *The Restless Breed*, 34–46.

36 Cheuk Pak-tong, "The Characteristics of Sixties Youth Movies," in Law and Teo, *The Restless Breed*, 66–79; Rex Wong, "Looking for Rebels in Sixties Cantonese Movies," in Law and Teo, *The Restless Breed*, 89–94.

37 Sek Kei, "The War between the Cantonese and Mandarin Cinemas in the Sixties, or, How the Beautiful Women Lost to the Action Men," in Law and Teo, *The Restless Breed*, 32–33.

38 Sek Kei, "The Development of 'Martial Arts' in Hong Kong Cinema," in Lau, *A Study of the Hong Kong Martial Arts Film*, 32–36.

39 Ng Ho, "Kung-fu Comedies: Tradition, Structure, Character," in Lau, *A Study of the Hong Kong Martial Arts Film*, 42–55.

40 Ng, 43, 46.

41 Chan has said of his apprenticeship: "The days at opera school were very long. Every day we would train from dawn to midnight, and anyone caught taking it easy would be whipped and starved. I don't know how the intense training affected me as a child or shaped me as an adult. I *do* know that I draw all my creativity for fight directing from those years of arduous training. But I would never put my kids through it, and I would never tell anyone to do the same thing." Quoted in Craig D. Reid, "An Evening with Jackie Chan," *Bright Lights* 13 (1994): 20.

42 As has frequently been noted, among Chan's classmates at the drama academy were other future Hong Kong film performers, action directors, and directors, most prominently Sammo Hung and Yuen Biao. Chan himself provides a colorful, if maddeningly fragmentary, account of his childhood in his autobiography,

I Am Jackie Chan (New York: Ballantine, 1998). A marginally less superficial discussion may be found in Clyde Gentry, *Jackie Chan: Inside the Dragon* (Dallas: Taylor, 1997).

43 The director and producer Lo Wei gave him his present Cantonese stage name, Sing Lung, an homage to Bruce Lee which translates as "Be the Dragon."

44 Yuen has achieved a measure of international recognition recently by virtue of his work as martial arts director during the production of *The Matrix* (1999), which features Keanu Reeves and Lawrence Fishburne performing simulations of moves and gestures previously associated with Chan, Jet Li, and other Hong Kong action stars with whom Yuen has worked.

45 Joseph Straubhaar, "Beyond Media Imperialism: Asymmetrical Interdependence and Cultural Proximity," *Critical Studies in Mass Communication* 8, no. 1 (March 1991): 39–59.

46 Roger Garcia, "The Autarkic World of Liu Chia-liang," in Lau, *A Study of the Hong Kong Martial Arts Film*, 113–34; Tony Rayns, "Resilience: The Cinema and Liu Jialiang," in Li, Lam, and Leong, *A Study of Hong Kong Cinema in the Seventies*, 51–57.

47 Roger Garcia, "The Doxology of Yuen Wo-ping," in Lau, *A Study of the Hong Kong Martial Arts Film*, 137.

48 See "Jackie Chan and the Cultural Dynamics of Global Entertainment." My discussion in that essay was guided significantly by the ideas and observations of Jenny Kwok Wah Lau in "A Cultural Interpretation of the Popular Cinema of China and Hong Kong," in *Perspectives on Chinese Cinema*, ed. Chris Berry (London: British Film Institute, 1991), and "A Cultural Interpretation of the Popular Cinema of China and Hong Kong, 1981–1985" (Ph.D. diss., Northwestern University, 1989).

49 Ng, 45.

50 For a detailed discussion of Chan's physicality and its significance, see Mark Gallagher, "Masculinity in Translation: Jackie Chan's Transcultural Star Text," *Velvet Light Trap* 39 (1997): 23–41.

51 Chan returned to Hong Kong to shoot a film for the first time in almost five years with his 1999 release *Gorgeous*, in which he plays somewhat against type as a wealthy capitalist wheeler-dealer (albeit one in the recycling business) and playboy. His prodigious martial arts skills are almost ancillary to the film's main storyline, a variation on the Kevin Costner vehicle *Message in a Bottle* (and I have no idea which project was out of the gate first). That is, *Gorgeous* is primarily a romantic comedy that also features elaborate but awkwardly grafted action sequences.

52 David Morley and Kevin Robins, *Spaces of Identity* (London: Routledge, 1995), 109, 113.

53 Ibid., 110.

54 Jim Hillier, *The New Hollywood* (London: Studio Vista, 1992), 32; Janet Wasko, *Hollywood in the Information Age* (Austin: University of Texas Press, 1994), 220.

55 Justin Wyatt, *High Concept: Movies and Marketing in Hollywood* (Austin: University of Texas Press, 1994).

56 Tony Bennett and Janet Woollacott, *Bond and Beyond* (London: Macmillan Education, 1987), 206–7.

57 In Hong Kong, *Mr. Nice Guy* was exhibited both in the "original" English version and in a dubbed Cantonese version.

58 Liz Hodgson, "Nice Guy Gets to Come First," *South China Morning Post,* 3 March 1997.

59 The term "design professional" is Anthony King's, from "Architecture, Capital, and the Globalization of Culture," in *Global Culture,* ed. Mike Featherstone (London: Sage, 1990), 397–411. I discuss the concept in relation to the Hong Kong movie industry in "Home, Migration, Identity: Hong Kong Film Workers Join the Chinese Diaspora," in *Fifty Years of Electric Shadows,* ed. Law Kar, Twenty-first Hong Kong International Film Festival (Hong Kong: Urban Council, 1997), 126–34.

CHAPTER SIX

Tsui Hark: National Style and Polemic

Stephen Teo

Local Settings

Like his great compatriot, erstwhile collaborator, and current rival, John Woo, Tsui Hark has gone Hollywood. Having secured a place for himself as a commercially dependable director in the Hong Kong cinema and gained cult status in the West with films such as *Peking Opera Blues [Dao Ma Dan]* and *Once Upon a Time in China [Huang Feihong]*, Tsui Hark's place in the pantheon of outstanding directors is guaranteed. His credentials as both a commercial director and a cult filmmaker with a New Wave upbringing paved his way to Hollywood. Critics at home may flinch at Tsui's unnerving ability to spew forth images as no one else can, but it is this facility that probably endeared him to a foreign audience. Tsui's visual imagery is so strong and fluent that the language he speaks is readily accessible. *Double Team*, his first Hollywood feature, entertains as ably as his best Hong Kong films, but I believe that it signals a turnaround in the direction of his career in more ways than one.

In 1981 the Hong Kong New Wave was thought to be floundering as Tsui Hark "sold out" and turned mainstream with his Cinema City comedy, *All the Wrong Clues . . . for the Right Solution [Guima Zhiduoxing]*. That film has proven to be a key work in denoting and developing Tsui's postmodern cinema, if we mean by that a cinema that integrates the aesthetics of avant-garde pop styles and the commercial instincts of genre cinema. *All the Wrong Clues . . .* presents a kind of vulgar commercialism that Hong Kong critics have derided as the "Cinema City" style. Tsui's career up to that point was in danger of losing commercial viability. He had to recut and reshoot *Dangerous Encounter—1st Kind [Diyi Leixing Weixian]* in the wake of censorship concerns about the film's violence and antiforeign attitudes. *Dangerous Encounter* is the most outstanding example of the director's ability to blend a hyperkinetic style with the uncontrolled emotions of his characters,

143

firmly grounding them in a local environment that is as much a part of the characters' psyches as it is a place where they live.

This "local" factor seems to me to be the most outstanding quality in the sum total of Tsui Hark's works. Later in this essay, I will attempt to define broadly just what constitutes Tsui Hark's localism — mutated since *Dangerous Encounter — 1st Kind* to a level that in the 1990s goes beyond mere settings for his characters. In 1997 Tsui even went international. If we see *The Blade [Dao]* (1995) as the picture that marks some kind of turning point in Tsui's "local" career, *Double Team* marks the post-1997 phase of Tsui's "international" career. Before *Double Team*, Tsui's career as a director was floundering on a series of box office and critical disappointments. *The Blade* was one of Tsui's two most notable achievements of the 1990s (the other was *Once Upon a Time in China*). The picture was reviled by critics in a curiously hard-hitting manner, a reaction that could have been provoked by the violent nature of the film itself. To quote the critic Li Cheuk-to: "The mood is hysterical, the soundtrack an incessant hubbub, the shots are faster than lightning, the rhythm infuriating."[1]

Hysteria and violence are the conventions of the genre on which Tsui Hark clearly has a point to make. Li's criticism therefore has the effect of "decentering" Tsui Hark's input as the auteur of the picture and his virtual reinvention of the conventions constituting the *wuxia pian* genre that he unabashedly draws on. *The Blade* is a remake of Zhang Che's Shaw Brothers blockbuster, *The One-Armed Swordsman [Dubi Dao]* (1967). Zhang's picture is set in the Shaws' movietown China, a milieu of artificial sets that convey the atmosphere of a China of legend. By contrast, Tsui eschews artifice and relocates his film in a China that is a crossroads of many cultures. The conventional patterns of the genre as defined by Zhang Che's *wuxia pian* films of the late 1960s onward are detected by Tsui's camera eye, roving and focusing on homoerotic motifs and sexual innuendo during the opening section of the picture, which unfolds from the perspective of Siu Ling, the naive girl who narrates a monologue about her romantic interest in the two male protagonists of the film. The voyeuristic shots of male buttocks and frontal shots of naked male bodies from the waist up are certainly evocations of convention for those who are familiar with the work of Zhang Che, Lau Kar-leong, and other directors of the genre. But Tsui treats these evocations almost cursorily and moves on to denote violence, which, he makes clear, is based on sexual emotion. The first such scene shows a monk fighting off a group of redneck hunters molesting women in the streets. The multiangled perspective of the sequence immediately conveys Tsui Hark's versatility as a craftsman.

破天荒携手

徐克 導演

陳家蓀 被為

馮愛慈 陳少玲 程小東 武術指導

客串主演 鍾志文 錄音

特別邀請美勒明星 史提夫勒沙 林榮 剪接

車保羅・龍天生
施露華・胡大鵬
葉德嫻・溫燦華
陳華南・麥大成
楊又薜・朱承彩
余頌允・余慕蓮
周國基・曹廣慶
馮潤泉・馮芹漢
盧家智・區樹湛
布魯士白龍
姬約翰・占美蕭

第一類型危險

Dangerous Encounter ~ 1st Kind

羅烈 林珍奇 區瑞強 呂良偉
領銜主演 領銜主演

監製 馮永發

影藝電影有限公司
Fotocine Film Production Limited

創業百萬鉅製

Figure 1.
Tsui Hark's antiforeign attitudes in *Dangerous Encounter—1st Kind* (1980) met with censorship.

The sequence is marked by jagged but graceful cutting between close and medium shots that maintains the continuity of the action and brief, frequent pans of the camera. The camera records the action from all angles. There are, in fact, very few subjective camera shots, and the action is covered quite literally from all perspectives save the subjective one. The audience sees the action as the camera swoops into it, panning or tilting from an "objective" shot to the action itself, such as, for example, from on top of a roof, or, on ground level, from the feet of people running away. The violence that we see takes on the quality of animation, an effect Tsui achieves by keeping his camera perspectives remarkably objective and maintaining them despite the ferocious movements that appeared so distracting to Tsui's critics. This way, the camera never loses track of all its perspectives, describing the action in toto. This "objective" camera stance makes the action more realistic, indeed more violent.[2] It also signals an attempt by Tsui to make his cinema universe more transcendent of "locality." Tsui gives us a vision of China that has never looked so multicultural or so alien to the mythical conception of a homogenous Han China most often depicted in the genre. Even while giving us such an uncommon vision, Tsui Hark never loses the context of "locality," embedding his vision in a dense depiction of background and foreground with a keen eye to realistic detail, as underscored by the market scenes, the costumes worn by Southern and Central Asian tribes, the wind, the sand, and the mud.

Thus, there seems to be an underlying tension between the image of a multicultural China and its "local" scenes of conflict and incompatibility. In other words, multiculturalism is offset by its context of locality—by Chinese nationalism and xenophobia. *Once Upon a Time in China* proffers the theme of foreigners engulfing China, provoking violence and xenophobia. In *The Blade*, Tsui plays a more harmonious theme of a China acting as host to multicultural communities and ethnic influences even though the images of violence seem to militate against harmony. The violence in *The Blade* may stem from the environment of a China heterogenized by multiculturalism—the hysteria and violence resulting from the trauma thrown up by disparate cultures and peoples, it may be argued—but it is symptomatic of human affairs. *The Blade*'s violence is diagnostic rather than prescriptive, as in *Once Upon a Time in China*, where the citizens' militia that Wong Fei-hung has organized acts as a bulwark against imperialist violence.

The Blade grounds its violence in sexual emotion, but it also explores the convention of heroism in the genre. Tsui Hark works with the theme of outrage against injustice and the intervention of heroes against the villains who are responsible for it. The hero is haunted by his father's death, asking his mentor, "Was his death worth it?" "Was he a good man?" The final duel between the hero and his father's killer takes on heroic proportions, becoming a struggle that decides the nature of man and his character. This duel sequence is one of the most extraordinary in martial arts cinema, its effect and significance perhaps second only to the final sequence in King Hu's *The Valiant Ones [Zhonglie Tu]* (1975). Tsui's contribution to the genre ultimately lies in the depiction of a climactic battle that explodes the mythic conventions of flying heroes: the arbitrary images of protagonists who defy gravity by leaping, somersaulting, levitating in midair, and flying down to confront opponents. The villain in *The Blade* carries the nickname of "Flying Dragon," but his putative power of flight is reinterpreted by Tsui Hark as a figurative connotation. Flying Dragon gets his feet off the ground with the aid of ropes. He is never seen suspended in midair. Tsui overturns the convention of flight and substitutes it for speed; the battle between hero and villain literally defeats the eye, as the hero taunts Flying Dragon with the words, "You're not fast enough!" In *The Blade* Tsui assembles a montage sequence to equal the incredible technical effect King Hu achieved in *The Valiant Ones*. The emotional impact of both sequences derives from the auteurs' quest to redefine the genre and from the characters' quest to confront injustice and redefine the nature of their characters.

Figure 2.
The Valiant Ones (King Hu, 1975) set many precedents for swordplay films.

Figure 3.
Once Upon a Time in China III (Tsui Hark, 1993) shows China as a crossroads of many cultures.

Tsui's sequence seems to do King Hu's one better. Tsui assembles many more shots and puts them over faster, along with the objective camera eye that covers all the action. However, for all its technical virtuosity, this last sequence does not equal the emotional intensity of the corresponding sequence in *The Valiant Ones*. Tsui's notion of speed overrides the consistent theme of nationalism in his own pictures as well as the patriotic nature of King Hu's last duel sequence between Chinese heroes and a Japanese pirate-villain. In fact, *The Blade* appears to consider questions of nonnational substance, as in the question that the young female narrator asks, "What is *jianghu*?"[3] Tsui provides an answer just before the final duel occurs that places the *jianghu* in abstract time rather than in the context of a real local-ity (country or community) and links it with the personal motivation of the hero's revenge and his quest for justice. Where the final duel sequence in *The Valiant Ones* is heroic by virtue of its concept of valor, the final duel se-quence in *The Blade* is heroic purely because of its abstraction of time and space.

The Nationalism of Tsui Hark

Rather like the question "What is *jianghu*?," the asking of which is designed to increase its mystery and vagueness, Tsui's theme of nationalism construes more misunderstanding than empathy. I have spoken of the "local factor" in Tsui Hark's works. The final duel in *The Blade* begins with a declaration, through the young woman's narrative, of the *jianghu* as a consequence of a hero's search for vengeance and justice through time, however long it takes. Personal motivation is paramount in the *jianghu*, and when one is in the *jianghu*, he or she is supposedly a person without a country. However, the question "What is *jianghu*?" in *The Blade* might as well be phrased, "What is a man's character?" or "What makes up his character?" The answer to these questions, in Tsui's best films, is almost indubitably that a man's character is determined by his circumstances and his locality, whether it be Hong Kong or some unnamed locality in a mythic China. In this regard, Tsui Hark's char-acters are far from abstract. That Tsui Hark has taken to asking the question "What is *jianghu*?" in his films is a natural consequence of his exploration of the nationalism theme in Hong Kong cinema.

The nationalist sentiment behind all of Tsui's films stems, I believe, from Tsui's own background. Born in Vietnam in 1951, Tsui came to Hong Kong in 1966 at the age of fifteen. He was educated in Hong Kong and then went on to further his studies in the United States. The experience of growing up as a Sino-Vietnamese teenager in the territory must have been formative. One can detect in Tsui's films a certain sensitivity to the fact that he is an overseas Chinese; they seem to tell everyone who cares to listen that his films are very Chinese indeed, referring as they do to Chinese history and culture, a Chinese environment. The role of Tsui's nationalism, therefore, is mainly to signify his "Chineseness."

In large part, Tsui's advocacy of nationalism must be seen in the context of selling Hong Kong cinema to outsiders. How, as a fledgling filmmaker in Hong Kong in the latter half of the 1970s, can one put across one's personal style and content to audiences? Tsui Hark had to think long and hard about

Figure 4.
Speed and nationalism
in Tsui Hark's *Once
Upon a Time in China*
films.

how to define certain characteristics of his style. Influences from King Hu and from Japanese directors with international reputations would have pointed Tsui toward defining a personal style through some form of "national style." Nationalism, in terms of what the *Encyclopaedia Brittanica* defines as "loyalty and devotion to the state such that national interests are placed above individual or global interests," is not particularly evident in Tsui's first works. However, if the term "nationalist" is used to define a style, then it clearly applies to Tsui Hark.

Tsui Hark is, of course, not alone in trying to define a national style. Hong Kong cinema in the 1970s went through a period of restructuring as Cantonese cinema declined and the new genre of *kungfu* hit the market. The rise of Mandarin cinema meant that the Hong Kong film industry had almost complete access to the Taiwan market through the notion of *guopian* (national cinema). As such, Hong Kong's Mandarin films were given a national identity. The debate on finding a "national style" is aptly expressed in the title of an article, "National Style and Reason in the Art of Film," written by an obscure critic, Huo Sen, and published in a Hong Kong film magazine in the 1970s.[4] The author attributes the development and progress of Chinese films to the fact that "Chinese films have deep and profound national sentiments" that could not be duplicated in Hollywood films or other foreign cinemas. "It is difficult for foreigners to film our national style because it is something that not only has a shape but also is fully possessed of a spiritual life style." Attempting a definition of national style, the author links it to the tenets of multiculturalism and critical reasoning based on rational thought.

> In a multicultural system, the impact of different nationalities increases the diversity of entertainment. It is easy to reach common ground with such entertainment derived from diverse national styles. This is due to the rationalization of drama. Even though the works of drama may be different, from a rational point of view, they are able to touch people and bring them together. Therefore, those works that have earned international recognition are mostly motion pictures with national styles that are rational. The Japanese films *Rashomon* and *Harakiri* are works of national style, but their appeal, which is appreciated by international critics, lies in their critique of antirationalism.[5]

Though the mood of the times twenty years ago might have conditioned national cinemas that were "rational" and well reasoned (the style of foreign art cinema most appreciated in the West from the 1950s onwards), Hong Kong cinema at the time was hardly known to foreign audiences as a "rational" cinema, at least through the martial arts films exported to the West. Ringo Lam made the same point: "The imagined world of the *jianghu*, the irrational arrangements of fighting scenes, the Old World romantic ambience, all went against the thoughts of the logical, scientific mentality of the Western audience."[6] How does all this relate to Tsui Hark's quest for a national style in the late 1970s? One must go back to *The Butterfly Murders [Die Bian]* (1979) to see that Tsui Hark was so immersed in the film culture of the 1970s — particularly "the imagined world of the *jianghu*," with its "irrational arrangements of fighting scenes . . . [and] Old World romantic ambience" — that it is not hard to observe the link he is trying to make between the New Wave and the old film culture of Hong Kong; and this, as *The Blade* makes clear, is an ongoing process.

As a New Wave filmmaker in Hong Kong cinema, Tsui Hark has dealt with the quest for identity with a hard-nosed toughness not found in any other New Wave director. The "local factor" in his pictures has come across, in pictures like *We Are Going to Eat You [Diyu Wu Men]* (1980) and *Dangerous Encounter—1st Kind*, as a crude, unrefined grossness in terms of both aesthetics and character behavior, behavior so gauche that it intensifies the irony of Tsui's status (why is somebody so authentically "local" at the same time a New Wave artist?). It is almost as if Tsui is challenging the tastes of foreign audiences well conditioned to the "rational national styles" that the article above refers to, but yet, in taking up this challenge, Tsui has not abandoned the principle of creating a national style. From *The Butterfly Murders* to pictures like *Zu, Warriors of the Magic Mountain [Xin Shu Shan Jianxia]*, *Shanghai Blues [Shanghai zhi Ye]*, *Peking Opera Blues*, *Once Upon a Time in China*, and *The Blade*, as well as in countless other minor pictures, Tsui makes allusions to classic Hong Kong and Chinese cinema genres, showing a typical movie brat's digestion of the classics. He comes up with his own distinctive style, to be sure, but the fun in watching a Tsui Hark picture is how it relates to the work of the old masters (such as Zhang Che and King Hu, among others). Tsui Hark's national style is thus related to the old Hong Kong cinema, but the periods that he evokes (the late 1960s and the 1970s) are quite different from the "rational dramas" of other national cinemas.

Oriental Abstractions Inverted

The thesis of rational drama as the constituent of national style is an understandable reaction when considered against the "dogmas of Orientalism" as propounded by Edward Said. According to Said, one of the principal dogmas of orientalism is "the absolute and systematic difference between the West, which is rational, developed, humane, superior, and the Orient, which is aberrant, undeveloped, inferior."[7] What Said calls a dogma is a truism among many Asians. The point is driven home when Huo Sen, the author of "National Style and Reason," freely confesses that "on the level of production, our films, on average, are not up to those produced by the foreigners."

The notion of rational drama and national style attacks the other dogma that "abstractions about the Orient . . . are always preferable to direct evidence drawn from modern Oriental realities."[8] In the postmodernist 1980s and 1990s, Tsui's style of national cinema offers contradictions about Orientalist abstractions in an inverted manner, on the one hand breaking down these abstractions from the Western standpoint, but on the other, bolstering other myths and abstractions from the Chinese standpoint. The classic exposition of this juggling act is *Once Upon a Time in China*, a film that reinvents the myth of Wong Fei-hung while drawing on the same arbitrary signs of genre cinema that feed Hong Kong pictures as a whole as well as stereotypes familiar from Hollywood cinema. The myth of Wong Fei-hung sustains the portrayal of Tsui's hero as a man who incorporates both conservatism and progressive tendencies, a man who is both a Chinese patriot and a bold thinker who tinkers with the idea of a Westernized China.

As played by Jet Li, Wong Fei-hung is a simple hero, but his all-round virtuosity and straddling of East and West reflects the rich complexity of *Once*

Upon a Time in China. The film works in part as a virtual textbook of Orientalist abstractions that have been passed down from both Hollywood and Chinese pictures, from Fu Manchu to Charlie Chan, from *The Opium War* (1959) to *Fifty-Five Days at Peking* (1963),[9] from *The Last Emperor* (1981) to *Tai-Pan* (1986). Tsui positively dwells on these "abstractions"; he goes as far as he can to depict arrogant, uncouth, bellicose Westerners. They are abstract characters, the typical heavies of propaganda melodramas of both sides: in countless Hollywood pictures, they are manifested as buck-toothed Orientals who kidnap white girls for white slavery; in *Once Upon a Time in China*, they are *gweilos* who kidnap Chinese girls to become sex slaves in the Gold Mountain.

Tsui is equally abstract about straight characterizations. Wong Fei-hung personifies *ren*, the ideal human. *Ren* is the same phonetic pronunciation of the word for "man" and for the word meaning "kindheartedness," "nobility," or "benevolence." All Chinese are *ren*, while all foreigners are "devils" (*gweilos*). Tsui depicts China as a mythic land whose potential strength remains in limbo, bounded by tradition and curbed by the refusal of talented individuals to come to terms with a new world. It is a vision that is nearer the truth than the conventional idea of a strong, bellicose China setting out to bully its neighbors, though this is the classic line of resistance against Chinese nationalism, particularly in Southeast Asia, where fear of China lingers. It can be seen from the film that Tsui Hark uses the concept of nationalism as a preexisting text for cinematic events, putting his characters into the context of nation and people. But this does not necessarily constitute Tsui's national style. Tsui's mastery of mise-en-scène and storytelling "deconstructs" his national style, as it were, due to the power of cinema as a universal language. However, the mise-en-scène "re-constructs" the national style by its references to the arsenal of arbitrary signs in Hong Kong cinema. Among these signs is one marked "nationalism."

Tsui Hark is never interested in defending a mythic or homogeneous image of China, or even one of China as a victim. Instead, this is a China that is often riven by internal disparities (among both ethnic groups and power groups), by the influx of technology (medicine, gunpowder, the camera, etc.) that heightens the awareness of difference (Chinese acupuncture, martial arts, and opera), and by the notion of fighting for a position of hegemony (in the martial arts world, within the bureaucracy, etc.). Thus, Tsui Hark's films make a diagnosis of nationalism, but at the same time, he uses the icons, appearances, and forms that are conventionally identified (even in Hollywood movies) as Chinese, in order to integrate them into a mise-en-scène that is entertaining to outsiders. All contemporary Chinese are also outsiders to, and voyeurs of, this earlier Chineseness. As a Chinese born in Vietnam, Tsui

Hark is the most consistent director of the New Wave to acknowledge such "Chineseness" as an intrinsic quality of Hong Kong cinema.

The Tsui Hark Cult

The argument of "Chineseness" as a "national style" cannot ignore the fact that Tsui Hark has an international cult following, one that has contributed to Tsui's entry into Hollywood.[10] A Tsui Hark cultist in the West could reasonably say that there is nothing specifically Chinese about the director. And for critics who are put off by the idea of nationalism in cinema, an international cult following should act as a countervailing force. One must ask, therefore, why Tsui has attracted a cult audience. Someone else will have to come up with a study of the reasons for Tsui's cult following, what social groups form the cult, how the cult functions in regard to Tsui's themes, as stated above, and what exactly spawned the cult (which of his pictures are considered "cultish," while others are not).

The corpus of work that illuminates the Tsui Hark cult includes *Peking Opera Blues* and films that Tsui has produced, including *A Chinese Ghost Story [Qiannu Youhun]*, *Swordsman II [Xiao'ao Jianghu II Dongfang Bubai]*, and *Swordsman III: The East Is Red [Dongfang Bubai zhi Fengyun Zaiqi]*, the last two featuring Brigitte Lin as the androgynous Dongfang Bubai, or "Asia the Invincible." Feminism and transsexuality are covered by the exploits of Asia the Invincible in the two *Swordsman* sequels, but the themes develop from the use of Peking opera stereotypes that make Asia both a *huadan* (a pretty heroine) and a *wudan* (a military hero). The picture sparkles with role reversals where good guys become bad guys and the chief protagonist is ambiguous in gender and covers the spectrum from villain to hero, from female to male, from man to eunuch to woman. This protagonist is called Asia the Invincible, a somewhat ironic name under the circumstances, and she/he seeks to dominate China, thus the world. Just what the Tsui Hark cultists make of all this is not known. Yet more Orientalist abstractions about gender? Inverted Orientalism? A parody of the nation?

To analyze the reasons for Tsui Hark's cult following, I propose to start with the notion of localism in his works. Tsui's cult following should by implication reinforce the notion of localism, since cult audiences tend to focus on a specific genre, actor, director, even perhaps the fact that Tsui Hark is a director dealing with exotic, local themes that are not found anywhere else. However, the wider the cult, the more universal Tsui's art should appear. This forms one more aspect of the irony inherent in the cinema of Tsui Hark: in sustaining the local factor that underlines his putative crudity, vulgarity, and gaucherie, not to mention his violence and hysteria, in films such as *We Are Going to Eat You, Dangerous Encounter—1st Kind,* and *The Blade,* we ultimately find a universal dimension in his art.

The theme of gender bending in its literal run of the gamut of sexual identity acts as a kind of wicked metaphor for this universality, and Brigitte Lin's performance as Asia the Invincible is a more adventurous throwback to the (bisexual?) character she plays in *Peking Opera Blues.* The transmutation of gender is part of Tsui Hark's quest for identity and nation inherent in the query "What is *jianghu?,*" a theme that is not denied by the apparent universality that bolsters the foundation of the director's cult following. Tsui Hark's world is inclusive, blending the outrageous with the normal, the paranormal (as in his horror films) with the natural world (as in *The Blade,* with its contortions of mud, sand, and wind), and the supernatural (the notion of flight) with the mundane (the notion of speed). Similarly, Tsui's mood tends to change even within a film: from comedy to tragedy (as in *The Butterfly Lovers* [*Lang Zhu*]), from romance to adventure (as in *The Blade* or *Love in the Time of Twilight* [*Huayue Jiaqi*]), and so on. The shifts of mood in synchronous cinematic time recall the Chinese expression *beihuan lihe* (joys and sorrows in equal measures, reflecting the vicissitudes of life) and conform to Tsui's fluidity with images and narrative mise-en-scène. The basis of Tsui's cult, therefore, must be wide even if the cult narrows down to only a part of Tsui's inclusive world.

We may refer to the multicultural world of *The Blade* as one more symbol of Tsui's universality. The film deals with sexual passion predicated on voyeuristic perspectives of homoeroticism as well as conventional heterosexuality, but it is not limited to these themes or desires. In *Swordsman II,* Asia the Invincible is not purely a sexual creature: in the event, sex is perhaps the least of her concerns. Identity, naturally, is one aspect; the role of women in the conventional world of men is another; and the question of political power involving the moral worth of character (Asia is evil, ambitious, and amoral but becomes a sympathetic, romantic, human, and even moral character of a sort). Such transmutations make Asia a kind of beacon in the cult worship of Tsui, for both men and women. The point here is that Asia is all things to all men and all women. In the scheme of Tsui's nationalism, Asia, as played by Lin in the transmutation of a woman, represents woman's aspirations to play a more prominent role in Chinese history. In the guise of a strong woman, Asia is clearly different from the sexist interpretations of women, say, in Hollywood cinema.

If Asia, as a character, is difficult to pin down, it is because Tsui Hark revels in the irony of mixing forms, unaware or perhaps uncaring of the contradictions that he conjures up. He is an auteur who has moved from New Wave status to that of a pioneer of Hong Kong's postmodernist cinema, clearly one more dimension that illuminates his cult reputation. While his style has always tended to the ephemeral, Tsui has advanced with each picture, and clearly his cult reputation has not kept up with him. *The Blade*, for example, does not seem to have been taken up by a cult audience as his other films have been. The reasons for this are unclear, nor should it be an issue. *The Blade* may well cultivate a cult reputation in time.

I am tempted to think that time and speed lie behind Tsui Hark's cult reputation, simply as a blatant consideration of tempo: Tsui's films move so much faster than the normal run of films. However, the notion of speed acts like a bullying boy in his pictures: recall the final duel of *The Blade*, where the one-armed hero taunts the Flying Dragon, "You're not fast enough!" That taunt is directed at all of us classicists who seek some rhyme and reason to tempo. Tsui does not let up; in the cult film *The Wicked City [Yaoshou Dushi]* (1992), an end-of-century cyberpunk nightmare derived from Japanese *manga*, the human hero does battle with a clock and says, "Time is a pain in the arse." The preoccupation with time is Tsui Hark's concession to Fredric Jameson's "inverted millenarianism," from the first sentence of "Postmodernism, or The Cultural Logic of Late Capitalism."[11] To Tsui Hark, while time is obviously some kind of twilight marking "the end of this or that," speed is of the essence, and the end of time is not necessarily a clear break. The element of speed makes Tsui Hark somehow a *Chinese* postmodernist — more specifically, a *Hong Kong* postmodernist.

The End of the Nation

Will Hong Kong revert to an atavistic cult of the nation after the handover to China, a notion inscribed in *The Wicked City*, where a father seeks the death of his son as both men are locked in conflict on top of a jumbo jet hovering above the Bank of China building? Tsui's answer to this question is developed in *The Blade*, which also has a (muffled) father-and-son. The one-armed swordsman manifests as the son, albeit a crippled son. This hero is an outsider who does not inspire narcissistic identification; rather, he represents a more human figure in a multicultural context embellished by realism.[12] And his speed makes him even more evasive. Misplacement is further generated by speed and a sense of uprootedness from the environment — the "transcendent locality" that lies behind the question "What is *jianghu*?" The multiculturalism of *The Blade* is one of the key signifiers of this uprootedness, but it also means considerably more in Tsui Hark's universe: for once in his career, Tsui Hark has actually sublimated the idea of Chineseness.

In reference to Leni Riefenstahl's *Triumph of the Will* (1935), Siegfried Kracauer writes about the director's attempts to achieve the "metamorphosis of reality" through "endless movement . . . produced by cinematic techniques." "There is a constant panning, travelling, tilting up and down — so that spectators not only see passing a feverish world, but feel themselves uprooted in it. The ubiquitous camera forces them to go by way of the most fantastic routes, and editing helps drive them on."[13] As with Riefenstahl, so with Tsui Hark. Tsui employs cinematic techniques to turn his genre upside down in the same way that Riefenstahl turns the documentary upside down. While Riefenstahl sought to transfigure reality, Tsui addresses the "unreality" of the martial arts film genre.

The feverish world of *The Blade* is a multicultural one in contrast to the traditional, homogeneous China usually dictated by the genre. However, the fantasy underpinnings of the genre are made over by a realist treatment of violence through the "objective camera eye" and Tsui's depiction of a multicultural bazaar. We see China as a continental landmass where different cultures collide, and this eclectic China challenges the stereotype of a changeless China ruled by Confucian values and ancestor worship. The realism of *The Blade* counteracts the *jianghu*, the transfigured world of the genre as seen in the *Swordsman* series, where Spanish conquistadores (in the third of the series) also ask, "What is *jianghu?*" There, an answer would only beg the question, reinforcing the almost Buñuelian surrealism of the moment. In *The Blade*, the *jianghu* exists in various manifestations that are no longer so abstract. It is country, community, locality; it is the person's character; it is the hero who knows how to develop his talent and achieve victory through the human dimension of speed rather than the superhuman one of flight.

The Blade works as a rejoinder to all the conceits of the genre that Tsui himself has exploited in the past. While it is a key work that departs from a well-trodden path, it is by no means atypical of Tsui Hark's work. It contains all the trademarks of the typical Tsui opus in his best style. But *The Blade* is marked by a particular hubris that seems to isolate it from other Tsui Hark pictures. Its critical and commercial failure may have relegated it to the category of *films maudit*, films consigned to oblivion because they are a "hard watch." *Double Team* followed in the wake of *The Blade*, with more than a hint that the film owes debts to the vulnerable one-armed hero. Jean-Claude Van Damme plays a hero so traumatized by failure in catching the villain that he is exiled to "the colony," where misfits and misplaced persons reside. It is easy to see through the allegory of "the colony" and the sense of alienation that pervades the film. The question is whether Tsui is beating a last retreat from his "colony" as he seeks greener pastures in the international playing field.

Tsui's agenda for post-1997 Hong Kong cinema will be interesting to watch. What will be his themes in relation to a Hong Kong integrated into the motherland? And where will his international career lead him? *The Blade* and *Double Team* are transitional works to a mature phase where new configurations may be played out in regard to his main themes. If we say *The Blade* presents a vague concept of nation, *Double Team* is an interpositive duplicate of that vagueness. It presents a view of the colony, a nonnation of men who belong nowhere, the end of the nation. In this new vagueness, sons are crippled or killed and fathers are emasculated figures.

It matters that we follow Tsui's development. Tsui Hark has what Hong Kong critics call a "devil's talent" (*gui cai*), a talent so broad and brilliant that it does not seem human. He is one of the prime movers in the industry and an original New Wave director who pushes his commercial instincts to the limit. He has been able to keep in step and in tune with the times, evoking the kind of postmodern energy that marks him as a representative Hong Kong filmmaker. What is most disconcerting about Tsui is the way he seems to come across as an eternal "movie brat," rather than growing and maturing as a filmmaker with precise messages to impart. Add to this his expansive interference in all departments of the creative filmmaking process (particularly scriptwriting) and his commercialism, and the devil's talent cooks up a brew that is too much for his critics to swallow and his defenders to digest. The cinema of Tsui Hark teaches us that time does not stand still and that speed is of the essence. But we may need to make some kind of Faustian compact with this devil, a compact that will give us some wind to catch up with all he conjures up so as to redeem his work.

Notes

1 Review by Li Cheuk-to published on the Web page of the Hong Kong Society of Film Critics, http://zero.com.hk/filmcritics.

2 The other action sequences in the film are similarly handled with the characteristic "objective camera eye" that marks this first one. What must be noted here is that there are indeed very few subjective camera shots in all of the other action sequences. When the subjective camera shots do occur, it is for only a brief second, as with the hero Ding-on's flashback to his own torture at the hands of the "foreign bandits" during the battle scene in which Ding-on defeats the bandits.

3 The literal translation of *jianghu* is "rivers and lakes"; the term refers to an abstract, if not imaginary, realm where mythic heroes dwell and conduct their business based on a meritorious code of honor and righteousness.

4 *Hong Kong Movie News* [in Chinese], 3 March 1970, 50–51. The author of the article may have been a film director writing under a pseudonym, a common practice in Chinese film criticism. The article is thus chosen here as a representative sample of the debate on "national style" that would tax the minds of film directors throughout the decades of development of both Hong Kong and Taiwan cinemas.

5 Translations of all quotes are by the author.

6 In a taped interview presented at the Conference on Hong Kong Cinema, organized by the Hong Kong International Film Festival, 10–12 April 1997. See the published catalog of proceedings of the conference, Hong Kong Urban Council, 1997.

7 Edward Said, *Orientalism* (London: Penguin Books, 1978), 300.

8 Ibid.

9 *55 Days at Peking* (1963), a Samuel Bronston epic directed mainly by Nicholas Ray and Andrew Marton, along with the 1959 Chinese picture *Lin Zexu* (variously known under the English titles of *Commissioner Lin* and *The Opium War*), appear to be the seminal references that bear upon *Once Upon a Time in China*. The film opens with a prologue in which Wong Fei-hung says farewell to a Lin Zexu–like figure (Lin being the historical character who provoked the Opium War by confiscating and burning the opium of British merchants in Guangzhou). The film then moves on to the after-credits scene, where Western missionaries repeatedly sing the word "Hallelujah" of the Handel chorus to counter the Chinese music and sounds reverberating from around them; the scene parallels the famous opening scene in *55 Days at Peking*, in which assorted national anthems of Western occupying powers in the Chinese capital vie to be heard as the respective national flags are hauled up the flagpoles, the resulting din causing a Chinese onlooker to comment that all the foreign nations sing the same tune: "We want China."

10 Tsui was offered the assignment to direct *Double Team* by the producer Moshe Diamont, who promptly informed Tsui that he had a cult following in the United States, at which, according to an interview in *City Entertainment* magazine [in Chinese], 1–14 May 1997, 46–68, Tsui affected surprise.

11 See Jameson's article in *New Left Review* 146 (1984): 53–92.

12 The castration symbol of the severed arm is used in cinema to signify Otherness, being outcast from the crowd, as in the 1951 Howard Hawks production *The Thing (from Another World)*. Tsui Hark may not have consciously copied Howard Hawks, but these signs are so embedded in cinematic language that Tsui, as a precocious "movie brat," would have no problem drawing on them as a kind of supertext. The problem lies in Tsui's critics, who insist on using identification principles that place Tsui in the narrower confines of society, group, gender, and so on, neglecting the supertextual parameters of the cinema.

13 Siegfried Kracauer, *From Caligari to Hitler* (Princeton: Princeton University Press, 1947), 302.

CHAPTER SEVEN

Hong Kong Hysteria: Martial Arts Tales from a Mutating World

Bhaskar Sarkar

To a Distant Observer

I have never been to Hong Kong. Yet the so-called capital of Asian capitalism glistens like a pearl in my sense of the emergent transnational imaginary. The city has become a signifier of dynamism and growth. It is the ideal to which other megalopolises like Kuala Lumpur and Bombay are compared.[1] For many Asians, upward mobility is coterminous with a one-way ticket to Hong Kong. Deepa Mehta's film *Fire* (1997), an Indo-Canadian coproduction, dramatizes this tendency in the figure of a video-store owner from Delhi who loves martial arts films, has a Chinese girlfriend, and dreams of migrating to Hong Kong.

Living in Los Angeles, I have many opportunities to watch Hong Kong martial arts films, which enjoy cult status among hip Angelenos. My sense of the Hong Kong world derives largely from these generic tales, often described as "cool" (which, in characteristically noncommittal Southern California lingo, denotes a whole range of qualities).[2] Yet, at times, I cannot help worrying that behind this fond and enthusiastic description is a thorough dismissal of the reality of Hong Kong, of the lived experiences and sensibilities of its people; that, like so many other cool postmodern artifacts, these films are being consumed without much understanding of the contexts in which they were produced. Signs emptied of all material significance travel better, generating more capital in their global wake.

This essay is an attempt to engage with certain martial arts films coming out of Hong Kong in the 1990s. My own precarious position as an Indian film scholar living in the United States, with no comprehension of the Chinese language, rules out a contextual reading attuned to the local specificities of the city. Instead, I offer one possible way of making sense of these films, an approach that may also be useful in comprehending many popular Bombay films. The perspective I adopt can be described loosely as "transnational   159

Asian," a description admittedly fraught with problems. While a thorough interrogation of such a position is beyond the scope of this essay, I hope to bring up some of the salient issues.

I have chosen to focus on films that are marked not by modernist, critical explorations of the Hong Kong milieu, but rather by postmodern excess. These recent works evince an accentuated, dizzying pace: the typical attributes of Hong Kong martial arts films — the dynamic camera movements, the dramatic framings, the oblique angles, the soaring music, the percussive underscoring of action, the choreographed fights, the flying leaps — began to intensify in the 1990s. These texts resonate with confusion, ambivalence, tension — attributes that make them "cool" only in a sizzling, urgent way. What follows is a reading of recent Hong Kong martial arts films as hysterical texts,[3] in which hysteria is linked intimately with the recent history and material conditions of the territory.

Through an Ambivalent Lens

My ideas about Hong Kong are colored by the hysteria in the Western media about the 1997 handover of the British colony to China. I keep reminding myself that the Western press cannot overcome its blind spots regarding the menace of communism and the inscrutability of the Oriental; that all the hype is aimed mainly at producing a media event that provides for good copy and compelling televisual spectacle for a couple of days. People around the world, with no direct link to Hong Kong, learn little about the experiences and concerns of the inhabitants of the territory; instead, they are offered a staged occasion for rehashing certain preconceptions and archetypes that were purveyed by the media in the first place.[4] The city is delivered temporarily as a consumable package, to be supplanted soon by the next sensational news item.[5]

Having spent the first two decades of my life in Calcutta, I am as much a Calcuttan as an Angeleno. Subjected to and through multiple displacements, both real and figural,[6] I understand the fears and concerns of Hong Kong residents who once ran away from mainland China, only to be handed back to the Communist regime after so many years. The specter of the disruption of an established way of life — with its aura of prosperity and freedom — is daunting, especially when the future seems nebulous. However, my own syncretic identity does not allow the unproblematic acceptance of Western capitalist notions of prosperity and freedom. Among other problems, the entire notion of the Pacific Rim smacks of economic, social, and cultural hegemony. In the background of this geopolitical configuration one can hear the incessant triumphant clucking: "they learnt it from us!" Even as Asia comes into its own as a region of rapid development, the West attempts to steal Asia's thunder and reposition itself as the perennial leader by insert-ing itself back into the region—not as archaic colonizer but as hegemonic cohort.

The Asian Miracle

The very idea of an Asian economic miracle remains controversial. Can we really lump Hong Kong, Taiwan, and South Korea together with Singapore, Indonesia, and Thailand? The construction of the notion of a resurgent, trans-national Asia elides the differences that exist at various levels.[7] In the drive to develop according to a Western capitalist teleology, the planners and resource owners seem to be forgetting the bulk of their populations. The in-ternational apparatus (the International Monetary Fund [IMF], the World Bank, the Western media) is dishing out awards (in the form of capital in-vestments, transfers, and low-interest loans) and praise (like the hype about Asia being "the place"). *Fortune* magazine devoted an entire special issue in 1994 on the emerging Indian market; analysts were smacking their lips at the prospect of a 200-million-strong Indian middle class by the end of the twentieth century with an appetite for conspicuous consumption. But what about the balance of the Indian population, the other eight hundred million? The Western media portray political upheavals in Korea or Indonesia as pop-ular attempts to further democratic rights; the discontent among the masses over increasing economic disparities is overlooked in these accounts.

The celebration of the Asian miracle is tied to the elision of its costs: the dislocation and disorientation of large masses of people. Stock market in-dices and gross domestic product growth rates do not give us any indication of the affective aspects of everyday life. Policy makers do not take into ac-count the sense of displacement among workers who travel thousands of miles in a "borderless" Asia from Kuwait to Kyoto to take low-paying jobs in the service sector, or the disorientation of Southeast Asian women who travel to Hong Kong to work as domestic help or to sell their bodies: is their lot much different from that of the "comfort women" rounded up in a different colonial era for the Japanese colonial army?

Even if we go by stock market indices, the experiences of Asian economies in 1998 put the supposed miracle into question. The vicissitudes of capitalist expansion besieged the Asian scene: as financial markets came crashing down, investors saw their portfolios wiped out overnight. With expectations of sustained economic expansion rudely shaken, erstwhile miracle performers — even the "tigers" — confronting ruinous balance of payment problems, and populations made uneasy by the specter of economy-wide downsizing, the rhetoric of a regional triumph took on a haunting ring.

Transformation, Cognition, and Representation

If there is one common trend that characterizes "Asia," it has to be the intense pace of transformation that the region is experiencing as a whole. Whether in Manila or Mumbai, Asians can barely keep up with the continual shifts in their realities: by the time they have some grasp over the situation, the ground has shifted again. Adrift in a world mutating at such an alarming rate, how do people make sense of their lives?

In the spatialized explications that dominate contemporary social theory,[8] such changes translate into a problem essentially of *locating* oneself subjectively in a complex social milieu. How do we map our world, and where do we fit into such a cognitive scheme? According to Fredric Jameson, the problem arises due to

> a growing contradiction between lived experience and structure, or
> between a phenomenological description of the life of an individual
> and a more properly structural model of the conditions of that
> experience.[9]

Jameson goes on to observe that as people's "lived experience" — their *lebenswelt* — keeps constantly slipping beyond their comprehension, the "structural coordinates are no longer accessible" and are often "not even conceptualizable" for most of them. How does one keep up with such dispersal, and how does one put up resistance? What forms of aesthetic representation are feasible and appropriate in this context?

For Jameson, the proper form of representation is *figuration*, which involves not a faithful mimetic copying of reality, but an attempt to comprehend the complex social relations that constitute the Real. In this scheme, all representations of reality will be inherently inadequate; in other words, the Real will always elude total cognition. In that sense, the Real remains an "absent cause" for our lived experiences. Figurations provide subjects with "imaginary solutions to real contradictions," or approximate maps that help them come to terms with the disjunctures and fragmentations in their lives.

Note the self-consciously abstract quality of such figurations or imaginary solutions; in this, they are similar to the literary category of the allegory. How does the allegorical relate to the notion of mapping? Cognitive maps or figurations may be seen as allegorical structures that attempt to produce an imaginary space, rather than a true (perfectly mimetic) representation of the Real. The relationship between such a map and reality is analogous to the relationship between a geographical map and the geographical space it represents; in either case, no "true" or "pure" map is possible.[10] Moreover, the imaginary space produced through such mapping operations is properly understood as a field of relations rather than an actual place. A mapping of Hong Kong, for instance, produces a figurative domain of material forces and social relations (Hong Kong as a cognitive space), not the actual city (Hong Kong as a place).[11]

The Realm of Popular Film Genres

In an earlier era, popular novels served as cultural arbiters of conflicts in people's daily lives, elucidating meaning and providing structure to their existence. Such arbitrations were carried out in generic settings, the relevance of tales being maintained through topical accommodations. Now that function of cultural negotiation is performed largely by popular films. In Hong Kong cinema, horror and martial arts have been the most popular, creative, and enduring genres.

Commentators often lament the untimely demise of the Hong Kong New Wave, which is supposed to have lasted from 1979 to the mid-1980s.[12] The standard estimation is that New Wave directors (most notably, Tsui Hark) sold out and focused their energies on producing generic films with strong box office potential. But Hong Kong cinema has remained vital well beyond the mid-1980s. Judging by the tremendous creative spurt it displayed in the early 1990s, it has remained topical, firmly grounded in its milieu, inventive in addressing sensitive subjects and in formal experimentations. If there is a difference, it is in the unabashedly populist tenor of the new films.

Indian cinema experienced similar transformations: compared to the Indian New Wave auteurs of the 1970s (Mani Kaul, Kumar Sahani, and Shyam Benegal), the filmmakers who came into prominence in the 1980s (Sai Paranjpye, Govind Nihalani, and Ketan Mehta) evince more accessible, audience-friendly styles. These directors practice what is often called "middle cinema"; they continue to make socially conscious films without eschewing the pleasure factor, in a vein closer to Bombay's *masala* products (exemplified in the works of Mammohan Desai, Yash Chopra, and Subhash Ghai). Underlying this shift is a recognition of the overarching importance of formulaic, commercial films in the quotidian lives of Indians.

In analyzing the role of popular cinema in the Indian milieu, Ashish Rajadhyaksha emphasizes the extent to which "Bollywood" films have been able to conjure up a "realm of belonging" that rivals the official Indian nation-state.[13] Ashis Nandy claims that commercial cinema reflects the implicit cultural values of the vast majority of Indians, not those of the cultural elite. Further, it

> romanticizes and, given half a chance, vulgarizes the problems of the survival sector, but it never rejects as childish or primitive the categories or worldviews of those trying to survive the processes of victimization let loose by modern institutions.[14]

I bring up Indian cinema because it bears some striking similarities to its Hong Kong counterpart. Both industries pitch their products primarily to audiences preoccupied with survival and upward mobility; both mediate worlds that boast of robust cultural traditions and yet keep changing, worlds in which people have to learn to cope with fresh traumas and to keep reinventing themselves. The negotiations between tradition and modernity supply the conflicts that primarily fuel the various film genres. The need for such mediations arises largely from the transnational circulation of Indian (in Africa and the Middle East) and Hong Kong (in Southeast Asia) films: diverse audiences have to be roped in, and their values and concerns need to be addressed. Both cinemas draw on narrative traditions that are rich in mythic components, elements that became more salient in the 1990s.

Swordplay

Martial arts films—*wuxia pian*—constitute one of the main genres within Hong Kong cinema. The mythic figure of the *xia* or wandering swordsman is inherently subversive: he evinces a contingent, provisional sense of justice and often comes into conflict with the law and the regime. Indeed, these chivalrous heroes are best understood as icons conjured up to be moral arbitrators in an anarchic, confusing world. The Hong Kong critic Ng Ho provides an interesting historical insight regarding the *xia*:

> The more chaotic the era, the greater the demand of the legendary *xia*. The popularity of the martial arts novels in the late Qing era

could probably be attributed to the intense longing for superhuman heroes strong enough to resist foreign aggression and to counter the repression of the Manchu government.[15]

Such an embedded understanding of the icon of the swordsman, related to social and political aspirations, may help us contextualize the remarkable revival of the subgenre of swordplay films in the 1990s.

After a period of relative dormancy in the 1970s, when *kungfu* (mainly unarmed combat) films dominated, swordplay films started making a comeback in the 1980s. In recent years they have reestablished themselves as one of the most popular subgenres, but in dizzyingly hybridized forms (as in the works of Tsui Hark, Yuen Kwai, Ching Siu-tung, and Raymond Lee). The typical swordplay film of the 1990s incorporates a whole range of martial art styles and evokes a magical, fantastic realm that can coexist with real, historical characters and situations. This interpenetration of the mythic and the historic, the fantastic and the realistic, is part of a postmodern turn that calls into question the very demarcations between these categories. As a result, the iconography of fighters flying through the air becomes acceptable as "realistic" in the context of these fabulous narratives.

Watching the *Swordsman* films of the early 1990s is often a breathtaking, reeling experience. The realities of the Hong Kong film industry partly account for the fast-paced quality, often bordering on incoherence: cutthroat competition and fears of video piracy necessitate rapid production under a tight schedule and prompt distribution.[16] But the films also intimate the vertiginous experience of history in the making. Ever since the Sino-British Joint Declaration of 1984, the countdown to the 1997 restitution of Hong Kong to mainland China has cast a shadow over every aspect of the territory's life. More generally, the ideas of capitalist expansion and modernization have been stretched beyond the modern all over Southeast Asia, producing a hypermodern realm in which the here-and-now is a leap into uncharted space and time. A reality that keeps churning and slipping away beyond the cognitive grasp of its inhabitants is likely to generate cultural responses marked by desperation, ambivalence, and abstractness. The return to the abstract world of martial arts and the recent generic transformations make sense when viewed against such a backdrop.

The intense creativity evident in the *Once Upon a Time in China [Huang Feihong]* series, the *Swordsman [Xiao'ao Jianghu]* trilogy, *Fong Sai-yuk [Fang Shiyu]* (1993), *Ashes of Time [Dong Xie Xi Du]* (1994), and *The Blade [Dao]* (1995) disproves the accounts of pervasive paranoia and resignation in the post–Tiananmen Square era. Perhaps it is more interesting to see any such paranoia and creativity not as antithetical, but as coexisting impulses: we can productively think of the 1990s as a period of transition, when the territory of Hong Kong faced a crisis of identity and its denizens responded by engaging culturally with the issues at stake in surprisingly creative ways. Indeed, these films reveal a spirited engagement with the crucial questions facing Hong Kong and a playing out of various anxieties at an allegorical level.

Encounter with Modernity: Postcolonial Takes

The *wuxia pian* of the 1990s takes on the function of mediating two inter-linked histories: China's encounter with modernity and its emergence as a nation. The *Once Upon a Time in China* series depicts its hero, Wong Fei-hung as a righteous martial artist, traditional healer, and champion lion dancer, who becomes the metonymic figure for China encountering moder-nity and the West. He learns to sift through what the West has to offer, elim-inating whatever does not suit his needs and worldview. The series manages simultaneously to criticize superstitious behavior and extol Chinese medici-nal practices like acupuncture. Many of the recent swordplay films reveal such discerning attitudes; their plots become postmodern negotiations of seemingly antithetical ideas such as tradition versus modernity.

Once Upon a Time in China I [Huang Feihong] (1991) presents mainly hu-morous confrontations: the traditional Chinese band and the "Hallelujah"-singing Christian missionaries try to drown each other out in the market-place, until they are both overwhelmed by the toot of the steamship (tradition and religion lose out to mercantile capitalism); the flashbulb of Aunt Thir-teen's foreign camera kills a pet bird in the marketplace; we hear "Yankee Doodle" at what looks like a vaudeville show, "The Battle Hymn of the Re-public" on the American ship, and Mozart in the colonial restaurant, where the waiters and doormen are all Indian.

Underlying the frivolity is an ominous tone (charges of white slavery, the murder of a European priest) that takes over in *Once Upon a Time in China II [Huang Feihong II: Nan'er Dang Ziqiang]* (1992). The confronta-tions become more serious: the fanatically nationalist White Lotus Clan goes around wreaking havoc and destroying everything Western. The Clan's ritu-alistic and superstitious ways are in direct contrast to Dr. Sun Yat-sen's insis-tence on building a nation through the amalgamation of classical Chinese knowledge and Western rationality. In a pivotal sequence, the British em-bassy in Canton becomes the refuge for progressive, anti–Qing dynasty Chi-nese forces. For Hong Kong audiences, these films are rich in local allusions

Figure 1.
Once Upon a Time in China II (Tsui Hark, 1992) evokes similarities between the White Lotus Clan and the anti-British riots of 1967 in Hong Kong.

Figure 2.
A fanatically nationalist White Lotus Clan wreaked havoc in *Once Upon a Time in China II*.

and inflections; take, for instance, the idea of a British space becoming a haven for people persecuted by the Chinese government, or the similarities between the excesses of the White Lotus Clan and the anti-British riots of 1967 in Hong Kong during the heyday of the Cultural Revolution.

In the *Swordsman* trilogy, produced around the same time as the *Huang Feihong* films, we find stronger anticolonial sentiments. The world of martial arts emerges as an abstract, philosophical space that is beyond the comprehension of Westerners. Mythical weapons and techniques (with names like "essence-absorbing stance" and "whirlwind blow") are pitted against Western scientific weaponry. The *xia* characters can catch the bullets fired from Western guns in their palms, rendering them harmless. The prayers of the Western priest—who is fearful of oriental spirits—cannot stop Asia, the transsexual warrior of the trilogy. After vanquishing the Spaniards, she declares that the biblical God is useless and should be replaced by her. Western categories are deployed to parody the West and to point to the limits of Western rationality.

Nationhood

The Nation and Its Fragments

Contemporary swordplay films often adopt an interrogating stance vis-à-vis the concept of a Chinese nation. *Fong Sai-yuk* plays up the regional differences between Canton and the rest of China. The merchant Tiger Lu, who speaks a different dialect, is depicted as an outsider in Canton—all his wealth cannot shield him from the derision and ridicule of the townspeople. The cocky merchant arouses ambivalent feelings: while his attempts to buy up the town mark him as an intruder, his refugee status elicits sympathy. His ultimate humiliation by imperial forces struck a chord in Hong Kong audiences; many of them had run away from a coercive regime and made a new life for themselves, only to face the prospect of another round of political and economic persecution.

The *Swordsman* trilogy points to the marginalization of minorities that becomes an intrinsic part of attempts by hegemonic groups to forge unity. *The Swordsman II [Xiao'ao Jianghu II Dongfang Bubai]* (1992) focuses on the highlander clans, who, oppressed by the Han people, occupied a subaltern position in imperial China. Asia the Invincible, who belongs to the Sun and Moon sect of highlanders, learns martial arts from the sacred scrolls and gains supernatural abilities by castrating himself. She/he unites the highlanders with exiled Japanese—fleeing persecution at home—in a transnational coalition of the oppressed. Thus a hope for transnational unity is articulated from a subnational, subaltern level, calling into question the absolute dominance of the national as a category of political organization. Interestingly, the diegesis takes place at the point in history when the weakest of all Han peoples—the Ming dynasty—was in power. The film registers the possibility that all regimes and dominant groups are vulnerable to incursions by the oppressed.

The Question of Power

Power emerges as a major concern in many recent films, particularly in those associated with Tsui Hark in his various capacities as producer, director, and screenwriter. The *Swordsman* films present a dystopic vision of the world

Figure 3.
Swordsman III: The East Is Red; Ching Siu-tung and Raymond Lee, 1993) may be read as a cautionary tale of transnational alliances.

torn asunder by vicious power struggles; the cynical outlook is reflected in lines like "There is no justice: power defines the truth." Battles rage not just between traditional enemies such as the Hans and the highlanders, but also within each group. The trilogy seems to suggest that power corrupts all political movements, irrespective of their original intent. Even regional coalitions, aiming to destabilize established hegemonic patterns, are likely to end in bitter squabbles.

It is possible to read these films as cautionary tales of transnational alliances. New regional leagues often become ways of reconfiguring geopolitical hegemonies; hence the recent mobilization of pan-Asian rhetoric has to be carefully evaluated. After all, the two significant pan-Asian movements of this century have been spearheaded by Japanese imperialism (with its promise of common prosperity) and Chinese communism (with its rhetoric of a common resistance to capitalist exploitation). Moreover, roving mercenaries are some of the most powerful figures in recent films; perhaps they stand in for the new transnational corporations, which operate without strong affiliations to any particular nation[17] and whose brand of exploitative transnationalism is often mistakenly lauded as post-statist progress.

Lacerations of the Body Politic

The tropes of physical amputation and castration in films like *Swordsman II* and *Blade* exemplify how apprehension about the future relations among the People's Republic of China, Taiwan, and Hong Kong works its way into

cultural forms. In the *Swordsman* series, Asia is castrated, disorienting her/
his followers and lovers. With a proliferation of impostors Asia's identity gets
obscured, producing confusion even in her/his own mind.[18] Caught in the
web of her/his own transgressions, she/he becomes more aggressive and
ruthless: after vanquishing the Spaniards she/he declares herself/himself
"Asia and Europe the Invincible." Often such plot twists are indirect invocations of a crisis in national identity and of contemporary political tensions,
especially the fear of forcible unification. Castration alludes not just to the
crisis of a partitioned China but also to the West's conception of Asia as
feminine, spiritual, and mysterious. At another level, the castration may be
interpreted as the abandonment by the various Asian nations of their avowed
socioeconomic policies and their capitulation to the West's schemes for a
global economic order. Similarly, it is possible to appreciate *Blade* as an allegory for surviving the historical truncation of the country: the protagonist
loses his right arm in battle and learns to fight with only one arm. We can
also read the film as a narrative of the constant struggle to overcome the
trauma induced by a mutating world. The one-armed hero relearns fighting,
using his father's broken sword and following a half-burnt manual. Improvi-
sation and reconstitution become essential strategies of survival under conditions of duress.

Unruly Allegories

The *wuxia pian* of the last decade is characterized by expressionist stylistics
that convey a sense of breathless pace and dizzying energy: the camera movements and editing have become faster; the angles are more askew, the special
effects more spectacular; and there is a fascination with cross dressing and
gender bending as part of the heightened emphasis on sheer performativity.
As Li Cheuk-to puts it, recent Hong Kong films evince a "no-holds-barred approach to action, gags, and stirring up emotions, even to the point of loss of
control and total overload."[19] The evolving hyperstyle of the genre is in keeping with the hypermodern world, where everyone is always trying to outpace
everyone else.

Taking my cue from their formal and stylistic excesses, I propose that we
read these texts allegorically. But such a reading strategy does not seek to reclaim martial arts films as modernist texts, with self-conscious strategies for
articulating social contradictions. The complex forms, the dizzying styles
cannot be reduced wholly to modernist inventions, as they verge on "the
point of loss of control and total overload." What needs to be read allegori-

cally is this excessive trait that is beyond the planned, that remains largely intuitive. Xudong Zhang, who has adopted an allegorical reading strategy to interpret reform-era films from mainland China, maintains that Chinese filmmakers employed modernist film forms to articulate developments that they could not fully grasp, an approach that also helped in the international art house circulation of their works.[20] Commercial Hong Kong cinema evinces no such determinate modernist strategy: it is far more incoherently eclectic, prompting commentators with a modernist hangover to find its output lacking in comparison to the "superior" new cinemas of mainland China (the Fifth Generation directors) and Taiwan (such as Edward Yang and Hou Hsiao-hsien).[21]

Indeed, recent martial arts films have a distinctly absurd or hysterical quality about them. In this, they become allegories of their context: anxieties over the new economic realities, the effects on social and cultural life, and the emerging political alignments are played out onscreen with hysterical abandonment. Hysteria often executes a parodic function against repressive social structures. In this case, the historical structures are being threatened by emergent ones that cannot be grasped and articulated easily. This constellation of ever-shifting grids is found to be oppressive in its effect; hence it becomes the object of parodic criticism. Unable to imagine the new structures adequately, the films articulate the anxieties by parodic repetitions of symbolic structures (myths).

One significant characteristic of these allegories is that they are often incomplete. The films abound in metaphoric allusions and metonymic figurations that are abandoned midway. The tentative, conjectural tenor of my interpretations in the previous section arises in part from this incompleteness of the texts. The result is a cornucopia of fleeting references that remain largely facetious. Nevertheless, they speak with a sense of urgency to local audiences and provide a forum for popular debates. As Tony Rayns points out, "The comparisons are too flip and facetious to amount to serious political comment, but the Hong Kong audience is quick to pick up the resonances."[22] What I am arguing is not that local audiences have a shared, overarching understanding of these intemperate and fragmented narratives, but that even cursory and loose allusions may enjoy some specific significance— if only in a diffuse way—in the local public sphere.[23]

The films are also incoherent, a fact that is reflected in the frequent suspension of the parodic stance in favor of nostalgia for older times and traditional values (such as chivalry and righteousness). Nostalgia becomes a collective strategy for weathering the maelstrom of change. What is really interesting is that the same film can exhibit both a parodic function and a nostalgic investment, giving rise to a form of schizophrenic incoherence. This incoherence sets martial arts films of the last decade apart from their classical counterparts.

The provisional nature of these allegories reflects the impossibility of mapping an accelerating reality in which the ground rules keep changing. The people of the region are finding their own cultural strategies — playful, excessive, schizophrenic — to deal with their disorientation. Jameson, with his interest in totalized mapping, pathologizes this schizophrenia and laments the lack of a historical consciousness.[24] I would argue that a very different kind of historical consciousness is at work in Asia and the Pacific, one that admits the possibility of overlapping temporalities and spatial imaginations and that finds expression in unruly allegories.

Hysterical Materialism or Hysteria as Materialist Resistance

Writing about postmodernity, Jean Baudrillard describes the dual processes of the "forced extroversion of all interiority" and the "forced injection of all exteriority."[25] On the one hand, "the most intimate processes of our life become the virtual feeding ground of the media"; on the other, "the entire universe comes to unfold arbitrarily on your domestic screen."[26] This condition, which he calls "obscene," marks the end of all "scenes," as there is nothing "hidden, repressed, forbidden and obscure."[27] Here he is claiming that the hidden scenes of psychoanalysis — always the source of trauma — are now out in the open. Since the structures have become visible, Baudrillard maintains that the "drama of alienation" is also over.

However, information overload does not necessarily imply deep comprehension: even when everything is all too visible, the structures may not be discernible. Indeed, from a materialist perspective, the "drama of alienation" is far from over. Jameson, for instance, points to alienation arising from the lack of a full cognitive grasp of reality.

Baudrillard does concur with Jameson in one important respect: both present pathological takes on schizophrenia, although they start from different perspectives. Baudrillard's assumption of the end of alienation leads him to claim:

> No more hysteria, no more projective paranoia, properly speaking, but this state of terror proper to the schizophrenic: too great a proximity of everything, the unclean promiscuity of everything which

touches, invests and penetrates without resistance, with no halo of private protection.[28]

Here Baudrillard leaves real historical subjects no way of dealing with reality. It is not that the real is lost to the schizophrenic subject; rather, it inhabits and "traverses him [*sic*] without obstacle." As a result, "[h]e can no longer produce the limits of his own being, can no longer play or stage himself, can no longer produce himself as mirror."[29] I find this description convincing to a certain extent: postmodern conditions do problematize the production of the "limits" of our "being." But is that problem necessarily deleterious?[30]

For Baudrillard, such disorientation entails schizophrenia — pathological fragmentation — as a negative psychic effect. However, it is possible to imagine a more optimistic scenario: resistance through hysteria (as in the readings by the French feminists of Dora's case).[31] Baudrillard defines the condition as "the pathology of the exacerbated staging of the subject, a pathology of expression, of the body's theatrical and operatic conversion."[32] If alienation or the incomprehension of totality plunges one into realms of excess, then hysteria — as a play of excess — becomes another possible psychic effect. The accentuated performativity of recent Hong Kong martial arts films — their hysterical abandon — makes sense in such a framework.

Concluding Remarks

In this essay I propose that, in the absence of a clear cognitive grasp of the vast transformations of their lives, many Asians turn to generic narratives and mythic structures to make sense — allegorically — of their lived experiences. As a formalist, Jameson laments the slippage of representation into "sheer theme and content" in generic texts.[33] I argue that it is not just at the level of thematics, but also in their form and style, that recent martial arts films coming out of Hong Kong allegorize the contemporary situation in that part of the world.

I have presented a reading of recent martial arts films as hysterical texts, imploding under the burden of multiple anxieties. By their very hysterical nature, these texts resist totalized readings. The hysteric thematically exposes the limit of structures; in a world of disconcertingly rapid changes, in the absence of coherent structures, old symbolic structures become the target of parody. In the process, any emergent structure is also contested. While the anxieties are played out at a mythic register, the performativity can produce real affect (comfort) because of the nebulous borders between the real and the figural.

One could argue that the incoherence and the hysteria result in part from the imperatives of a postmodern cinema. Hong Kong cinema is a highly competitive industry that requires rapid production under a tight schedule. The giddy generic spinoffs are shaped as much by the dictates of the marketplace as by any proclivity for critical parody.

The commercial success that Hong Kong martial arts films enjoy all over East and Southeast Asia points to their ability to tap into certain common concerns. Surely people's experiences in various parts of the region are marked by local differences; yet, these genre films seem attuned to certain commonalities in their structures of feeling in the wake of similarly destabilizing changes. Notions of a pan-Asian sensibility — even identity — gain credence from such evidence, although local differences rule out the unproblematic celebration of these kinds of transnational conceptions. How the particular texts are received or decoded, what place they occupy in popular discourse, and what kinds of intensity and pleasure they generate in different milieux remain a rich area of study.

Notes

This paper would not have materialized without the help of Chia-chi Wu. I am also indebted to Bishnupriya Ghosh, David James, Roland Tolentino, and especially Esther Yau for their suggestions and feedback.

1 Of course, in the aftermath of the economic and financial crises of 1998, these Asian megalopolises have experienced a pronounced deceleration in growth, unambiguously intimated by plummeting real estate values. More on this slowdown below.

2 These might include interesting, hip, smart, most excellent.

3 My friends who are native inhabitants of Hong Kong and Taipei tell me that these films are often described in popular discourse as hysterical.

4 For instance, the cover of the 19 May 1997 issue of *Newsweek* showed a Chinese (presumably Hong Kong) model blindfolded with a Chinese flag, with the caption "China Takes Over: Can Hong Kong Survive?" The issue goes on to harp on the "ring of romance" that marks the hype around "the End of Empire" (3); it characterizes Hong Kong as "one of the world's freest places" and China as "a nation in transition, but hardly free," and then opines conclusively that "6 million people will be placed on the wrong side of the fence" (32). The tenor of the cover story is encapsulated in the recurring speculation about China's "true face" (30), whether it can be "truly trusted" (3).

5 Indeed, in the post-handover dog days of 1997, I noted with mordant postcolonial satisfaction that the cityscape of Hong Kong was fading fast behind mug shots of

the serial killer Andrew Cunanan, who became a household name by murdering the fashion designer Gianni Versace.

6 In a sense, I was born displaced. Years before my birth, with the 1947 partition of India, my family had to abandon its ancestral home in East Bengal and move to Calcutta in West Bengal as refugees.

7 See Mark Borthwick, *Pacific Century: The Emergence of Modern Pacific Asia* (Boulder, Colo.: Westview Press, 1992); Masao Miyoshi, "A Borderless World? From Colonialism to Transnationalism and the Decline of the Nation-State," *Critical Inquiry* 19 (summer 1992); Arif Dirlik, ed., *What Is in a Rim? Critical Perspectives on the Pacific Region Idea* (Boulder, Colo.: Westview Press, 1993).

8 Edward Soja, *Postmodern Geographies: The Reassertion of Space in Critical Social Theory* (London: Verso, 1989); Arjun Appadurai, "Disjuncture and Difference in the Global Cultural Economy," *Public Culture* 2, no. 2 (1990): 1–23.

9 Fredric Jameson, "Cognitive Mapping," in *Marxism and the Interpretation of Culture*, ed. Cary Nelson and Lawrence Grossberg (Urbana: University of Illinois Press, 1988), 349.

10 Robert Tally Jr., "Jameson's Project of Cognitive Mapping: A Critical Engagement," in *Social Cartography: Mapping Ways of Seeing Social and Educational Change*, ed. Rolland Paulston (New York: Garland, 1996), 405–6.

11 On cognitive mapping, see Jameson, "Cognitive Mapping"; Colin MacCabe, preface to Fredric Jameson, *The Geopolitical Aesthetic: Cinema and Space in the World System* (Bloomington: Indiana University Press, 1992); Crystal Bartolovich, "Mapping the Spaces of Capital," in Paulston, *Social Cartography*, esp. 380–81.

12 See, e.g., the opening paragraph of Li Cheuk-to, "The Return of the Father: Hong Kong New Wave and Its Chinese Context in the 1980s," in *New Chinese Cinemas: Forms, Identities, Politics*, ed. Nick Browne et al. (Cambridge: Cambridge University Press, 1994), 160–79.

13 Ashish Rajadhyaksha, introduction to Rajadhyaksha and Paul Willemen, *Encyclopaedia of Indian Cinema* (New Delhi: Oxford University Press, 1994), 10.

14 Ashis Nandy, "An Intelligent Critic's Guide to Indian Cinema," in *The Savage Freud and Other Essays on Possible and Retrievable Selves* (Princeton: Princeton University Press, 1995), 203.

15 Ng Ho, "*Jiang Hu* Revisited: Towards a Reconstruction of the Martial Arts World," in *A Study of the Hong Kong Swordplay Film (1945–1980)*, Fifth Hong Kong International Film Festival (Hong Kong: Urban Council, 1981), 84.

16 According to Tony Rayns, "A fortnight from the close of the shooting to the premiere is quite usual"; see Rayns, "Hard Boiled," *Sight and Sound* 12, no. 4 (August 1992): 20.

17 See Miyoshi, "A Borderless World?"

18 Interestingly, several other characters are marked by vacillation and duplicity: Swordsman Ling is never sure of his retirement from the world of martial arts; the ninja general turns out to be of dubious origins; Snow has to take on the identity of her lover.

19 Li Cheuk-to, "Tsui Hark and Western Interest in Hong Kong Cinema," *Cinemaya* 21 (autumn 1993): 51.

20 Xudong Zhang, *Chinese Modernism in the Era of Reforms: Cultural Fever, Avant-Garde Fiction, and the New Chinese Cinema* (Durham, N.C.: Duke University Press, 1997).

21 See, e.g., the opening paragraph of Li Cheuk-to, "The Return of the Father: Hong Kong New Wave and Its Chinese Context in the 1980s," in Browne et al., *New Chinese Cinemas*, 160–79. To continue the comparison with Indian cinema, we may recall the international reception of Satyajit Ray's films, and the simultaneous dismissal of even the most successful commercial directors as people who lack command over "film language," since they do not follow either of its two "standard" versions (Hollywood and modernist idioms).

22 Rayns, "Hard Boiled," 21.

23 With Tsui Hark's films, sections of the narrative may be as incomprehensible to Hong Kong audiences as they are to European or American audiences, in which case this local/foreign or inner/outer dichotomy in terms of audience does not really work. Then the *form* becomes more important: what do we have to learn from the "content of the form" of these inscrutable texts?

24 Fredric Jameson, "Postmodernism, or the Cultural Logic of Late Capitalism," *New Left Review* 146 (July–August 1984): 53–92.

25 Jean Baudrillard, "The Ecstasy of Communication," in *The Anti-Aesthetic: Essays on Postmodern Culture*, ed. Hal Foster (Seattle: Bay Press, 1983), 132.

26 Ibid., 130.

27 Baudrillard writes: "We are no longer a part of the drama of alienation; we live in the ecstasy of communication. And this ecstasy is obscene. It is no longer the obscenity of what is hidden, repressed, forbidden or obscure; on the contrary, it is the obscenity of the visible, of the all-too-visible, of the more-visible-than-the-visible. It is the obscenity of what no longer has any secret, of what dissolves completely in information and communication." Ibid., 130–31.

28 Ibid., 132.

29 Ibid., 133.

30 Here I have in mind criticisms of standard Western rationality and the Enlightenment model of Man. It is possible to learn from postmodern problematizations of the production of rigid boundaries of the self and to imagine new notions of identity and community. Feminists have provided some pointers in this direction, as have philosophers such as Immanuel Levinas and Giorgio Agamben.

31 See Jane Gallop, *The Daughter's Seduction: Feminism and Psychoanalysis* (Ithaca: Cornell University Press, 1982).

32 Baudrillard, "The Ecstasy of Communication," 132.

33 Jameson, "Cognitive Mapping," 356.

CHAPTER EIGHT

Women on the Edges of Hong Kong Modernity:
The Films of Ann Hui

Elaine Yee-lin Ho

The career and films of Ann On-wah Hui over the past three decades have inscribed the transitional history of Hong Kong cinema from domination by imported English-language and Mandarin films to the production of a corpus of indigenous-language films of artistic quality and merit. Hui herself has, in turn, acted to bring this history into being. In significant ways, this cinematic history bears witness to a critical juncture in Hong Kong's recent history: a rapid urbanization that radically redrew the physical and socio-cultural contours of the territory; the emergence of an indigenous middle-class elite, newly aware and confident of itself and largely oriented to local issues and concerns; and the domination of bourgeois aspirations toward material well-being among a majority of those who had yet to share the territory's growing prosperity. Ann Hui, who made thirteen films between 1979 and 1996, is the only woman filmmaker of her generation to have been consistently active in Hong Kong cinema.[1]

A number of systemic features, underpinned and guaranteed by continuous economic growth, characterize Hong Kong's recent modernity. British colonialism nurtured, in both conscious and unconscious ways, the identification of modernity with Western forms of bureaucratic and institutional management and the embrace of Western technology, despite the fact that the colonial administration, backed by the local elite, was averse to the development of Anglo-American forms of democratic politics. A Westernized and increasingly technologized corporate culture began to make significant inroads into the inherited cultural traditions and practices of the majority Cantonese population in Hong Kong and to be manifest at all cultural levels. The continuous negotiation of contact and conflict between the imported and the inherited, local and Western, became the quotidian reality of Hong Kong. The myriad forms that such negotiation took not only left indelible marks on the physical landscape but also generated the push toward a Hong Kong cultural identity in which entrepreneurial brinkmanship and flexibility, as much as a sense of in-betweenness and unbelonging, are writ large.

Ann Hui's education and training as a filmmaker show a distinctly Westernized orientation characteristic of the middle-class generation that came of age in the 1960s. After completing her undergraduate and master's degree studies in English and comparative literature at the University of Hong Kong, she enrolled in the London Film School.[2] But right from the start of her cinematic career in 1979, her films attempted recurrently to distance, dislocate, and disrupt the corporate push toward economic success, Western lifestyles, and technology that characterizes Hong Kong's modernity. In configuring cinema as critical practice, Hui's optic frequently turns to the forms of inherited Chinese cultural life as they endure in Hong Kong and to Chinese history framed by Hong Kong's location on the temporal and spatial edge of two empires. This "Chineseness," mediated by a Hong Kong vantage point, constitutes the counterdiscourse to modernity in Hui's films. But Hui's ethnic scenes and narratives are never merely celebratory, or triumphalist, or nativist and retrogressive. In composing them, she shows the same hesitation and anxiety that characterize her doubtful reception of modernity.

Looking both to the West and to Chinese traditions, Hui visualizes the complex transactions of modernity and countermodernity out of which Hong Kong's cultural identity develops its special features. She has a sharp eye for contest and conflict; in her narrative and visual thematics, she remembers the voices, scenes, and rituals that are marginalized and suppressed, at times conjuring the phantasms of what modernity has interred. Her films make visible a critical social discourse that has to contest, often in unequal combat, with the corporate momentum toward a Westernized and technologized modernity under colonial patronage. Hui and her contemporaries in the Hong Kong New Wave cinema, Tsui Hark and Alex Cheung, whose first films appeared in 1979, were not the first in Hong Kong filmmaking to think of cinema as a social medium.[3] What distinguished their films was an intense reflexiveness about forms of cultural identity that were recognizably local but subsumed by the dominant bourgeois imaginary. Hui's early films symptomatize the discontent of her generation, with its nascent consciousness of a so-called Hong Kong identity hybridizing inherited Chinese and imported Western characteristics, but that also places itself against the glamorized spectacles of economic success and social advancement that dominate official and commercial media. In a public sphere heavily, if never overtly, regulated by colonial censorship laws, and with civil society yet unformed and thus absent, the New Wave cinema directors assumed the mantle of cultural workers, chiseling and mining at the edges of Hong Kong's modernity, locating fissures where they existed and bringing them into public view.

Like her New Wave contemporaries, Hui began her career not in local film studios but in television. After returning to Hong Kong from London, she first worked for Television Broadcasting Limited (TVB), where she shot a few travel programs, then moved on to the government-funded Radio Television Hong Kong (RTHK). In its conscious, if not overt, inculcation of civic values and the concept of a Hong Kong identity and community, RTHK really came into its own in the 1970s. The three RTHK docudramas of the period — *Social Worker [Beidou Xing]*, *Below the Lion Rock [Shizi Shanxia]*, and *ICAC [Lianzheng Gongchu]* (ICAC is the acronym for the Independent Commission Against Corruption, set up in 1974) — put into circulation the images of Hong Kong's "progress" from a refugee haven to a distinctive social system in which both inherited Chinese values and modern institutional management work hand in hand under the guidance of colonial rule. Within the constraints of its institutional role, RTHK did try to present itself as critical and pluralistic and, as such, modeled itself on the British Broadcasting Corporation (BBC), against the Americanized TVB. Like the BBC, RTHK had always claimed autonomy from the government in its programming decisions and did not adopt the overtly propagandist agenda evident in other state-sponsored media in the region. In its attempts to constitute Hong Kong as what Benedict Anderson (1991) has called an "imagined" and "communicative" community, its cautious tolerance of criticism and dissent generated a quasi-public sphere blurring the boundaries between government and civil society. In this respect, it departs from other state media in the region, which are driven by unitary functions to the exclusion of difference (Dissanayake 1994, xii–xxi).

But while it offers the simulacrum of a diversified public sphere, RTHK has to operate within the government's censorship powers, which are wide ranging.[4] Ann Hui's own productions for RTHK were subject to censorship. "The Bridge" ["Qiao"], in the series *Below the Lion Rock*, was nearly held back for its perceived criticism of the policy and bureaucracy of the Housing Authority, and two of the *ICAC* episodes she made in 1977 were actually banned because they supposedly attacked the police and civil servants. Hui had never explicitly connected her move from television to cinema with these experiences of censorship, but a cynicism about governmental and quasi-official institutions permeates her first film, *The Secret [Feng Jie]*, and works in tandem with its broader critique of colonial modernity. As a woman filmmaker, Hui quickly established herself as a pioneer in a profession monopolized by men; as a social critic, her films centralize and individualize women subjects in ways that the earlier Cantonese cinema had rarely attempted.

Drawing their inspiration from the aesthetics of Western avant-garde filmmaking and their audience from a burgeoning young middle class, Hui's films, like those of the New Wave cinema, broke decisively with the Cantonese-language films of the past. In the poverty and privation of the 1950s and early 1960s, realist Cantonese cinema was the main source of entertainment for the majority working-class population, while the more affluent preferred imported English-language or Mandarin films. There is no question that this cinema was replete with stereotypes of women, but in their representations of women's subordination they spoke to the realities of women incapacitated by a patriarchal culture of labor and by the complicity of Chinese patriarchy with colonial rule and economy.[5] During this period, studios with left-wing affiliations, while still technically conservative, also produced films that tried to critique women's victimization, and it is in these productions, rare though they may have been, that the emergence of women's countercultural agency was best visualized.[6] But in the aftermath of the 1967 riots, many of those who worked in the left-wing studios were either imprisoned or joined the commercial television stations, and the profession as a whole witnessed, as a constituent of Hong Kong's structural transformation, the defeat of an incipient socialist modernity.[7]

The tentative visualizations of socially progressive female figures in left-wing cinema disappeared as the commercially productive but ideologically conservative media moved into public consciousness, fueling and communicating the dominant work ethic of early modern and capitalistic Hong Kong. During this period women continued to receive less pay than men, and their dependent, subordinate, and at best supportive roles in both the family and the workplace were taken for granted not only by men, but often by the women themselves. Veronica Pearson and Benjamin Leung (1995) have delineated the three mutually supporting reasons for women's low sociocultural status:

Gender inequality in Hong Kong is intricately related to and sustained by several distinct features of the society: it is a predominantly Chinese society; it is a British colony; and it is a capitalist economy whose well-being has been heavily dependent on low labor costs enabling its exports to compete successfully in overseas markets. . . . These three dimensions interrelate in providing the context in which individual women in Hong Kong seek to play out the script of their lives, and in which they search for meaning to their experience. (4)

Patriarchal control underpinned and integrated inherited Chinese, colonial, and capitalistic cultures, circumscribing and defining individual woman subjects and their places in early modern Hong Kong. An emergent Hong Kong cultural identity that hybridized Chinese and Western cultural elements was unmarked by gender consciousness until the women's movement in Hong Kong took shape and gathered momentum in the 1980s.[8]

The New Wave filmmakers were beneficiaries of early modern Hong Kong, which had produced a small but growing middle-class cinemagoing public like themselves. As such, the social and critical discourse in the films of Hui and her New Wave contemporaries could not avoid inflection by the bourgeois paradigm itself. One of the strongest signs of this inflection in Hui's early films is the way in which women subjects continue to figure as subordinate to men or as victims of patriarchal domination, or to define their identity exclusively by romance.[9] The complex interiority of these women subjects and their spectacular visuality coexist in uneasy conjunction with narratives that by and large rehearse their traditional discontents.

In her public statements, Hui has denied time and again that she is either political or interested in women's subjects and feminist issues.[10] Her earlier projects exemplify the gender blindness that underpins Robin Wood's claim, made two decades ago, that for the cinema director and critic "to 'live' historically need not entail commitment to a system or a cause; rather, it can involve being alive to the opposing pulls, the tensions, of one's world" (1977, 46). In these earlier films, Hui's preoccupation with the cultural contestation that underlines everyday or topical events, though often focalized by women protagonists, tends to neglect issues involving women and gender. This neglect can be seen as a sign of the incorporative power of capitalistic discourse in Hong Kong's early modernity: Hui's insightful mappings of the fissures of modernity fail to take into account the continued sociocultural inequalities that afflict women both at home and in the workplace and that underpin industrial production and economic progress.

In Hui's more recent films, there is a very noticeable difference, and it can be said that these films have taken a distinctly feminist turn. The focus on woman's history and agency in these recent films imbricates an urgent political self-recognition that complicates and transforms Hui's earlier critique of modernity. Through visual narratives of women's histories and subjective transformations, these films fracture the patriarchal determinations of old and also chart recognizable passages toward a horizon of the "modern" in which utopian ideals of equality, compassion, and sociality are never lost sight of.[11] In relocating women, Hui's more recent films also renew the inspiration of modernity when its achievements, at a critical historical moment in Hong Kong, seem to be under particular threat from the resurgence of essentialistic ethnic rhetoric and ethnocultural orthodoxies. At moments of existential and ontological crisis, these female figures speak to the cultural and political instability that has afflicted Hong Kong in the passage to 1997. It is a significant aspect of these recent films that in narrating women's struggle to become autonomous subjects, Hui invokes the past in order to mobilize its energies in the present; often these energies are visualized as disruptive, and at times they develop fearful tyrannical power, but in mobilizing them, the films also focus and refocus on the possible sources of cultural change and renewal within Chinese ethnic traditions and practices.

To substantiate the claims I have made, I will in the next section explore in detail four of Hui's films: the first, *The Secret* (1979); *Princess Fragrance* [*Xiangxiang Gongzhu*] (1987), from her middle period; and the later films, *Song of the Exile* [*Ketu Qiuhen*] (1990) and *Summer Snow* [*Nuren Sishi*] (1995). This detailed exploration is crucial in order not to simplify and reduce the films to transparent social records of changes in women's situation in Hong Kong during the past two decades. The films are not merely cinematic texts foregrounded by a larger contextual backdrop; they are in themselves cultural documents that fuel the dynamics of Hong Kong culture as much as they draw on such dynamics for inspiration and energy. Mediatized and widely circulated, they have significant visibility and, in turn, make visible certain complex transactions of women in society, enabling them to enter into dialogue with other contemporaneous cultural narratives and discourses. In the 1990s, the dominant tendency of studies on women and gender in Hong Kong, at least in sociological discourse, is linear and progressivist, moving from earlier moments, when women's issues and the women's movement were hardly visible and received scant attention in the public sphere, through the critical massing of women's groups, to their current vigorous participation in both the public sphere and civil society.[12] My selection and discussion of Hui's films, in the main, map onto this modernist narrative. But through detailed studies of the films, I also wish to show how Hui delineates the woman question in different locations, and how the changes in her artistic optic enact the falterings and disruptions of the modernist narrative.

WOMEN ON THE EDGES OF HONG KONG MODERNITY | 183

The Secret, set in Hong Kong in 1970, is based on the murder of a couple whose defaced and mutilated bodies were found on a deserted hillside frequented by monkeys. The sensationalized reports in the local press contained hints of simian interference. Seizing on the topicality of the murder, Hui shoots the film as docudrama but focuses her narrative through the juxtaposition of two women figures, Yuan, the apparent murder victim, and Ming, her friend, who takes on the role of detective. Since the murdered woman is discovered wearing Yuan's clothes, both the police and her family assume that Yuan has been killed together with her fiancé, Cheuk. Before long Yuan's ghost starts to haunt the neighborhood; and while it thoroughly unnerves others in the community, Ming initiates an investigation that leads to the discovery that Yuan is still alive and in hiding. Ming uncovers Yuan's predicament as the third point of a triangulated relationship with Cheuk and another woman, a ballroom hostess, and Yuan's culpability in the murder that necessitates her feigned death and ghostly return. The last violent sequence in the film revisits the clearing in the wood where Ming has finally located Yuan, heavily pregnant with Cheuk's child. The film cuts from the present confrontation of the two friends to flashbacks of the murder, in which the ballroom hostess, enraged by Cheuk's decision to abandon her for Yuan, runs him through with a long barbecue fork and is in turn struck repeatedly with a stone by Yuan. Yuan, by now completely unhinged by the murder and her fugitive existence, turns on Ming. Only through the timely intervention of an old woman who lives near the crime scene is Ming saved and Yuan able to give birth to her child before her own exhausted death.

Yuan is figured as the traditional Chinese woman, suffering, silenced, the victim of patriarchal sexuality, while Ming seems to embody her modern antithesis, active and self-determined. Through this superficial juxtaposition, the film excavates the subterranean dynamic of modernity and countermodernity and the way in which the interlocking of the two frames women's subjectivities.

Yuan's spectral return, which provides the film with some of its most gothic and visually spectacular sequences, is linked with scenes of the necromantic rituals of her blind grandmother. Immobilized within a room, restrictive and claustrophobic in its gloominess, the old woman strikes a figure of maternal loss and desolation whose only recourse to action is through an atavistic spiritualism. But the film also suggests, through the reaction of the other characters in the neighborhood, that the old woman's necromancy has invoked Yuan's return, and the first hints of Yuan's haunting of her home community come through the old woman's report that she has felt her granddaughter's presence in the room. Through Yuan and her grand-mother, Hui visualizes a specific bond between women that fuses the ties of blood with their inherited roles as bearers of an ethnic Chinese primitivism that is marginalized, repressed, and rendered invisible by the city's moder-nity, but that continues to structure the life of women, of the old, and of the small backwater community in which they live. As Yuan's alter ego, Ming seems to have moved away, at least partially, from this community of women and the sub-urban space it occupies, and in her investigation she operates in the quotidian and apparently transparent spaces of modern institutions and discourses — hospitals and forensic and police procedures. Unlike the female detectives of earlier Cantonese cinema, who are frequently endowed with superhuman cognition and martial expertise, Ming appears in the mode of the Western detective, acting within the bounds of human and everyday possibilities, motivated by curiosity but remaining detached and objective even as she is drawn deeper and deeper into the mystery of her friend's sup-posed death.

The recurrent site of narrative action is composed in frames of a group of prewar buildings in an older quarter where both Yuan and Ming live. "Home," as the film signifies, is the in-between cultural space on the fringes of urban modernity where primordial significations continue to circulate. Their presence is invoked in ritual, spectralized as haunting, and symptom-atized in the inhabitants' fearful reaction to Yuan's ghostly revenance. As the film's visualization of Hong Kong, this home space clearly departs from the celebratory images of the colony thrust into public consciousness by the official media and the predominantly glossy exteriors of the commercial cinema.[13] In another spatial configuration in the film's narrative, this home community is intermediate between two alternative visual locations: the clearing in the wood where the bodies were found, which in the film's flash-backs figures as the primitive space of ritualistic sacrifice, and the hospital and police station, which signify modern institutional spaces. Yuan's self-consuming desire for Cheuk and her submission to his chauvinistic fantasy lead to her communal exile and the ultimate alienation of being an outcast in the land of the dead. Ming's move away to the modern institutional spaces shown in the film to be controlled mainly by men is highly circumscribed by their lack of interest, if not their outright hostility. The women's dislocations imply the gradual fragmentation of the home space and, by further implica-tion, of a traditional Hong Kong within the orbit of residual, and decadent, ethnic Chinese archaisms. But the film also eschews the bright-light images of modern urbanization, and the film's spatiality, with respect to the space of

Figure 1.
The Secret (Ann Hui,
1979) depicts maternal
loss and desolation in
claustrophobic spaces
haunted by the spectral
return of dead persons.

woman and of the home, is tinged overall with a gloomy indeterminacy that signals woman's social disaffiliation and subliminal derangement as subjects, as well as Hong Kong in its passage through an ambivalent modernity.

In the final sequence of the film, Ming is saved, not through her own actions, but by the intervention of an old woman who lives in an isolated shack nearby. The appearance of this old woman has been prepared for in earlier scenes, where she hysterically protests against the arrest of her idiot son, whom the police originally believe to be the murderer. Her hysteria, which contrasts with the silent isolation of Yuan's grandmother, speaks of an alternative and quasi-anarchic maternalism that the film projects as awesome and transgressive. If Yuan and Ming are coopted, in their different ways, into the film's ambivalent modernity, the two maternal figures present women subjects whose resistance to the "modern" has cast them into extreme marginality. Both maternal figures appear to have privileged access to primitive forces that endure at the very edges of the city, but that erupt periodically to contest their own disappearance. This second old woman lives outside of the local community, together with her idiot son, in a ramshackle dwelling near the wood without any modern conveniences. The son is first characterized by simian manners and gestures and then shown dressed fantastically in the clothes, no longer worn by "modern" young women like Ming and Yuan, of ancient village women. In their appearance, the way they live, and the perception of them by the local community as "mad," the mother and son embody and gather, in one direct thrust, the film's countercultural discourse. The old woman's hysteria and the son's apelike contortions disrupt the rational logic of Ming's investigations and haunt the main narrative as another ineffable reminder of the film's own chthonic impulse. In the suspicion of the idiot as murderer and his mother's violent outbursts, the film insinuates the alignment of this impulse with violence. Ultimately, however, this alignment is shown to be the mistaken prejudice of those who are framed by rationality and modernity as "normative": the police are wrong about the idiot, and even Ming herself, for all she manages to discover through her quotidian investigation, could not have escaped death without the intervention of his mother. Cheuk's masculine objectification of Yuan, and the patriarchal insidiousness of institutional procedures that underpin the narrative of the murder and its investigation, are counteracted, challenged, and disrupted by the film's visualizations of maternity and its discontents.

But it is precisely the film's alignment of maternity with both Chinese cultural primitivism and extreme social marginality that is dark and troubling. As a critique of the repressions of patriarchy and modernity, this alignment develops its own argumentative force and spectacular visuality, and the film contemplates the place of women amid the dissolution of ancestral structures with an aesthetic thoughtfulness previously unseen in Cantonese cinema. But as a projection of woman's resistance, poised at the beginning of Hong Kong's recent modernity, it is, even for its own time, regressive and self-consuming. *The Secret* lays down the contours of Hui's initial filmic ambivalence about women's position and subjectivity, in which the exploration of agency is heavily circumscribed by a continued investment in what inherited strictures will both allow and afford and increasingly reincorporated into an ethnocultural determinism that is, by history and definition, patriarchal in its social exemplifications. As such, her films tread the narrow path between the critique and reinvention of tradition and estrange it even while affirming its continued power to structure, coopt, and exclude women's subjects. Despite the experimental and auteurish treatment of her films, and their eschewing of the melodramatic and stereotypical narratives about women in earlier Cantonese cinema, they articulate a pragmatic realism in the imagination of the possibilities of and, always, the limitations of change and newness. This in itself not only typifies an ideological scrupulousness in her own films but forecasts the highly negotiated discourses on Hong Kong cultural identity in the 1980s as 1997 begins to cast its long shadow.

Hui's films of the middle period, which include *Love in a Fallen City* [*Qingcheng zhi Lian*], *Romance of the Book and Sword* [*Shu Jian Enchou Lu*], and its sequel *Princess Fragrance*, move away from a Hong Kong setting to the broader contours of recent Chinese history in continued attempts to locate transitional moments when the modern impacts, complicates, and dislocates the binding structures of tradition. *Love in a Fallen City* begins in Shanghai in the 1930s and moves to colonial Hong Kong—two cities that stood, albeit differently, at the vanguard of China's experience of Western modernity at the time. Based on a novel by Eileen Chang Ai-ling, *Love* retrieves, remembers, and memorializes the checkered history of modernity as it struggles to emerge on China's geographical and cultural frontiers. *Romance* and *Princess* move further back in time to narrate the moment when the Manchus, under the Qianlong emperor, conclusively overwhelmed the political resistance of the remnants of the preceding Ming dynasty and their allies, the Huei ethnic minority. In narrating the defeat of resistance, *Princess* underlines the recent politics of Chinese history as the triumphal history of empire. The fact that the Manchus were "foreigners," as opposed to the Ming loyalists, who were ethnically Han Chinese, carries the resonances of contact and conflict between Chinese and other ethnocultures that are central to Hui's thematics. But more significantly, the films problematize resistance in the context of an asymmetrical relationship between dynastic power, with the organization and technology it commands, and marginalized communities, whose strengths and resources are minimal by comparison.

Through their complex thematics, these films develop an optic on Hong Kong's contemporary situation in the mid-1980s. Ever since the signing of the Sino-British Joint Declaration in 1984, which guaranteed no change in Hong Kong's way of life for fifty years after 1997, debates on Hong Kong's cultural and political identity, suppressed by corporate identification with capitalistic enterprise and restrictive colonial laws on freedom of expression since the 1960s, have returned with a vengeance.[14] Hui's films constitute Hong Kong cinema's thoughtful interventions in this public debate, and her paradigms of cultural destabilization take on a recognizable political inflection. In *Princess*, for instance, the antiquated structures of belief first narrated in *The Secret* are mapped onto the struggle of the minority Huei community, allied with the remnants of the Ming dynasty, against the Qing imperial juggernaut. The antiquated and the residual: the alignment of these two discourses constitutes that fragile space of cultural and political resistance, while Qing imperial "modernity" is projected as ruthlessly masculinist and politically and militarily brutal. In the defeat of the former, the film develops allegorical inferences about Hong Kong's contemporary situation and is full of foreboding about Hong Kong's reincorporation into Chinese sovereignty after 1997.

At the same time these films rehearse, in separate but related ways, the Chinese woman's involuntary passage between multiple subjectivities and "homes"—natal, ethnic, patriarchal—and how she plots a trajectory of her own self-fulfillment amid great adversity. They configure a number of vantage points on women's predicament in the tortuous passages of Chinese modernity: unconscious derangement by the split in patriarchal culture between a nascent modernity and traditional authoritarianism, or their mutual reinforcement, which strains women's psyches under patriarchal bondage to the breaking point. A conscious self-alienation, along with its corollary, an alienated self-consciousness, produces a failure not only of corporate identification but also of community with other women. Hui's women characters, in their subjective and social estrangement, figure as outposts marking but also displaced on the edges of modernity at different times and places in China's recent history. Some of them embody what Julia Kristeva, in a different but related discourse on the stranger and estrangement, calls "an agonizing struggle between what no longer is and what will never be": others try to live "neither before nor now but beyond . . . bent with a passion that, although tenacious, will remain forever unsatisfied" (1991, 10). Hui's vantage points on women's identity, past and present, exemplify the complicated transactions of this difference grounded on Hong Kong's own decade of uncertainty in the 1980s.

While both *Romance of the Book and Sword* and *Princess Fragrance* are relentlessly bleak in their staging of the defeat of women's perspective on history and of women's history, it is in *Princess* that Hui focalizes the contests between men and women, between empire and periphery, and between empire and its others, through the female subject. The titular heroine of *Princess* is Hasili, the second daughter of the chief of the Huei minority ethnic community, which is under threat of conquest and genocide from Qing imperialism. In the original novel by Louis Cha (writing under the pen name Jinyong) on which the film is based, the beautiful, semimythical Hasili is important but not central. Another crucial departure from the original novel is the insertion in the film of the myth of Mamier, whose grip on the imagination of the Huei, and especially of the princess, signifies the film's historical determinism. *Princess* begins with the meeting between Hasili and Chen Jialuo, the hero of Cha's novel and the leader of the Red Flower Broth-

香港金像獎大導演
許鞍華
最新傑作

香香公主
改編自《書劍恩仇錄》

Figure 2.
The Huei minority ethnic community is under threat of conquest and genocide from Qing imperialism in *Princess Fragrance* (Ann Hui, 1987).

erhood, the predominantly male band of Ming loyalists who are rebelling against Manchu rule and whose exploits are the focus of the prequel, *Romance of the Book and Sword*.

In the opening sequences of *Princess*, Chen is on his way to the desert homeland of the Huei to inform them of an imminent Qing attack; at the edge of the oasis where Chen bends down to drink, he catches his first, fascinated glimpse of Hasili. Their romance unfolds as Hasili leads Chen to her tribal camp through the Huei homeland, composed as an arcadian space where the natural and the pastoral are integrated; where water is the enduring source and symbol of an ancient way of life; where men and women have their own roles, which foster gendered initiatives but are also compatible; and young women have autonomy in choosing their male partners. This visual geography of utopia, detailed and consummate, is unsurpassed in any of Hui's movies; the rituals of spiritualism that in *The Secret* symbolize a suppressed and atavistic cultural heritage are replaced by the verdant and life-enhancing images of the Huei homeland on the margins of the Qing empire. Utopianism, marginality, community: through the Huei, Hui maps the ground of minority resistance, the contours of which are embodied in the princess, a woman subject who, more than any other in Hui's films, articulates a political idealism justified in inherited beliefs. These beliefs are twofold, looking in one direction toward the Huei's Islamic faith and in another toward contemporary bonds of kinship. The threat of Qing conquest becomes a historical crisis when religious faith, faith in life and community survival as sacrosanct, and faith in romantic love coordinate as exigent pressures on Hasili, establishing at once her inalienable subjectivity and its ultimate proof in self-sacrifice.

It is the paradox of selfhood and sacrifice, and selfhood in sacrifice, that exemplifies the dilemmas of estrangement outlined by Kristeva. In her historical situation, Hasili is poised on the cusp of "what no longer is" (that is to say, a life justified in an inherited tradition that is unsustainable under the encroachments of empire) and "what will never be" (the realization, no matter how partial, of political and romantic utopianism), in an autonomous peripheral space. Her narrative in the film is a movement from the now to the "beyond," to borrow Kristeva's terms again, a narrative of passion unfulfilled and inimical to fulfillment within her historical circumstances. As the Qing forces mobilize on the borders of the Huei homeland, Hasili, accompanied by Chen, volunteers as an emissary to convey the Huei message of defiance to the Qing commander. Before they leave, she confesses her love to Chen and her readiness to lay down her life for her people. This will to act in both the private and the public sphere makes Chen's indecision in the military campaign look unheroic and his self-control in love, prudish. The asymmetry between the artless princess with her loyal band of tribesmen and the cruelty of the Manchu commander pitches primordialized innocence and community against a barbaric primitivism made even more savage because of its access to technology. The advantage of the former is revealed in an exemplary display, when the Huei manage to drive back the Qing attack and win moral and poetic justice, in the first half of the film.

The second half of the film attempts to visualize and communicate an aura of Hasili's greatness, but it is here that its failure is most obvious. This failure was misconstrued by some early reviewers as the result of an unsuitable choice of actress, but it actually raises far more complex issues. The aura of the princess should derive fullness from the sequence right at the heart of the film when she and Chen lose their way in a sandstorm, until they eventually stumble on the ruins of the lost city where Mamier, the mythical Huei heroine, was once captive. In the ruins, the princess and Chen read an inscription on a stone tablet and reconstruct Mamier's tragedy in the present. Mamier's voice is heard narrating her capture, rape, and impregnation by a tyrant and her forced separation from her Huei lover; she goes on to describe how Huei resistance against the tyrant ended in defeat and her own suicide. As she speaks, the scenes of her tragedy are enacted, but the sequence is hurried, histrionic, and garishly colored, completely at odds with the aversion to melodrama habitual in Hui's films and with the significant thematic import the sequence is supposed to carry in *Princess*. In trying to be mythical and dreamlike, it only manages to achieve a kind of comic-book slow-motion effect. The cuts to the princess are equally hurried, reducing her and her companion to whispering, prying voyeurs of the ancient revelation, rather than awestruck visitants initiated into an ancient communal myth of which they are also supposedly the latest inheritors. The symbolic significations of the sequence—as the prophecy of the princess's and the Huei's tragic fate and mythical structuration of history—are undermined by the inadequate visual texture and rhetoric. This seriously diminishes the princess's tragic grandeur, which might otherwise counterpoint the film's portrait of Qing triumphalism.[15]

In their second imperial campaign, Qing forces destroy the Huei community, and the princess is captured and brought to the imperial capital, where she at first resists the lecherous designs of the emperor Qianlong. Persuaded by Chen to put community before self, Hasili acquiesces, but at the purification ceremony in the mosque before her marriage to Qianlong, she stabs herself. She thus reenacts Mamier's suicide as ritual in the present and fulfills an ancient myth as prophecy. Huei cultural myth and narrative point toward a determinism structuring the community's history and woman's subjectivity and disable both communal resistance and woman's agency. The princess appears as the doomed challenger of the fatal order of things, the woman in love, the shaman who crosses the ethnic spaces of Huei and Qing and the temporal boundaries between the historical present and mythical past and is destroyed by her passage. Her suicide, an act she commits to preserve her purity in the first instance, enacts the extinction of Huei heritage and imperial history's bloody purification of its Others. In the final scenes of slaughter, the leaders of the Red Flower Brotherhood are outmaneuvered by Qianlong and fall one after another in a massacre. Only Chen is left unhurt; the last dramatic confrontation shows him throwing away his sword with the parting words to Qianlong that to kill him would only mean that a worse emperor will follow. In this recognition of defeat, marginality and minority resistance confirm the irresistible triumph of the juggernaut of empire. It is a bleak diagnosis. Resistance is weak, flawed, and pointless; modernity is hateful, and the only thing to be said for it is that it might be even worse.

With *Princess*, Ann Hui seems to have exhausted the politicized cinematics of her middle period. Perhaps it would be more accurate to say that the films of this period exemplify an aestheticized politics,[16] in that they seek to construe the problematic of Hong Kong's identity under Chinese rule while obfuscating the relationships between the cinematic sign and its cultural and political referents. *Princess* relocates the themes of Hong Kong identity in a distant geography and imperial history, and in repeatedly denying an interest in politics, Hui treads a canny middle path between cinema's sociopolitical significations and its aesthetics. As cinema, *Princess* is a very uneven work; its bleak optic on Chinese history as the history of empire and the closures it imposes on resistance and woman's agency suggest a cul-de-sac vision in the long road ahead to 1997 and beyond and strike a particularly hesitant note in the local discourse, emerging in the mid-1980s, on Hong Kong's identity as different from both traditional and mainland China and from the West.

The three later films, *Starry Is the Night [Jinye Xingguang Canlan]*, *Song of the Exile*, and *Summer Snow*, return to Hong Kong locations and focus, in a conscious contemplation, on woman in Hong Kong's history in the decade before 1997. This does not mean a turning away from Chinese cultural identity in Hong Kong's modernity, or from the remapping of primordial meanings that is the burden of *The Secret* and *Princess*. But the routes of cultural memory take a more distinctly woman-centered and feminist turn in these three recent films as they cross, once again, the boundaries between Hong Kong and China and the terrain of individual and community narratives.[17] *Starry Is the Night* concludes Hui's imagination of women in love. The other two films marginalize romance as the determinant of woman's subjectivity. Gender relations continue to be important, but the space vacated by the drama of romantic love is taken up with explorations of filial and kinship bonds and by forms of love between men and women that speak to a more inclusive sociality. The films visualize women's subjectivity through a plurality of sociocultural mediations, and in so doing they open up an engagement with the Hong Kong of the recent past and its changing identities that is more direct than in Hui's previous films. Politics, understood as the contestation of power in the public domain, also recedes as a narrative dynamic, and woman's empowerment takes place across a number of sites and discourses, in the home and in the workplace, both traditional and modern.

What remains consistent with the earlier films and is further augmented is the force of memory and history: both *Song of the Exile* and *Summer Snow* show women confronting the paradoxes of memory—their own and that of other characters who have the most impact on their efforts at self-determination. Through the thematics of individual memory, Hui implicitly narrates the collective memory of Hong Kong's recent modernity against the push of the rhetoric of oblivion, which seeks to cast recent constructions of Hong Kong identity as inauthentic and colonialist.[18] In the nascent nationalistic discourse of Hong Kong's return to the "motherland," the narratives of the past three decades of Hong Kong's modernizing experience and the sociocultural bonds they generate are exiled and replaced with narratives that stress ethnic, cultural, and political continuities between Hong Kong and the mainland. The emergence of a nationalist discourse of return speaks of assimilation rather than difference, of centristic reincorporation rather than the accommodated autonomy of "one country, two systems."

Song of the Exile implicitly confronts this discourse with an alternative narrative of return and homeland.[19] It also takes up the earlier themes of women's struggle against male-centered histories framed by romance, as in *Starry Is the Night,* or epical conflicts of power, as in *Princess Fragrance.* Memory is the site of this struggle, and *Song of the Exile* maps the tortuous, circuitous, and above all, ex-centric routes that this struggle takes as the woman protagonist, Hueyin, tries to negotiate her own past with that of her parents and, through them, with the historical conflict between China and Japan in the twentieth century. The film begins with Hueyin's last days as a student in London. She is summoned back to Hong Kong for her sister's marriage, which causes her to miss an interview for a job at the BBC. This is the first of the film's many returns, each framed by the unfolding history of Hueyin's family and her own changing self-identification within it, especially as it relates to the bond between her and her mother. Beginning with Hueyin's narrative, the film extends its reach to the story, hitherto unarticulated within the family, of her mother's past. The two women's narratives are folded into one another to become the complex sign of Hui's reconstruction of contemporary Chinese history from women's vantage points.

On her return to Hong Kong, the longstanding conflict between Hueyin and her mother quickly resumes, and the film unravels the complicated history of this conflict through flashback sequences of the family's life in Macao during World War II. In these flashbacks, the young Hueyin appears as an unwitting accomplice in her mother's marginalization by her in-laws. The mother is figured as silent, cold, and detached, in contrast to the grandparents' loving care, and the child turns away from the mother, refusing to join her and her father when they leave Macao for Hong Kong. Even when Hueyin finally rejoins her parents, the alienation continues, and when her father dies and her younger sister marries and emigrates to Canada, mother and daughter are left to confront each other and their conjoined but also conflicted past within a "home" space emptied of natural and familial bonds. The film shows the difficult process of their reaffiliation. It begins when Hueyin first discovers her mother's Japanese nationality. As she accompanies

her mother on her return to Japan after three decades of exile, Hueyin's disjointed memory of affliction is reconnected in a new narrative that bonds the
two of them in a common history. Most of the second half of the film is shot
in Japan, where Hueyin, unable to speak the language, watches her mother
reenact the communal affiliations of her youth; marginalized and excluded,
she begins to understand her mother's early silence and internal exile in the
marital home and from the Chinese community. The immobilizing ties of
childhood and youth inscribed in her mother's behavior toward her brother
and friends in Japan impel Hueyin to assert her difference; she begins to
revalue the narrative of their mutual alienation and moves to overcome
the physical and emotional barriers between them. In this part of the film,
the mother's narrative takes over in flashback sequences of her distraught
reunion with her kinfolk and her ex-lover and oral accounts of her meeting
with Hueyin's father in China during the last days of the Japanese occupation in the 1940s. Hueyin perceives that change is her prerogative; her
mother is too old and entrenched in her parental dignity to make the move
toward reconciliation.

In the final scenes, mother and daughter return to Hong Kong, where
Hueyin, stabilized in a reconstituted narrative of affiliation, finds her own
place in a career as a producer of news programs for a local television station.
The exile has returned to her first home — Hong Kong in the 1970s — but this
Hong Kong is substantially different from that visualized in *The Secret*.
Through news flashes edited by Hueyin of local protests against corruption
that led to the establishment of the Independent Commission against Corruption, the sequences in *Song of the Exile* that deal with Hong Kong summarize its early modernity as a period of nascent social consciousness and activism toward reform and change.[20] This strong sense of place is augmented
by Hueyin's visit to her ailing grandparents, who moved back to China shortly
after 1949. While both women's early subjectivity is scripted by their hybridized Chinese and Japanese histories and the conflict between the two, it
is through Hueyin, the young Hong Kong woman, that the film bears witness
to an autonomous desire toward change and self-invention, and to her commitment to finding her own place in a changing Hong Kong community. In
mapping this dynamic of individual change onto Hong Kong's early modernity, *Song of the Exile* inscribes both the woman and the community's liberation from history as an inherited parental or nationalistic determination. Of
all Ann Hui's films, it strikes the most positive note about the will to change
and woman's agency in putting change in place, in a reaffirmation of the enduring bonds of family and community.

Figure 3.
Mother and daughter
confront the paradoxes
of memory in *Song of
the Exile* (Ann Hui,
1990).

Summer Snow accentuates the historical consciousness that Hui has displayed and explored in all her films and its domestication in the individual family. But unlike *Song of the Exile, Summer Snow* refocalizes the contest between narratives of woman's subjectivity through a gendered relationship that pits an ordinary, lower-middle-class working woman and housewife against her father-in-law. At the same time, *Summer Snow* is located in Hong Kong and shows the quotidian realities of life and hardship of the contemporary Hong Kong woman in situ. What is equally significant and timely is that the film implicitly argues for the endurance in Hong Kong of inherited and quotidian Chinese cultural practices, especially as they relate to women, that have not been erased by colonial history; but it also imagines their renewal in the contemporary moment.

Unlike Hueyin, the protagonist of *Summer Snow,* Mrs. Suen, is neither young nor Western-educated, but she lives the multiple and often conflicted life of women under the sign of modernity. She is a housewife burdened not only by domestic chores and the task of looking after her father-in-law, husband, and teenage son, but also by her work in a small business importing toiletry items from mainland China. In the central conflict between her and her father-in-law, the patriarch of the family, *Summer Snow* interweaves gendered narratives of memory and visualizes their contest. She endures the overt dislike of her father-in-law, who at the beginning of the film appears as a detestable authoritarian demanding her total submission and goes out of his way to humiliate her. In these early moments, Suen is abject, "colonized" by patriarchal tyranny; and her abjection intensifies when her mother-in-law, her only source of support in the family, dies suddenly.[21] Most of the film narrates in meticulous and often humorous detail Suen's slow and hesitant transformation from abjection, during which she maintains her traditional place as mother, wife, and daughter-in-law but also renews it in ways that signal the film's perception of cultural change as it takes place within individual families, and how it entails a more equal partnership between woman and man, wife and husband, mother and son.

After his wife's death, the patriarch is diagnosed as suffering from Alzheimer's disease, and the family members, especially Suen, exhaust themselves trying to protect him from his own life-threatening behavior. The patriarch's mental confusion is symptomatized by short-term memory loss. He fails to recognize his children and grandchild and obsessively reenacts his earlier career as a fighter pilot in the Nationalist air force battling the Japanese in World War II. His sense of self, and the patriarchal narrative of history he embodies, contracts into a truncated narrative of epic heroism. Such diminishment is at first difficult for Suen to resist, for only in becoming part of his narrative — and playing along with the fantasies created by his disturbed memory — can Suen access his interiority and contain the disruptiveness of his behavior. This entails the displacement of the ongoing narratives of her own subjectivity as wife, mother, and worker and leads to sudden disruptions in her family life. She finds herself in conflict with her husband and son and marginalized by a younger female competitor in the office, a glamorous new immigrant from mainland China. One by one her support systems fail: her husband and son become frustrated and unhelpful, and the day-care center that initially accommodates the patriarch rejects him because of his vagrant tendencies.

While the film visualizes Suen's predicament and exhaustion, it focuses above all on her strength under duress, amplifying an ordinary woman's fortitude with vignettes of other women who strive, despite their straitened circumstances and privation, to care for men who are old and sick in their own families and the community. In its consistent attention to women's patience and endurance, the film interweaves and makes visible a narrative of their heroism that counteracts, displaces, but also works in tandem with the patriarch's epical memory. In this respect, *Summer Snow* is Ann Hui's most detailed and accomplished project to date in retrieving and liberating Chinese women's history from its patriarchal determinations and her own earlier defeatist optic. At the same time, it reconciles, through the growing imaginative and emotional empathy between daughter-in-law and father-in-law, the

Figure 4.
An enduring Mrs. Suen
makes a slow and
hesitant transformation
from abjection in
Summer Snow
(Ann Hui, 1995).

conflict of gendered histories, positing this reconciliation as the source of the family's rapprochement and renewal. The apparently limited scope of the domestic narrative belies the complex ambition of *Summer Snow*: it relocates history as women's history and visualizes cultural regeneration predicated on the intimate revolutions in women's place within individual families.

In the office subplot, the young immigrant contests Suen's indispensable assistance to the male boss. Again the contest is focalized by memory; Suen is used to keeping an inventory of the company's stock, clients' orders, and dates of delivery in the private storehouse of her memory. But the younger woman pushes for computerization and for a time wins the boss's confidence with her glamorous appearance and technological expertise. Through the two women, the film reverses the oppositions between Hong Kong and mainland subjects and aligns the former with the contemporary renewal of traditional practices while embodying in the latter the frenzied rush toward a technologized modernity. When the computer breaks down, the business operation has to rely once more on Suen's prodigious memory. In this narrative, the film's skepticism about technology's necessary displacement of inherited forms of memory pushes into the contemporary moment Hui's earlier critiques of Hong Kong's bourgeois modernity. *Summer Snow* revisits most of the preoccupations that I examined in the earlier films. Now, a modernity that is entrepreneurial and led by technology is seen as subject to amnesia, as disabling in its way as the pathology of a ghostly traditionalism —

like the patriarch, a captive of the dead past. *Summer Snow* enacts a critique of both; in it and in the person of a family woman and clerk in a toiletries company, Hong Kong's modernity finds its latest and not unworthy embodiment.

In *The Secret* and *Princess Fragrance*, Hui maps the intersecting contours of patriarchy and modernity as the grid within which women both are confined and struggle to stake claims on their own subjectivity. These women are figured as bearers of veridical details or ethical ideals but defeated as social agents and, as such, situated in uneasy and anxious relationships with the material world — in extreme instances, perpetual and irreversible exile from it. It is a paradox of these early films that they figure women as central even as the spectacle insistently indicates a vantage point that sees their past and present decentering from society and culture.

In her films of the 1990s, Hui seems to have turned away from the broad canvases of politics and society to the milieu of family and home. Along with this one sees a perceptible shift in her stance on women as agents of change. In their traditional places as daughters or daughters-in-law, these women seek self-transformation and enable the reparation of disrupted kinship and social bonds. But despite its ostensible focus on individual and familial renewal, this feminist turn has broader social implications, for it posits the dislodging of women from traditional positions of dependency within the family as the basis for their social empowerment and agency. Hueyin's liberation from her mother's memory is coterminous with their reaffiliation, and the narrative sequencing of the film proposes that this reinvigorated bond between the two generations of women becomes the ground of Hueyin's engagement with a reformist agenda through her work as a journalist. From a different generational perspective, *Summer Snow* reconfigures Mrs. Suen as the cohesive force of family renewal, and she also returns to a position of centrality in the workplace. While the films of the 1990s of other directors, such as Wong Kar-wai, celebrate postmodernist dislocations and symptomatize urban decadence and transitional hysteria, Hui's recent films of the 1990s, such as *Song of the Exile* and *Summer Snow*, have become increasingly realistic in their optic on women's continuous struggle to unsettle and disrupt the orthodoxies that prescribe relationships within the Chinese family as an inherited social institution, and to imagine and enact its restructuration. Through the narratives of the two women, one young and the other middle-aged, one from the middle class and the other from the lower middle class, the films point toward the emergent formation of Hong Kong civil society from the bedrock of individual and familial changes wrought by women in different locations and the collective strength of their aggregation. For all Ann Hui's narrative peregrinations, her films have in the main been configured as social critiques and utopian projects. Her future cinematic passage, post-1997, into the ambivalent intersections of postmodernity and ethnic and nationalistic corporatism will certainly be worth waiting for.

Notes

1   I have periodized Hui's films in the following order: the early period includes *The Secret* (1979), *The Spooky Bunch* (1980), *The Story of Woo Viet* (1981), and *Boat People* (1982). I have considered *Love in a Fallen City* (1984), *Romance of the Book and Sword* (1987), and *Romance's* sequel, *Princess Fragrance* (1987) films of the middle period, while the more recent films include *Starry Is the Night* (1988), *Song of the Exile* (1990), *My American Grandson* (1991), *The Zodiac Killers* (1991), *Summer Snow* (1995), and *Ah Kam* (1996). This essay will focus on films in which women play significant roles and leave out those in which they are insignificant or simply act out cinematic, gender, and cultural stereotypes. The latter include the women characters in *The Story of Woo Viet* and *Boat People*, two films that are otherwise of considerable interest in their handling of the topical issue of the exodus of refugees from Vietnam in the early 1980s and questions of diasporal Chinese identities. Hui's penchant for the topical can degenerate into purely market concerns, as in *The Zodiac Killers* and *My American Grandson*, two recent films with insignificant women characters. In her response to my comment that these two are her most "commercialized" films, Hui agrees: "Yes. [They] were made not really with the market in mind, but I listened more to my boss." *Ah Kam*, her latest film, once again displays this tendency. It is ironic that while a number of her more "artistic" films did not earn enough money at the box office to please their investors, the films shot to appease the financiers or the market fared no better.

2   It is interesting to note that Hui's 1972 master's thesis was on the novels and films of Alain Robbe-Grillet. She explored Robbe-Grillet's "main concern — a denial of all 'significance' or pre-established 'values'" — and showed special interest in the antitraditional devices he employed in different "phases" of his work (Hui 1972, i). The conscious search for alternative spaces and identities and experiments with montage and temporal dislocations in her cinematic narratives, especially in the early films, resonate with Hui's graduate academic work.

3   For preliminary studies of the Hong Kong New Wave and its cinematic context, see Kung and Zhang 1984, Ma 1988, and Lui 1988. At the moment, there is no extended work in English on the subject.

4   Through the Television and Films Authority, and latterly, the Television and Entertainment Licensing Authority (TELA), the government vets all mediatized productions. Television programs are regulated by powers enshrined in the *Television (Standards of Programmes) Regulations* (Hong Kong Government 1964).

Paragraph 4 of the subsidiary legislation, for example, states that "[p]rogrammes broadcast by a licensee shall exclude material which is likely (a) to offend against good taste or decency; (b) to mislead or alarm; (c) to encourage or to incite to crime, civil disorder or civil disobedience; (d) to discredit or bring into disrespect the law or social institutions including any religion; and (e) to serve the interest of any foreign political party." The government has invoked these laws on a number of occasions to prevent the shooting or showing of films that are perceived to be potentially destabilizing locally or that might lead to trouble with China.

5 As Janet Salaff observes, while women's labor had been central to "an export-dependent economy, beginning with the labor-intensive textiles and garment machining in the 1950s," their participation in the workforce continued to be seen as transient and superfluous, subject to the fluctuations of external demand for locally made goods and unprotected by any governmental legislation against their employers' exploitation through enforced redundancy when there was a downturn in trade (Salaff 1981, 20). Their wages were also kept low, "and young women are assumed by management and the Department of Labor to be indifferent to long-term job security" (20). That is to say, despite their crucial presence in the industrial and manufacturing sectors, women were still largely identified by their places within the Chinese family, which was and continued to be patriarchal in its structure. The Hong Kong Council of Women, set up in 1947, was largely an expatriate, upper-middle- and middle-class group whose charity work was confined to members of their own class. They would not have been part of the audience of the indigenous Cantonese cinema.

6 See, e.g., *Love and Passion* (1964), produced by the left-wing studio Chi Luen, which targets the destructive impact of capitalistic modernity on familial bonds and women's intellectual and social advancement. The woman protagonist is a Western-educated architect who contests patriarchal and colonial authority and attains a measure of self-sovereignty through suffering and subterfuge. In another popular genre—that of martial arts films—the gothic mood and charismatic countertraditionalism of the heroine in *Green-Eyed Demoness* (1967) is particularly interesting. The eponymous demoness has prodigious martial arts skills and is positioned as the cultural outsider, battling against three villains figured as the standard-bearers of Chinese cultural orthodoxies and patriarchal authority: a Confucian scholar, a Buddhist monk, and a Taoist priest. In separate modern and traditional settings, the two films narrate women's fulfillment through social and cultural transgression, and insofar as the women protagonists emerge triumphant, they provide unusual counterblasts to the conformist visual thematics of most of the Cantonese films of the time, which place a premium on male social agency and masculine satisfaction in gender relationships. Informative studies on the Cantonese films of the earlier period include Lai 1982, Lin 1982, Law 1984, Du 1986, Ma 1988, and Chan and Law 1996.

7 In 1967, riots inspired by anticolonial sentiment and the ideology and rhetoric of the Cultural Revolution exploded into violence on the streets of Hong Kong. After the riots, in its heightened anxiety about civil disorder and social discontent, the government took the initiative in fashioning an environment where

some form of local and communal identity could be nurtured, without, however, the need to open legal channels for public debate on or popular participation in the political process (Turner 1995). In this executive-led project, Hong Kong belatedly exemplifies, despite its colonial situation, what Jürgen Habermas observes of Western modernity: "The modern state, that is the tandem of bureaucracy and capitalism, has turned out to be the most effective vehicle for accelerating social modernization" (Habermas 1996, 282). The riots of the 1960s mark a watershed in many aspects of Hong Kong's passage to modernity, not least for the cinema. For a study of Chi Luen and the work of other studios with left-wing sympathies, see Yu 1982, Fonoroff 1988, and Lai 1982.

8   See *The Other Half of the Sky* (1992) and other annual reports from 1985 of the Association for the Advancement of Feminism in Hong Kong, Choi 1993, Wu 1995, and the essays in Pearson and Leung 1995.

9   Besides Hui's *The Secret*, the two other classics of the New Wave in 1979, Tsui Hark's *The Butterfly Murders* and Alex Cheung's *Cops and Robbers*, are equally uninnovative in their imagination of women subjects.

10 In an interview in 1982, Ann Hui said, "I really do not understand politics. I don't know if it's too simple so I don't care to understand it, or it's too complicated, so I can't understand it" (Li 1982, 20; my translation). More recently, Hui has distanced herself and her films from the issue of 1997 when she was asked what she thought about using the medium of film to raise questions about the handover and Hong Kong's future: "The biggest problem is that this involves the whole of society, and you don't know where to begin. . . . My personal view is that without sufficient time, there is no way one can filter the issues, and so it's impossible to shoot a film. There has to be enough time for research; it takes patience. There is no need to rush into films about the question of 97" (Wei and Lao 1990, 17; my translation). Earlier, in 1988, on the subject of herself as a woman director, Hui said, "If you don't ask for social advantages as a woman, you don't get the disadvantages. . . . Women directors are not even an issue now [in Hong Kong]. You don't hear people saying 'Ah, there's an interesting woman director. Look what a woman can do'" (Lam 1991, 6). In answer to my questions as to whether she is especially interested in making films on women subjects, she has said, "No, I'm not," and adds, "I seldom reflect on my identity as a woman."

11 These films exemplify John Orr's contention, in speaking of the aesthetics of Western cinema, that "the reflexive nature of the modern film, in its capacity for irony, pastiche, for constant self-reflection, and for putting everything in quotation marks, is not 'postmodern' at all, but on the contrary, has been an essential feature of cinema's continuing encounter with modernity" (1993, 2). My own discussion has a more specific reference point in Hong Kong's recent history but also distances itself from recent discussions of Hong Kong culture within "postmodernist" frames (Abbas 1997).

12 Choi Po-king's 1995 study of the period between the mid-1980s and mid-1990s, which begins "with the building up of the local women's movement in the process of decolonization, and ends with its diversification in its confrontation with problems associated with political transition" (102), is an outstanding example of this tendency. See also Hong Kong Association for the Advancement of

Feminism 1992 and 1993; Choi 1993; Wu 1995; and the essays in Pearson and Leung 1995.

13 The Government Information Service performs a crucial function, as an ideological apparatus, in composing and disseminating images of Hong Kong as economically vibrant and politically consensual (see Chan 1987, chapter 6). The involvement of the government in the design and manufacture of the bourgeois imaginary is discussed by Turner 1995.

14 The past five years have seen an increasing, and urgent, self-reflexiveness in Hong Kong on questions of a local identity. In the domain of literature, the arts, and culture, see especially Ho 1995; Leung 1995; Sinn 1995; Turner and Ngan 1995; and Clarke 1996.

15 For debates on the film among reviewers, see Shu 1987.

16 I have borrowed and adapted Walter Benjamin's phrase "aestheticization of politics" (1970). In 1987, three years after the signing of the joint declaration in which Britain and China agreed on the transfer of sovereignty and launched the long transition to 1997, the problematic of Hong Kong's political future was just beginning to take shape. Without a tradition of public debate, serious discussions over the future were confined to small, elite groups that were involved, directly or indirectly, in working out the complicated mechanics of the transition. In the months to come, these groups came under increasing public pressure to define and formulate their positions vis-à-vis political and constitutional development up to and beyond 1997. *Princess Fragrance* represents not only an individual artistic vantage point but is also evocative of the anxiety over engagement in the mid-1980s, when filmmakers had to reassess their own cinematics and, like other cultural workers, explore relocations with the rapidly shifting contours of sociopolitical change. Hui and her New Wave contemporaries took different routes: the cinematic career of Alex Cheung, for instance, stuttered, while Hui, like Tsui Hark, continued to work within the parameters of commercial cinema while trying to expand its capacity for self- and social reflexiveness.

17 Recent works mapping ethnic and feminist contestations in different locations include Spivak 1987 and Mohanty, Russo, and Torres 1991. For specific discussion of such mappings in contemporary Chinese cinema, see Chow 1991.

18 In his discussion of films like Louis Malle's *Lacombe Lucien* and Liliana Cavani's *The Night Porter*, Michel Foucault (1989) discusses cinema as the site at which popular memory contests its erasure by official "histories" and re-members the dispersed imaginations of resistance.

19 See Choi 1995 for a discussion of the politics of the women's groups in Hong Kong as they diversify between those with pro-China and nationalistic orientations and others with a strong sense of Hong Kong identity.

20 Lui (1995) offers a detailed account of women's participation in politics.

21 In Mrs. Suen's relationship with her father-in-law early in the film, certain traces of Kristeva's complex constitution of the subject as abject can be seen: "It is not the white expanse or slack boredom or repression, not the translations and transformations of desire that wrench bodies, nights, and discourse; rather it is a brutish suffering that 'I' puts up with, sublime and devastated, for 'I' deposits it to the father's account . . . : I endure it, for I imagine that such is the desire of the other" (1982, 4). "Abjection," Kristeva further observes, "is always brought

about by that which attempts to get along with trampled-down law" (19). As the film goes on to show, the patriarch, as the embodiment of immutable cultural power and hegemonic historical narrative, has become deranged and incoherent, although this fact is unknown to Mrs. Suen and the family in the film's opening sequences.

Filmography

Chan Lit-bun
1967 *Green-Eyed Demoness*. Hong Kong Film Co.

Hui, Ann On-wah
1979 *The Secret*. Unique Film Co.
1980 *The Spooky Bunch*. Hi-Pitch Co.
1981 *The Story of Woo Viet*. Pearl City Films.
1982 *Boat People*. Pearl City Films.
1984 *Love in a Fallen City*. Shaw Brothers (Hong Kong)
1987 *Romance of the Book and Sword*. Yangzijiang Film Co., Tianjin Film Studio, Yindu Corp.
1987 *Princess Fragrance*. Yangzijiang Film Co., Tianjin Film Studio, Yindo Corp. Ltd.
1988 *Starry Is the Night*. Shaw Brothers (Hong Kong), Thomson (Hong Kong).
1990 *Song of the Exile*. Gaoxi Film Co., Zongyiang Film Co.
1991 *My American Grandson*. Taiwan Golden Film Co., Shanghai Film Studio.
1991 *Zodiac Killers*. Taiwan Golden Film Co.
1995 *Summer Snow*. Golden Harvest Entertainment Co.
1996 *Ah Kam*. Golden Harvest Entertainment Co.

Wong Yiu
1964 *Love and Passion*. Chi Luen Film Co.

Works Cited

An asterisk indicates that the work was published in Chinese. All English titles of printed Chinese texts are my translations. Titles of Cantonese-language films are the standard English translations.

Anthologies
Hong Kong Cinema Survey, 1946–1968. 1979. Hong Kong: Urban Council.
A Study of Hong Kong Cinema in the Seventies. 1984. Hong Kong: Urban Council.
Changes in Hong Kong Society through Cinema. 1988. Hong Kong: Urban Council.
The China Factor in Hong Kong Cinema. 1990. Hong Kong: Urban Council.
The Restless Breed: Cantonese Stars of the Sixties. 1996. Hong Kong: Urban Council.

Abbas, Ackbar. 1997. *Hong Kong: Culture and the Politics of Disappearance.* Minneapolis: University of Minnesota Press.

Anderson, Benedict. 1983. *Imagined Communities: Reflections on the Origins and Spread of Nationalism.* London: Verso.

Benjamin, Walter. 1970. *Illuminations.* London: Jonathan Cape.

Chan, Cindy, and Law Kar. 1996. "Cantonese Movies of the Sixties: An Oral History by Chan Wan." *Hong Kong Urban Council Publications:* 107–14.

Chan Hoi-man. 1994. "Culture and Identity." In *The Other Hong Kong Report,* edited by Donald H. McMillen and Man Si-wai, 443–68. Hong Kong: Chinese University Press.

Chan, Man Joseph. 1987. *Shifting Journalistic Paradigms: Mass Media and Political Transition in Hong Kong.* Hong Kong: Centre for Hong Kong Studies, Chinese University of Hong Kong.

Chan, Man Joseph, with Chin-chuan Lee. 1991. *Mass Media and Political Transition: The Hong Kong Press in China's Orbit.* New York: Guilford Press.

*———. 1987. "Fame Stopping Short of Reality: Why Defend *The Romance?*" *Film Biweekly* 221: 37–38.

Choi, Po-king. 1993. "Women." In *The Other Hong Kong Report,* edited by Choi Po-king and Ho Lok-sang, 370–400. Hong Kong: Chinese University Press.

———. 1995. "Identities and Diversities: Hong Kong Women's Movement in 1980s and 1990s." *Hong Kong Cultural Studies Bulletin* 4 (winter): 95–102.

Chow, Rey. 1991. "Violence in the Other Country: China as Crisis, Spectacle, and Woman." In *Third World Women and the Politics of Feminism,* edited by Chandra Talpade Mohanty, Ann Russo, and Lourdes Torres, 81–100. Bloomington: Indiana University Press.

Dissanayake, Wimal, ed. 1994. *Colonialism and Nationalism in Asian Cinema.* Bloomington: Indiana University Press.

*Du, Yuenji. 1986. *Seventy Years of Chinese Cinema, 1904–1972.* Taipei: Zhonghuaminguo dianying tushuguan chubanbu.

Foucault, Michel. 1989. "Film and Popular Memory." In *Foucault Live: Collected Interviews, 1961–1984,* edited by Sylvère Lotringer, translated by Lysa Hochroth and John Johnston, 122–475. New York: Semiotext(e).

Fonoroff, Paul. 1988. "A Brief History of Hong Kong Cinema." *Renditions* 29, no. 30: 293–308.

Habermas, Jürgen. 1989. *The Structural Transformation of the Public Sphere: An Inquiry into a Category of Bourgeois Society.* Translated by Thomas Berger. London: Polity Press.

———. 1996. "The European Nation-State, Its Achievements and Its Limits: On the Past and Future of Sovereignty and Citizenship." In *Mapping the Nation,* edited by Gopal Balakrishnan, 281–94. London: Verso.

*Hau Si Kit. 1980. "Ann Hui Playing Hide and Seek with the Audience." *Film Biweekly* 35: 22–24.

Ho, Elaine Yee-lin. 1994. "Women in Exile: Gender and Community in Hong Kong Fiction." *Journal of Commonwealth Literature,* 29, no. 1: 29–46.

———. 1995. "Women in Exile: A Study of Hong Kong Fiction." In *Culture and Society in Hong Kong,* edited by Elizabeth Sinn, 133–59. Hong Kong: Centre of Asian Studies, University of Hong Kong. [Revision and reprint of Ho 1994.]

Hong Kong Association for the Advancement of Feminism. 1992. *The Other Half of the Sky: Women's Movement in Hong Kong since the Post-War Years.* Hong Kong: Association for the Advancement of Feminism.

*———. 1993. *The Hong Kong Women's File.* Hong Kong: Association for the Advancement of Feminism.

Hui, Ann On-wah. 1972. "The Phases of Alain Robbe-Grillet." Master's thesis, University of Hong Kong.

Kristeva, Julia. 1982. *Powers of Horror: An Essay in Abjection.* Translated by Leon S. Roudiez. New York: Columbia University Press.

———. 1991. *Strangers to Ourselves.* Translated Leon S. Roudiez. New York: Columbia University Press.

Kung, James, and Zhang Yueai. 1984. "Hong Kong Cinema and Television in the 1970s: A Perspective." *Hong Kong Urban Council Publications:* 10–14.

Lai Kit. 1982. "Cantonese Cinema in the 1960s: A New Perspective." *Hong Kong Urban Council Publications:* 25–31.

Lam, Perry. 1988. "Women Shoot in a New Direction." *Hong Kong Sunday Morning Post Guide*, 31 July, 6.

Law Kar. 1984. "The 'Shaolin Temple' of the New Hong Kong Cinema." *Hong Kong Urban Council Publications:* 110–14.

———. 1990. "The Shadow of Tradition and the Left-Right Struggle." *Hong Kong Urban Council Publications:* 15–21.

* Liang Huasang. 1987. "On Traveling North for the Shooting of the *Romance of the Book and Sword.*" Part 1, *Film Biweekly* 219: 6–9. Part 2, *Film Biweekly* 220: 7–10.

*Li Cheuk-to. 1982. "Survival Is the Most Important: An Interview with Ann Hui." *Film Biweekly* 96: 19–23.

*———. 1986. "An Extensive Study of Four of Ann Hui's Films." In *Six Film Directors of Hong Kong and Taiwan*, 170–200. Taipei: Independent Evening News Press.

*———. 1987a. "Ann Hui on *Romance.*" Part 1, *Film Biweekly* 220: 3–4. Part 2, *Film Biweekly* 221: 26–28.

*———. 1987b. "Ann Hui's *Romance of the Book and Sword.*" *Film Biweekly* 217: 3–4.

*———. 1993. *Viewing the Rebels: An Anthology [Guanyiji].* Hong Kong: Qiwenhuatang.

Lin Nien-tung. 1982. "Cantonese Cinema in the 1960s: Some Observations." *Hong Kong Urban Council Publications:* 32–40.

Lui Tai-lok. 1988. "Home at [sic] Hong Kong." *Hong Kong Urban Council Publications:* 88–93.

Lui, Terry T. 1995. "Political Participation." In *Women in Hong Kong*, edited by Veronica Pearson and Benjamin K. P. Leung, 133–66. Hong Kong: Oxford University Press.

Ma, Teresa. 1988. "Chronicles of Change: 1960s–1980s." *Hong Kong Urban Council Publications:* 77–80.

Mohanty, Chandra Talpade, Ann Russo, and Lourdes Torres, eds. 1991. *Third World Women and the Politics of Feminism.* Bloomington: Indiana University Press.

*Ngai, Jimmy. 1979. "Pokfield Road Aesthetics: To Hui On Wah." *City Magazine* 40: 6.

Orr, John. 1993. *Cinema and Modernity.* London: Polity Press.

Pearson, Veronica, and Benjamin K. P. Leung, eds. 1995. *Women in Hong Kong.* Hong Kong: Oxford University Press.

Salaff, Janet W. [1981] 1995. *Working Daughters of Hong Kong.* Cambridge and New York: Cambridge University Press. Reprint, New York: Columbia University Press.

Scott, Janet Lee. 1980. "Action and Meaning: Women's Participation in the Mutual Aid Committees, Kowloon." Ph.D. diss., Cornell University Press.

*Shu Kei. 1987. "We Didn't Wait in Vain." Part 1, *Film Biweekly* 219: 4–5. Part 2, *Film Biweekly* 220: 5–6.

Spivak, Gayatri Chakravorty. 1987. *In Other Worlds: Essays in Cultural Politics.* New York: Routledge.

Teo, Stephen. 1988. "Politics and Social Issues in Hong Kong Cinema." *Hong Kong Urban Council Publications:* 38–42.

Turner, Graeme. 1988. *Film as Social Practice.* London and New York: Routledge.

Turner, Matthew. 1995. "Hong Kong Sixties/Nineties: Dissolving the People." In *Hong Kong Sixties: Designing Identity,* ed. Matthew Turner and Irene Ngan, 13–34. Hong Kong: Hong Kong Arts Centre.

Turner, Matthew, and Irene Ngan, eds. 1995. *Hong Kong Sixties: Designing Identity.* Hong Kong: Hong Kong Arts Centre.

*Wang Jianyie. 1990. "Ann On-wah Hui: Changing Rhythms of an Environmental Paranoia." In *In Search of a People's Cinema,* 177–81. Taipei: Yuanliu.

*Wai Heen and Lo Man-sing. 1990. "An Interview with Ann Hui." *Film Biweekly* 289: 12–15.

Wood, Robin. 1977. "Ideology, Genre, Auteur." *Film Comment* 13, no. 1: 46–51.

Yu Mo-wan. 1982. "A Study of Zhong Lian Film Company." *Hong Kong Urban Council Publications:* 41–50.

Part III

A Culture of Disappearance

Nostalgia, Nonsense, and Dislocation

CHAPTER NINE

A Souvenir of Love

Rey Chow

We don't know what love is. Sometimes people even think it is a "local custom."
—LEE BIK-WA/LI BIHUA, *YINJI KAU/YANZHI KOU*

Any visit to Hong Kong in recent years tells one that strong feelings of nostalgia are at work in the general consumer culture. As *waigau/huaijiu* [1] —the most commonly used Chinese term for nostalgia—becomes a trend, the city culture of Hong Kong takes on the appeal of an ethnographic field. Landmarks such as the Repulse Bay Hotel, the Peak Restaurant, and the Western Market have been rebuilt or renovated in such ways as to resurrect their former colonial "flavor." Exhibitions were held in 1992 of Hong Kong postcards from the late nineteenth to the early twentieth century, of Hong Kong film posters dating back to the 1950s, and of Hong Kong cigarette and groceries posters dating back to the 1930s, as well as of various kinds of mass culture publications and daily wares from the 1950s and 1960s. Furniture, music, clothes, shoes, and cosmetics of the past decades are being revived, and it has become fashionable to collect "antiques" such as pocket and mechanical watches, records, old newspapers, old magazines, old photographs, old comic strips, and so forth, in addition to the more traditional collector's items such as coins, stamps, snuff bottles, utensils, paintings, calligraphy, and carpets. The nostalgic hold on history, tradition, and culture has made way for the endless production of commodities.

As a Hong Kong journalist writes, "For the nostalgic class and its rapidly expanding club membership, what is beautiful has to be in the past tense; to appreciate the beautiful is like entering a time tunnel in order to reach for hidden secrets" (*Chan Bing-chiu/Chen Bingzhao*). Is the upsurge of nostalgia in Hong Kong "the flight of the owl of Minerva," a desperate reaction to the approach of 1997, when Hong Kong will return to China and thus, for many, lose its identity? Is it not also because Hong Kong, as one of the last outposts of European territorial colonialism, merely shares the ongoing worldwide trend of simultaneously raiding and idealizing the past—a trend that has long been present in both elite and mass culture, in the form of art and ethnographic museums, auctions, films, music, retro-dressing, and much more?[2] If one of the strategies of colonialism and Orientalism has been that of nativism — of conferring upon colonized peoples the status of local natives with local histories and customs, in contrast to the universalized, "cosmopolitan" status of "First World" colonial powers — then it seems that the recent waves of nostalgia in Hong Kong constitute a cultural politics of self-nativizing that is as complex and as deserving of attention as critiques of colonialism and Orientalism themselves.

A full discussion of this cultural politics will obviously require much more than the space of one essay. My reading of the film *Rouge [Yanzhi Kou]* (Golden Way Films, 1987) will hopefully offer some useful starting points. Several things inform this reading: (1) the relationship between nostalgia and one of the most widely accessible instruments of communication and entertainment, the filmic image; (2) the mutual implication between romantic love and ethnography; (3) the agency of chance; and (4) the question of nostalgia as an alternative temporality for fantasizing a "community" amid the identity-in-crisis of contemporary Hong Kong.

The Nostalgic Filmic Image

What is nostalgia? It is commonly understood to be a longing for the past or, etymologically, a homesickness. The Chinese *huaijiu* literally means missing or reminiscing about the old. Nostalgia is often assumed to be a movement backward in time: The past happened, time passed, we look back to the past from the present, we feel that the past is more beautiful but we can no longer return to it; in this longing for the past, we become "nostalgic." As Caryl Flinn writes in regard to nostalgic trends in American pop culture: "Classical and contemporary accounts alike riddle their conceptions of the present with lacks and deficiencies, obliging the past to function as a site of comparative cohesion, authority, and the hope of 'something better'" (152).

In classical Chinese poetry (*shi* and *ci*), the convention for expressing nostalgia was often that of a lack/loss projected onto physical space. Poets lamented that while the seasons, scenery, architecture, and household objects remained unchanged, the loved ones who once shared this space with them were no longer around. Idioms such as *taohua yijiu, renmian quanfei* — "the peach blossoms are there as always, but the human faces have completely changed" — summarize the feeling of lack/loss peculiar to this kind of nostalgia by contrasting the stability of the environment with the changefulness of human lives.

For Hong Kong people, as for people elsewhere in the "developing" world, the main problem with nostalgia defined in the classical poetic way is the constant disruption of their physical and architectural environments and thus of their sense of the stability of place. (In *Rouge*, the protagonist's first major shock is precisely the disappearance of her original surroundings.) In the 1980s and 1990s, the omnipresence of real-estate speculation means not only that "original" historic places are being demolished regularly, but also that the new constructions that replace them often do not stand long enough — to acquire the feeling of permanence that in turn gives way to nostalgia — before they too are demolished. In the midst of a chimerical concrete jungle, where one's senses are forever jolted by the noise of wrecking balls, bulldozers, pile drivers, air hammers, and power drills, how does one begin to be nostalgic? If the expedience of technology means that human separation itself need no longer be mournful because of diminished travel distances, it also means that our relations to the past are drastically altered because of the unprecedented disintegration of stationary places. Nostalgia now appears differently, working by a manipulation of temporality rather than by a simple projection of lack/loss onto space. If and when the past is to be (re)collected, it is (re)collected in compressed forms, forms that are fantasies of time.

Two sets of questions, then: First, instead of thinking that nostalgia is a feeling triggered by an object lost in the past (a mode of thinking that remains linear and teleological in orientation), can we attempt the reverse? Perhaps nostalgia is a feeling looking for an object? If so, how does it catch its object? Could the movement of nostalgia be a loop, a throw, a network of chance, rather than a straight line? Second, how can nostalgia be "represented" in film? What is the relation between nostalgia and the filmic image? I will approach the second set of questions as a way to return to the first. This requires an examination of the status of images that are the most explicit "sites" of nostalgia in *Rouge* — the *recollections*.

In the novella *Yanzhi kou*, the story is narrated by Yun Wing-ding/Yuan Yongding, the journalist. It begins when Yu Fa/Ruhua, the female ghost, appears in Yongding's office asking to place a personal ad in the newspaper. The use of Yongding as the narrator helps anchor the narrative firmly in the contemporary time frame; following Yongding, we read "about" Ruhua as a character described and recorded by him. In *Rouge*, however, the more stable narrative perspective of Yongding is abandoned. In a way that is more appropriate for the film medium, the text of the film progresses with a double narrative, with scenes from the contemporary time interspersed with scenes from the past.

In *Rouge*, we begin, in fact, with Ruhua's story, but only later do we know that it is her story, recounted from her point of view. The opening shots show

Ruhua, dressed in an old-style *kei po/qipao* with a high round collar, in the process of putting on makeup. Instead of a lipstick, she uses a piece of red dye-paper that women used in the olden days. This small gesture alone becomes the definitive mark of a different time, opening onto several scenes in a *jauga/jiujia*,[3] or restaurant, frequented by prostitutes and their patrons. The time is about 1934; the place, Shek Tong Tsui/Shitangzui, a Chinese "red light district" of Hong Kong during the 1920s and 1930s. Henceforth alternating between the past and the present, the film juxtaposes the two temporalities without offering us the stable anchorage in the present that is offered in the novella. The past—that is, Ruhua's story—is given to us in beautiful golden colors that contrast sharply with the mundane documentary tones of the present. The extravagantly sensuous images of the 1930s demonstrate the logic of the flashback, which Gilles Deleuze describes as "an inexplicable secret, a fragmentation of all linearity, perpetual forks like so many breaks in causality" (49).

By moving Ruhua to the place of a narrator rather than letting her remain a character within Yongding's narration, director Stanley Kwan (*Kwan Gum-pang/Guan Jinpeng*) makes maximum use of the effects of the cinematic image as a type of "free indirect discourse." As Pier Paolo Pasolini argues in his classic essay, "The Cinema of Poetry," the free indirect discourse, used frequently in modernist literature to present a character's inner thoughts and feelings as if they are there without the author's mediation, can also be applied to the understanding of film, in which images are used to signify particular characters' perspectives. In *Rouge*, the past is beautiful and romantic because it is remembered by Ruhua as such. Whereas in the novella Yongding has to deduce or interpret from Ruhua's tone of voice or facial expression the kind of emotion she attaches to the past she is narrating, in the film Ruhua's "narration" *is* the images in front of us. (The ingenuity of the film script lies in the fact that there is no voice-over.) As Pasolini writes, the free indirect discourse is most effective when the character whose "view" we see is an abnormal one. It is thus by using Ruhua, a ghost and an insanely passionate woman, that Kwan intensifies the perspectival and idiosyncratic but enchanted quality of the images of the past.

However, these "recollection" images or flashbacks are not simply subjective and private. If they constitute the story as told by Ruhua the narrator, they do not *only* present her as narrator. On the screen, Ruhua is present not as the voice/gaze of an invisible storyteller but as an image. She is a character in the story *supposedly told by herself*. Because she appears as a character, we are watching these images as if they were *told* from the viewpoint of a narrator who is not Ruhua. Strictly speaking, therefore, the status of these recol-

Figure 1.
A ghost—a madly passionate woman—intensifies the enchanted quality of the images of the past in *Rouge* (Stanley Kwan, 1987).

lection images is neither completely subjective (belonging to one character, Ruhua) nor completely objective (belonging to no one and thus to everyone). At once private and public, the recollection images occupy a peculiar space between the character and the author, between a single consciousness and an omniscient one. While Ruhua is their "subject," she is also present as one of their objects. The best parallel to this is the dream in which one *sees oneself* as a persona, in which one is both the dreamer and the dream(ed).

Memory and dream are precisely the analogies Pasolini draws with cinematic images. In a way that differs sharply from great structuralist film theorists such as Christian Metz, Pasolini thinks that if one is to speak of a "language" of cinema, that language is not a "grammar" (as proposed by Metz and others) but an inscription of an irrational kind. The cinematic language, Pasolini writes, is oneiric and concrete at once (545). Unlike written texts, cinema constructs its materials not from verbal language but from images; such materials, which Pasolini calls prelinguistic or pregrammatical, are "brute." And yet, in their brutality and physicality, images nonetheless have a long and intense history that is derived from the "habitual and consequently unconscious observation of environment, gestures, memory, dreams" (547).

The most interesting aspect of Pasolini's essay concerns the relation between images understood this way and the possibility of the "free indirect discourse" in film. As I already mentioned, in literature, free indirect discourse is usually produced by the author's adopting the "psychology" of a particular character and presenting events in that character's language without quotation marks. The abstract nature of language makes it quite possible for it to capture the specificity of a character without losing track of the author's voice. This is why, for instance, Mikhail Bakhtin could theorize the novelistic discourse of Dostoyevsky in terms of what he calls the "struggle" between the author and character. The abstractness of language means that the boundary between the "inside" and "outside" of any perspective — and hence between author and character — is blurry and potent grounds for contention. In cinema, Pasolini argues, the implications of the free indirect discourse are quite different. While directors do, as we see in *Rouge*, adopt the "voices" or "gazes" of particular characters, the abstract effect achievable in a written text is not possible on the screen because of the filmic image's concreteness. Thus, when a director creates a particular vocabulary for a particular character, Pasolini writes: "But, even this particular vocabulary ends up a universal language; for everybody has eyes" (551). Through a comparison between verbal and imagistic "free indirect discourse," thus, Pasolini highlights the physicality and palpability of the cinematic image as qualities that are especially adept for the metaphoric expression of the unconsciously remembered relations we have with reality.

We are now able to define the relation between nostalgia and the filmic image in *Rouge*. Like directors mentioned by Pasolini, such as Antonioni and Bertolucci, Kwan here adopts the perspective of an "abnormal" character in the creation of his film's images. This "abnormality" allows him a certain liberty. The images from Ruhua's memory are intoxicating because of their absorbed, obsessive, narcissistic quality. But precisely because of the physical and palpable nature of these images, the emotion that accompanies them — nostalgia — becomes collective as well as completely private. In those scenes from the past, the full gestural, physiognomical, and thus societal nature of the image is deployed: apart from the colors, architecture, costumes, and interior decor, there are all the bodily movements, the facial expressions, the eye-to-eye exchanges between the lovers that strike us as at once familiar and exotic, at once belonging to the present (the moment we are watching) and the past (the time of Ruhua's story). As Pasolini would say, such images constitute a reality in which objects are "charged with meanings and utter a brute 'speech' by their very presence" (544). That brute speech would be the pre-linguistic "long and intense history" — the unconsciously remembered relations with "reality" that are shared and dreamed collectively by a community.

If Ruhua's imagistic recollections are the "sites" of nostalgia, then what can we say about nostalgia? Nostalgia is not simply a reaching toward the definite past from a definite present, but a subjective state that seeks to express itself in pictures imbued with particular memories of a certain past-ness. *In film*, these subjectively pictorialized memories are there for everyone to see: nostalgia thus has a public life as much as a purely private one. The cinematic image, because of its visible nature, becomes a wonderfully appropriate embodiment of nostalgia's ambivalence between dream and reality, of nostalgia's insistence on seeing "concrete" things in fantasy and memory. One could perhaps go as far as saying that Ruhua's recollections are not simply images of nostalgia; rather they contain a theory of the *filmic-image-as-nostalgia*. It is against this theoretical understanding of the filmic-image-as-nostalgia that the two predominant components of *Rouge*, the love story and the sociology of prostitution, come together. I will now turn to these components.

Love, a Local Custom

As pointed out by some critics, the love story in *Rouge* is a traditional and hackneyed one.[4] Its narrative turns, its fascination with the amorous relationship between a virtuous prostitute and a romantic youth, its assignment of the fateful burden of love to femininity, and its sorrowful ending remind us of typical features of the Mandarin Duck and Butterfly novels of the early twentieth century. A brief summary of its story goes as follows. In the 1930s, when prostitution was still legal in Hong Kong, Ruhua was one of the most famous prostitutes in the Shitangzui district. She met Chan Chun-bong/Chen Zhenbang, a young man from a wealthy family who was known to his friends by his familial title of Sup Yee Siu/Shier Shao (twelfth young master). Ruhua and Shier Shao fell madly in love, but Shier Shao's family objected to their marriage because of Ruhua's background; they also wanted him to marry his cousin. Ruhua and Shier Shao made a brief attempt at living on their own, with him becoming an apprentice to a Cantonese opera master, while she tried to make as much as possible by "bleeding" rich clients.[5] Angered by the sight of their son in the socially despised role of a minor stage performer, Shier Shao's parents interceded and demanded that he return home. Realizing that there was no escape from family pressure, the two lovers decided to commit suicide together by swallowing opium. At 11 P.M. on 8 March, the hour at which they were supposed to make their exit together from this world, Ruhua asked Shier Shao to remember "3811" as their secret signal of communicating with each other in the life to come. Ruhua died and has been waiting for fifty-three years for her lover to show up in the underworld, but Shier Shao has not appeared. It is now 1987 and Ruhua is tired of waiting. She traded some of the years of her future life (one year for each day spent in the living world) and came back to look for him, hoping that he would respond to her newspaper ad indicating the meeting time of 3811 "at the same old place."[6]

Clearly, Ruhua is an interesting character because of her *chi qing*, her excessive capacity for being faithful in love. During the flashback that shows Ruhua and Shier Shao making love for the first time, we hear Shier Shao describe her: "You are very *yum/yin*" — the Chinese term for the quality of excessiveness that has, in common parlance, become the word for "lewd" or "lascivious." *Yin*, however, is precisely the rare quality that was used to describe a lover like Jia Baoyu in *The Dream of the Red Chamber*. As used in the context of *Rouge*, it is meant to signify Ruhua's essential difference from other people.

The love story from the 1930s is consciously juxtaposed with the relationship between Yongding and his girlfriend, Ling Chor Gu/Ling Chujuan, a tabloid reporter. Instead of a tenacious love like that once shared by Ruhua and Shier Shao, the contemporary lovers strike us as having a relationship of convenience, in which they are not eager to form a permanent union, and in which even the expression of affection and intimacy can be disrupted by professional duties. (Near the beginning of the film, for instance, Yongding gives Chujuan a surprise present of a pair of shoes, but she is too much in a hurry to do her tabloid assignment to appreciate his thoughtfulness.) In contrast to Ruhua, Chujuan seems boisterous, self-centered, and inattentive to her loved one.

Throughout the film, Ruhua alludes to her past and future as if the meaning of her life, rather than beginning and ending at any one point, were repeating and recurring continually. A feeling of cyclical time, in which the past and the present intermingle as if in a dream, in which the debts of the past may be paid in the present, and in which unfinished events of the present may be completed in the future, accompanies Ruhua's endeavor of returning from the dead. By contrast, Yongding and Chujuan are much more bound to their time. Being journalists by profession, the contemporary lovers are acutely conscious of time as a limit. As Ruhua's first encounter with Yongding shows, an ad in the newspaper costs so much, takes so much time to be placed, will appear for so much time, and so on. The contemporary, mediatized world is one in which time is measured and evaluated accordingly. Time is money. Time is also the linear movement of speed, the unidi-rectional, irreversible movement of modernity that goes forward incessantly. This is the time of progress—fast food, brief sex, and short-lived romances.

After the initial feelings of fear, anger, and suspicion, Yongding and Chu-juan are eventually so moved by Ruhua's love story that they decide to help her find Shier Shao. As they become drawn into the details of Ruhua's life, they also become aware of their own ordinariness. In the film, there are these dialogues between them:

CHUJUAN: Would you fall in love with Ruhua?
YONGDING: Her emotions are too strong; I would not be able to take it.
CHUJUAN: Would you kill yourself for me?
YONGDING: How could we be so romantic?
CHUJUAN: Just say yes or no!
YONGDING: No. How about you?
CHUJUAN: No.

CHUJUAN: . . . Nowadays, who would be as faithful as Ruhua? It's difficult being a woman; even when you try your hardest you don't know what it's all for. I am jealous of Ruhua, she has really won me over. What she dared to do, I won't dare for the life of me—I haven't even thought of it.
YONGDING: Yes. We are ordinary people. We just need to feel good when we are together. For us there is no such thing as killing oneself for love; there is no such grand plan as risking lives.

Like a number of other characters created by Li Bihua, such as the im-mortal terra cotta warrior in *Chun Yung/Qin Yong* [*Terra Cotta Warrior*] and the Peking opera actor Ching Dip-yee/Cheng Dieyi in *Ba Wong Bit Gei/Bawang Bie Ji* [*Farewell My Concubine*], Ruhua not only embodies a dif-ferent time and value, but represents an otherness that is absolute. Her *chi qing* makes her a peculiar object of the past which is no longer available. This, then, is the additional meaning of her "timelessness"—Ruhua is time-less not only in the sense of a time that is repetitive and cyclical, but also a time that has stood still or evaporated. This is why Ruhua is so "well-preserved." As Yongding comments:

She is forty-eight years older than me. Forty-eight years—that's a whole lifetime for many people. If Ruhua had been merely living, she would now have become a frail old woman, her skin all wrinkled, her eyes without luster. If she had been reincarnated, she would still have been over forty—the embarrassing age that is neither "middle" nor old. And yet, she is standing beside me in her lovely youthful beauty, simply because she is stubbornly faithful in love. (*Yanzhi Kou*, 28)

Rouge is, in this regard, not only the story of a ghost talking nostalgically about a past romance, but is itself a romance with Ruhua, a romance that is nostalgic for superhuman lovers like her.

Whereas the Mandarin Duck and Butterfly novelists of the 1910s and 1920s would have moralized didactically and warned us against the destructive nature of Ruhua's love as such, Li Bihua finds in it the occasion for a different kind of project. For Li Bihua, Ruhua's *chi qing* is interesting in ways that exceed purely romantic and literary reasons. Ruhua is an anthropological type that has become extinct. In the novella, thus, we find this observation by Yongding: "We don't know what love is. Sometimes people even think it is a 'local custom'" (*Yanzhi Kou*, 49). This short remark revealingly brings together the romantic and the sociological strands of *Yanzhi Kou*.

For readers and viewers of the late 1980s, this Mandarin-Duck-and-Butterfly-style story is intriguing not least because of its social setting. Li Bihua had clearly done a great deal of historical research for the writing of her text, which contains all kinds of interesting details about prostitution as a profession in early-twentieth-century Hong Kong. *Yanzhi Kou* can, among other things, be read as a re-creation of a particular historical period through its practices, mannerisms, linguistic uses, costumes, architecture, and peculiar brand of human relations based on the commodification of sex. To its own success, the film makes ample use of these historical details. Among the gifts sent by Shier Shao to seduce Ruhua, for instance, are a pair of scroll-like tablets decorated with fresh flowers—what was called a *fa pai/huapai*—on which is written a couplet beginning and ending respectively with the two characters in Ruhua's name, and an imported brass bed, indicating his exclusive rights to her. As audiences, we watch with voyeuristic pleasure the enticing scenes of Shier Shao removing Ruhua's layers of clothing when making love to her and of the lovers "chasing the dragon" in bed together. The hairdo, makeup, clothing, and shoes worn by men and women of the 1920s and 1930s, together with their etiquette, vocabulary, and body gestures, are attractively displayed on the screen.

The social details from the past constitute a kind of ethnography, a culture-writing. In the process of conjuring up a different time, the details become

Figure 2.
The brothel becomes
the locational evidence
of the past in *Rouge*.

native witnesses and aboriginal evidences that fascinate and persuade the contemporary viewer. But most interesting of all is the type of enclave Li Bihua chooses for her culture-writing. Of all possible sites of production, it is a brothel which becomes the locational evidence of the past; of all possible culture workers, it is a prostitute who becomes that past's witness, with an obstinate faithfulness in love that is exemplary of a kind of heroism. If the Confucian ancients taught us the "great" virtue of *she sheng qu yi*—a readiness to give one's life for justice—Ruhua teaches us the "small" virtue of a readiness to give one's life for love. While other Chinese directors conceptualize the past more "properly," then, the conceptualization of the past in *Rouge* is an improper one. While others use emperors, empresses, and major eunuchs (e.g., Li Han-hsiang, Tian Zhuangzhuang); sympathetic poor peasants in the countryside (e.g., Xie Jin, Chen Kaige, Zhang Yimou, Xie Fei, and other mainland Chinese directors); or smart, frustrated adolescents (e.g., Hou Hsiao-hsien, Edward Yang, and Wong Kar-wai), Li Bihua and Stanley Kwan use socially despised workers in a socially despised occupation to produce a past that is at once glamorous and trivial, earthshaking and inconsequential.

Notably, therefore, in spite of the abundance of the kinds of ethnographic details that could have filled the pages of the traditional *difang zhi*, the local gazetteers, what distinguishes *Yanzhi Kou* from a conventional writing of history is precisely Li Bihua's refusal to downplay its fictional component, the component of love. Instead, both the novella and the film suggest that conventional ethnography needs to be supplemented by fiction, for it is fiction which provides the most intriguing "historical" or "ethnographic" material. More so than all the arcane objects on display, it is the love embodied by Ruhua that makes this particular ethnographic account memorable. The thing that is no longer comprehensible to contemporary men and women, the exotic ethnographic object par excellence, is Ruhua's *chi qing* per se.

Once we see this mutual implication between ethnography and fiction, the many "clichéd" features typical of the love story—the initial encounter, the mutual attraction, the repartee, the tactics of romantic conquest, the obstacles created by familial objection, and finally the suicide—take on the significance of inevitable but irretrievable customs and rituals. Conversely, the notion of ethnography as a scientific and objective account of a "primitive" society is now constructed as lacking in any consideration of fiction and fantasy. The effect of the signification of nostalgia in *Yanzhi Kou* and *Rouge* is that neither fiction (love) nor ethnography (history) can be understood without the other. The degree of our "historical" interest in the world of the 1930s is in many ways in direct proportion to the degree of our "irrational" mesmerization by a passion we feel is foreign to our time. Ruhua is, on the one hand, a "native" long thought to have gone extinct, who suddenly turns up in the modern metropolis and who insists on reliving the practices of her society. On the other hand, she is also the romantic ethnographer, intent on a certain belief in the past, only to discover that the native object she vows to find is irredeemably lost.

Upon seeing that the man in her dream has vanished precisely because he is still alive,[7] Ruhua returns to him a locket of rouge. Shier Shao had given this pendant to her at the climax of their relationship, when they knew that they were about to be forced apart. Like all souvenirs of love, the locket was intended for promise and trust. But like all allegories of times past, the souvenir is also emblematic of the death of what it commemorates. Ruhua the lover and ethnographer returns to her "field" only to discover that it has long dissolved, and that the souvenir she has been wearing for fifty-three years is . . . a corpse of love. As she "wakes up," she disappears into the haze of darkness and from our sight.

Chance Encounters

Whose fault is the truth? Who or what is the agent for final revelation of the pathetic sight of a senile Shier Shao, an opium addict working as a mere extra, pissing and smoking in the dark and deserted corner of a movie studio? This is one of the multiple-layered questions that the rich, inexhaustible text of *Rouge* asks us. If love is indeed a promise, an infinitely reciprocal exchange of faith, who has broken the terms of the promise? Shier Shao, obviously, because he did not die. But is Ruhua herself not also a "culprit," because she came back to look for him? Within the terms of trust, her return amounts to *dis*trust, a refusal to wait forever and unconditionally. It is also a transgression of the taboo implied in any memory of a beautiful experience, the taboo against turning back. Her "discovery," thus, is a kind of punishment: because she returns, because she looks twice, she loses what (she has hitherto thought) she has. It is important to note that Ruhua's distrust does not begin now, fifty-three years later, but was already present at the time of the lovers' suicide. Ruhua's love did not blind her to her lover's cowardice. In the film we are told that before they committed suicide together, Ruhua, out of fear that Shier Shao would be too timid to swallow the opium, had secretly put an overdose of sleeping pills in the wine he drank. Her logic was that if he should back down from the opium, he would still have died from the sleeping pills, but if he took the opium and died, then the pills would not have mattered. This way, she made sure that he would be (dead) with her forever.[8] (On first discovering Ruhua's murderous act, Chujuan was scandalized; only later does the younger woman accept that even this act was one of love.)

However, if we accept that Ruhua is punished, it is not possible to say who is punishing her. The only agency indicated by *Rouge* is fate or chance, the mysterious network of coincidences that in due course bear pertinent meanings. Hence, if Ruhua's separation from Shier Shao in 1934 was caused by his family's chance rescue of him that she could not have planned, her way back to Shier Shao in 1987 is led by an equally unpredictable coincidence. In an age when everyone has countless numbered documents and possessions, how could Shier Shao be located simply with "3811"? After ruling out identity cards, phone numbers, driver's licenses, and other possibilities, Yongding and Chujuan finally wonder: "What about beepers?"[9] Using the code 3811, they are eventually connected, as if by miracle, to Shier Shao's son, who tells them his father's whereabouts. (After being rescued in 1934, Shier Shao married his cousin and, well before the birth of his son, had squandered his family's fortune. His wife is long dead and his son has nothing but contempt for him.) Do we call this "reunion" of Ruhua and Shier Shao "chance" in the sense of a purely arbitrary happening, possible only "in fiction"? And yet, does not chance strike us precisely when what it brings bears an uncanny recognizability and an uncanny accuracy in hitting home? What is "home"? To be nostalgic, we remember, is to be homesick.

There is a way in which the truth-yielding work of chance has announced itself long before Ruhua sees the truth. This work is not metaphysical but literary, textual, and mediatized.

Consider, once again, the beginning of the film. As I already mentioned, the film differs from the novella by beginning with Ruhua's story rather than Yongding's. The visual staging of Ruhua and Shier Shao's first encounter emphasizes chance as the most active agent in the events of this tragic story. As we go back to the 1930s, we see Ruhua dressed as a man performing a song in front of her patrons. Against the noisy, lively background of the restaurant, the young Shier Shao appears. He ascends the stairs, exchanging interested glances with passing prostitutes. He is captivated by the music. As he enters the room where his friends and their prostitute companions are drinking, the music stops: Ruhua and he discover each other. As she resumes singing with the line, "Look at the pair of swallows against the setting sun," the world has changed for him. The song is a well-known "southern tune" (nam yum/nanyin) sung in Cantonese, "Hak To Chau Hun"/"Ke Tu Qiu Hen" ["A Melancholy Autumn away from Home"].[10] In retrospect, it was as if the song were flowing down the stairs looking for an object, and it found Shier Shao.

The words of "Ke Tu Qiu Hen" tell of the love of a scholar and a courtesan-songstress. Alone under the cool autumn moon, the scholar sings nostalgically of his lover's beauty and talent, of the memorable times they spent together, and of his worries about the dangers that presently surround her. Despite her loved one's poverty, this woman, unlike the mercenary members of her occupation, chose to remain absolutely faithful to him. Is not this old love story like the tune itself, a "chance" *and* pre-scripted happening that catches not only Shier Shao but also Ruhua the singer/seducer? For audiences who do not recognize the tune, this opening scene is by itself a beautiful capturing of the elusive romantic encounter of a prostitute and a dandy; but for those who do, the preordained *and thus* nostalgic nature of the encounter is remarkable. This encounter signifies how the "spontaneous" love between Ruhua and Shier Shao—the "original" story from the 1930s—is itself already a modern (re)enactment, a nostalgic (re)play of older tales, legends, and romances. Behind one encounter is another encounter: as they sing and listen while exchanging fateful glances with each other, Ruhua and Shier Shao are also being sung by the song and its literary romance, which, we might say, has been waiting to meet them. If romance is a matter of "being

Figure 3.
Ruhua (Anita Mui)
dresses as a man
performing a song in
front of Shier Shao
(Leslie Cheung) in
Rouge.

caught" unexpectedly, what we have here is not only the romance of the two lovers catching each other, but also the romance of the past catching human beings unawares. In their encounter with the text that is the past, the lovers become, as it were, that text's actualization and self-fulfillment.

This encounter between the past (fiction?) and the present (reality?) is demonstrated in other scenes of the film. Toward the end, when Ruhua and the contemporary lovers have almost despaired of finding Shier Shao, we find Ruhua watching a Cantonese opera song being performed on the street. The camera indicates that although the actor on the stage is a stranger, Ruhua sees him as her lover. This dreamlike identification of her lover takes place once again against the background of a story of love—the song being performed this time is "San Bak Lum Chung"/"Shanbo Lin Zhong" ["Shanbo on the Eve of his Death"], the last words supposedly sung by the faithful poor scholar Leung San-bak/Liang Shanbo mourning his love affair with Chuk Ying-toi/Zhu Yingtai, who has been forced to marry someone else. And finally, where would the lovers from the 1930s meet again but in a movie studio, where Ruhua in her lovely youthful self appears as surreal as the actress in the background, who is flying about in a *kungfu* movie being shot on the spot? In a way that is characteristic of many unexpectedly funny moments in the film (most of which are lost in the Mandarin and English translations), the actress is instructed by the director: "You are both a female knight-errant and a female ghost. You must act both awesome and spooky!" Is this "real" movie a replay of or a play on the movie we have been watching, or vice versa?

The predominant feeling that our time in this world is but a matter of stumbling upon things and events long inscribed in an unconscious ancient memory distinguishes Li Bihua's sense of nostalgia from other contemporary Chinese writers. Unlike many who seek the past in terms of *xiangtu*, the idealized and often "earthy" homeland in the countryside, Li Bihua's writings are always characterized by a fascination with the materials of past *literature*—with words, phrases, idioms, legends, history books.[11] In Li's writings, what is perceived to be lost is never rural, "innocent," or even "original." Basing her narratives on urban, literate culture (and often the culture of Hong Kong), Li constructs loss as something that is not specifiable and yet traceable in the intertextual relations between the past and the present. This traceability owes itself, precisely, to the alluring work of chance, the agent that is the equivalent of "God." "God" is now a labyrinth.

Nostalgia, an Alternative Temporality for a Community?

If cinema is an index to our contemporary culture at large, then the nostalgia we see in Chinese cinema may well be the *episteme* of Chinese cultural production in the 1980s and 1990s. Nostalgia links the otherwise diverse intellectual and artistic undertakings of the mainland, Taiwan, and Hong Kong. In mainland Chinese films and writings since the early 1980s, nostalgia often takes the form of a contemplative inquiry into China's rural, mythic origins, as well as a renewed interest in the China of pre-Communist days. In Taiwan, nostalgia expresses itself in the massive concern over the suppressed wounds of Taiwan's local history.[12] In Hong Kong, apart from protean appearances in the plenitude of commodity culture, nostalgia often becomes, as in the case of *Rouge*, an aesthetic emotion in which the idealization of the past functions side by side with a submission to chance, fate, physiognomy, cy), and other varieties of *shushu* (techniques of calculat-

omance with the past seems to offer a way of imagining alternative to the one imposed by the rationalist, con- world, nostalgia is nonetheless most acutely felt not as an to the past as such, but as an effect of temporal disloca- g having been displaced in time. Nostalgia is first and fore- the movements of temporality. This is why the narrative structure of *Rouge*, like many films made in Hong Kong in the 1980s and 1990s, is itself nostalgic. These films are not, despite their often explicit subject matter, *nostalgic for the past* as it was; rather, they are, simply by their sensitivity to the movements of temporality, nostalgic *in tendency*. Their affect is interesting precisely because we cannot know its object for sure. Only the sense of loss it projects is definite.

Apart from being seen on its own terms, then, *Rouge* should also be seen in conjunction with a host of relatively recent Hong Kong films, such as *Ying Hung Boon Sik/Yingxiong Bensi* [A Better Tomorrow] I, II, III; *Choi Suk/Cai Su* [The Raid]; *Hak To Chau Hun/Ke Tu Qiu Hen* [Song of the Exile]; *Sheung Hoi Ga Kei/Shanghai Jiaqi* [My American Grandson]; *Bai Ho/Po Hao* [To Be Number One]; *A Fei Ching Chun/A Fei Zhengzhuan* [Days of Being Wild]; *Gup Dong Kei Hup/Ji Dong Qi Xia* [The Iceman Cometh]; *Yun Ling-yuk/Ruan Lingyu* [Center Stage]; and others. Representing a range of genres and made by directors as different as Tsui Hark, Ann Hui, Poon Man-kit, Wong Kar-wai, and Johnny Mak, as well as Stanley Kwan, these films collectively exhibit a nostalgic tendency in their explorations of alternative times and alternative values. What they have in common is an attempt to fantasize the past, which is usually embodied in some character who, like Ruhua, is a larger-than-life "other" with strong, insistent moral beliefs that are out of sync with those of contemporary times. In the comical *The Iceman Cometh*, for instance, the past and the present meet when two soldiers who have been frozen in ice in a fight since the Ming dynasty are defrosted in contemporary Hong Kong. After completing his duty of killing his enemy, the good iceman returns to the Ming by a reincarnation machine. Like Ruhua, this righteous iceman brings with him a nostalgic romance with the past; like Ruhua's loyalty to her lover, the iceman's loyalty to his emperor makes him an irreproducible curio in the age of mechanical human relations.

The ways of looking at the world unique to such characters—their "gazes," as it were—are arguably the most important objects of fascination presented by these films. As Slavoj Žižek writes in a different context: "In nostalgic retrofilms, . . . the logic of the gaze qua object appears as such. The real object of fascination is not the displayed scene but the gaze of the naive 'other' absorbed, enchanted by it" (Žižek 1991, 114). What we really see when we watch these nostalgic films is "the gaze of . . . the one who was 'still able to take it seriously,' in other words, the one who 'believes in it' for us, in place of us" (112). Ultimately, therefore, "[t]he innocent, naive gaze of the other that fascinates us in nostalgia is . . . always the gaze of the child" (114). Li Bihua, described by one critic as the writer who set in motion the entire nostalgic trend in Hong Kong,[13] has herself authored many stories experimenting with the idea of reincarnation, in which memorable characters with childlike credulity appear. For instance, there are the aforementioned *Qin Yong* and *Bawang Bie Ji*, as well as *Ching Se/Qing She [Green Snake]*, *Poon Gum-lin Ji Chin Sai Gum Seng/Pan Jinlian Zhi Qianshi Jinsheng [The Past and Present Lives of Pan Jinlian]*, *Moon Chau Gwok Yiu Yim: Chundo Fongji/Manzhouguo Yaoyan: Chuandao Fangzi [Femme Fatale from Manchukuo, Kawashima Yoshiko]*,[14] and others. Like chance, the credulous, stubborn, childlike "gaze" signifies a temporality that is irrational, repetitive, mischievous. Like chance also, the child can be a tyrant who loves to play hide-and-seek and who demands absolute submission. If nostalgia may be considered an alternative way of conjuring up a "community" amid the ruthless fragmentations of postcoloniality, the community being conjured up is a mythic one. The love of love, of fate and chance, and of the childlike gaze are some of its dimensions.

Like any elaborate form of emotion, nostalgia as presented in *Rouge* and other recent Hong Kong films is the product of a materially well-endowed world. That is why, perhaps, it finds its expression so appropriately in the cinematic image, the technical convention that requires for its continual existence the supply of enormous wealth. (The leading characters in *Rouge* were played by Anita Mui Yim-fong/Mei Yanfang and Leslie Cheung Kwok-wing/Zhang Guorong, two of the highest-priced showbiz figures in Hong Kong.) In the nostalgic filmic image, the entire world turns into a sadly beautiful souvenir. But if its compressed images always convey a sense of loss and melancholy, nostalgia also works by concealing and excluding the dirty and unpleasant elements of social hardships. The degenerate, seductive, and tortuous forms of nostalgia's labor are things with which any critique of the "identity crisis" in a postcolonial space such as Hong Kong must come to terms. The point of this essay has been to provide a beginning for such a critique.[15]

Notes

1 Many of the Chinese words and names quoted in this essay were originally meant to be read in Cantonese. The first time such words and names appear in the essay, I will give both Cantonese and pinyin transliterations, and thereafter repeat in pinyin. Even though *Yanzhikou* is the title for both the novella and the film in Chinese, I will use it to refer only to the novella, which was scripted by the Chenghe chuangzuo zu [Chenghe writing team] and entitled *Rouge* in English.

2   In her study of the relations between music and Hollywood films, for instance, Caryl Flinn writes: "The point is, [nostalgia] is still going strong today. Contemporary art music audiences [*sic*] get more opportunities to hear Beethoven performed than they do Steve Reich; commercials promote everything from regional health centers to champagne using the tired-and-true war-horses of Western art music. Pop culture in the United States takes us back through retro dressing, contemporary television shows like *China Beach* and *The Wonder Years* (not to mention reruns), and the golden oldie programs that saturate radio airwaves on weekends" (Flinn 1992, 151).

3   According to one account, the term *jiujia*, which literally means "wine house," originated with the famous Jinling Jiujia in Shitangzui in the early part of the twentieth century. Most Chinese restaurants at that time used the term *jiulou*. See Ng Ho/Wu Hao 1989, 13.

4   See "Minutes" 1992, 8. One critic mentioned that the story of *Rouge* is a reproduction of classical *chuanqi* and popular folklore stories.

5   It is clear from the contexts of both the novella and the film that Ruhua no longer "slept with" her clients at this point. Instead, as a few scenes with a rich patron show, she let him touch certain parts of her body, such as an ear and a lower leg, at deliberately inflated prices. When this patron tried to mock her loyalty to Shier Shao by lying down in the brass bed the latter had bought to indicate his own possession of Ruhua, she responded subtly but defiantly to the rich man: "I did not lie down (with you)."

6   There are some minor alterations between the film and the novella. In the novella, the time of the suicide is 7 past 7 on 8 Mar., and the secret signal between the lovers is 3877.

7   In the novella, we read descriptions of extras walking about in the movie studio but are given no clear indication that Shier Shao is among them. Ruhua simply disappears at this point, leaving behind the locket, which Yongding afterward finds in his pocket. The next day, Yongding reads in the newspaper that someone by the name of Chen Zhenbang was prosecuted for smoking opium and fined $50. In the film, Ruhua identifies her lover among the movie extras, follows him to a dark corner, and finally approaches him as he falls asleep. Bending down near Shier Shao, she hums the line she was singing when they first met. As the old man awakens in shock, Ruhua speaks to him briefly and returns the locket to him before disappearing.

8   In the novella, Ruhua first lets Shier Shao drink the wine with the sleeping pills in it, then takes the opium herself, waiting to see if he would follow suit; her last memory is of him raising the spoon to his lips. In the film, the lovers drink the wine together before Ruhua takes some opium herself and offers some to Shier Shao. Seeing that he is hesitant, she gives him more wine and then spoons the opium into his mouth. The two then get dressed, walk into the next room, and embrace each other at the approach of death.

9   In the novella, they are struck by the possibility of finding Shier Shao through the beeper when they hear someone else's beeper go off.

10 Well known to Cantonese audiences in Guangdong, Hong Kong, and overseas, "Ke Tu Qiu Hen" was originally sung in the 1910s and 1920s by Bak kui-wing/Bai

Jurong (1892–1974), one of the most highly acclaimed male Cantonese opera singers in the first few decades of the twentieth century.

11 See, e.g., Lee Cheuk-hung/Li Zhuoxiong 1991–92 (I am very grateful to William Tay for providing me with copies of this essay). A slightly shorter version of the essay is also available in Chan Bing-leung/Chen Bingliang 1989, 285–330. In a discussion of the relation between popular literature and Hong Kong's current political and economic situation, Li Zhuoxiong analyzes Li Bihua's writings in terms of the latter's fondness for words and names. This fondness, argues the critic Li, leads Li Bihua sometimes to base her narratives entirely on fascinating words and to include information that is often out of place in the story line. Li compares such love of words to the love of opium, since both enable one to see only the world one needs to see. Li's meticulous attention to Li Bihua's use of words could have led to a reading in which words themselves become signs that open up areas usually neglected by the conscious mind, so that "unconscious" meanings return to interrupt the surface of rational thinking. But this is not the reading he produces. Instead, in a manner characteristic of the historiographic tendencies of traditional Chinese literary criticism, Li ultimately charges Li Bihua for sacrificing a broad "historical vision" to an indulgence in words (that is, we might say, an indulgence in the literary). Li Bihua's fondness for "words and names" thus becomes, for Li, a limitation and a dangerous, self-destructive kind of pleasure. The antifiction moralism of this criticism is obvious, but I find it especially disturbing in an account that is supposedly about popular/mass culture and literature.

12 Especially since the lifting of martial law in 1987, Taiwanese people from different walks of life have been demanding full knowledge of the controversial events surrounding the bloody origins of Chinese Nationalist rule, events that are commonly abbreviated as the "February 28 Taiwan Incident" of 1947. Hou Hsiao-sien's *Beiqing Chengshi [A City of Sadness]* is exemplary of this popular passion for (the truth of) the past.

13 Leung Ping-kwan/Liang Bingjun, "Minutes" 1992, 6.

14 For an English translation of the last title, see Lee 1992.

15 This essay is for Pearl Chow, in appreciation of her assistance with locating some of the materials mentioned in my discussion, her opinions about *Rouge* and other films, and her delightful companionship during a month of intensive film- and video-watching in the summer of 1992.

Works Cited

Bakhtin, Mikhail. 1984. *Problems of Dostoyevsky's Poetics*. Ed. and trans. Caryl Emerson. Introd. Wayne C. Booth. Minneapolis: University of Minnesota Press.

Chen Bingliang, ed. 1989. *Xianggang Wenxue Tanxiang [An Investigation and Appreciation of Hong Kong Literature]*. Hong Kong: Sanlian shudian.

Chen Bingzhao. 1992. "Ningding Guoqushi de Metgan" ["Beauty in the Condensed Past Tense"]. *Xin Bao [Hong Kong Economic Journal*, overseas edition], 16 August, 6.

Deleuze, Gilles. 1989. *Cinema 2: The Time-Image*. Translated by Hugh Tomlinson and Robert Galeta. Minneapolis: University of Minnesota Press.

Flinn, Caryl. 1992. *Strains of Utopia: Gender, Nostalgia, and Hollywood Film Music*. Princeton: Princeton University Press.

Lee, Lilian. 1992. *The Last Princess of Manchuria*. Trans. Andrea Kelly. New York: William Morrow.

Li Bihua. 1986a. *Qing She*. Hong Kong: Cosmos Books.

———. 1986b. *Yanzhi Kou*. Hong Kong: Cosmos Books.

———. 1989. *Qin Yong*. Hong Kong: Cosmos Books.

———. 1991. *Bawang Bie Ji*. Hong Kong: Cosmos Books.

———. N.d. *Pan Jinlian Zhi Qianshi Jinsheng*. Hong Kong: Cosmos Books.

———. N.d. *Manzhouguo Yaoyan: Chuandao Fangzi*. Hong Kong: Cosmos Books.

Li Zhuoxiong. 1991–92. "Mingzi de Gushi: Li Bihua *Yanzhi Kou* Wen Ben Fenxi" ["The Story of Names: A Textual Analysis of Li Bihua's *Yanzhi Kou*"]. Part 1, *Su Ye Wenxue* 30 (November 1991): 22–29; Part 2, *Su Ye Wenxue* 33 (February 1992): 38–47.

"Minutes from the Seminar on Two Hong Kong Films: *Days of Being Wild* and *Rouge* Button." 1992. *Jintian [Today]* 2: 2–11.

Pasolini, Pier Paolo. 1976. "The Cinema of Poetry." Trans. Marianne de Vettimo and Jacques Bontemps. In *Movies and Methods*, vol. 1, ed. Bill Nichols. Berkeley: University of California Press. 542–58.

Wu, Hao. 1989. *Fengyue Tangxi [Snippets from the Shitangzui Era]*. Hong Kong: Publications (Holdings).

Žižek, Slavoj. 1991. *"Looking Awry": An Introduction to Jacques Lacan through Popular Culture*. Cambridge, Mass.: MIT Press.

CHAPTER TEN

Film and Enigmatization:
Nostalgia, Nonsense, and Remembering

Linda Chiu-han Lai

Enigmatization and Memory

The ruthlessly beautiful evening skyline during the handover week leading to 1 July 1997 harbored all yearnings to remember — once and for all — the end of the territory's colonial history, as if those intense, concentrated moments of festivity would allow the people of Hong Kong to let go from then on, finally to free themselves from the burden of coloniality. The neon lights along the shores of the harbor promised a bright, rosy future. The grand ceremonies, headed by the two sovereigns of China and Great Britain, strummed with unprecedentedly dignified civility. And the alternative handover "ceremony" put up by the Democratic Party on the balcony of the Legislative Council invoked the vanishing star of Madonna's Evita Perón bidding her people, "Don't cry for me, Argentina." All of these manifest signs played out in the public sphere were to be appropriated as token images by the dominant, global discourse of Hong Kong's handover. The displacement and replacement of signs have marked the countdown years: the shift from (China's) takeover to (Hong Kong's) handover in local press reportage; the final "resurrection" of the bohemia, the city flower that had practically symbolized the governor's residence more than the territory itself, now made the permanent emblem on the SAR (Special Administrative Region) flag; the blue dolphin that replaced the Chinese fishing junk as a symbol of the city's vitality; the visible presence of festive slogans proclaiming Hong Kong's "return to its roots"; and the list goes on. At the very moment of the handover, the official rhetoric of Hong Kong's sovereignty that had developed over the years concluded in a burst of visuality that reasserted a set of common quotables for easy consumption by the international media.

There are the discourses produced and reproduced by the dominant institution of political power. But they often distract us from other perspectives on the historical transition and the dissemination of other views on local life

231

below that official rhetoric. This essay explores the way many Hong Kong films, starting for the most part in the early 1990s, are carefully designed to harbor multiple layers of meanings, so that they produce messages coded in ways that the local audience alone can interpret but that remain comprehensible to an international audience on a more general level. This practice I shall characterize as "enigmatization," that is, the selection and reorganization of existing images from popular culture in order to distinctly select the local audience as a privileged hermeneutic community, thus facilitating a state of internal dialogue, distinguishing those within from the "outsiders" by marking who partakes in a shared history of popular culture. Enigmatization is necessary, I argue, to preserve a textual domain where local expressions, memories, and contentions that may potentially contradict official views will find articulation. Enigmatization preserves freedom — of sentiments, thoughts, and speech — from below. I shall identify two groups of films that carry enigmatizing functions for detailed examination — the "nostalgia films" and the comedian Stephen Chiau's "cinema of nonsense."

The nostalgia film produces enigmatization by addressing a distinctly local viewer with quotations of popular stereotypes, stock characters, recognizable plot lines, and other conventions from classical Cantonese and Mandarin films, either in a period context or a contemporary setting. Stephen Chiau's films recode genre conventions, conventional configurations of scenes and characters in the local cinema, and, significantly, Cantonese slang, which he executes with a "rhetoric of subversion" (as opposed to "subversion"). In this sense, my claim that Chiau's nonsense films and the nostalgia films function as a site of identity formation has to be argued from a position beyond the manifest themes and moral statements of the films. For it is the formal construction of the films that addresses the Cantonese-speaking Hong Kong insider as a privileged viewer who alone can understand the puns, jokes, and generic allusions of the films, thus fulfilling the function of collective identity formation.

With stock material that alludes to earlier films, the nostalgic films and Chiau's together constitute a shared textual horizon that addresses anxiety over the potential degeneration of Hong Kong's self-sufficient cultural identity beyond 1997. Such a shared horizon comes into place in the actual moments of viewing, as well as in the very act of remembering, invoking a history that is also the history of popular culture. However, in this essay I also point out that the substance of popular memory is centrifugal to the dominant discourse of Hong Kong's economic success story, which has been made the official grand narrative of "Hong Kong history." Thus the so-called alternative discourse of history that films of enigmatization produce is complex—more than simply subversive and resistant. In fact, in the conclusion of this essay I caution against any easy populist celebration of the cinema of enigmatization.

One important issue to address is to what degree rhetorical strategies of the cinema are valorized to produce a specific mode of appropriation of social or collective identity that consciously counteracts the high-low cultural rhetoric prevalent in local discourses on local culture. In the concluding section of this essay, I will argue that the act of enigmatization culminates in a historiographic function in the form of "ritualistic commemoration." "Commemoration," because both groups of films correspond to a contingent and deeply felt yearning for an affirmative local Hong Kong identity—though residents are deeply suspicious that it will gradually be coopted after 1997— that therefore function as acts of remembering, the object and site of which is the territory's popular cultural arena. "Ritualistic," because each type, the nostalgia film and the cinema of nonsense, has its own unique mode of communication to achieve the quest for a history that has yet to be articulated, and they both do so by gathering the local people before the screen, turning film viewing into a concentrated act of recalling the shared memory of a shared culture. Ritualistic commemoration emphasizes the "surface"—stock images and representational norms, and the immediate recognition of them—without necessarily involving "an imaginative grasp of the subjective experience"[1] of the authors or any intersubjective exchange of psychological significance. Ritualistic commemoration is effected by what I call "solidarity through shared signs," whereby the intentional domain of the author is bracketed to foreground signs, images, and representations as "the public medium of social being."[2] Enigmatization, or the selective process of solidarity membership, pertains to a consensus theory based on communicative competence as well as cultural literacy of the popular. The resulting popular historicist discourse, I propose, draws from the formal innovativeness of the discussed film texts and finds total effectuation in the interpretive domain of the critics and the everyday consumers.

Nostalgia . . .

People in the local film industry sometimes explain the "nostalgic" film as a result of the lack of high-quality scripts or good local literary works available for adaptation. In the popular press, local film critics and academics have also defined certain films as "nostalgic," laying down a genealogy of the phenomenon that accounts for the recent fad as a response to the threat of 1997. For the sake of a more productive discussion, this essay will avoid any definitive characterization of nostalgia with essential properties, instead taking a communicative approach to the use of the term: that is, to capture those films that have been identified and talked about as nostalgic. The similarities and contrasts between these films can be described, and their implications reconstructed, without suggesting anything like an overarching or global definition of the nostalgic impulse. The emergence of nostalgia and the roll call of the "nostalgic film" within the territory indeed call for attention to the family resemblance of those films already identified as nostalgic rather than the philosophical nature of the category.[3] Most writings to date have emphasized mood and period setting as distinctive of the nostalgic film. Many describe certain films as nostalgic by reason of their "wistful or excessively sentimental yearning for the return to some past period,"[4] while the more academic writings read these films in the light of postmodernity. In this essay, I prefer to call these films "nostalgia films." They are worth examining not so much because they are nostalgic in content, but because of their narrative machinery, which articulates carefully crafted identity values far beyond mere nostalgic sentiments. My real emphasis, then, is to trace the performative variations of the narrative machinery — the nostalgic mode or structure that transposes, transforms, and negotiates with "original" meanings from the past. What also cuts through the category of nostalgia films is the pleasure taken in re-presenting stock material from the popular media.

A key example of nostalgia expressed through genre recycling and transformation is *He Ain't Heavy, He's My Father!* [*Xin Nanxiong Nandi*] (1993). The plot has a time-travel structure resembling that of *Back to the Future* (1984), gradually indigenized through replacement by localized conventions of Hong Kong cinema. In the film, Chu Yuan, a skeptical young man resentful of his father's moralizing disregard for material success, suddenly travels back in time to the 1960s, where he meets his father as a young man (thus the obvious reference to the Robert Zemeckis film) and the entire neighborhood community that once gave meaning to his father's life. The collectivist world he suddenly discovers is that of Hong Kong's Cantonese classics: Li Tie's *In the Face of Demolition* [*Weilou Chunxiao*] (1953) and Yang Gongliang's *The Apartment of 14 Families* [*Yilou Shisihuo*] (1964). In these representative Cantonese oldies, tenants struggle against the threat of homelessness caused by a greedy landlord's rent increase; a wealthy man's daughter rebels against her parents' "feudal" decision to marry her to an idiotic rich cousin instead of her working-class boyfriend; a gambler who attempts suicide to get away from loan sharks is saved by his neighbor's sacrificial love and mutual assistance; and an orphan girl is constantly threatened by her lascivious stepfather while her true love, an educated and sensitive but extremely timid teacher, cannot effectively protect her.[5] In this world, manual laborers barely manage to make ends meet but nonetheless manage to live happily, whereas the educated schoolteacher still must suffer from tuberculosis, from which he never recovers.

He Ain't Heavy, He's My Father! explicitly recalls three other Hong Kong films bearing the same Chinese title, *Nanxiong Nandi* (literally, "faithful brothers in a time of crisis"). These films—Qin Jian's *Intimate Partners* [*Nanxiong Nandi*] (1960), Chen Wen's *Colorful Partners* [*Qicai Nanxiong Nandi*] (1968), and Karl Maka's *It Takes Two* [*Nanxiong Nandi*] (1982)—all share a celebration of fraternal loyalty between two young men.[6] Often discussed as an example of "the sub-genre of the [1960s] urban comedy," the first recounts "the story of two down-and-out bachelors making ends meet and chasing girls" while "overcoming obstacles through collective effort."[7] It belongs to a period when the celebration of communal solidarity in the cinema was gradually being eroded by growing petit-bourgeois individualism. One of the two protagonists gives up the idea of suicide to join the other as a real estate broker and, later, grocery store owner. The story maps out Hong Kong's economic transformation during the 1960s while holding on to the collectivist, neighborly ethic of mutual help characteristic of the subgenre.

The search for this lost sense of moral community is precisely what underpins the 1990s' nostalgic recuperation of the genre in *He Ain't Heavy*. The film celebrates historical anachronism by recovering a communitarian ethos in opposition to the alienated individualism of contemporary Hong Kong. This statement can only be fully appreciated by an insider familiar with the stars and genre conventions of the local film industry during the 1950s and 1960s.

He Ain't Heavy also retrieves the male lead from *In the Face of Demolition*, best known for his typically communitarian motto "one for all and all for one," an attitude that Chu Yuan initially resents but eventually learns to love in his own father. The father's own name, Chufan, evokes the old actor most closely associated with this ethos of "mutual assistance," Wu Chufan, while Chu Yuan is the name of the popular director of a similar urban comedy, *The House of 72 Tenants* [*Qishi er jia Fangke*] (1973). The real Chu Yuan in fact appears in *He Ain't Heavy* (albeit his character has a different name), which provokes some rather obvious insider jokes. Other supporting characters also adopt the names and mannerisms of various well-known movie stars from the classical Cantonese era. In addition, the filmmakers allude to a series of local celebrities: Lee Rock, a famous Chinese chief police inspector in the 1950s; the Democratic party politicians Martin Lee and Szeto Wah in their childhood; the local business tycoon Li Ka-shing as a humble young man; and so on. These well-known personae are imagined (fictionally) as having a shared childhood and adulthood in one neighborhood.

In a few instances, dialogues are structured in an elliptical fashion, which requires viewers to fill in the gaps with their knowledge of the conventions of Cantonese cinema. Ellipses actively encourage the film's native spectators to recover their personal memory of their own cinema. What is characteristic of such moments is their heightened self-consciousness, rooted in an extreme awareness of Hong Kong cinema traditions.

Another instance of a nostalgic structure is Derek Yee's *C'est la vie, mon cheri* [*Xin Bu Liao Qing*] (1993), a melodramatic romance-tragedy about a struggling pop musician and a young songstress dying of cancer.[8] The film's Chinese title, literally "The New Love without End," clearly functions to differentiate viewers on the basis of their knowledge of Hong Kong popular culture. It alludes to Tao Qin's famous Mandarin melodrama *Love without End* [*Bu Liao Qing*] (1961) and, more generally, to the "songstress" genre, which originated in the Shanghai film industry of the 1930s and was later transplanted to Hong Kong after the Communist Revolution on the mainland. The fact that the reference is only clear in the Chinese (rather than the English) title indicates an exclusive address to a specific public that can recognize the generic allusion. Familiarity with popular culture again becomes a criterion of belonging to the community of ideal viewers.

One of the key motifs of the songstress genre was that of the self-sacrificing woman condemned to a life of poverty, suffering, and humiliation in the entertainment industry because of economic pressures, or in order to protect her family or her lover.[9] *C'est la vie, mon cheri* self-consciously splits the figure of the songstress into four different female characters that embody a complex historical temporality. The narrative juxtaposes past and present through the contrasting associations evoked by the different female characters. On the one hand, Min's mother, once a famous nightclub singer who now performs in a neighborhood street, is a figure suggestive of the 1960s and 1970s, a time when pop artists were often depicted as condemned to a life of poverty and decadence. In almost exactly the same situation is Ling, the prima donna of an opera troupe who has devoted all her life to the impossible dream of making her debut in a real theater. The superstar Tracy is associated with a more contemporary scene. Talented, versatile, self-confident,

Figure 1.
C'est la vie, mon cheri
(Derek Yee, 1993)
brings back the
songstress genre to
express the gap
between the 1960s
and the 1990s.

earthy, and independent, she is ready to grab every opportunity that gives her maximum happiness and autonomy within the constraints of a commercial industry. Min, the female protagonist, is the other side of the same coin: a Tracy fan who makes a living by dubbing her idol's voice in pirated cassette tapes and yet retains a firm grasp of the 1990s way of life. *C'est la vie* expresses the gap between the 1960s and contemporary Hong Kong while nonetheless holding on to a nostalgic, modified version of old genres.

The one director who has most frequently indulged in a nostalgic mode is Clifton Ko. His last three films, *I Will Wait for You [Nian Nian You Jinri]* (1994), *The Umbrella Story [Renjian You Qing]* (1995), and *The Mad Phoenix [Nanhai Shisan Lang]* (1997), all take up a storytelling structure that collects forgotten moments of ordinary life and popular cultural history in the territory. *The Umbrella Story*, while sounding a euphuistic and eulogistic note of traditional humanism, has its real pleasure in the Forrest Gump–style fetishism of old photographic images of the past, showing vested interest in technology's possibilities to reclaim (or refabricate) the past. As for the aspect of nostalgia, *The Mad Phoenix* is textual machinery for nostalgia, providing the audience with some pleasant recreation by allowing them to meet popular cultural celebrities whose name they have barely heard of, accompanied by readily consumable moral messages. *I Will Wait for You, The*

Umbrella Story, and *The Mad Phoenix* all evidence similar characteristics: they flirt with epic scale to cover a large span of years, thus tracing social changes in the territory; they combine historical figures and events with fictional ones; and they are full of references to popular culture — film, television, and opera — recycling and transforming well-known genres and images.

Ko's *I Will Wait for You* follows a thirty-year affair between a man and woman, each of whom is married to someone else. The relationship is sustained by their annual rendezvous in an isolated hotel on an outlying island. The affair was an accidental product of the territory's most severe storm, the famous Typhoon Wendy of 1963, and the dynamics of their relationship move in parallel with major local events, changing with the climate of the decade. The long and winding development of the affair is a clever device for inserting various collages of photographic images and popular songs. Thus, between 1963 and 1973, the cradle years of Hong Kong's evolution into a financial center, we see news footage and stills of two top movie actresses, Lin Dai (who acted in Mandarin films) and Lin Feng (of the Cantonese cinema), both of whom committed suicide; we see the typical weather-forecasting icon of early commercial television, the "weathergirl" standing in front of a transparent wall of air-pressure contours; the long-running evening variety show "Enjoy Yourself Tonight," which played every weekday evening on Jade, TVB's Chinese channel; *Meng Duan Qing Tian* (literally, "the broken dreams of love"), the first popular television melodrama series; the comedians and brothers Sam and Michael Hui; the martial arts star Bruce Lee; and "Princess Hong Kong," the winner of an annual beauty pageant who then became a prominent television actress. The film is divided into four more periods: 1973–78, 1978–84, 1984–87, and 1987–94. These follow a similar pattern — a bit of everything is shown, from headline news incidents, representative television stars, and dramatic series to new developments in the entertainment arena. Ko's project of nostalgia depicts individual lives as products of epic history. The key turning points of the life of *I Will Wait*'s protagonists, understandably, were shaped by signal events. The female protagonist's own husband, for example, went from selling cars in the 1970s (during the oil boom) to dealing in computer equipment in the 1980s. He has to immigrate to Canada, and she accompanies him, which forces the two lovers to separate. And the female protagonist's economic status rises from anonymous white-collar worker to millionaire as a result of speculation in the stock market in the 1980s. Most of the selections are integral to the collective memory of the local people of Hong Kong but are basically unknown to the "outsider." More crucially, the film works to reassert the dominant rags-to-riches narrative of Hong Kong's "economic miracle," imposing its rhetoric on the lives of the protagonists; their affair is seen as a reflection of the colony's success story.

In all three of these films, Ko's nostalgia project constructs pseudo-epics in order to search for an imaginary past. What he accomplishes is not a retrieved past based on historical knowledge, but a satire on the effects of monumental historical moments, whether from official or popular discourses, on individual lives.

The films discussed so far are only some of the many instances of enigmatization. *C'est la vie* and *He Ain't Heavy* achieve it through genre recycling and transformation. Similar gestures characterize Joseph Chan's more subversive '92 *Legendary la rose noir* [*Jiuer Hei Meigui Dui Hei Meigui*] (1992) and Jeff Lau and Corey Yuen's *The Black Rose* [*Hei Meigui Yi Jie Jinlan*] (1997). Both films recall the popular "Black Rose and White Rose" series of the 1960s depicting two female Robin Hoods in contemporary Hong Kong who rob the rich to feed the poor, in stern opposition to the Royal Hong Kong Police. Two science-fiction action films, Johnnie To's *The Heroic Trio* [*Dongfang Sanxia*] (1993) and *The Executioners* [*Xiandai Haoxia Zhuan*] (1993), do not have obvious genre precedents, but they display a swordplay ethos rooted in the values of chivalry and philanthropy. Both films integrate the female Robin Hood with the detective or crime film, employing comic book–style visual effects and the action choreography of Japanese television cartoons. And Tsui Hark's *Once Upon a Time in China* [*Huang Feihong*] series revises the story of the famous Cantonese *kungfu* master Wong Fei-hung, whose life has become an interpretive arena in itself. Earlier versions, mostly embodied in the paternalistic persona of the actor Kwan Tak-hing, find the fatherly authority figure of Master Wong exemplifying a Confucian, patriarchal moral paradigm as a protector of Chinese traditions. Tsui's remake in the 1990s freely turns Wong into a handsome, energetic young man, witty, versatile, and open to Western ideas. Tsui's anachronistic treatment also allows Master Wong to reside in crucial moments of modern Chinese history, from the Opium War in the mid- to late nineteenth century and the 1911 Rebellion led by Sun Yat-sen to the era of the legendary Hong K Cheung Po-tzai, who actually lived much earlier, in the early century, and was active around 1807–1810. These moments b temporaneous events, which provides Tsui with a convenient de verting the official interpretation of these events.

As mentioned earlier, many local writings in Hong Kong account for nostalgia as a sign and product of the territory's postmodern phase. Postmodernism is a complex label that demands immediate clarification once the term is evoked. The extant literature has advanced many versions of postmodernism — as the close of an episode in human history, as a social mood, as a socioeconomic reality, as a set of new types of political, social, and aesthetic philosophy, or as new ways of making art; and postmodern cultural theories center on the "effacement of the older frontier between high culture and so-called mass or commercial culture, and the emergence of new kinds of texts infused with the forms, categories and contents of that very industry so passionately denounced by all the ideologues of the modern." [10] A key component of many definitions of the term "postmodern" is the erosion of the modern idea of irreversible, unidirectional historical progress. A full-blown capitalist consumer culture, in which the principle of thrift is dissolved by the expansion of advertising, and the evolution of an information society are perhaps the most obvious traits of Hong Kong's postmodernism. [11] But beyond economic postmodernism, does Hong Kong share that postmodern social mood that forfeits the modern faith in progress? In terms of political, social, and aesthetic beliefs, postmodernism rejects objective or universal standards of morality and knowledge and the clear distinction between reality and representation, asserting instead that knowledge is intrinsically connected to power. These views have increasingly infiltrated local cultural and intellectual activities, which subsequently conjoin in the celebration of the popular. In Western scholarship, this claim signals a revolt against classicism, which, according to Jameson, has been processed into the discourse of the "problematic" decade of the 1950s, the postmodern era's imaginary enemy in the United States. [12] The 1950s, Jameson claims, was a period when high culture was "authorized to pass judgment on reality, to say what real life is and what is mere appearance." [13] A similarly authoritative high culture has not manifested itself in Hong Kong. Although the academic community has always furbished the cognitive texture of Hong Kong's social cultural reality, this was not a self-conscious vocation on a collective level and therefore did not carry much weight in shaping the descriptive discourse of local events on a broader communicative scale. The situation did not change until the mid-1980s, when the domain of cultural criticism was suddenly charged with zealous writings from academia, which took unprecedented interest in the popular and was willing to write for the general public, often in columns for the local Chinese newspapers. In this way, rather than forming themselves into a powerful high culture tearing down the popular, these intellectuals situated themselves within popular writing, wavering somewhere between condemnation and celebration. The postmodern condition Jameson describes may be a revolt against the modernist phase of authoritative grand narratives, and perhaps American nostalgia functions to reclaim the interpretation of past decades from below. But Hong Kong has not yet sufficiently articulated its object of resistance for any real revolt to take place. If the postmodern is partly a social mood that forfeits the modern faith in irreversible historical progress, then Hong Kong, by contrast, is still deeply immersed in a sense of pride in its economic progress. Nostalgia films and other cultural practices, deliberately or not, collaborate in further engraving that discourse into the minds of the viewers. The discourse of nostalgia in the Hong Kong cinema is, in other words, closely linked with the discourse of progress.

In short, Hong Kong is still very much driven by its own success story. Popular efforts on all fronts look out for as many local stories as possible to furbish and substantiate this grand narrative, which in turn subjugates the multitudinous, often underrepresented facets of local life and public ventures to the story of progress. The nostalgia film's self-configuration as a counterforce to the grand narrative of economic success is at best ambivalent. At the core of all these stories lies the pride of Hong Kong and its people. This same success myth is at the heart of Peter Chan's *Comrades, Almost a Love Story* [*Tian Mimi*] (1997), a big hit both at home and overseas. *Comrades* chants the sad song of permanent exile to the question of where home really is for the Hong Kong citizen. But the material actions of the film weave paradigms, almost with pedagogic tenacity, of what qualifies one as a citizen of Hong Kong; and behind the assertion of a collective social identity lie the integral components of the typical Hong Kong legend, such as overnight success, overnight downfall, economic opportunities for all, flexibility in crisis management, and so on. In congruence with the assertion of a Hong Kong identity, the pop singer Teresa Tang, the unifying force of *Comrades'* romantic saga, is turned into an equivocal cultural marker in the film that selects only those "insiders" who have experienced the significance of Tang's leap from Hong Kong idol in the 1970s to a mainland celebrity in the 1990s. The power of the many films discussed so far lies in their assembly of recognizable cinematic codes in actual moments of congregation, which situates the viewers as beholders and makers of history on a collective level. The nostalgia film executes enigmatization and produces a solidarity underpinned by the remembrance of a shared popular tradition. Yet it also works to reassert the discourse of economic progress, the most widely perpetuated "Hong

Kong story" in all public dominant discourses, and at the core of everything resides the pride of the Hong Kong citizen—a discursive object that has yet to be defended. And indeed, what do we have other than the mythical economic success story the official discourse has written for us? And what do we have other than popular culture, where the sentiments of the ordinary people are imagined?

Stephen Chiau's Logic of Nonsense

Just as fleeting as memories that dwell in popular fiction is Stephen Chiau's parody of power and established norms through the creation of Cantonese slang, from which Chiau's films draw their enigmatizing power. The power of Cantonese slang is instantaneously differentiating at the moment of utterance: it distinguishes not only Cantonese from Mandarin speakers, but also Cantonese speakers in Hong Kong from those who live in places like Singapore, Malaysia, Canton, Canada, and so on—part of the Cantonese diaspora.

Cantonese slang is not a written language, and neither, like most local slangs, is it translatable. Although Chiau's films have always been subtitled in both English and written Chinese (Mandarin) for foreign markets, subtitles are almost impossible with the new Cantonese slang he creates. Whereas the general idea of the jokes is preserved, very little of the fun of his parody of Cantonese sounds or his subversion of grammar and linguistic norms can be made available to non–Hong Kong people. The intensive use and constant re-creation of Cantonese slang privileges a distinct viewing community comprised of not just any Chinese person, nor just any permanent citizen of Hong Kong, but only those residents who partake of everyday life and popular culture in the territory now. For only they can have up-to-date knowledge of contemporary linguistic practices and an appreciation for the comic defamiliarization of ordinary popular language.

Chiau creates slang by taking common Cantonese expressions and attaching new meanings to them, literalizing metaphoric expressions or producing intentional nonsense and thus overthrowing established meanings and dominant values.[14] The collective identity thus produced of the Hong Kong person incorporates a fantasmatic quality rooted in the ephemeral, transient quality of the language employed. Unlike Mandarin, Cantonese is mainly circulated in a spoken form that largely eludes written transcription. In contrast to the printed text, it only reproduces itself in the here-and-now contexts of actual utterances, escaping storage and recording (except on a soundtrack). The local identity enacted through Cantonese is embodied in the instantaneous and transient moment of its performance.

But linguistic solidarity is not all. The "word" aspect—that is, the play of Cantonese slang and catchphrases—has a "play" counterpart, which is the performative aspect of the film as well as the dramatic configuration of comic moments reminiscent of children's games. "Word" and "play" together constitute Chiau's rhetoric of subversion directed against norms of social propriety. Chiau's rhetoric, then, can be characterized as a move from general comic conventions toward a specific grammar of laughter whereby "word" and "play" split into two rhetorically distinct but interactive domains. What the grammar of laughter produces is not humor or satire, but parody and curses.

At least three stylistic features compound the "play" aspect. Most of Chiau's main characters are either characterized by idiosyncratic mannerisms or presented as acrobatically versatile, often with robotic precision—all of which produces a masking effect that detaches the behavioral dimension of the characters from even the most minimal traits of psychological interiority. That leads to a second aspect: obsession with the human body as a site of mystical science and with its fusion with the machine,[15] which is often tied to Chiau's lip service to consumerism. In Yip Wai-man's *Sixty Million Dollar Man [Baibian Xingjun]*, (1995), in which a scientist-magician has the ability to turn human beings into everyday objects, and in Stephen Chiau and Vincent Kok's *Forbidden City Cop [Da Nei Mitan Linglingfa]* (1996), whose hero is a great inventor of household utensils, techniques are presented as power tools able to critique civilization. These tools form a burlesque of commodities in his films, guffawing, "Consumerism saves!" In *Sixty Million Dollar Man*, it is a microwave oven that—thanks to the wisdom of "old Mrs. Wong," the representative persona in the Park'N Shop grocery's television commercial—finally conquers the bad guy. In *Forbidden City Cop*, a simple magnetic bar in a period setting becomes a miraculous lifesaver. The message of all this remains equivocal: wholehearted celebration of consumerism or deliberate inversion of "proper" values, such as the denunciation of the materialistic lifestyle by critics of popular culture?

The films are also obsessed with orality, ranging from playing with food[16] to the oral intake of human waste (feces, etc.),[17] daily utensils,[18] or, symbolically speaking, the devouring of the "world" through the mouth. Orality, too, is extended to other forms of mischief—the celebration of anti-etiquette, sexual displays in public settings, excessive play with the grotesque, the ugly, and the disgusting, marketplace shrewdness that embarrassingly violates social norms of honesty and good citizenship, and anything that is banned in proper, respectable representational practices.

In this sense, on the one hand Chiau entrenches himself in a culture of folk humor, shaped over many centuries, that defended ordinary people's creativity in unofficial forms.[19] On the other hand, by highlighting the line dividing the high and the low, the proper and the inappropriate, and the cultured and the banal, he is actually playing with these boundaries and visualizing their collapse. In this way Chiau's films celebrate a kind of humanity that is different from that of humanism.[20] What he lets shine through is that aspect of humanness often suppressed or condemned by social etiquette, norms, and rationality, as well as pedagogic programs delimiting proper civic conduct that are geared toward effective government. The rhetoric of Chiau's films is that of nonsense and "festive speeches," free and jocular, destructive and yet creative. With Chiau, comedy demarcates the very location that stands in opposition to the official public domain — the latter largely organized and ruled by the logic of economic success and progress, the imperative of submission to authority, and faith in social stability guaranteed by colonial rule.

Many of the word-and-play characteristics just described are composite features of what Bakhtin called the carnivalesque in the Renaissance.[21] In a nutshell, Chiau's films bear the mark of a carnival's "grotesque realism" — which turns conventional aesthetics on its head in order to locate a new kind of popular, convulsive, rebellious beauty, each thing containing its opposite.[22] The difference is that the Renaissance carnival was "schizophrenic," as it embraced both an "official" theocratic social structure and "unofficial" forms of folk expression; but Chiau's intent, overt and determined in privileging the low over the high, needs no camouflage. *Sixty Million Dollar Man*, for example, carnivalizes the place of the university, science, and the scientist. Chiau's films not only collapse the high-low boundary, but also overthrow established social orders, corroding the high while blatantly inhabiting the space of the low.

It is crucial, above all, to read Chiau's word-and-play formula of laughter in the context of his consistent parodic references to genre conventions in order to elucidate his own form of enigmatization. Chiau's later works, starting more or less with his and Lee Lik-chi's *From China with Love [Guochan Lingling Qi]* (1994), itself a sinicized James Bond story, are all explicitly genre conscious. *Sixty Million Dollar Man* is an extravaganza of local and Hollywood cinematic clichés, such as the norms of filial piety, and includes a reference to a rescue scene from *Pulp Fiction*. *Forbidden City Cop* opens with

Figure 2.
Stephen Chiau
carnivalizes science
and the scientist in
Sixty Million Dollar Man
(1990).

Figure 3.
Stephen Chiau
entrenches himself
in subversion and a
culture of folk humor in
Sixty Million Dollar Man.

Figure 4.
From China with Love
(Stephen Chiau, 1990)
has a sinicized James
Bond story.

a scene invoking a number of famous, handsome knights-errant from various Chinese swordplay novels who turn out to be ugly and deformed despite their exquisite reputations.[23] As the audience watches, puzzled, Chiau's voice is heard in the midst of the fight: "Handsome? That's only ordinary people's wishful thinking!" *Forbidden City Cop* also phenomenally defies any expectation of a unified dramatic whole, with its deliberately convoluted, discursive plot line that changes direction at the most unlikely moments, swinging back to an almost forgotten idea whenever the director feels like it. The film is at times publicity demo shorts of the latest home appliances or Master Wong Fei-hung's renowned charity clinic, at other times a family romance, a showcase of martial arts styles, the local film award presentation ceremony, and so on, juxtaposed at random. Chiau's films are highly conscious of generic hierarchies, acknowledging a simple high-low dichotomy in order to demolish it via performance. Chiau's grammar of laughter, therefore, alienates his films distinctly from the tradition of high comedy.

In brief, the performative essence of the word-and-play carnivalesque in Chiau's films is integral to the politics of commemoration vis-à-vis rhetorical conventions; one may call it, in rhetorical terms, the location of solidarity-in-the-making. The continuous (re-)affirmation of individual membership in a community is valorized via speech as well as a shared visual generic heritage. Like the nostalgia film, Chiau's nonsense weaves its own communicative system of internal commemoration.

Cinema: Mnemonic Schemes[24] and Commemorative Rituals

Both the nostalgia film and Chiau's works force us to recognize that the most enduring and widespread experience of Hong Kong's local history inhabits the domain of popular culture, especially since various mass media rushed into a historicist fad in the mid-1980s. The marketplace had witnessed disparate but growing attempts to capture a local history believed to be on the verge of dissolution or erasure from above. Popular anecdotal accounts of Hong Kong's early colonial life sprouted in the form of pocket-size paperbacks, and pop lyricists began to inject social commentary into their work. The family histories of local Chinese tycoons and the success stories of younger entrepreneurs also emerged as a fashionable feature genre in news journalism. In the midst of all this, cinema was found to be a privileged vehicle of collective memory.[25]

Commemoration is a key notion in contemporary historiography, which takes a special interest in memory and its relationship to the production of historical knowledge.[26] The writing of history as such departs from regime or monumental history, which looks at dominant political events alone. Commemoration attends instead to the microlevels and more everyday domains of human life, such as habits of mind, (structures of) feeling, conventions of speech, customary practices, and other material forms left out of the framework of monumental history. Commemoration in particular directs the historian's attention to specific forms of communication that tie contemporary people to a world that is gradually passing.

Enigmatization, as I have argued, has formed the basic grammar of the mnemonic schemes of the nostalgia film and the cinema of nonsense, culminating in commemorative practices. The nostalgic trend, therefore, should be inscribed within the general impetus to recover a subterranean local history inseparable from the genres and traditions of popular culture. But, as with the commemorative function of Stephen Chiau's films, the "history" produced by nostalgia films does not relive or re-present the physicality of the past but instead reconstructs the past for the present.

To grasp the full sense of commemoration, one must have firsthand experience of viewing these films with the local audience to feel what they feel. Commemoration practices are founded on living memories, which, as Hutton contends, involve an interplay between repetition and recollection. By repetition, he means that memories are not transmitted intact but conflated, being continually subject to revision over time. Expressions of memories coalesce into stereotypical images to give form to collective memories. In turn, particular memories are reduced or compressed into idealized images to constitute a social and textual framework by which individual memories can be located. As for recollection, images of the past, when retrieved, are perceived not as they were in the original context, but as they fit into our present conception. As the historian Eric Hobsbawm noted, an image, once invented, tends to proliferate into myriad reconfigurations.[27] That is especially true of the fictional stock characters, archetypal plot lines, and so on from local films in the 1950s and 1960s, since, once detached from their original spatiotemporal context, they go through a resignification process to codify a certain state of the past consumable by contemporary viewers, and notably to signify change as progress. Collective memory thus reflects the social role of a particular group consuming selected images.[28] Indeed, around the early to mid-1990s, Chiau's films were especially appropriated by young local viewers as pleasurably empowering and supplying a new source of solidarity. By abiding in the ever-expanding vocabulary of Cantonese slang, they marked out for themselves a distinct territory of enigmatic wordplay, impenetrable to those who did not take part in the exercise in the present continuous tense.

Notes

This essay was first presented as a paper at the Annual Film Conference of the University of Ohio in November 1994, with an emphasis on the films in question as a manifestation of postcolonial resistance. This reading, which I increasingly found too triumphant and detached from reality, was abandoned in a later version, published in *Fifty Years of Electric Shadows*, ed. Law Kar, Twenty-first Hong Kong International Film Festival (Hong Kong: Urban Council, 1997), in which I shifted my focus to the historiographic dimension. The present essay is an elaboration and revision of that version bearing a more critical look: I suspend my overt affirmation of the historiographic power of the films discussed for more specific discursive functions. Special thanks to Hector Rodriguez for his stimulating comments, especially his warning against easy populism; and to Esther Yau for encouraging me to rework the essay.

1 I borrow the expression from Anthony Giddens, "Habermas's Critique of Hermeneutics," in *Studies in Social and Political Theory* (New York: Basic Books, 1977), 135–64, at 136.

2 Ibid., 137.

3 For more on the definitive characterization of "nostalgia" and an inventory of "nostalgia films," readers may want to refer to Luo Feng, *The Decadent City* (Hong Kong: Oxford University Press, 1995), 60–75; Li Cheuk-to, *Guan Ni Ji: Hong Kong Cinema* (Hong Kong: Sub-culture, 1993), 133–36, 165–68; Li Cheuk-to, *Guan Ni Ji: Chinese and Foreign Cinema* (Hong Kong: Sub-culture, 1993), chapter 1; and Jiao Xiongping (Peggy Chiao), ed., *Xianggang Dianying Feng*

Mao, 1975–1986 [*The Outlook of Hong Kong Cinema, 1975–1986*] (Taibei: Shibao Chibuan, 1987), 191–96.

4 See *Merriam-Webster's Collegiate Dictionary*, 10th ed. (Springfield, Mass.: Merriam-Webster, 1994), s.v. "Nostalgia."

5 One other important precedent is Wang Weiyi's *The House of 72 Tenants* (1993), a Hong Kong–mainland coproduction. The prototype can be traced back to Cheng Bugao's *Old and New Shanghai* [*Xing Jiu Shanghai*] (1936), made by Mingxing Co. in Shanghai.

6 The latest addition to the list is Cho Gin-laam's *Those Were the Days* (1997), featuring four "faithful brothers in a time of crisis." The film alludes to the 1990s director Wong Kar-wai, whose contempt for Hong Kong cinema of the 1960s met the vengeance of the 1960s director Chu Yuan. Chu took him back in time to the 1960s, where he met the good and bad members of the cursed film community. Wong's view was "reformed" in the end.

7 *Cantonese Cinema Retrospective (1960–1969)* (Hong Kong: Urban Council, 1982), 145.

8 A fuller discussion of *He Ain't Heavy* and *C'est la vie* by this writer appears in *Fifty Years of Electric Shadows*, 95–98.

9 The songstress prototype can be traced back to the Shanghai cinema of the 1930s; it was immortalized by the actress Zhou Xuan.

10 Fredric Jameson, *Postmodernism, or, The Cultural Logic of Late Capitalism* (Durham, N.C.: Duke University Press, 1991), 2. The quote, in the original text, is a description of what Jameson considers the "one fundamental feature of all the postmodernisms," which the writer of this essay reads instead as the unifying feature of postmodern cultural inclinations.

11 Research published in Geneva in 1987 shows Hong Kong second among the world's cities (after Tokyo) in its cost of living. See *Ming Pao Daily News*, 5 August 1997.

12 Jameson, 279–82.

13 Ibid., 280.

14 *Fight Back to School*, *All's Well Ends Well*, *Justice, My Foot*, and his earlier films are pregnant with such language.

15 This is evident in almost all of Chiau's films. The most interesting examples include *From China with Love* (1994), *Sixty Million Dollar Man* (1995), and *Forbidden City Cop* (1996).

16 The most explicit example is *The God of Cookery* (1997).

17 See, e.g., *Out of the Dark* (1996).

18 This is most apparent in *Sixty Million Dollar Man*, in which the carnivalesque masks appear in the form of domestic household appliances such as an iron, a rice cooker, a toilet, toothpaste, a shower hose (functioning as an elongated penis), a microwave oven (as the ultimate killer of the wicked), and so on. *Forbidden City Cop* demonstrated similar practices.

19 Some local film critics identify Chiau's cinematic predecessor as Michael Hui, a comedian famous in the 1980s for such films as *Security Unlimited* (1981), *Teppanyaki* (1984), and *Chicken and Duck Talk* (1988).

20 By humanism, I refer particularly to a mode of thinking, predominant in the West since the eighteenth century, that emphasizes the use of the human mind

and its application in social and political matters, celebrating individual creativity and a participatory lifestyle. This brand of humanism has significantly informed China's history of modernization.

21 John Docker, *Postmodernism and Popular Culture: A Cultural History* (Cambridge and New York: Cambridge University Press, 1994), 177.

22 Robert Stam, *Subversive Pleasure: Bakhtin, Cultural Criticism, and Film* (Baltimore: Johns Hopkins University Press, 1989), 305.

23 All of them have been popularized in television drama series.

24 The term was originally used by the historian Pierre Nora. See Patrick Hutton, *History as an Art of Memory* (Hanover: University of Vermont, 1993), 10.

25 True-crime stories from the distant past are sometimes turned into television dramas, while legends of local heroes and celebrities form a unique genre of biographical movies such as Lawrence Ah Mon's *Lee Rock I* (1991) and Poon Man-kit's *To Be Number One* (1991). The territory's early colonial days, which to most Hong Kong people is a blank, has been fantasized by the territory's popular directors, most prominently in Jackie Chan's *Project A, Part II* (1987) and Leung Po-chih's *Welcome* (1985).

26 My discussion of commemorative practices is based on Hutton's discussion of the role of memory in contemporary historiography in the first chapter of *History as an Art of Memory*, 1–26. "Commemoration" can be traced back to the French Annales School's emphasis on cultural history and everyday life, which is developed by other historians into the study of the role of memory.

27 Ibid., 4.

28 Ibid., 7. Hutton's discussion is based on the work of the historian Maurice Halbwachs.

CHAPTER ELEVEN

Transnational Exchanges, Questions of Culture, and Global Cinema: Defining the Dynamics of Changing Relationships

Gina Marchetti

In recent years, the terms "nation" and "culture" have provided the fuel for countless discussions involving borders, border crossings, transnationalism, and globalization in media studies. There seems to be general agreement that changing economic, political, social, and other relationships precipitated by new technologies have dramatically changed the cultural landscape. However, moving down from the theoretical plane to the level of scholarly practice, established categories tend to dominate research. In the case of motion picture studies, for example, books on "national" cinemas abound, and the idea of "culture" as self-evident, self-contained, bordered, and monolingual is still taken for granted.

Scholarship coming from a variety of disciplines has sought to engage this dilemma. Postcolonial theory has contributed the notion of hybridity to these debates, and a call to place all notions of an "essential" identity into question within the multiple identities available in the postmodern metropolis. Others call for a "radical" multiculturalism that refuses to disguise the issues of power and struggle behind the "melting-pot" veneer of contemporary culture. Within these debates, the centrality of the economy and globalization of the culture industry cannot be neglected. Filmmakers, for example, may live in one country, make all their films in a second country, and find financing in a third, while hoping to address a global, polyglot audience with what may be a localized narrative. Because of the transnational nature of these films, a new, "transcultural" politics of representation needs to be elucidated.

This is an investigation of some of the attempts to rethink cultural relationships within the dynamics of an increasingly globalized media environment, using transnational motion picture production as the specific case in point. To ground the discussion in a specific case study, the work of Evans Chan will be taken as an example of the difficulty and the necessity of developing a transcultural approach. Chan is a New York–based filmmaker, 251 born in mainland China, bred in Macao, and educated in Hong Kong and America, who makes independent narrative films primarily for a Hong Kong, overseas Chinese, "greater China" audience. His films straddle the gulf between the international art film and Hong Kong commercial cinema and thus have gotten some art film viewers globally. In addition, several Asian American film festivals in the United States have picked up his work. To date, Chan has completed two features, *To Liv(e) [Fushi Lianchu]* (1991) and *Crossings [Cuoai]* (1994). Both of these films openly address issues that find only a marginal voice in the mainstream cinema of Hong Kong, the United States, and other Chinese cinemas globally.

Both films feature Rubie (Lindzay Chan) as a Hong Kong woman who confronts and crosses various literal and figurative borders. In *To Liv(e)*, Rubie becomes angered by a statement made by Liv Ullmann in December 1989 about the inhumane treatment of Vietnamese refugees by the Hong Kong authorities. In the wake of the events in Beijing that June, Rubie questions Ullmann's timing in a letter she composes and addresses to the Scandinavian actress. Passages from the letter punctuate the rest of the film as Rubie must decide, along with members of her family and circle of Hong Kong artists and intellectuals, whether to stay or leave Hong Kong before 1 July 1997. Throughout the film, Rubie talks to a range of people about their feelings regarding the handover. In *Crossings*, she has settled in New York City as a social worker. She befriends Mo-Yung (Anita Yuen), who has illegally come to the United States to look for her wayward, drug-trafficking boyfriend, Benny (Simon Yam). Joey (Ted Brunetti), a psychotic schoolteacher with a fetish for Asian women, stalks Rubie, whom he has seen as a community spokeswoman on television. Mistaking Mo-Yung for Rubie, he kills Mo-Yung on a subway platform.

With one foot in the United States and the other in Hong Kong, Chan can freely address issues as diverse as Hong Kong's return to China in 1997, the legacy of the events of 4 June 1989 in Tiananmen Square, the role of women in the world economy (in both the "official" economy and the "informal sector," which can include prostitutes and traffickers in narcotics), and the processes of immigration and dispersal involving the Chinese globally. While fears of censorship arising from Hong Kong's laws and the unofficial censorship of the marketplace in the United States place a boundary around what can and cannot be said in the cinema, Chan, with his transnational production team, manages to seriously explore controversial issues. In this way, Chan creates a transnational, transcultural discourse through the medium of the motion picture, pointing to a new type of cultural sphere that must be noted in media studies.[1]

To Liv(e) and *Crossings* can be seen as works suspended between the modern and the postmodern;[2] indeed, their textual strategies rely on this deeply rooted indeterminacy to explore people and issues that are themselves difficult to delineate. Chan is profoundly influenced by European art cinema. The English title *To Liv(e)*, for example, conjures up both Jean-Luc Godard and Jean-Pierre Gorin's *Letter to Jane* (1972), as well as Ingmar Bergman's many works with Liv Ullmann. Chan characterizes the film as "inevitably a response to both Bergman and Godard,"[3] and Patricia Brett Erens outlines the various ways in which the film draws on Godard in her insightful essay "The Aesthetics of Protest: Evans Chan's *To Liv(e)*."[4]

The impact of Godard is very clear in the scene in which Rubie reads her first letter to Liv. Using a shot of boats as a transitional device, the tinny, hollow sound of a recording of Cui Jian's "Nothing to My Name" comes up on the soundtrack. The film pans across a crowded auditorium; Rubie is seated in the audience. A dance performance ("Exhausted Silkworms"), inspired by the events of 4 June in Tiananmen Square, is taking place on the stage. Three male dancers, dressed simply in white shirts and black pants, tear their clothes to form gags and, later, nooses. A red scarf is pulled out of one of the dancer's shirts, like spurting blood. As "Nothing to My Name" ends, one dancer falls as if shot. Suspended for a moment with a freeze frame, he finally lands on the ground as the audience applauds.

This performance is layered by the inclusion of Rubie's first letter as a voice-over. As the dancers perform, Rubie's address to Liv Ullmann (and, through her, to the world at large) adds another dimension to both Cui Jian's rock music, which says nothing explicit about "democracy" or politics at all, and to the performers' reenactment of the Tiananmen Square demonstration and its suppression. As the dancers act out this violence, accompanied by Cui Jian's harsh, direct vocals, Rubie likens Liv Ullmann to a respected, distant portrait coming to life and slapping her in the face with accusations of cruelty and indifference. Rubie complains not only of Ullmann's ignorance about the situation in Hong Kong that this public condemnation of the treatment of the Vietnamese displays, but also questions her timing. Coming just months after Tiananmen Square, an event that was taken by many in Hong Kong as a barometer of what to expect after 1997, Rubie reminds Ullmann that the people of Hong Kong may soon find themselves in the same boat, so to speak, as the Vietnamese.

Figure 1.
Dancers reenact the
Tiananmen Square
demonstration and its
suppression in *To Liv(e)*
(Evans Chan, 1991).

However, it may be too tempting, at this point, to conclude that *To Liv(e)* is simply imitation Godard. Another element to the scene takes the film in a radically different direction. While Rubie is presented as an agent addressing Ullmann, as a spokesperson for Hong Kong, and as a spectator of a dance piece (and, by extension, a political event), Rubie is also depicted as distracted. Near the beginning of the scene, she checks her watch and looks around the auditorium. Later we learn that Rubie is waiting for her brother, Tony. Rubie's relationship with her brother, his fiancée, and her family propels the film into another, totally different arena: the realm of the love story and family melodrama. Rubie may be the voice of Hong Kong, but she also plays the roles of daughter, sister, lover, and friend in other parts of the narrative.

While less directly indebted to the European New Wave, *Crossings* still bears the marks of cinematic modernism. Again, fiction and nonfiction overlap as actual footage of Tiananmen Square in 1989 is cut into newscasts in which the film's fictional characters appear. Dance presentations divide the diegesis further into self-contained fictional realms. Characters again function as mouthpieces for policies or ideas as well as fictional creations involved in narrative events. Rubie (again played by Lindzay Chan) reappears to serve this function once more: she is featured on New York television as the public voice of the Chinatown community and, through voice-over excerpts from a diary, as the personal voice of the Hong Kong emigrant. However, while *To Liv(e)* has more clearly demarcated divisions between the various layers of the discourse, *Crossings*, which is closer to Edward Yang's

Terrorizer and other works of the Taiwanese and Hong Kong New Wave, experiments with time and space to a much larger degree. In fact, it is often difficult to figure out whether the location is New York or Hong Kong—before or after the characters come to America.

The films, as Fredric Jameson might say, have a "schizophrenic" quality that can be seen in their titles. Not only is the English title, *To Liv(e)*, a deconstructed play on words referring to Liv Ullmann, *Letter to Jane*, and a heartfelt desire for the people of Hong Kong to somehow endure and "to live," the Chinese title, which translates roughly as "Love Songs from a Floating World," seems to refer to another face of the film that deals with romantic relationships and a Chinese tradition of misdirected and/or impossible love. *Crossings* offers a similar case in point. The English title conjures up images of immigration, exile, nomadism, and the modern metropolis as a crossroads, while the Chinese title, "Wrong Love," refers to unhappy affairs of the heart. As the titles imply, these polyglot films offer a divided address and, potentially, multiple interpretations, or at least a divided ordering of narrative hierarchies, for the English-speaking film audience at festivals and art cinemas globally, for the slowly expanding circle of Asian American film spectators, and for the Chinese-speaking audience seeing the films in relation to the standard Hong Kong commercial product.

However, it is wrong to view the films exclusively in this way, as split discourses, because there is another possibility that needs to be taken into consideration. Rather than operating as a dialectic between the art film and the commercial love story, between English and Chinese, the films can be taken as palimpsests where the elements overlay one another, obscuring meaning for some, illuminating a different kind of meaning for others. A new meaning is not created through the clash of contradictory discourses, as can be seen in the work of Godard. Rather, layers sit on top of one another, some (almost) postcolonial in English, some diasporic and accented in American English, some (almost) post-socialist in Chinese, some modern and part of the tail end of an international New Wave, others postmodern and part of contemporary global cinema culture.

Although *To Liv(e)* and *Crossings* are quite different, more than a single director links the works together. Taken as a set, they comment on certain common themes (e.g., Hong Kong in 1997, immigration, changing family and social relationships in "Greater China," etc.) from two different temporal and spatial perspectives. *To Liv(e)* primarily looks at the edginess of Hong Kong residents who are able to leave but may or may not do so before July 1997. *Crossings* looks primarily at newly transplanted Hong Kong

Figure 2.
Edgy Hong Kong
residents before
July 1997 in *To Liv(e)*.

émigrés in New York City, that is, at immigration as a fait accompli rather than as a possibility.

Rubie appears in both *To Liv(e)* and *Crossings*, and her character can be pieced together from information found in each film. Her roots are found among the poorer quarters of Hong Kong society. Rubie is a journalist who becomes a community activist and social worker in New York. Her brother Tony is a highly skilled radiologist, and their eldest brother has successfully established himself in Canada. Unlike their parents, the children have the education and skills to move outside a Chinese environment into a global, English-based, diasporic community of postcolonial professionals and intellectuals plying their trades along the path of the former British empire — from Canada to Australia, the United States, and South Africa. They come from an impoverished China, but they move now in other circles. Ironically, it is the experience of colonialism that makes this movement and this upward mobility possible.

Rubie speaks in two voices, in fluent Cantonese and in impeccable British-accented English. Like Hong Kong itself, sometimes she looks Western, British, and Caucasian, and sometimes she looks Chinese and Asian. For example, in *To Liv(e)* she reads several of her letters in English, directly addressing the camera in medium shots, seated against a British Union Jack, the American stars and stripes, and the flag of the People's Republic of China. Interestingly, when she is shot in front of the red Chinese flag, the lighting of her hair accentuates its reddish highlights. The light allows her to

Figure 3.
Displaced women as
the voice of Hong Kong
and beyond in *Crossings*
(Evans Chan, 1994).

blend in with the flag at the same time it emphasizes her distinctiveness as a Eurasian performer. Rubie plays the roles of a British subject, an ethnic Chinese, an Asian American immigrant, and, most importantly, a character of an indeterminate identity.

In *Crossings*, Rubie tells another story about her origins. She explains her Caucasian features to another displaced woman, Mo-Yung, as a throwback to the Tang dynasty, when she must have acquired some European ancestor from exchanges on the Silk Route. Rubie, then, functions as the voice of Hong Kong and as the voice of the Chinese beyond Hong Kong and China, expressing, through her letters in *To Liv(e)*, and her diary and appearances on the television news as an "expert" insider in *Crossings*, the hopes and fears of her community. Her identity and the identity of that community, however, are difficult to pin down as they slip among Britain, America, Hong Kong, and China, between the lower small-merchant classes and the upwardly mobile professionals, between a "traditional" older generation and a more urbane younger one. Still, Rubie manages to embody this cacophony of "voices."

However, Rubie is more than a "mouth"—she is also an "ear." Rubie functions as a public, intellectual ear that is able to hear and validate the various voices that present themselves, and she also serves as a private, personal ear. In both films, Rubie listens to an array of personal problems voiced by those in her circle of family, friends, and acquaintances. Perhaps because of the very nature of her indeterminate identity, all the characters in both films feel free to express themselves in her presence. With few exceptions, all the films' characters talk to Rubie, and Rubie listens. As this narrative ear, Rubie holds the plots of both films together.

Although Chan works, like Bertolt Brecht, Sergei Eisenstein, and Godard, to alienate his characters from the audience, using them often as types to illustrate particular points, the filmmaker also employs these characters in more conventional ways, underscoring their individuality, allowing them to speak not only as representatives of ideological positions and abstract social categories, but also as distinct entities.

To illustrate this point, it might be instructive to look at a scene from *Crossings*. Rubie meets Mo-Yung in a café near Times Square. The camera is positioned outside as the scene begins, then moves inside to frame Rubie and Mo-Yung, silhouetted against the café window as the New York traffic passes by outside. Throughout the scene, the camera moves between the two women, using a vase with dried flowers on the table as a pivotal point. Mo-Yung talks about coming from Suzhou; Rubie talks about her features and the imagined Silk Route ancestor. Both laugh that they are "two barbarians invading New York." The camera cuts away to a shot of Mo-Yung framed through the café window, and the mood changes. Rubie fills Mo-Yung in on her own situation and her desire to get a green card and open America as a possibility for her son. Mo-Yung asks, "What if your son doesn't like America and blames you?" When Rubie replies that he can always go back, Mo-Yung counters, "Do you think you can recreate the past just like that?" The scene ends on a close shot of Mo-Yung putting out her cigarette in an ashtray near the dried flowers, flanked by the empty coffee cups.

This scene highlights elements that move the narrative into the realm of the women's film. The emphasis is on the relationship between women, their solidarity in the face of the trials of immigration and in the face of changing sexual mores and family relationships. Here, as friends, mothers, lovers, ex-wives, fiancées, and confidantes, Rubie and Mo-Yung illustrate the personal dimension of the political concerns of 1997. Women experience a different type of "crossing" than men. Traditional roles for women dissolve in the diaspora. Families become unhinged, scattered; romantic relationships become more fleeting. Cast adrift by a desire to escape from rigid families, ex-husbands, and the feeling of being alienated from the traditional world in which they were born and bred, these women move off with a different sense of loss, different fears, and for reasons that go far beyond the political dynamics of 1997. Following Rubie as the "ear," the camera invites the spectator to share these intimate moments.

Like the in-between, transnational, transcultural characters they depict, *To Liv(e)* and *Crossings* also defy easy classification. However, while identities may be uncertain and fluctuating, the issues these characters embody remain concrete and disturbingly fixed.

Chan's treatment of these issues involves ambivalent feelings. *To Liv(e)* concludes with cautious optimism on two fronts. In her last letter to Liv Ullmann, Rubie ends with the hope that China, Vietnam, and, by extension, Hong Kong will improve their respective situations so that all, including Rubie and Liv, will be able to meet as friends. In fact, she signs her letter, "Love, Rubie." The last image of the film shows Rubie's brother and his fiancée, saved from near suicide and break-up, alighting from their taxi at the airport, baggage in hand, on their way to Australia. *Crossings*, on the other hand, ends on a pessimistic note. Rubie burns incense in memory of Mo-Yung on the subway platform where she was murdered.

While *To Liv(e)* ends with death averted and hope in the future, *Crossings* concludes with the finality of death and the uncertainty of Rubie's future. She returns to Hong Kong with Mo-Yung's bones, but it is not certain whether she will return to New York, stay in Hong Kong, or go elsewhere. Since, after death, even bones continue to drift between continents, Rubie's continued "crossings" between roles and professions, among nation-states, and between Asia and the West also seem to be one of the few certainties in a very uncertain fictional world. That global filmmakers themselves will continue to drift and make films about this "floating world" of displacement and hybridity also seems fairly certain. To bring Chan's pessimism back around to a more hopeful note, I conclude with a quote from Homi Bhabha's "DissemiNation: Time, Narrative and the Margins of the Modern Nation":

> For it is by living on the borderline of history and language, on the limits of race and gender, that we are in a position to translate the differences between them into a kind of solidarity.[5]

Notes

A version of this paper was originally presented at the Pre-Conference Proceedings of the Sixth AMIC Annual Conference, Kuala Lumpur, 19 June 1997. A longer version of this essay is published in "Transnational Cinema, Hybrid Identities and the Films of Evans Chan," *Postmodern Culture* 8, no. 2 (January 1998), at http://jefferson.village.virginia.edu/pmc/current.issue.

1   The transnational dimension of Chinese film has been noted by a number of film scholars, including Sheldon Lu, ed., *Transnational Chinese Cinemas* (Honolulu: University of Hawaii Press, 1997), and Steve Fore, "Golden Harvest Films and the

Hong Kong Movie Industry in the Realm of Globalization," *Velvet Light Trap* 34 (fall 1994): 40–58, among others.

2 Fredric Jameson makes a similar point about Edward Yang's *The Terrorizer* in *The Geopolitical Aesthetic: Cinema and Space in the World System* (Bloomington: Indiana University Press, 1995).

3 Evans Chan, "Forward to *To Liv(e)*," in *Evans Chan's "To Liv(e)": Screenplay and Essays*, ed. Tak-wai Wong (Hong Kong: University of Hong Kong, Department of Comparative Literature, 1996), 6.

4 Patricia Brett Erens, "The Aesthetics of Protest: Evans Chan's *To Liv(e)*," in Wong, 109–16.

5 Homi Bhabha, "DissemiNation: Time, Narrative, and the Margins of the Modern Nation," in *The Location of Culture* (London: Routledge, 1994), 170.

CHAPTER TWELVE

Transnationalization of the Local in Hong Kong Cinema of the 1990s

Kwai-cheung Lo

The notion of transnationality opens up a new possibility of studying the social and cultural conditions of Hong Kong cinema in the 1990s and poses a daunting challenge for us to rethink the concept of the local. Hong Kong, the second largest source of film exports in the world, is undergoing an unprecedented process of decolonization and at the same time is engaged in forming a newly unified national identity under the regime of Communist China in the name of "one country, two systems." It is understandable that films produced in Hong Kong would be harnessed with a more distinctive national image after 1997. In fact, Hong Kong cinema has since the early 1980s been infiltrating the mainland by coproducing with Chinese studios and importing films (and also through video piracy).[1] But this kind of cooperation and interaction does not necessarily create a stronger sense of unity in the cultural and cinematic productions of the two Chinese communities; it does reveal a freer flow and more pervasive penetration of transnational capital in the mainland market.

The Hong Kong film industry has a much closer tie with Taiwan than with the mainland, not only in terms of capital investment and market distribution, but also in the areas of talent exchange, story materials, and even legal status.[2] Many Hong Kong productions have been directly financed by Taiwanese capital ever since Hong Kong commercial films began to dominate Taiwan's film market in the early 1980s and Taiwanese businessmen found it more profitable to invest in Hong Kong films. Over the last decade, Hong Kong also served as a middleman for Taiwanese investment in the mainland film industry because the Nationalist government in Taiwan strictly regulated the screening of films shot in China. In the 1990s some Taiwanese companies even began moving their main offices to Hong Kong in order to facilitate their transnational investments both in Hong Kong and on the mainland.[3] Some Chinese films with international reputations, such as Zhang Yimou's *Raise the Red Lantern* [*Dahong Denglong Gaogao Gua*]

(1990) and *To Live [Huozhe]* (1995), and Chen Kaige's *Farewell My Concubine [Bawang Bieji]* (1995) and *Temptress Moon [Fengyue]* (1996), were financed by Taiwanese companies registered in Hong Kong.

The direct financing of Hong Kong movies enables Taiwanese investors to dictate casting, genre, and other production decisions. Taiwanese investors have a strong voice in the logistics of Hong Kong productions, and it is arguable that Taiwanese capital is really capable of steering the development of Hong Kong film industry. Meanwhile, Hollywood has imported a number of Hong Kong directors, such as John Woo, Ringo Lam, Tsui Hark, and Stanley Tong, to shoot actions and comedies. At the same time, Hong Kong films starring Jackie Chan, Jet Li, and Chow Yun-fat are able to draw big crowds on American college campuses and major cities. The idiosyncratic style of Hong Kong cinema — its cartoon violence and fast editing — has already had a visible impact on some mainstream Hollywood films such as *Desperado* (1995), *Mortal Kombat* (1995), and *From Dusk till Dawn* (1996). Yet, the cross-cultural achievement of Hong Kong cinema also comes at a time when the local industry is suffering a severe decline. Even though some Hong Kong filmmakers become successful in Hollywood, Hong Kong cinema is actually losing its competitive edge to Hollywood productions in its Asian markets.

The Local Constituted in the Transnational

Hong Kong cinema seems to be entering a transnational space in which tensions and ambivalence resulting from encroaching national representation and borderless capitalization have generated a new kind of complexity in its filmic production. Does Hong Kong cinema become more national or more transnational in these changing times? How do local filmmakers react to the increasing influence of mainland China and the economic pressures of other foreign investors? This essay is concerned with how some Hong Kong films, in this transnational situation, attempt to constitute a "local" site in the field of relationships shaped by those contradictory pressures and tendencies. What the "local" implies in this context is no longer a realm of resistance to global capital, nor is it a form of desire to return to one's cultural origins or to a lost past. Rather, the "local" constructed in Hong Kong cinema of the 1990s is an area of negotiation within which dominant, subordinate, and oppositional cultural, economic, and ideological elements are mixed, in various permutations.

In terms of the antagonistic relationship between the local and the global, the former is always designated as the primary source of national identity against the penetrating forces of multinational capitalism and cultural imperialism. It is also considered a site of resistance to the coercive linear and teleological development of Western modernization. But the local constructed in Hong Kong cultural and filmic production may not necessarily meet this definition. On the contrary, the local site, rather than being an enclosed place for delineating a well-established homogeneous identity, is relatively fluid and porous to the infiltration of alien elements. I would like to argue that the meaning of the Hong Kong local is always already overdetermined by the framework of the transnational that structures our perception of its reality. In the case of Hong Kong, the local is the transnational itself in its becoming. It emerges in between the national discourse and global structuralization and remains fluctuating and unsettled rather than being fully articulated and self-present. The local is a moment not of closure but of openness or undecidability that can even disrupt and call into question some fundamental structures and preconceptions of self-identity. This may explain why the local in Hong Kong filmic production is never asserted as a nationalistic entity against the universalistic drive for modernization. Instead, the Hong Kong local is always accompanied by a tinge of modernity in the sense that the capitalist narrative and the claim of Westernization are not easily repudiated.

In other words, there is a correlation or codependence between the transnational and the local, which, however, is not merely an objective correlative to the global force. It is the transnational itself, in its changing and pliable existence, that serves as a kind of stand-in for the local, which cannot be recuperated in a simple positive form. Thus, the conception of the local always goes hand in hand with transnational development and resists a separated comprehension.[4]

A trend of transnationalizing of the local was evident in *kungfu* movies early in the 1970s. The martial arts films or swordplay films made in Hong Kong, inheriting the local opera tradition, emphasized the tactical skills of the *kungfu*-master actors and closely captured in cinema minute changes in the actors' posture, stance, and appearance. As David Bordwell points out, this aesthetic of highlighting the concreteness and clarity of each gesture in *kungfu* cinema must come from traditions of martial arts and Peking opera.[5] It is precisely this localism that differentiates Hong Kong action cinema from its Hollywood counterpart and intrigues many Western audiences. Paradoxically, Bruce Lee, the superstar who used the localist *kungfu* film genre to fight his way into international markets, making Hong Kong martial arts films fascinating to the Western gaze, was not so local himself. The first internationally known Hong Kong movie star, Lee always combated foreign villains on screen, though the characters he played were more generically "trans-Chinese" than distinguishably Hong Kong local. Lee's cultural and racial background further complicated the "local identity" that his action movies brought to the Hong Kong people.[6]

Esther Yau observes that action directors like Zhang Che in the 1970s urged Hong Kong filmmakers to work on a new kind of localism, a combination of native legends, *yanggang* masculinity, and modern cinematic mise-en-scène, in order to compete internationally.[7] The "local" boosted in Hong Kong *kungfu* cinema is not really intended to empower native awareness. Rather, it is more a strategy of overseas marketing undertaken to serve commercial purposes. Although Bordwell convincingly argues that the concrete and powerful action sequence in Hong Kong *kungfu* cinema is mostly manifested by a pause-burst-pause pattern in which the actor's continuous movements are separated by intelligible breaks of stasis,[8] the main rhythm of this action genre is still predominantly characterized by unimaginable speed—a speed that, as Tsui Hark's films abundantly demonstrate, can no longer be performed by human bodies but has to be supported by special effects and advanced technology. It is also a speed that can easily merge into the highway of the multinational flow of capital, becoming synonymous with transnational circulation, progress, and change.

Hong Kong films of the late 1980s and early 1990s provide more reflections on the concept of the local. For New Wave directors and filmmakers like Allen Fong, Ann Hui, Stanley Kwan, Mabel Cheung, and Clara Law, localism no longer pertains to the culture and customs of a particular place. It is thought of in relation to other cultures and other localities, rather than simply being a thing that stresses its selfsame identity. The construction of the local relies on what differentiates. In short, the local consists of a sequence of representations that are all by definition differentiated. In Allen Fong's *Just like Weather* [Meiguoxin] (1986), Ann Hui's *Song of the Exile* [Ketu Qiuhen] (1989), Stanley Kwan's *Full Moon in New York* [Renzai Niuyue] (1987), Mabel Cheung's *An Autumn's Tale* [Qiutian de Tonghua] (1987), and Clara Law's *Farewell China* [Ai zai Biexiang de Jijie] (1990) the local is scrutinized in terms of its being displaced in different spaces and different times. These films were mostly shot in foreign locations and deal with the problem of local subjectivity through the relationship of the local to the other. Though they could be considered transnational in their inclinations, these works still see the foreign other as a differentiating entity from which a distinct Hong Kong or Chinese identity is constituted. However, in other productions of the 1990s that I will discuss shortly, the local culture or identity depicted has a much-blurred boundary with the foreign. The other is always incorporated as an essential part of the local. Never is the local a single, unified given; rather, it is a multiplication of various cultures and different times. What is revealing about these productions is that the so-called Hong Kong localism is becoming more ambivalent in the further transnationalized context of the last few years of the twentieth century and the first few of the twenty-first.

Creating Transsubjectivity

Hong Kong cinema went through a slump in the early 1990s. The uncertainty attending Hong Kong's return to China in 1997 exacerbated the loss of talent and the take-the-money-and-run attitude in filmmaking that were in turn helping to create a flood of slapdash productions, which resulted in a serious drop in ticket sales. But the most critical factor contributing to the industry crisis was the rapid shrinking of its overseas market shares, which traditionally made up 30 to 80 percent of the total income of each production. The increasing loss of overseas markets was caused by the decreasing standards of many Hong Kong productions and keen competition from Hollywood cinema.[9] The crisis in the film industry, however, created opportunities for new talents and new companies to renovate conventional genres and explore innovative new ideas. Spending large amounts of money on stunts and explosions for action thrillers became far less common in the local cinema of the 1990s. Hong Kong filmmakers, knowing that their movies had fallen out of favor among foreign film buyers, have been attempting to give priority once more to the local audience. They believe, with a certain arrogance and pride despite the adverse circumstances, that what is popular in Hong Kong will be widely appreciated by other Chinese.

As one producer puts it, "The Chinese communities in Southeast Asia always see Hong Kong as their role model. They accept almost everything that is popular in Hong Kong. This means that the tastes of the people of Hong Kong would be warmly received by other Chinese communities. It is only a matter of time."[10] In the new marketing strategies of the Hong Kong film industry, the local stands for the transnational Chinese. This notion of Chinese transnationality is, however, different from that of the Chinese diaspora. The concept of the Chinese diaspora is still built upon the "Middle Kingdom complex," in which the hierarchical relationship between the Chinese cultural core and the peripheral status of the dispersed Chinese communities dominates,[11] whereas transnationality depends more on economic and informational-cultural deterritorializing drives than on the centripetal force of Chineseness. Thus, the transnational character in Hong Kong cinema of the 1990s was not exactly a manifestation of the cultural identification of the Chinese diaspora. It was less a symbol of ethnic unity than a form of desire for capital growth. For instance, a diasporic Chinese may be eager to find another space to relocate the ethnic community, but a transnationalized local would attempt to remake or dislocate a given space in order to loosen it for more fluid economic and cultural flows.

The current Hong Kong filmmakers have refocused on the concerns of the local market, but their works are not confined to narrow parochial interests. They endeavor to simulate the quality of Hollywood productions with a much lower budget and, consciously or unconsciously, imitate the characteristics of the globalist American cinema, with its emphasis on movement and ease of crossing frontiers, a concern with communication and service, and a relative downplaying of subtle emotions in human interaction but focusing on violent action or sexual activity.[12] The popularity of their movies may tell us about the changing cultural conditions of the local community. The producers and directors Peter Chan and Lee Chi-ngai and the production company United Filmmakers Organization (UFO), founded in 1990, are outstanding examples of this new trend in Hong Kong cinema. Meanwhile, some other, less prominent companies founded in the 1990s are producing films in which the interplay of transnationalization and localism can be tracked. These companies' films have in common low budgets, contemporary settings (for the most part), commercial orientation (though with good artistic considerations), and close ties to the current issues of Hong Kong daily life — for instance, the problems of cultural identity and migration. Nevertheless, UFO relies more on the star system, which may explain why the company is doing better in terms of box office receipts and attracting more media attention.

Back to Roots [Guitu] (1994),[13] directed by Ray Leung, is a film that touches on nationhood, but anachronistically: a Hong Kong gangster running away from a murder charge ends up in a primitive Shaanbei village on the loess plateau of northern China. The film's images of the yellow rural landscape, the hardships of peasant life, and women's subordination to the patriarchal system, all accompanied by a soundtrack of folksong, repeatedly remind the viewer of another film, Chen Kaige's *Yellow Earth*, set in 1939. For the contemporary citizen of Hong Kong, what signifies China — an estranged homeland to which Hong Kong Chinese have to return — is still the loftiness of the

natural landscape, poverty, and primitive living conditions, as well as harmony and intimacy in human relationships. The typical "Chinese features"
presented in imagistic terms in *Back to Roots* do not necessarily generate the
same effects of cultural identification as those in the works of the Fifth Generation directors from mainland China did among audiences in the West.
Perhaps it is not simply that a Hong Kong film is incapable of correctly representing authentic and pure "Chineseness." Precisely because of its powerful technology, capable of recreating a rural China as visually impressive as
the real thing on the mainland, Hong Kong film transforms Chinese local
culture into a simulacrum for the tourist's gaze and renders its authenticity
suspicious.

The message of *Back to Roots* is "politically correct": the Hong Kong exile
and prodigal recognizes his identity in the Chinese homeland and is determined to go back there after serving his sentence in a Hong Kong prison. But
that identity is never place-bound and has no community loyalty to any particular locale; instead, it is constituted by simulated images from contemporary Chinese cinema. It is a Hong Kong transnational fantasy of the Chinese
local, created by privileging its isolated ethnic signifiers while depoliticizing
the cultural and native experiences. Invoking not only the dichotomy between the evil city and the saintly countryside as a political message, the film
also implies the opposition between the Communists and the Nationalists
(the Hong Kong gangster is the grandson of a deceased Nationalist soldier
who had been exiled to Hong Kong, while the father figure he meets in
Shaanbei village is a retired Communist soldier participating in the Long
March). Yet, it is an opposition that can be overcome by the myth of a shared
"Chineseness" and by male bonding (the Hong Kong gangster sees in the retired Communist his own Nationalist grandfather and regains from him
lost fatherly love and meaning in his life)—a fantasy often upheld in Hong
Kong cinematic productions, like Alfred Cheung's *Her Fatal Ways [Biaojie
Nihaoye]* (1990) and its sequels. In a way, this film reconstructs an exotic but
hospitable China in terms of surface imagery and simulated concepts. But
the last shot is ambiguous: the protagonist, who wears decent modern clothing and carries an Adidas bag, walks away from the camera in the direction
of the village. Is he abandoning corrupt Hong Kong society for the new horizon of the idyllic China? Or does he bring with him the global impulse of
the late capitalist city to penetrate the nature of that precapitalist enclave?

At a first glance, Gordon Chan's *First Option [Fei Hu]* (1996)[14] appears to
be an attempt to reassert the integrity of the local in the face of threatening

internationalism: international terrorists (mainly ex–U.S. Marines) traffic in drugs and challenge the local police force. Instead of remasculinizing the loner hero, a Special Unit cop who is suffering after being ditched by his girl-friend, the film emphasizes the spirit of teamwork and collective discipline. The film differs from the Hollywood terrorist genre in that the hero of *First Option* is not rewarded with a woman (that is to say, he does not again become the "real man" he once was) after winning the battle with the terrorists. Localism is not delegated by any individual masculine hero. On the contrary, the local world is represented by various members of the law enforcement group, especially the female customs officer, who knows she is no match for the terrorists in terms of military training and weaponry but still insists on doing her duty. However, even though the unified local triumphs over the internationalist threat, the film exemplifies certain globalist attitudes. First of all, the male lead, played by the half English, half Chinese Michael Wong, suggests the hybrid and multicultural nature of the local subject. The local is never in a truly antagonistic position with respect to the global culture. The hero himself is an American-trained specialist who transfers his foreign knowledge to the local officers in order to combat the terrorists. The film stresses the performativity rather than the origins of ideas, things, and people. Second, the terrorists are portrayed as rapacious thieves who have no commitment to any global cause. Even though these global professionals have done the evil deeds, there is no direct linkage to the transnational system itself. The film is by no means about the antagonism between localism and globalism. Rather, it is about which system could be more effective for managing crisis—which, of course, allegorizes the utilitarian attitude of the Hong Kong locals.

Interest in the creation of transnationalism is better demonstrated in Peter Chan's popular comedy, *He's a Woman, She's a Man* [*Jinzhi Yuye*] (1994), UFO's greatest hit, which plays on the gimmick of (mistaken) sexual identity and projects a fantasy of the global power of Hong Kong's music industry. The film begins with an ordinary local teenage music fan, Wing, who idolizes the glamorous female vocalist Rose and her composer boyfriend, Sam. Sam's record company organizes an open audition to look for a new talented male performer. Seeing it as an opportunity to get close to her idols, Wing poses as a man to go to the audition. "He" wins the contest and, in this disguised identity, becomes a popular teen idol; "he" even gets involved romantically with Sam. Apparently, the film's humor is based mainly on false identity gags and gender confusion. It could be read as subversive, since it

Figure 1.
Michael Wong suggests
the hybrid and
multicultural nature
of the local subject
in *The First Option*
(Gordon Chan, 1996).

provides an antiessentialist understanding of sexuality by revealing gender identity to be an artifice or a performance. The director makes a concrete claim, through Wing's male pose, that gender identity is more a costume than a given, more a social construction than a biological essence. But another myth is built upon the film's deconstruction of the gender myth. As a local nobody, Wing is reconfigured by the transnational capitalist power into a new, decorporealized "transsubject." Her unbound sexual identity is, in fact, more compatible with the fantasy of the global flow of capital than with criticism of traditional notions of gender. The film also calls the audience's attention to the fact that the logic of commodification dominates the local popular culture: the individual style and talent of the artist is simply a package produced by the music industry, while the fans are not so innocent that they would not take advantage of their idols by selling photos of them and accessories they have used. Hence, the local culture is depicted as totally capitalized and commercially exploited. The only uncontaminated place left is exotic "Africa," to which Sam is always longing to go. He identifies with Paul Simon, who uses African music as a new source for his creativity. He falls for Wing because she is Africa for him. In this respect, *He's a Woman,*

She's a Man is in line with many Hollywood movies that join in the privi-leged and globalist appropriation of peripheral, localist cultures for main-stream reimagining.

Although the film looks forward to a new transsubject whose identity can blur into another's and who is no longer constrained by any frontiers, it dresses itself in a nostalgic ambience. Its Chinese title, "Golden Branch and Jade Leaf," is the Chinese translation of the title of the 1953 American film *Roman Holiday*, starring Audrey Hepburn. The sweet Mandarin melodies of the 1950s and the Beatles songs incorporated in *He's a Woman*'s soundtrack induce an emotional yearning for Hong Kong's past and at the same time remind the viewer of a local identity that is always already multicultural.

Recognition of the Transnational as Home

Another Peter Chan blockbuster, *Comrades, Almost a Love Story [Tian Mimi]* (1996), also makes good use of old music. The old song here is pres-ent not only for nostalgia and narrative comprehension but also for the con-templation of identity. The Chinese title of the film, "Sweetness," is a popu-lar song by the female Taiwanese vocalist Teresa Tang (Deng Lijun). Tang's songs swept through Taiwan and Hong Kong during the 1970s, but their influence subsided in the 1980s. However, thanks to mainland China's ver-sion of a market economy, outmoded popular cultural goods from the two capitalist Chinese communities, namely Hong Kong and Taiwan, can always get a new lease on life in the People's Republic.

Tang's oldies became huge hits among the mainlanders in the early 1980s. Her popularity was even comparable to another Deng: the engineer of the modernization campaign and the political leader at that time, Deng Xiaoping. Because of this time lag in the reception of the same cultural prod-ucts among the Chinese, their choices and tastes easily reveal their different local identities. Chan's film cleverly appropriates this delicate difference in tastes in pop song to rethink the question of Chinese cultural identity. *Com-rades, Almost a Love Story* is a romance of two mainlanders who first meet in Hong Kong and, ten years later, reunite in New York. Like many formulaic movies, the plot puts much emphasis on chance and coincidence. The film begins on 1 March 1986 in the Kowloon train station, where the two protag-onists, Li Xiaojun and Li Qiao, both arrive at the same time, at this point still strangers to each other. The closing scene of the film reruns the opening scene by showing that they actually fall asleep on each other's back on the same train, which reiterates the myth of fate in a romantic relationship. It is

Figure 2.
Comrades, Almost a Love Story (Peter Chan, 1996) uses popular Taiwanese songs to narrate a fluid trans-Chinese identity.

rather a commonplace in popular romances that the other person contingently encountered always, predictably, turns out to be the love object prescribed by providence. But the "magic element" that thematically and structurally ties the couple together across all the boundaries is Tang's songs, which are heard both diegetically and nondiegetically.

The film makes apparent the audience's cognition of Teresa Tang as well as her songs' narrative functions. Unlike films that affirm their music's self-effacement and unobtrusiveness, the sweet voice of Tang is foregrounded in *Comrades* to help the audience notice structural unity and narrative coherence. Tang's song first appears nondiegetically when Xiaojun is giving a bicycle ride to Li Qiao in the busy streets of Hong Kong. Xiaojun, who has a mainlander's skill in maneuvering the bicycle, inscribes a transnational space into the congested traffic of the colonial city and turns the urban area into a pastoral field, with Tang's music in the background while the noise of the city street is totally unheard. Li Qiao, sitting behind him on the bike, enjoys the ride so much that she is humming Tang's song, unconscious of the fact that she is thereby revealing that she herself is a mainlander, a fact she wants to conceal from Xiaojun.

This inscription of a different space in the local site of Hong Kong could be interpreted as the desire of homeless Chinese to construct their own sense of locality. It destabilizes the binarism between city and country, homeland and hostland, self and other. The spatial reconfiguration of the bicycle ride in the urban city is imbued with eruptions of memory and nostalgia for a cultural identity the protagonists miss. Thus, the newly inscribed space is not only transnationalized but also nationalized. As new immigrants suffering from culture shock, poverty, and discrimination, the protagonists have achieved a transcendent unity and a community of one not by any traditional folk-cultural forms but, ironically, through an "alien" commercial Taiwanese song.

There is another bicycle-ride scene, roughly near the end of the film, in which the transnational spatial reconfiguration is considered. By this time Xiaojun and Li Qiao have already gone their separate ways, but, coincidentally, both are in New York City. When Li Qiao is deported by U.S. immigration officers and is on the way to the airport (she is on the run with a Hong Kong mob boss, who is, however, accidentally killed in a random street crime), she catches a glimpse of Xiaojun. He is a bicycle deliveryman for a Chinese restaurant in the busy streets of New York. She unhesitatingly jumps out of the car, chasing Xiaojun's bike as well as running away from the immigration officers. She cannot catch Xiaojun, nor can the officers catch her. The bicycle ride indirectly saves her from being deported from the locale of her lover. On the other hand, it also keeps her from reuniting with him, since she is not fast enough to catch up with the bike. Unlike the first bicycle scene, which conveys a (temporary) sense of harmony and suggests a growing intimacy and emotional bond between the protagonists, the bike scene in New York produces feelings of alienation, loss, and anxiety owing to separation and the tensions of acculturation. However, even in a Western metropolis, the trajectory of the Chinese-food delivery bike ridden by Xiaojun becomes

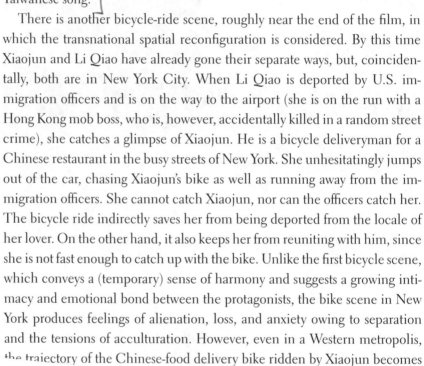

Qiao from the hands of foreigners. The rootless Chi-
st in an adopted country since there is always a nation-
route for them to tread whereby they may find tempo-
ntually, a home.
ally intended to make a film about Hong Kong natives
, Peter Chan said he was really talking about "the root-
ese as a people, and of their continuing search for a new
ntly," he elaborated, "I realized that the story is also a
ves of Hong Kong natives of my generation, people like

me who are trying to cope with a deadline called 1997. The story of Hong Kong natives is told in the story of mainlanders within a transnational context, and the specific issue of 1997 is universalized into a problem of exile and the loss of home. In this way, the local question is reconsidered by the filmmaker in the light of an intertextual, cross-cultural, and translational vision.

As I mentioned earlier, Teresa Tang's song, besides ensuring continuity, creating atmosphere, and providing background music, performs a narrative function in the film. Its primary function is to narrate and reinvent a fluid and multiple trans-Chinese identity of social migration and transcultural production. Repeatedly, it is Tang's songs that diegetically bring the protagonists together romantically. It first happens when Li Qiao sells Tang's cassette tapes in the Chinese New Year's Eve market. Being a big fan of Tang, Li Qiao forgets that Tang's songs are no longer popular in Hong Kong and that new immigrants from the mainland would avoid buying Tang's tapes in public in order not to reveal their not-so-respectable backgrounds. Her business flops, but she gains a deeper understanding of Xiaojun, and they begin their relationship and sleep together that night. When the second diegetic cue of Tang's song appears, it is several years later; Xiaojun has married his fiancée and Li Qiao has become the mob boss's mistress. Obviously they still have strong feelings for each other. On the way home with Li Qiao, Xiaojun (the two have met in Li Qiao's bridal shop) turns on the car radio, and Tang's song is on the air. As if to remind the viewer even more of the importance of Tang's music in the film, the protagonists run into Teresa Tang on the road. Xiaojun gets out of the car to ask her to autograph the back of his jacket. The appearance of Tang and her melodies triggers Xiaojun and Li Qiao's repressed passions, and they start their love affair again.

The last noticeable instance of Tang and her music in the film is the announcement of her sudden death. The news plunges the protagonists into deep reminiscence, and they wander the streets of New York in this reverie. Each stops in front of a shop window to watch a television program reviewing Tang's life, and right there they have their final reunion. Tang's songs have a crucial representational and expressive function in the film, intensifying the protagonists' love affair. The style and cultural connotations of Tang's love songs allow the viewer to easily attribute a particular emotional cast to the musical accompaniment of various scenes in the film. But what is telling about the film score is that the identification of the musical expression always already involves transnational cultural codes and differences under a seemingly unified national representation. The romantic desire for unity is overdetermined and structured by a transnationalized musical mode rather than by any indigenous folksongs.

The filmmaker never really uses the national image and the ethnic tradition to construct cultural identity. In fact, the local represented in the film always enacts the reconfigured space of national deterritorialization and reinvention. Xiaojun's aunt, Rosie, a prostitute who runs a brothel, is constantly indulging in her memory of the happiest day in her life — one she spent with William Holden while he was shooting *Love Is a Many-Splendored Thing* (1955) in Hong Kong. And the brothel is a multiracial place where Thai girls work and where Westerners stay. In addition, the protagonists have their first rendezvous at McDonald's, the multinational fast-food restaurant. In a way, the film paints a utopic picture to show that different races can get along well and dreams can cross cultural and national boundaries. This transnational and transcultural fantasy is indeed very common in Hong Kong cinema of the 1990s. It is not merely a conscious strategy of transnational marketing but also a hybridized production process. As Yau succinctly puts it, Hong Kong filmmakers "have refashioned a cinema that is eclectic in cultural imagination: modern, local and Americanized, but also premodern, Westernized, Japanese and Chinese. A complex hybridization has been taking place for the last two decades that is more conducive to a theory of chaos . . . than the lateral model of cross-fertilization between East and West, or the critical model of colonial hegemony and subjugation." [16]

The reimagining of the local realm into a hybrid wonderland is evident in other works produced by UFO — for example, the collective neighborhood modeled on Cantonese classics in *He Ain't Heavy, He's My Father!* [*Xin Nanxiong Nandi*] (1993), the Japanese comic–inspired local street in *Dr. Mack* [*Liumang Xiayi*] (1995), and the corrupted fin-de-siècle city waiting for a savior in *Heaven Can't Wait* [*Jiushi Shengun*] (1995). These imagined spaces cannot be understood simply as the anachronistic or atemporal worlds of fairy tales. Indeed, they are like a loop: by moving toward the past or toward an alien culture, they come back to where they always already are. Far from being the kind of fantasy spaces that offer the audience the illusion of escape from immediate reality, these dreamlands provide a defamiliarized perspective from which to view the present. If localism is understood as a desire to return home, what the films discussed above designate is a home that is ultimately always a fantasy. It is a home imagistically built, through the mediations of transnational capital, more on deterritorialized cultures than national, on reinvented memories than inherited ones, on forms of creolization than a unified and integrated ethnic content. The sense of the local, in Hong Kong films of the 1990s, is sustained through the syncretization of images and information whose origins are external with the existing forms of cultural life. What is discovered at the kernel of the local is always a self-estrangement. Thus there always remains, in the construction process of the local, a nonlocal that can provide a viewpoint from which the local can identify itself as something other than itself. These estranged, transnational elements are the local's Otherness, which, however, is closer to the local than anything it can set against itself.

[The notion of the local in Hong Kong cinema exists in the form of a desire to become what it is not, in the hope of losing as well as simultaneously reconstituting itself in the process of globalization, which marks a new possibility of self-representation.] The full power of the idea of the local is reached in the sense of aggregates and conglomerations of various cultural particulars — national or global — enmeshed together on the same field. Hong Kong cinema of the 1990s does not necessarily demonstrate that, under the dynamic changes brought by the forces of globalization, all cultures become more creolized and more pluralistic in relation to their origins. But the more the Hong Kong filmmakers invest in constructing a site of the local in the field of relationships, the more they find the local to be inseparable from the transnational modes of living and imagining. This portrayal of the local in the Hong Kong film industry of today as constant mutability in the terrain of continuous cultural and political intervention and reformulation may have nothing to do with the homogeneous synthesis of late capitalism. Instead, it may lie much deeper in the nature of the passing experience of constructing the local itself.

Notes

1 See Hu Ke, "The Influence of Hong Kong Cinema on Mainland China," in *Hong Kong Cinema Retrospective: Fifty Years of Electric Shadows*, ed. Law Kar, Twenty-first Hong Kong International Film Festival (Hong Kong: Urban Council, 1997), 171–78.

2 Hong Kong films are considered by the Taiwanese government as domestic products that may be exempted from the quota restriction on foreign-made movies. See Liang Hai-chiang, "Hong Kong Cinema's 'Taiwan Factor,'" in Law, *Hong Kong Cinema Retrospective*, 163.

3 For the history of Taiwan's investment in Hong Kong cinema, see Liang, 158–63; Shiao-ying Shen, "Where Has All the Capital Gone: The State of Taiwan's Film Investment," *Cinemaya* 30 (autumn 1995): 4–12.

4 Ackbar Abbas argues that the "local" in Hong Kong is "already a cultural translation." See his *Hong Kong: Culture and the Politics of Disappearance* (Hong Kong: Hong Kong University Press, 1997), 12.

5 David Bordwell, "Aesthetics in Action: Kung Fu, Gunplay, and Cinematic Expressivity," in Law, *Hong Kong Cinema Retrospective*, 81–89.

6　Bruce Lee's mother is Eurasian, and he was born in San Francisco; he married an American and was himself an American citizen. The Hollywood production *Dragon: The Bruce Lee Story* even tried to claim Lee as an incarnation of the myth of the American dream. In the film, Lee is portrayed as a struggling immigrant who is able to overcome racial discrimination and merge into mainstream American life. The image that Lee provides for local identification is never immanent, but comes from outside. His "foreignness," however, gives a new symbolic meaning to the local community even though he is not an integral part of it. What Lee's image offers is not a solid ground for locating a specific entity but a symbolic void around which the invention of the local is structured. See my "Muscles and Subjectivity: A Short History of the Masculine Body in Hong Kong Popular Culture," *Camera Obscura* 39 (1996): 105–25.

7　Esther Yau, "Ecology and Late Colonial Hong Kong Cinema: Imaginations In Time," in Law, *Hong Kong Cinema Retrospective*, 111.

8　Bordwell, 84.

9　See Grace Leung and Joseph Chan, "The Hong Kong Cinema and Its Overseas Market: A Historical Review, 1950–1995," in Law, *Hong Kong Cinema Retrospective*, 136–51.

10　He Wenlong, "Chen Kexin yaozhuahui yiliushi de guanzhong" ["Peter Chan Wants to Regain the Confidence of the Audience"], *City Entertainment* 388 (February 1994): 50.

11　For the discussion on diasporic Chinese culture, see the special issue, "The Living Tree: The Changing Meaning of Being Chinese Today," *Daedalus* 120, no. 2 (spring 1991). For a pointed and vigorous critique of the Chinese centrism, see Rey Chow, *Writing Diaspora: Tactics of Intervention in Contemporary Cultural Studies* (Bloomington: Indiana University Press, 1993).

12　For a discussion of the new American global cinema, see Dana Polan, "Globalism's Localisms," in *Global/Local: Cultural Production and the Transnational Imaginary*, ed. Rob Wilson and Wimal Dissanayake (Durham, N.C.: Duke University Press, 1996), 255–83.

13　This production was from Media Asia, a Hong Kong company that, like UFO, was founded in the 1990s.

14　This box office success was another production from Media Asia.

15　Athena Tsui, "Interview with Peter Chan," in *Hong Kong Panorama 96–97* (Hong Kong: Urban Council, 1997), 26.

16　Yau, 111.

The Intimate Spaces of Wong Kar-wai

Marc Siegel

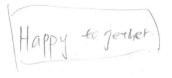

Happy Together [Chunguang Zhaxie] (1997), Wong Kar-wai's first film to focus on a homosexual relationship, is also the director's first film to take place outside of Asia. The interrelatedness of these two "firsts"—homosexuality and flight from Hong Kong—is articulated right from the start of the film. The first images, which appear even before the title, are two jerky close-ups of the passports of the protagonists, Ho Po-wing (Leslie Cheung) and Lai Yiu-fai (Tony Chiu-wai Leung), as they are stamped for entry into Argentina. Immediately following the title, we are treated to a grainy black-and-white sequence in which the two men, clothed only in underwear, are having sex on the bed in a seedy hotel room. These opening moments, together with Lai Yiu-fai's voice-over telling us that the two lovers came to Argentina to "start over," initiate a somewhat disjointed narrative in which the invocation of homosexuality is linked to the dis/articulation of nationality.

Wong attributes his interest in setting the story in Argentina to a desire to evoke the Latin America of South American novelists, namely Manuel Puig, whose work had already influenced the structure of the director's earlier film *Days of Being Wild [A Fei Zhengzhuan]* (1990).[1] When Wong and his crew went to Argentina in August 1996 to begin work on *Happy Together*, they sought the spaces of 1970s Buenos Aires. Financially incapable of recreating the earlier period and style, they gravitated instead to that aspect of contemporary Argentina that resembled Hong Kong. As the film's cinematographer, Christopher Doyle, notes in his shooting diary:

> We came to Argentina to "defamiliarise" ourselves by moving away
> from the spaces—and we hope the preoccupations—of the world
> we know so well. But we're out of our space and depth here. We
> don't even know the city well. So why do we still tend towards
> bars, barbershops, fast-food joints and trains? What happened to
> the inspiration from Manuel Puig's structures and Julio Cortázar's
> conceits? We're stuck with our own concerns and perceptions.[2]

277

Figure 1.
Filming homosexuality
in *Happy Together*
(1997). Courtesy
of *City Entertainment*
and Christopher Doyle.

Unacquainted with Buenos Aires, Wong and his crew found themselves returning to the transient spaces that are familiar to any international traveler. These bars, barbershops, fast-food joints, and trains, as well as the temporary, fleeting human encounters associated with them, are also familiar to viewers of Wong's other urban films — *Days of Being Wild, Chungking Express [Chongqing Senlin]* (1994), and *Fallen Angels [Duoluo Tianshi]* (1996). In this sense, *Happy Together* does not really tell us very much about Buenos Aires. Instead, it uses certain Argentine spaces in order to localize Hong Kong concerns and perceptions. As Wong has put it, "[I]t's more like I'm remaking Hong Kong *in* Buenos Aires."[3]

Wong and Doyle have also suggested that the film doesn't really tell us very much about homosexuality either. Though ostensibly a story about the trials and tribulations of two male lovers, *Happy Together*, we are told, is actually about human communication in general. As Wong stated in a press conference at the 1997 Cannes Film Festival, where the film won a prize for mise-en-scène, "[T]his film is not merely about two men, but about human relations, human communication and the means of maintaining it. It's two men but it could have been any other couple."[4] On another occasion, Wong asserted: "In fact I don't like people to see this film as a gay film. It's more like a story about human relationships and somehow the two characters involved are both men."[5] Doyle reiterated the director's sentiments: "At a pinch, there are no gays. One is what one is and this film shows that."[6] One enthusiastic French critic seems to relish the opportunity to erase any traces of homosexuality whatsoever from the film, claiming that

> the presence of the two central male characters does not signify at
> all that this film, like many others, flaunts the ostentatious signs of
> a homosexuality worn on its sleeve. Concerning the question of a
> "gaytto," Wong Kar-wai settles his account conclusively: the film deals
> with a couple: and whether the actors were two women, a man and a
> woman, two men, a man and a wardrobe, a woman and a transsexual
> would in any case not change a thing.[7]

While Wong's statements have made it clear that he does not have any stake in producing films that might be labeled "gay," his account is by no means settled as conclusively as the implicitly homophobic (and transphobic) statements of the above critic would imply.[8] Wong has noted elsewhere, for example, the significance that a gay specificity brings to the film. Distinguishing the depiction of homosexuality in *Happy Together* from that of heterosexuality in his other films and from that of homosexuality in other Hong Kong films, Wong notes that "the few Hong Kong films that treat homosexuality do so within the context of comedy. I wanted to take on the subject without making people laugh."[9] Doyle notes as well that at one point during production, after viewing the rushes, Wong even worried that the film was "not gay enough."[10]

This ambivalence about the ostensible subject of *Happy Together*—about how gay the film really is and about the film's relationship to Hong Kong—is emblematic of Hong Kong cinema as it confronts what Ackbar Abbas has called "the problematics of disappearance."[11] Because of Hong Kong's position in the global economy, its experiences of colonialism and imperialism, and its anxiety over 1997, the city, according to Abbas, has been marked by elusiveness, defined by spatial and temporal disjuncture, and characterized by disappearance. The filmmakers of the Hong Kong New Wave—most notably Wong, Stanley Kwan, Ann Hui, Tsui Hark, John Woo, and Allen Fong—thus do not document the appearance of Hong Kong as a subject, but rather the elusiveness of Hong Kong's cultural space. These films thereby contribute to a redefinition of the local, expressed in part through the use of the Cantonese language. In Cantonese films of the early 1970s, according to Abbas, "the local was an ethic of exclusion: it defined a narrow homogeneous social space where foreigners and foreign elements had no place."[12] Films of the 1980s and 1990s, however, utilized the Cantonese that is spoken in Hong Kong today, "a Cantonese sprinkled with Mandarin, English, and barbarous sounding words and phrases—a hybrid language coming out of a hybrid space."[13] No longer stable and homogeneous, the local is now mutable and international, like spoken Cantonese itself. In fact, it is precisely the new Cantonese cinema's specificity as local that lends it its international quality.

If *Happy Together* is successful at achieving the local internationalism invoked by Abbas, then its success is not limited to its ability to articulate a Hong Kong localism in Argentina. The depiction of temporary, fleeting human encounters in public places resonates not only with similar images in Wong's other films—and thereby with the transient cultural space of Hong Kong—but also with that very "gaytto" so denigrated by the above French critic. By acknowledging the significance of homosexuality to *Happy Together*, by acknowledging what I would call the film's ghetto specificity, moreover, we can recognize these behaviors, spaces, and images as indicative of something other than "loneliness, insecurity, and [the] inability to commit," the typical qualities ascribed to Wong's films.[14] From a ghetto perspective, the images in *Happy Together*, as in Wong's other films, are instead indices of a public world of new intimacies.

Globalization and the Ghetto

As Ella Shohat and Robert Stam note, "the term 'globalization' usually evokes a complex realignment of social forces engendering an overpowering wave of global political, cultural and economic interdependency."[15] There are many ways in which sexuality is implicated in this situation of global interdependency. I'll cite two striking examples. First, the global AIDS epidemic has forced various levels of interaction and discussion about sex, sexual behavior, and sexual identity among individuals, community organizations, and governments across national borders.[16] Second, the explosion of gay and lesbian or queer film festivals around the world ensures that queer images will travel to and from places with significantly different conceptions of gender, sexuality, identity, and community. In this respect, it is useful to consider the comments made by Seo Dongjin, director of the First Seoul Queer Film and Video Festival, on the occasion of the banning of the festival by the Korean government:

> Our censorship regulations only recognize that there is gay or
> lesbian sexual behavior, not that there are gay and lesbian people
> who are citizens and form communities. . . . In terms of this logic,
> it is nonsensical to speak of a "queer" film festival for the "queer
> communities," because the regulations do not recognize the existence
> of such people.[17]

The movement of queer images across national borders thus highlights the isomorphic alignment of sexual behavior, sexual identity, and the development of sexual communities in different localities.

In *Modernity at Large: Cultural Dimensions of Globalization,* Arjun Appadurai offers one way of conceptualizing locality in a global context. In his analysis, locality is "primarily relational and contextual rather than scalar or spatial."[18] Not simply smaller in size or scope than the global, the local is rather a structure of feeling or a distinctive property of social life that ensures its own reproducibility. For Appadurai, this "phenomenological quality" of locality is linked to its material context, or to what he calls the neighborhood. "I use the term *neighborhood* to refer to the actually existing social forms in which locality, as a dimension or value, is variably realized."[19] In a destabilizing global economy, it is the neighborhood, according to Appadurai's analysis, that ensures the production and reproduction of local knowledges, local subjects, and local contexts. "Neighborhoods are contexts in the sense that they provide the frame or setting within which various kinds of human action (productive, reproductive, interpretive, performative) can be initiated and conducted meaningfully."[20]

Appadurai's theorization of locality may account for some of the ways in which particular ethnic communities have established and reproduced a sense of place despite global economic and cultural transformations. In his reliance on the concept of the neighborhood, however, he presumes that culture is produced and reproduced within the context of residence. Moreover, the implied residence in Appadurai's neighborhood is the private home of the nuclear family, which he refers to as "the most intimate arena" of cultural reproduction.[21] How relevant, then, is the neighborhood to a consideration of the localization of sexualities, especially those that are excluded from this "most intimate arena?"

In their exhilarating discussion of "the radical aspirations of queer culture building," Lauren Berlant and Michael Warner challenge the ideology of the neighborhood.[22] For them, the neighborhood as a social form does not adequately describe the context within which queer sexual subjectivity is produced. As they note, sexual subjects do not merely reside, and "the local character of the neighborhood depends on the daily presence of thousands of nonresidents."[23] Emphasizing the status of property owners and the condition of residence, the ideology of the neighborhood reproduces national divisions between public and private space, with intimacy relegated to the realm of the private. In the transient queer world described by Berlant and Warner, however, intimacy is neither constrained by the privatized form of the couple nor segregated within the privatized spaces of the bedroom, the apartment, or the home.

> Queer and other insurgents have long striven, often dangerously or
> scandalously, to cultivate what good folks used to call criminal
> intimacies. We have developed relations and narratives that are
> only recognized as intimate in queer culture: girlfriends, gal pals,
> fuckbuddies, tricks. Queer culture has learned not only how to
> sexualize these and other relations, but also to use them as a context
> for witnessing intense and personal affect while elaborating a public
> world of belonging and transformation. Making a queer world has
> required the development of kinds of intimacy that bear no necessary
> relation to domestic space, to kinship, to the couple form, to property,
> or to the nation.[24]

Following Berlant and Warner, we could say that a discussion of the localization of sexualities in a global context must be attentive to the potential intimacies in the "public world of belonging and transformation." To describe this queer experience of locality, I propose to use the term *ghetto*, instead of neighborhood. In the introduction to his 1980 travelogue *Le gay voyage*, the French writer, journalist, and activist Guy Hocquenghem invokes the importance of the ghetto to urban gay male life and to the gay male traveler.[25]

> I don't know cities. I only know ghettos. Interconnected ghettos that
> are barely interrupted by train stations or airports. City of night, said

the great American writer John Rechy. The Lungotevere comes to
an end at West Street, the Tiber flows into the Hudson River, the door
in the back of a sauna in Amsterdam opens onto the dark hall of a
cinema in Pigalle. The Tuileries and Central Park have the same
bronze lion, and the same shadows swirl in the alleys in the wee
hours of the morning.[26]

In what we might call Hocquenghem's translocal gay ghetto, the mist of a
sauna or the shadows in a nighttime park are imbued with a transforma-
tive power that seems literally to whisk the gay urbanite from ghetto to
ghetto. The locality of each ghetto is thus marked by dislocation, by a connection with other ghettos across national boundaries. Moreover, the ghetto
in Hocquenghem's formulation is not simply descriptive of a particular
spatially bounded section of town. Instead it refers to an assortment of public spaces — including saunas, cinemas, parks, and alleys — that are linked
together as places for potential sexual contacts. The ghetto is also the site
where one hones the skills necessary for navigating vastly different urban
landscapes — that is, where one learns the essential queer art of cruising.
Hocquenghem's sexual ghetto is thus a context within which the intimate
relations forged by queers are meaningful, legible, and reproducible. It is
a context that ensures the reproduction of sexual subjects and of queer
knowledges.

Published just after the beginning of gay liberation and just before the
emergence of the AIDS epidemic, Le gay voyage, with its sections on the
major European and American cities, is very much a product of its time.
The fact of global interdependency today suggests that Hocquenghem's
ghettos are interrupted not merely by train stations and airports, but also by
the flows of capital, politics, and the media. The knowledges and intimacies
of the ghetto are thus constructed in relation to the seemingly random influx
of images, ideas, and behaviors that come from elsewhere.

The Intimate Spaces of Wong Kar-wai

Wong has pointed out that Hong Kong fan magazines urged audiences to be
punctual to Happy Together so as not to miss the opening sex scene. "Otherwise," he says, "it's just a film about two brothers."[27] As one critic has observed, however, it is only a film about two brothers if one denies the strong
erotic tension between the male protagonists, most evident for that critic in
the scenes of Ho Po-wing teaching Lai Yiu-fai how to dance the tango.[28]

While there is a precedent in Hong Kong films for close bonding between male protagonists, perhaps most famously in the films of John Woo, the degree of intimacy between Ho and Lai in *Happy Together* does suggest a relationship of a different category altogether. Rather than argue for the queerness of the film by having recourse solely to the intimacy between Ho and Lai, however, I prefer to discuss the specific context within which their relationship takes place and indeed breaks down. *Happy Together* is clearly a queer film not simply because it depicts a sexual relationship between two men, but because it depicts and evokes the intimate behaviors, spaces, and images of a sexual ghetto.

The film tells the story of two male lovers from Hong Kong who leave for Argentina in order to "start over." After their failed road trip to find Iguaçu Falls, the lovers end up in Buenos Aires without enough money for the return trip to Hong Kong. Lai begins work as a doorman in a tango bar, and Ho becomes a hustler. Though Ho's hustling distances him from his coupling with Lai, it does serve to connect him with a sexual ghetto. As evidenced by his frequent nighttime cruising, Ho's ability to function in Buenos Aires relies on his skill at negotiating the unspoken codes and unformalizable gestures of a sexual ghetto.[29] For Wong, Ho's survival is evidence of "an animal instinct that keeps him more or less intact on the streets."[30]

After Ho's relationship with Lai breaks down, Lai engages in some cruising of his own. His skill at finding the porno theaters and the bathrooms attests to his ghetto knowledge. Lai's lengthy cruising sequence, scored to Frank Zappa's song "I Have Been in You," begins with a roaming camera catching him in interactions with other men at various public locations. As the sequence progresses, Lai begins to stare back at the camera. The camera thereby becomes implicated in the cruising it is supposedly documenting. In other words, Wong's camera does not merely document Lai's cruising spaces but actually produces them.

In addition to these explicit invocations of a sexual ghetto, *Happy Together* suggests another possible point of connection through its depiction of Lai's peculiar job in the abattoir. Lai begins working at the abattoir after his relationship with Ho is over, at a time when he is nostalgic for his lost love and for Hong Kong. His voice-over suggests that this work brings him closer to Hong Kong, both by allowing him to save money for his return trip and by forcing him to work at night and thereby adjust his daily schedule to Hong Kong time. The initial images of the abattoir sequence, however, are accompanied by a reprise of the Frank Zappa song from Lai's cruising sequence. Proximity to Hong Kong, we might say, is thus mediated by the markers of a

Figure 2.
Public space as
sexual ghetto in
Happy Together.
Courtesy of *City
Entertainment* and
Christopher Doyle.

sexual ghetto. Moreover, the narrative function and aesthetic impact of the sequence resonate with that of the abattoir scene in Rainer Werner Fassbinder's *In a Year of Thirteen Moons* (1978). *In a Year of Thirteen Moons* tells the story of a transsexual, Erwin/Elvira, whose melancholy over being abandoned by her lovers leads her to commit suicide. Thomas Elsaesser notes that in the abattoir scene, in which Elvira reminisces about her past life as a male butcher and her decision to transition, an association is made of "suffering with deliverance . . . amplified with a materiality — of steaming blood, of smells and cries."[31] Wong's abattoir is also marked by the materiality of the flesh — the racks of animals, the ravishing puddles of blood, but also the gratuitous naked male bodies in the shower. Regardless of Wong Kar-wai's intentions with this scene, the intimate images of an abattoir in a film dealing with homosexuality will, at least in a Western gay context, evoke a relationship to Fassbinder's images.[32]

In his depictions of cruising and the space of the abattoir, Wong produces the ghetto as the context within which the behaviors, spaces, and images in the film become meaningful. In *Happy Together* intimacy is not achieved within the couple and is not segregated to the private space of the apartment. Instead, the potential for intimacy exists outside in the public sexual world, whether that means watching pornography on television in a hotel room or movie theater or cruising for men on the streets, in cinemas, or in public toilets. Viewed within the context of a sexual ghetto, these actions are meaningful in that they are creative of potential new intimacies.[33]

This is not to say that the characters understand or experience random fleeting encounters in the public sexual world as intimate. Lai in particular expresses discomfort and confusion about this sexual world. When he unexpectedly encounters Ho while both are cruising in a public toilet, Lai expresses regret for his actions. His voice-over explains: "I've never liked hanging around toilets. Thought it was dirty. These days I use them as it's the easiest. Never dreamed I'd see Po-wing in there. I never went back. I thought I was different from Po-wing. Turns out lonely people are all the same." Despite his stated discomfort with this situation, Lai's acknowledgment of the ease of connecting with other men within the sexual ghetto—by "hanging around toilets"—attests to his awareness that such a world does exist. For the critic Larry Gross, the characters in Wong's films seem suspended in an "unfulfilled yet compelling dream, as if the movie opens out into a new reality just outside the frame of the screen."[34] Following Gross, we might say that Lai shares a trait with other Wong protagonists: a sense that there is a public world of possible intimate connections, but that one does not quite know how to access it.

Wong's other films, while not depicting the particular sexual ghetto that I have been describing here, do depict the random encounters and possible public connections that are recognized as intimate within a sexual ghetto. The structures of gay male cruising, the anonymous, often wordless encounters between men in public, and the intense affective images in *Happy Together* indeed recall Wong's earlier films. Christopher Doyle notes that one day during the shooting of *Happy Together*, he experienced déjà vu.

> The cars, the colours, the isolation, the trains, the (same) cast, the (same) crew, the weather and the unfamiliar language. We start to have a déjà vu feeling. It seems we're finally making that *Days of Being Wild Part II* that so many have expected from us for so long. Leslie even began humming the theme from *Days* as he prepared for a shot today.[35]

Happy Together shares with Wong's other films a concerted refusal to relegate intimacy to the private form of the couple or to the privatized space of the apartment. It is perhaps in this way that we could make sense of Gross's temptation to refer to Wong as "the last heterosexual director."[36] He is the last heterosexual director because his films picture the limits of heteronormative constraints on intimacy. In other words, Wong's films challenge the idea that intimacy can be confined within the form of the couple and within the realm of the private.

His films frequently focus on characters who randomly connect with others in public places. *Days of Being Wild*, for instance, opens with a series of brief meetings between Yuddy (Leslie Cheung) and Lai Jun (Maggie Cheung), an employee in a deserted cafe. The sequence culminates with Yuddy and Lai Jun watching the clock and agreeing to remember the single minute they spent together. As Lai Jun's voice-over indicates, that minute expanded until it became an hour (of sex) every day. Early in both *Chungking Express* and *Fallen Angels* we hear voice-overs suggesting the potential connections to be had in public places. The cop in *Chungking Express*, He Qi Wu (Takeshi Kaneshiro), and the killer in *Fallen Angels*, Wong Chi-ming (Leon Lai), express basically the same sentiment in almost identical voice-overs: "We rub shoulders with each other every day. . . . We may not know each other. . . . But we may become good friends someday."

The potential for public intimate connections is underscored by the lack of possibility for restricting intimacy to privatized spaces. In both *Chungking Express* and *Fallen Angels*, the apartment, for example, is not a place of residence, but of transience.[37] After the keys to cop no. 633's (Tony Leung's) apartment are left by a former girlfriend at the Midnight Express fast-food counter, Faye (Faye Wong) manages to get the cop's address and sneaks into his apartment in his absence. Frolicking alone in the apartment, Faye rearranges the room, changes the fish in the fish tank, and cleans up after no. 633. In *Fallen Angels*, Wong Chi-ming, a contract killer, has worked with his partner (Michelle Reis) for three years, though they have rarely met. When Wong is absent from his apartment, his partner enters, cleans up, takes out the garbage, and masturbates on his bed. She even rummages through the garbage to find clues about the killer's life. The seemingly private details of one's life are therefore not necessarily free from unsolicited inspection by others. Concerning his interest in disturbing the privacy of the apartment, Wong has noted, "Most people harbor a secret curiosity concerning the intimacy of others, and dream of penetrating their homes without being seen, in order to discover who they are, what they do."[38]

The destabilization of the divide between public and private that suggests to me a public world of potential new intimacies is described quite differently by Wong's other critics. In most accounts of his films an absence of privatized forms of intimacy attests instead to the failure of the individual characters to achieve *real* or *actual* intimacy. For Jean-Marc Lalanne, for example, Wong's films emphasize the solitary individual in contemporary urban society, one who is destitute and emotionally impoverished, without bonds to family or community.[39] For Chuck Stephens, Wong's characters experience "coincidental proximity and romantic bad timing [that] rarely add up to actual interaction."[40] And for Ackbar Abbas, every Wong Kar-wai film treats the theme of "proximity without reciprocity; that is to say, how we can be physically close to a situation or to a person without there being any intimacy or knowledge."[41] But does "proximity without reciprocity" necessarily suggest a failed interaction, an absence of knowledge? Might it not rather offer a different kind of knowledge? Finally, and most importantly, does intimacy demand reciprocity?

While these critics rightly acknowledge the fast-paced urban world of Wong's films, their analyses of this world betray their own anxiety about what counts as intimate in a global context. Abbas notes that Wong's films, like others of the Hong Kong New Wave, respond to the spatial transformations effected by globalism, and in particular by new technologies, with a challenge to realist cinematic strategies for depicting space. These films do not merely depict characters attempting to adjust to spatial transformations but produce images that are themselves marked by disjuncture. "It is as if all the ways of relating have somehow shifted, the bonds that join us to others as friends and lovers, as daughters and sons blurring like the lines on a television screen that is not tracking properly."[42] The skewing of affectivity that Abbas attributes to Wong's films thus finds itself inscribed in his very images. In his analysis, these images of proximate but nonreciprocal relationships are themselves mediated, disturbed by tracking problems, even, perhaps, nonintimate. Given this perspective, Wong's ingenious inventory of mediated connections between characters is bound to disappoint. But Wong's images are only disappointments to those who expect the affective relations between the characters to remain the same in a world of spatial and temporal disjuncture. If globalism generates the possibilities for new kinds of looking, does it not also offer the potential for new kinds of feeling, new kinds of intimacy?

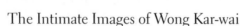

The Intimate Images of Wong Kar-wai

Critics are not alone in their discomfort with the intimacies of Wong Kar-wai; they disturb Wong's actors as well. Describing the shooting of the opening sex scene of *Happy Together*, Doyle notes: "It's a beautiful and sensual scene. Tony and Leslie really look great in bed. But Tony is devastated when it's all done. 'Wong said all I had to do was kiss,' he confides to me, 'now look how far he's pushed me.'"[43] Wong has a reputation for being particularly demanding of his actors, shooting a large number of takes and exhausting the performer in order to get the performance he wants. According to Wong, this strategy is a necessary one given the context of filmmaking in Hong Kong,

Figure 3.
Intimacy marked by
spatial and temporal
disjunctures in
Happy Together.
Courtesy of *City
Entertainment* and
Christopher Doyle.

where films are produced at such a quick rate and actors, who are making a
number of films at the same time, are not able to "enter the world" of the particular film Wong is shooting. "I have to get them to leave themselves in order
to prepare them for their role. I have to exhaust them so that they get rid of
the acting clichés that come out in their other films."[44]

By exhausting his performers, Wong is able to extract from them performances of great intensity and intimacy. Leung, who also appeared in
Days of Being Wild, Ashes of Time [Dong Xie Xi Du] (1994), and *Chungking
Express*, was, according to Wong, like many Hong Kong actors with television
experience; he was wonderfully expressive with his face, but did not quite
know how to utilize his body.[45] After thirty unsuccessful takes—for a sequence that was cut from *Days of Being Wild*—Wong finally managed to in-
still in Leung the necessity of concentrating on the most intimate bodily
gestures. In the case of Maggie Cheung, who began work with Wong on his
first film, *As Tears Go By [Wangjiao Kamen]* (1988), the director noticed that
she was quite expressive with her body, but not particularly gifted with dialogue. "So I cut the majority of her lines in order to concentrate on her actions, on her most intimate bodily movements, and her performance became
excellent."[46]

Wong's ability to solicit intimate performances is paired with the cinematographer Christopher Doyle's skill at producing intimate images. Doyle
is particularly known for his agility with a handheld camera. Working in this
way allows him mobility and the liberty to follow the actions of the performer
more closely.[47] "Our kind of camerawork is 'anticipation and response.' I

need to follow the actor or dancer as much as I need him or her to 'lead.'"[48] Doyle's images, which attempt to match or be in tune with the bodily gestures and movements of the performers, achieve an unusual kind of intimacy. Remarking on Doyle's work on *Temptress Moon [Feng Yue]*, the director Chen Kaige commented, "When you see Chris's shots, you feel the camera loves the characters—which makes it easy for the audience to love them too."[49] Noting Wong's use of music and the rhythmic, musical qualities of his images, the critic David Martinez writes that Doyle's "camera caresses the actors . . . enveloping them so that they become 'prisoners of the rhythm.'"[50]

The rhythmic, expressive world within which Wong's actors and characters are imprisoned is a world of intense affect. As Doyle notes:

> I don't know what to call our "trademark" shots in English. In Chinese we say "kong jing." They're not your conventional "establishing shots" because they're about atmosphere and metaphor, not space. The only thing they "establish" is a mood or a totally subjective point of view. They are clues to an "ambient" world we want to suggest but not explain.[51]

In this ambient world, affect and intimacy appear where one might not expect them, and the senses find themselves attuned to new purposes. In *Chungking Express*, no. 633's apartment is not flooded; it cries. In *Fallen Angels*, the female agent and Blondie (Karen Mok) identify each other in passing because they are wearing the same perfume, given to each of them by Wong Chi-ming. In *Happy Together*, Lai's Taiwanese friend, Chang, explains that because of a childhood accident, he can see much better with his ears. Able to hear conversations from across a noisy bar, Chang experiences intimacy independently of both proximity and reciprocity.

Far from depicting the impossibility of intimacy in a global context, Wong's films propose new kinds of intimacy. His films even suggest that intimacy is linked to creating images. In *Fallen Angels*, He Zhiwu's affection for his father is expressed through his incessant production of video images. *Happy Together* as well ends with an affirmation of the potential comfort of intimate images. As Doyle's shooting diary attests, Wong "feels that what the Chang Chen character gives Tony and Tony Leslie is not 'love' but 'courage' and a 'will to live.' It's our brightest film in all senses of the term and looks like it will have the happiest ending of any Kar-wai film."[52] At the end of the film, Lai returns to Asia, where he visits Chang's family food stand in Taipei.

Here he steals a photo from Chang's trip to the lighthouse in South America. Lai's return home to Hong Kong with Chang's photo in hand, far from signaling his solitude or melancholy, suggests rather his acknowledgment of a potential for new kinds of intimacy. What Chang gives Lai is thus not enduring physical proximity, but the comfort of an image.

In a global context, in which the movement of queer images across national borders facilitates the creation of a public world of belonging, the comfort of an image cannot be taken too lightly. With *Happy Together*, Wong Kar-wai's images have begun to circulate within a queer world. In the context of contemporary gay and lesbian films, these images are distinguished by an intimacy that is all too rare. As B. Ruby Rich notes in an article in which she singles out *Happy Together* for praise while bemoaning the current state of gay and lesbian filmmaking, "It's very much a gay story and one that no gay director has dared show. Why is that? Why are we still covering up the realities of our lives for the sake of a respectable image?"[53] The respectable images that Rich criticizes are those sterile depictions of gays and lesbians that are so prevalent among commercial films that treat homosexuality; these are images without tracking problems in which intimacy and sexuality—if depicted at all—are safely confined to the realm of the private. In contrast, Wong's unstable images of drunken, angry, sexually active characters and the public spaces where they find and lose one another suggest a depth of feeling and an imaginative array of affective relations. From the perspective of the sexual ghetto, these images attest to the rich possibilities for imaging and imagining intimacy in a global context.

Notes

1 See Bérénice Reynaud, "*Happy Together* de Wong Kar-wai," *Cahiers du cinéma* 513 (May 1997): 76.

2 Christopher Doyle, *Buenos Aires* (Tokyo: Prénom H, 1997), 53.

3 Quoted in Howard Feinstein, "Celluloid Takeover: Hong Kong's Miniwave of Gay-Themed movies," *Out*, October 1997, 40. Wong's remake of Hong Kong in Buenos Aires occurred just prior to the end of British rule in the colony in July 1997 and thus at a time of intense anxiety over the potential remake of Hong Kong by the Chinese government. As Wong notes in an interview with Jimmy Ngai, "One of the reasons that I chose Argentina was that it is on the other side of the world, and I thought that by going there, I would be able to stay away from 1997. But then, as you must understand, once you consciously try to stay away from something or to forget something, you will never succeed. That something is bound to be hanging in the air, haunting you." Jimmy Ngai and Wong Kar-wai, "A Dialogue with Wong Kar-wai," in *Wong Kar-wai*, ed. Jean-Marc Lalanne et al. (Paris: Dis Voir, 1998), 112.

4 Conférence de presse, *"Happy Together* de Wong Kar-wai" (Cannes, 17 May 1997), n.p. All translations from the French are my own.

5 Quoted in Richard Lippe, "Gay Movies, West and East," *CineAction* 45 (1997): 58.

6 Conférence de presse, n.p.

7 Thierry Jousse, *"Happy Together* de Wong Kar-wai," *Cahiers du cinéma* 514 (June 1997): 20.

8 Wong has stated: "Normally I hate movies with labels like 'gay film,' 'art film,' or 'commercial film.' There is only good film and bad film." Quoted in Lippe, 58.

9 Reynaud, *"Happy Together,"* 76.

10 Doyle, 130.

11 See Ackbar Abbas, *Hong Kong: Culture and the Politics of Disappearance* (Minneapolis: University of Minnesota Press, 1997), chapters 2 and 3.

12 Ibid., 28.

13 Ibid.

14 Tony Rayns, "Poet of Time," *Sight and Sound* 5, no. 9 (September 1995): 12. About *Chungking Express*, Ackbar Abbas writes: "[I]ts subject matter deals with the world of fast food, quick fixes and one-night stands; in other words, with a *throwaway culture*, where objects, people, and relationships are all marked in one way or another with an expiry date." Abbas, "The Erotics of Disappointment," in Lalanne et al., *Wong Kar-wai*, 67 (my italics). Abbas's haste in linking one-night stands with fast food as part of a throwaway culture gives me pause. By associating objects, people, and relationships that have categorically different temporal dimensions — one night of sex, a few months of canned pineapple, and twenty minutes for a quick hamburger, for example — he muddles the different values attending each of these terms. "One-night stands," or what I would prefer to call tricks, have for instance been indispensable for the creation of an intimate public culture that I am describing as a sexual ghetto, a culture that queers cannot afford to throw away.

15 Ella Shohat and Robert Stam, "From the Imperial Family to the Transnational Imaginary: Media Spectatorship in the Age of Globalization," in *Global/Local: Cultural Production and the Transnational Imaginary*, ed. Rob Wilson and Wimal Dissanayake (Durham, N.C.: Duke University Press, 1996), 146.

16 On AIDS and globalization, see Paul EeNam Park Hagland, "International Theory and LGBT Politics: Testing the Limits of a Human Rights-Based Strategy," *GLQ: A Journal of Gay and Lesbian Studies* 3, no. 4 (1997): 368–70; Cindy Patton, "Critical Bodies," in *Trajectories: Inter-Asia Cultural Studies*, ed. Kuan-hsing Chen (London and New York: Routledge, 1998), 314–29. On sexuality and globalization, see Chris Berry, *A Bit on the Side: East-West Topographies of Desire* (Sydney: EM Press, 1994); Dennis Altman, "Rupture or Continuity? The Internationalization of Gay Identities," *Social Text* 48 (fall 1996), and "Global Gaze/Global Gays," *GLQ: A Journal of Gay and Lesbian Studies* 3, no. 4 (1997): 417–36; Martin F. Manalansan IV, "In the Shadows of Stonewall: Gay Transnational Politics and the Diasporic Dilemma," in *The Politics of Culture in the Shadow of Capital*, ed. Lisa Lowe and David Lloyd (Durham, N.C.: Duke University Press, 1997); and Cindy Patton and Benigno Sánchez-Eppler, eds., *Queer Diasporas* (Durham, N.C.: Duke University Press, 2000).

17 "How Could It Happen? Seo Dongjin and Chris Berry Discuss the Banning of the First Seoul Queer Film and Video Festival," excerpt included in "Seoul Queer Film Festival Fights Back," press release, Seoul (30 October 1997), n.p. The complete text of the interview was printed in *Cine 21* 122 (7–14 October 1997): 24–25. At the time of the banning of the Seoul Queer Film Festival, *Happy Together* was also banned in Korea and therefore received only "restricted" screenings at the 1997 Pusan International Film Festival. For more on sexuality and globalization in relation to the Seoul Queer Film Festival, see Chris Berry, "My Queer Korea: Identity, Space, and the 1998 Seoul Queer Film and Video Festival," *Intersections* 2 (May 1999), http://www.sshe.murdoch.edu.au/intersections/issue2/Berry.html; I would like to thank Peter Limbrick for bringing these texts to my attention.

18 Arjun Appadurai, *Modernity at Large: Cultural Dimensions of Globalization* (Minneapolis: University of Minnesota Press, 1996), 178.

19 Ibid., 179.

20 Ibid., 184.

21 Ibid., 44.

22 Lauren Berlant and Michael Warner, "Sex in Public," in *Intimacy*, ed. Lauren Berlant (Chicago: University of Chicago Press, 2000).

23 Ibid., 327.

24 Ibid., 322.

25 Guy Hocquenghem, *Le gay voyage: Guide homosexuel des grandes métropoles* (Paris: Albin Michel, 1980). For an extended discussion of the notion of the ghetto in Hocquenghem and in the writer Guillaume Dustan, see Daniel Hendrickson and Marc Siegel, "The Ghetto Novels of Guillaume Dustan," *Paroles gelées* 16, no. 1 (1998): 97–119.

26 Ibid., 9.

27 J. Hoberman, "Happy Talk," *Village Voice*, 21 October 1997, 85.

28 Lippe, 59.

29 For more on the particularities of communication in a sexual ghetto, see the brilliant manifesto that concludes Cindy Patton's *Fatal Advice: How Safe-Sex Education Went Wrong* (Durham, N.C.: Duke University Press, 1996). Patton observes: "The ways of being within sexual cultures are difficult to articulate, their processes of acculturation—their practices—are to some extent unspeakable, unformalizable" (142).

30 Ngai and Wong, 106.

31 Thomas Elsaesser, *Fassbinder's Germany: History, Identity, Subject* (Amsterdam: Amsterdam University Press, 1996), 212. See also Douglas Crimp, "Fassbinder, Franz, Fox, Elvira, Erwin, Armin, and All the Others," in *Queer Looks*, ed. Martha Gever, John Greyson, and Pratibha Parmar (New York: Routledge, 1993), 257–74.

32 An intentional reference to Fassbinder, however, is not completely out of the question. Doyle mentions, albeit facetiously, that at one point they were considering titling the film "Fox and His Friends," after Fassbinder's most explicitly gay film. Doyle, 213.

33 For more on the variety of intimacies in a public sexual world, see Samuel R. Delany, *Times Square Red, Times Square Blue* (New York: New York University Press, 1999).

34 Larry Gross, "Nonchalant Grace," *Sight and Sound* 6, no. 9 (1996): 10.

35 Doyle, 38.

36 Gross, 10.

37 In this respect, Wong's films are engaged in a similar project to those of director Tsai Ming-liang.

38 Bérénice Reynaud, "Entretien avec Wong Kar-wai," *Cahiers du cinéma* 490 (1995): 38.

39 Jean Marc Lalanne, "Images from the Inside," trans. Stephen Wright, in Lalanne et al., *Wong Kar-wai*, 24.

40 Chuck Stephens, "Wong Kar-wai and the Persistence of Memory," *Film Comment* 32 (January–February 1996): 16.

41 Abbas, "Erotics of Disappointment," 43.

42 Abbas, *Hong Kong*, 27.

43 Doyle, 48.

44 Reynaud, "Entretien," 37.

45 Ibid., 38.

46 Ibid. Cheung agrees with Wong's assessment and has praised him for facilitating her acting career. In an interview with Bérénice Reynaud, Cheung notes that Wong "made me understand that acting is not just about expression, but comes from the inside. The whole body should follow, not just the face or eyes." See Reynaud, "I Can't Sell My Acting Like That," *Sight and Sound* 7, no. 3 (March 1997): 25.

47 Doyle has said, "Handheld camera-work is more intimate and liberating." Adrian Pennington, "Cinematographer Christopher Doyle," *Premiere*, September 1996, 38.

48 Doyle, 73.

49 "Motion and Emotion: Tony Rayns Interviews Chen Kaige about *Temptress Moon*," *Sight and Sound* 6, no. 3 (March 1996): 14.

50 David Martinez, "Chasing the Metaphysical Express," in Lalanne et al., *Wong Kar-wai*, 35.

51 Doyle, 24.

52 Ibid., 214.

53 B. Ruby Rich, "What's a Good Gay Film?" *Out*, November 1998, 57.

Directors, Actors, Screenwriters, Cinematographers, and Critics

Ah Mon, Lawrence	劉國昌	Cheung Kam-moon	張錦滿
Cha Chuen-yee	查傳誼	Cheung Kin	張　鍵
Chan, Benny	陳木勝	Cheung, Leslie	張國榮
Chan, Evans	陳耀成	Cheung, Mabel	張婉婷
Chan Fong	陳　方	Cheung, Maggie	張曼玉
Chan, Fruit	陳　果	Cheung Man-yee	張敏儀
Chan, George	陳樂儀	Cheung Wai-nam	張偉男
Chan, Gordon	陳嘉上	Cheung, William	張叔平
Chan, Hilda	陳燭昭	Cheung Wood-yau	張活游
Chan, Jackie	成　龍	Chiau, Stephen	周星馳
Chan, Joyce	陳韻文	(Chow Sing-chi)	
Chan, Lindzay	陳令智		
Chan, Peter	陳可辛	Ching Siu-tung	程小東
Chan, Philip	陳欣健	Chin Yong	金　鏞
Chan Po-chu	陳寶珠	Cho Gin-laam	曹建南
Chan Wun	陳　雲	Choi, Clifford	蔡繼光
Chan Yum	陳　任	Chor Yuen	楚　原
Chen Kaige	陳凱歌	Chow, Selina	周梁淑怡
Cheuk Pak-tong	卓伯棠	Chow Yun-fat	周潤發
Cheung, Alex	章國明	Chu Kong	朱　江

Chung, Cherie	鍾楚紅	Kwan, Stanley	關錦鵬
Chung, David Chi-man	鍾志文	Kwan Tak-hing	關德興
Chu Yuan. See Chor Yuen	楚原	Lai, David	黎大煒
Dai Tin	戴天	Lai, Neon	黎明
Deng Lijun. See Tang, Teresa	鄧麗君	Lam, Ben	林權
Do Do	杜杜	Lam, Ringo	林嶺東
Doyle, Christopher	杜可風	Lam Tak-Luk	林德祿
Fong, Allen	方育平	Lau, Andrew	劉偉強
Fong, Eddie	方令正	Lau, Andy	劉德華
Fong Yuen	方圓	Lau, Jeff Chun-wai	劉鎮偉
Fung, Wellington	馮永	Lau, Kar-leong	劉家良
Gu Er	顧耳	Lau Shing-hon	劉成漢
Ho, Josephine	何康喬	Law Clara	羅卓瑤
Hou Hsiao-hsien	侯孝賢	Law Kar	羅卡
Hui, Ann	許鞍華	Law Man	羅文
Hui, Michael	許冠文	Law, Wai-ming	羅維明
Hu, King	胡金銓	Lee, Bruce	李小龍
Hung, Sammo	洪金寶	Lee Chi-ngai	李志毅
Jin Rong. See Chin Yong	金鏞	Lee, Conan	李元霸
Kam Ping-hing	金炳興	Lee, Danny	李修賢
King, David Hoi-lam	敬海林	Lee, Dunn	李登
Kitano, Takeshi	金城武	Lee Kwok-chung	李國松
Ko, Clifton	高志森	Lee Lik-chi	李力持
Ku Chong-ng	古蒼梧	Lee, Lilian Bik-wah	李碧華
Ku Lung	古龍	Lee Pui-kuen	李沛權
Kwan, Apple Pak-huen	關柏煊	Lee, Raymond	李惠民

Lee, Waise	李子雄	Maka, Karl	麥 嘉
Lee Yiu-ming	李耀明	Mak, Johnny Dong-hung	麥當雄
Leung Po-chih	梁普智	Mak, Michael	麥當傑
Leong Noong-kong	梁濃剛	Mok, Karen	莫文蔚
Leung, Ray	梁本熙	Mok Tai-Chi	莫泰志
Leung, Tony Chiu-Wai	梁朝偉	Mui, Anita	梅艷芳
Leung, Tony Kar-Fai	梁家輝	Nam Hung	南 紅
Liang Hai-chiang	梁 良	Ng, Agnes	吳振明
Li Bihua. See Lee, Lilian Bik-wah	李碧華	Ng Ho	吳 昊
		Ng See-yuen	吳思遠
Li Cheuk-to	李焯桃	Ng Yu-shum. See Woo, John	吳宇森
Li Han-hsiang	李翰祥	Poon Man-kit	潘文傑
Li, Jet	李連杰	Qin Jian	秦 劍
Lin, Brigitte Ching-hsia	林青霞	Reis, Michelle	李嘉欣
Lin Dai	林 黛	Sek Kei	石 琪
Lin Feng	林 鳳	Shin, Stephen	冼杞然
Lin Niantong. See Lin Nien-tung	林年同	Shu Kei	舒 琪
Lin Nien-tung	林年同	Shum, Annette	沈月明
Li Tie	李 鐵	Shu Ming	舒 明
Liu Chia-liang. See Lau Kar-leong	劉家良	Shum, Lydia	沈殿霞
		Shu Shuen (Tang, Shuxuan)	唐書璇
Liu Fang	劉 芳	Siao, Josephine	蕭芳芳
Liu, Jerry	廖永亮	Sit Kar-yin	薛家燕
Lo Wei	羅 維	Siu Yeuk-yuen	蕭若元
Luk, Ada	陸 離	Szeto Cheuk-hon	司徒卓漢
Lung Kong	龍 剛	Tam Ning	譚 嬣

Tam, Patrick	譚家明	Wong, Manfred	文雋
Tang Shuxuan. See Shu Shuen	唐書璇	Wong, Michael	王敏德
		Wong Yiu	黃瑤
Tang, Teresa	鄧麗君	Woo, John	吳宇森
Tao Qin	陶秦	Wu Chu-fan	吳楚帆
Teo, Stephen	張建德	Wu Ma	午馬
Tian, Zhuangzhuang	田壯壯	Xie Fei	謝飛
Ti Lung	狄龍	Xie Jin	謝晉
Ti, Tina	狄娜	Xi Xi	西西
To, Johnnie	杜琪峰	Yam, Lambert	任國光
Tong, Stanley	唐季禮	Yam, Simon	任達華
Tsang Kong	曾江	Yang, Edward	楊德昌
Tse, Patrick	謝賢	Yang Gongliang	楊工良
Tsui Hark	徐克	Yau, Patrick	游達志
Wang Weiyi	王爲一	Yee, Derek	爾冬陞
Wong, Bill	黃仲標	Yeh, Sally	葉倩文
Wong, Calvin	黃敬強	Yeoh, Michele	楊紫瓊
Wong Chi	黃志	Yim Ho	嚴浩
Wong, Faye	王菲	Yim Wai	嚴維
Wong Fei-hung	黃飛鴻	Yip Wai-man	葉偉民
Wong, Freddie	黃國兆	Yu, Dennis	余允抗
Wong, Jing	王晶	Yuen, Anita	袁詠儀
Wong, Joey	王祖賢	Yuen Biao	元彪
Wong Kar-wai	王家衛	Yuen, Corey Kwai	元奎
Wong Ka-wah	黃家華	Yuen Wo-ping	袁和平
Wong, Kirk	黃志強	Yu Lik-wai	余力爲

Yung, Peter Wai-chuen   翁維銓

Yu, Ronnie   于仁泰

Zen, Rachel   單慧珠

Zhang Yimou   張藝謀

Zhang Che   張 徹

Films

Affairs   冤家

Ah Kam   阿金

Ah Ying   半邊人

All's Well Ends Well   家有喜事

All the Wrong Clues...for the Right Solution   鬼馬智多星

Apartment of 14 Familes, The   一樓十四伙

Arch, The   董夫人

Armour of God   龍兄虎弟

Armour of God II   飛鷹計劃

Ashes of Time   東邪西毒

As Tears Go By   旺角卡門

Autumn's Tale, An   秋天的童話

Back to Roots   歸土

Beasts, The   山狗

Below the Lion Rock series   獅子山下片集

Better Tomorrow, A   英雄本色

Better Tomorrow II, A   英雄本色續集

Big Boss, The	唐山大兄
Black Rose II	黑玫瑰義結金蘭
Blade, The	刀
Boat People	投奔怒海
Bodyguard from Beijing	中南海保鑣
Bridge, The	橋
Butterfly Lovers, The	梁　祝
Butterfly Murders, The	蝶　變
Call Girls, The	應召女郎
Casino Raiders	至尊無上
Center Stage	阮玲玉
C'est la vie, mon cheri	新不了情
Challenge of the Masters	陸阿采與黃飛鴻
China Behind	再見中國
Chinese Ghost Story, A	倩女幽魂
Chungking Express	重慶森林
CID series	ＣＩＤ第一輯
Club, The	舞廳
Colorful Partners	七彩難兄難弟
Comrades, Almost a Love Story	甜蜜蜜
Cops and Robbers	點指兵兵
Crossings	錯愛
Dance of the Drunken Mantis	南北醉拳
Dangerous Encounter — 1st Kind	第一類型危險
Days of Being Wild	阿飛正傳

Day the Sun Turned Cold, The	天國逆子
Dr. Mack	流氓醫生
Dragon Gate Inn, The	龍門客棧
Dragons Forever	飛龍猛將
Drunken Master	醉拳
Drunken Master II	醉拳（II）
Enchanting Shadow, The	倩女幽魂
Encore	喝采
Executioners	現代豪俠傳
Expect the Unexpected	非常突然
Extras	茄喱啡
Fallen Angels	墮落天使
Farewell Buddy	過客
Farewell China	再見中國
Farewell My Concubine	霸王別姬
Father and Son	父子情
Fearless Hyena, The	笑拳怪招
Fight Back to School	逃學威龍
First Option	飛虎雄心
First Strike	警察故事之簡單任務
Fist of Fury	精武門
Five Fingers of Death	天下第一拳
Fong Sai-Yuk	方世玉
Forbidden City Cop	大内密探零零發
From Beijing with Love	國產凌凌漆

Full Moon in New York	人在紐約
Gen-X Cops	特警新人類
God of Cookery, The	食神
Green-Eyed Demoness	碧眼魔女
Green Snake	青蛇
Happenings, The	夜車
Happy Together	春光乍洩
Hardboiled	辣手神探
He Ain't Heavy, He's My Father!	新難兄難弟
Health Warning	打擂台
Hearty Response	義蓋雲天
Heaven Can't Wait	救世神棍
Her Fatal Ways	表姐你好嘢
Heroic Trio	東方三俠
He's a Woman, She's a Man	金枝玉葉
Hiroshima 28	廣島廿八
Homecoming	似水流年
Hong Kong Tycoon	暴發戶
House of 72 Tenants, The	七十二家房客
House of the Lute	慾火焚琴
ICAC series	廉政公署片集
Iceman Cometh, The	急凍奇俠
Imp, The	兇榜
Interpol series	國際刑警片集
In the Face of Demolition	危樓春曉

In the Mood for Love	花樣年華
Intimate Partners	難兄難弟
It Takes Two	難兄難弟
I Will Wait for You	年年有今日
Joys and Sorrows of Youth	冷暖青春
Jumping Ash	跳灰
Justice, My Foot	審死官
Just Like Weather	美國心
Kawashima Yoshiko	川島芳子
Killer, The	喋血雙雄
Lee Rock I	五億探長雷洛傳 I 一雷老虎
Legendary Weapons of China	十八般武藝
Legend of the Mountain	山中傳奇
Little Cheung	細路祥
Longest Summer, The	去年煙花特別多
Love in a Fallen City	傾城之戀
Love in the Time of Twilight	花月佳期
Love Massacre	愛殺
Love Will Tear Us Apart	天上人間
Love Without End	不了情
Mad Phoenix, The	南海十三郎
Man on the Brink	邊緣人
Meng Duan Qing Tian Series	夢斷情天劇集
Mr. Nice Guy	一個好人
My American Grandson	上海假期

'92 Legendary la rose noir	'92 黑玫瑰對黑玫瑰
No Big Deal	有你有你
Nomad	烈火青春
Once a Thief	縱橫四海
Once Upon a Time in China	黃飛鴻
Once Upon a Time in China II	黃飛鴻 II：男兒當自強
Once Upon a Time in China III	黃飛鴻 III：獅王爭霸
Once Upon a Time in Triad Society	旺角揸 *fit* 人
One-Armed Swordsman, The	獨臂刀
Operation Condor	禿鷹行動
Operation Manhunt series	大丈夫片集
Operation Manhunt II series	新大丈夫片集
Ordinary Heroes	千言萬語
Out of the Dark	回魂夜
Peking Opera Blues	刀馬旦
Police Story	警察故事
Police Story II	警察故事續集
Police Story III: Supercop	超級警察
Pom Pom and Hot Hot	神槍手與咖喱雞
Princess Fragrance	香香公主
Project A	A 計劃
Project A, Part II	A 計劃續集
Raid, The	財叔之橫掃千軍
Raining in the Mountain	空山靈雨
Raise the Red Lantern	大紅燈籠高高掛

Reincarnation of Golden Lotus, The	潘金蓮之前世今生
Romance of Book and Sword	書劍恩仇錄
Rouge	胭脂扣
Rumble in the Bronx	紅番區
Running Out of Time	暗戰
Sacred Knives of Vengeance	大殺手
Secret, The	瘋劫
See-Bar	師爸
Seven Women series	七女性片集
Shanghai Blues	上海之夜
Sixty Million Dollar Man	百變星君
Snake in the Eagle's Shadow	蛇形刁手
Social Worker	北斗星
Song of the Exile	客途秋恨
Songs of Yuen Chau Chai	元洲仔之歌
Spacked Out	無人駕駛
Spooky Bunch	撞到正
Starry Is the Night	今夜星光燦爛
Stormriders	風雲之雄霸天下
Story of a Discharged Prisoner	英雄本色
Story of Woo Viet, The	胡越的故事
Summer Snow	女人四十
Superstars series	群星譜
Sup Sap Bup Dup	十三不搭
Swordsman	笑傲江湖

Swordsman II	笑傲江湖之東方不敗
Swordsman III: The East Is Red	東方不敗之風雲再起
Sword, The	名劍
System, The	行規
Taxi Driver series	的士司機片集
Teddy Girls	飛女正傳
Teenage Dreamers	檸檬可樂
Temptress Moon	風月
Ten Assassinations series	十大刺客片集
Ten Sensational Cases series	十大奇案片集
Teppanyaki	鐵板燒
Terra Cotta Warrior	秦　俑
Terrorizer	恐怖份子
Those Were the Days	精裝難兄難弟豪情蓋天
Thunderbolt	霹靂火
Tiger on the Beat	老虎出更
To Be Number One	跛豪
To Live	活著
To Liv(e)	浮世戀曲
Twin Dragons	雙龍會
Umbrella Story, The	人間有情
Valiant Ones, The	忠烈圖
Victim	目露兇光
Way of the Dragon	猛龍過江
We Are Going to Eat You	地獄無門

Welcome	補鑊英雄
Who Am I?	我是誰
Wicked City, The	妖獸都市
Wild Child	野孩子
Winter Love	冬戀
Wonderfun series	奇趣錄
Yellow Earth	黃土地
Yesterday, Today and Tomorrow	昨天今天明天
Young Dragons, The	鐵漢柔情
Young Master	師弟出馬
Zodiac Killers, The	極道追蹤
Zu, Warriors of the Magic Mountain	蜀山劍客

Terms

chiqing	癡情
ci	詞
feng shui	風水
gweilos	鬼佬
huadan	花旦
huaijiu	懷舊
jianghu	江湖
keipo/qipao	旗袍
kungfu	功夫

liang hsiang	亮相
manga	漫畫
she sheng qu yi	捨生取義
shi	詩
sifu	師父
taohua yijiu renmian quanfei	桃花依舊人面全非
toupan	偷片
wudan	武旦
wuxia pian	武俠片
xia	俠
yum/yin	淫
Hong Kong New Wave	香港新浪潮

Film Production Companies, TV Stations, and Film Publications

Asian Television (ATV)	亞洲電視
Chinese Student Weekly	中國學生週報
Cinema City Company Incorporated	新藝城影業有限公司
City Entertainment	電影雙週刊
Close Up Film Review [*Close Up Weekly*]	大特寫
College Cine Club Monthly Bulletin	大學生活電影會影訊
Commercial Television (CTV)	佳藝電視
Film Biweekly	電影雙週刊
Film Guard Association	衛影會

Golden Harvest (Hong Kong) Limited	嘉禾（香港）有限公司
Great Wall Production Company	長城電影有限公司
Hong Kong Youth Weekly	香港青年週報
Ming Pao Daily	明報
New Films Company	新電影公司
New Life Evening News	新生晚報
New Sensibility	新思潮
Phoenix Film Club	火鳥電影會
Radio Television Hong Kong (RTHK)	香港電台電視部
Rediffusion Television (RTV)	麗的電視
Seventies Weekly, The	七十年代雙週刊
Shaw Brothers Studio	邵氏兄弟製片廠
Studio One Film Society of Hong Kong	第一影室香港電影協會
Tabloid [*City Magazine*]	號外
Television Broadcasting Limited (TVB)	香港電視廣播有限公司
Youth Garden Weekly	青年樂園
Zhonglian Company	中聯影業有限公司

Selected Bibliography

Esther C. M. Yau

Since 1980, critics and journalists all over the world have produced numerous reviews and short essays on contemporary Hong Kong films, most of which appeared in local newspapers and popular magazines. Since the early 1990s, popular books as well as longer scholarly essays and book-length studies have appeared. Discussions of Hong Kong films have also become an integral part of scholarly writings on Hong Kong culture and identity, and many were written in the Chinese language — with participation from critics working in mainland China and Taiwan. In its "Hong Kong Cinema Retrospective" series, the Hong Kong International Film Festival has published a total of twenty-two collections, which together make up a highly informative bilingual (Chinese and English) resource on Hong Kong cinema. What follows is a selective list of writings on Hong Kong films and filmmaking of the 1980s and the 1990s that have been published in English, together with a small sample of major works on the topic published in Chinese. Given the number of publications that exist in these two languages alone on a subject of growing popularity, such a list is necessarily incomplete and certainly far from fulfilling the needs of transnational research. With some exceptions, mention is made of longer essays and book titles rather than short reviews and popular commentaries, and only a short list of Chinese-language publications has been included here.

Books and Essays

Abbas, Ackbar. 1994. "The New Hong Kong Cinema and *Déjà desparu*." *Discourse* 16, no. 3: 65–77.
———. 1997. *Hong Kong: Culture and the Politics of Disappearance.* Minneapolis: University of Minneapolis Press.
Atkinson, Michael. 1996. "Songs of Crushed Love: The Cinema of Stanley Kwan." *Film Comment* 32, no. 3 (May–June): 42–46, 49.

Aufderheide, Pat. 1988. "Dynamic Duo." *Film Comment* 24, no. 3 (June): 42–45.

Berry, Chris. 1992. "Heterogeneity as Identity: Hybridity and Transnationality in Hong Kong and Taiwanese Cinema." *Metro* 91: 48–51.

———, ed. 1991. *Perspectives on Chinese Cinema.* London: British Film Institute.

Block, Alex Ben. 1974. *The Legend of Bruce Lee.* New York: Dell.

Bordwell, David. 2000a. *Planet Hong Kong: Popular Cinema and the Art of Entertainment.* Cambridge, Mass.: Harvard University Press.

———. 2000b. "Richness through Imperfection: King Hu and the Glimpse." In *The Cinema of Hong Kong: History, Arts, Identity,* ed. Poshek Fu and David Desser, 113–36. Cambridge and New York: Cambridge University Press.

Borthwick, Mark. 1992. *Pacific Century: The Emergence of Modern Pacific Asia.* Boulder, Colo.: Westview Press.

Braester, Yomi. 1998. "Modern Identity and Karmic Retribution in Clara Law's *Reincarnations of Golden Lotus.*" *Asian Cinema* 10, no. 1: 58–61.

Browne, Nick, Paul Pickowicz, Vivian Sobchack, and Esther Yau, eds. 1994. *New Chinese Cinemas: Forms, Identities, Politics.* Cambridge and New York: Cambridge University Press.

Chang, Terence. 1993. "Woo in Interview." *Sight and Sound* 3 (May): 25.

Chan, Natalia Sui-hung. 2000. "Rewriting History: Hong Kong Nostalgia Cinema and Its Social Practice." In *The Cinema of Hong Kong: History, Arts, Identity,* ed. Poshek Fu and David Desser, 252–72. Cambridge and New York: Cambridge University Press.

Chen, Xiaoming. 1997. "The Mysterious Other: Postpolitics in the Narrative Chinese Film." *boundary 2* 24, no. 3 (fall): 123–41.

Cheuk Pak-tong. 1999. "The Beginnings of the Hong Kong New Wave: The Interactive Relationship between Television and the Film Industry." *Post Script* 19, no. 1 (fall): 10–27.

Chiao, Peggy Hsiung-ping. 1987. *Xianggang Dianying Fengmao [Style of Hong Kong Cinema].* Taipei: Shibao.

———. 1988. "Contrasting Images: Taiwan and Hong Kong Films." *Free China Review* (February): 12–19.

———. 1991. "The Distinct Taiwanese and Hong Kong Cinemas." In *Perspectives on Chinese Cinema,* ed. Chris Berry. London: British Film Institute.

———. 1997. "Happy Together: Hong Kong's Absence." *Cinemaya* 38 (October–December): 17–21.

Chow, Rey. 1995. *Primitive Passions: Visuality, Sexuality, Ethnography, and Contemporary Chinese Cinema.* New York: Columbia University Press.

Chu, Blanche. 1998. "The Ambivalence of History: Nostalgia Films Understood in the Post-Colonial Context." *Hong Kong Cultural Studies Bulletin* 8–9 (spring–summer): 41–54.

Chun, Allen. 1996. "Fuck Chineseness: On the Ambiguities of Ethnicity as Cultural Identity." *boundary 2* 23, no. 2: 111–38.

Chu, Rolanda. 1994. "*Swordsman II* and *The East Is Red*: The 'Hong Kong Film,' Entertainment, and Gender." *Bright Lights Film Journal* 12: 30–35, 46.

Chute, David. 1988. "Midsection: Made in Hong Kong." *Film Comment* 24, no. 3 (June): 34–56.

———. 1998. "New Maps of Hong Kong." *Film Comment* 34, no. 3 (May–June): 85–88.

Ciecko, Anne T. 1997. "Transnational Action: John Woo, Hong Kong, Hollywood." In *Transnational Chinese Cinema: Identity, Nationhood, Gender,* ed. Sheldon Hsiao-peng Lu, 221–37. Honolulu: University of Hawaii Press.

Ciecko, Anne T., and Sheldon H. Lu. 1999. "The Heroic Trio, Anita Mui, Maggie Cheung, Michelle Yeoh: Self-Reflexivity and the Globalization of the Hong Kong Action Heroine." *Post Script* 19, no. 1 (fall): 70–86.

Collier, Joelle. 1999. "A Repetition Compulsion: Discontinuity Editing, Classical Chinese Aesthetics, and Hong Kong's Culture of Disappearance." *Asian Cinema* 10, no. 2 (spring–summer): 67–79.

Corliss, Richard. "Stealing Stars." *Time Asia,* 26 January, 52.

Curtin, Michael. 1999. "Industry of Fire: The Cultural Economy of Hong Kong Media." *Post Script* 19, no. 1 (fall): 28–51.

Dancer, Greg. 1998. "Film Style and Performance: Comedy and Kungfu from Hong Kong." *Asian Cinema* 10, no. 1: 42–50.

Deng, To, ed. 1997. *1996 Xianggang Dianying Huigu [1996 Retrospective on Hong Kong Films].* Hong Kong: Hong Kong Critics Society.

Desser, David. 2000. "The Kung Fu Craze: Hong Kong Cinema's First American Reception." In *The Cinema of Hong Kong: History, Arts, Identity,* ed. Poshek Fu and David Desser, 19–43. Cambridge and New York: Cambridge University Press.

Donald, Stephanie. 1998. "Symptoms of Alienation: The Female Body in Recent Chinese Film." *Continuum* (April): 9–103.

Doyle, Christopher. 1997a. *Christopher Doyle's Photographic Journal of "Happy Together," a Wong Kar Wai Film.* Hong Kong: City Entertainment.

———. 1997b. *Buenos Aires.* Tokyo: Prénom H.

Eberhard, Wolfram. 1972. *The Chinese Silver Screen: Hong Kong and Taiwanese Motion Pictures in the 1960's.* Taipei: Orient Culture Service.

Einhorn, Bruce. 1998. "What Hit Hong Kong's Film Industry?" *Business Week,* 4 May, 34.

Eng, David. 1995. "Love at Last Site: Waiting for Oedipus in Stanley Kwan's *Rouge.*" *Camera Obscura* 32: 75–97.

Erens, Patricia Brett. 2000. "The Film Work of Ann Hui." In *The Cinema of Hong Kong: History, Arts, Identity,* ed. Poshek Fu and David Desser, 199–226. Cambridge and New York: Cambridge University Press.

Feinstein, Howard. 1997. "Celluloid Takeover: Hong Kong's Miniwave of Gay-Themed movies." *Out,* October, 40.

Fitzgerald, Martin. 2000. *Hong Kong's Heroic Bloodshed.* North Pomfret, Vt.: Trafalgar Square.

Fonoroff, Paul. 1997. *Silver Light: A Pictorial History of Hong Kong Cinema, 1920–1970.* Hong Kong: Joint Publishing.

———. 1999. *At the Hong Kong Movies: 600 Reviews from 1988 till the Handover.* Hong Kong: Film Biweekly.

Fore, Steve. 1993. "Tales of Recombinant Femininity: *The Reincarnation of Golden Lotus,* the *Chin P'ing Mei,* and the Politics of Melodrama in Hong Kong." *Journal of Film and Video* 45, no. 4: 57–70.

————. 1994. "Golden Harvest Films and the Hong Kong Movie Industry in the Realm of Globalization." *Velvet Light Trap* 34: 40–58.

————. 1997. "Jackie Chan and the Cultural Dynamics of Entertainment." In *Transnational Chinese Cinema: Identity, Nationhood, Gender,* ed. Sheldon Lu, 239–62. Honolulu: University of Hawaii Press.

————. 1999. "Introduction: Hong Kong Movies, Critical Time Warps, and Shape of Things to Come." *Post Script* 19, no. 1 (fall): 2–9.

Frank, Bren. 1998. "Connections and Crossovers: Cinema and Theatre in Hong Kong." *New Theatre Quarterly* 14, no. 35: 63–74.

Fu, Poshek. 2000a. "Between Nationalism and Colonialism: Mainland Emigres, Marginal Culture, and Hong Kong Cinema, 1937–1941." In *The Cinema of Hong Kong: History, Arts, Identity,* ed. Poshek Fu and David Desser. Cambridge and New York: Cambridge University Press.

————. 2000b. "The 1960s: Modernity, Youth Culture, and Hong Kong Cantonese Cinema." In *The Cinema of Hong Kong: History, Arts, Identity,* ed. Poshek Fu and David Desser, 71–89. Cambridge and New York: Cambridge University Press.

Fu, Poshek, and David Desser, eds. 2000. *The Cinema of Hong Kong: History, Arts, Identity.* Cambridge and New York: Cambridge University Press.

Gallagher, Mark. 1997. "Masculinity in Translation: Jackie Chan's Transcultural Star Text." *Velvet Light Trap* 39: 23–41.

Garcia, Roger. 1998. "The Touch of Hu." *Cinema* (winter–spring): 77–79.

Glaessner, Verina. 1974. *Kungfu: Cinema of Vengeance.* London: Lorimer.

Hall, Ken. 1998. "Hong Kong 1997, Mexico 1917: Motifs and Historical Perspective." *Asian Cinema* 10, no. 1: 51–57.

Hammond, Stefan, and Michelle Yeoh. 2000. *Hollywood East: Hong Kong Movies and the People Who Make Them.* Lincolnwood, Ill.: Contemporary Books.

Hampton, Howard. 1996. "Venus, Armed: Brigitte Lin's Shanghai Gesture." *Film Comment* 32, no. 5 (September–October): 48.

————. 1997. "*Once Upon a Time in Hong Kong*: Tsui Hark and Ching Siu-tung." *Film Comment* 33, no. 4 (July–August): 17–19.

Hastie, Amelie. 1999. "Fashion, Femininity, and Historical Design: The Visual Texture of Three Hong Kong Films." *Post Script* 19, no. 1 (fall): 52–69.

Havis, Richard J. 1997. "Wong Kar-wai: One Entrance, Many Exits." *Cinemaya* (October–December): 15–16.

————. 1998. "Hong Kong's John Woo Finally Does It His Way in Hollywood." *Cinemaya* (winter/spring): 10–16.

Heard, Christopher. 2000. *Ten Thousand Bullets: The Cinematic Journey of John Woo.* Los Angeles: Lone Eagle.

Henderson, Jeffrey. 1989. "The Political Economy of Technological Transformation in Hong Kong." *Comparative Urban and Community Research* 2: 102–55.

Hollander, Jane. 1987. "Jackie Chan: Risking Life for American Approval." *Inside Kung Fu* 14, no. 2: 36–41.

Hong Kong Film Archive. 1997. *Fifty Years of the Hong Kong Film Production and Distribution Industries: An Exhibition (1947–1997)* [catalog]. Hong Kong: Urban Council.

Hoover, Michael, and Lisa Stokes. 1998. "A City on Fire: Hong Kong Cinema as the Cultural Logic of Late Capitalism." *Asian Cinema* 10, no. 1: 25–31.

Hwang, Angela. 1998. "The Irresistible: Hong Kong Movie *Once Upon a Time in China* Series, An Extensive Interview with Director-Producer Tsui Hark." *Asian Cinema* 10, no. 1: 10–24.

Jarvie, Ian C. 1977. *Window on Hong Kong: A Sociological Survey of the Hong Kong Film Industry and Its Audience*. Hong Kong: Centre of Asian Studies, University of Hong Kong.

Joseph, May. 1999, "Kung Fu Cinema and Frugality." In *Nomadic Identities: The Performance of Citizenship*, 49–68. Minneapolis: University of Minnesota Press.

Keng, Chua Siew. 1998. "The Politics of Home: *Song of the Exile* (Ann Hui, 1990)." *Jump Cut* 42: 90–93.

Kowallis, Jon. 1997. "The Diaspora in Postmodern Taiwan and Hong Kong Film: Framing Stan Lai's *The Peach Blossom Land* with Allen Fong's *Ah Ying*." In *Transnational Chinese Cinema: Identity, Nationhood, Gender*, ed. Sheldon Hsiaopeng Lu. Honolulu: University of Hawaii Press.

Kwong, Powai. 1998. *Xu Anhua Shuo Xu Anhua [Ann Hui on Ann Hui]*. Hong Kong: Hong Kong Arts Development Council (sponsor).

Lai, Linda, and Kim Choi. 1997. "Interview with Stanley Kwan on Yang and Yin: Gender in Chinese Cinema." In *Twenty-first Hong Kong International Film Festival*, 42–43. Hong Kong: Urban Council.

Lalanne, Jean-Marc, et al., eds. 1997. *Wong Kar Wai*. Paris: Editions Dis Voir.

Lau, Jenny Kwok Wah. 1989a. "A Cultural Interpretation of the Contemporary Cinema of China and Hong Kong, 1981–1985." Ph.D. diss., Northwestern University.

———. 1989b. "Towards a Cultural Understanding of Cinema: A Comparison of Contemporary Films from the People's Republic of China and Hong Kong." *Wide Angle* 11, no. 3: 42–49.

———. 1998. "Besides Fists and Blood: Hong Kong Comedy and Its Master of the Eighties." *Cinema Journal* 37, no. 2 (winter): 18–34.

Lau, Shing-hon, ed. 1980. *A Study of the Hong Kong Martial Arts Film*. Fourth Hong Kong International Film Festival. Hong Kong: Urban Council.

———. 1981. *A Study of the Hong Kong Swordplay Film, 1945–80*. Fourth Hong Kong International Film Festival. Hong Kong: Urban Council.

Law Kar. 2000. "The American Connection in Early Hong Kong Cinema." In *The Cinema of Hong Kong: History, Arts, Identity*, ed. Poshek Fu and David Desser, 44–70. Cambridge and New York: Cambridge University Press.

———, ed. 1991. *Hong Kong Cinema in the Eighties: A Comparative Study with Western Cinema*. Fifteenth Hong Kong International Film Festival. Hong Kong: Urban Council.

———. 1996. *The Restless Breed: Cantonese Stars of the Sixties*. Twentieth Hong Kong International Film Festival. Hong Kong: Urban Council.

———. 1997. *Hong Kong Cinema Retrospective: Fifty Years of Electric Shadows*. Twenty-first Hong Kong International Film Festival. Hong Kong: Urban Council.

———. 1998. *Transcending the Times: King Hu and Eileen Chang*. Twenty-second Hong Kong International Film Festival. Hong Kong: Provisional Urban Council.

————. 1999. *Hong Kong New Wave: Twenty Years After.* Twenty-third Hong Kong International Film Festival. Hong Kong: Urban Council.

————. 2000. *Border Crossings in Hong Kong Cinema.* Twenty-fourth Hong Kong International Film Festival. Hong Kong: Leisure and Cultural Services Department.

Law Kar, Ng Ho, and Cheuk Pak-tong. 1997. *Xianggang Dianying Leixing Lun [On Hong Kong Film Genres].* Hong Kong: Oxford University Press.

Lee, Leo Ou-fan. 1994. "Two Films from Hong Kong: Parody and Allegory." In *New Chinese Cinemas: Forms, Identities, Politics,* ed. Nick Browne et al., 202–15. Cambridge and New York: Cambridge University Press.

————. 1996–97. "Tales of a 'Floating City.'" *Harvard Asia Pacific Review* (winter): 43–49.

————. 1998–99. "Hong Kong Movies in Hollywood." *Harvard Asia Pacific Review* (winter): 30–34.

Lent, John A., ed. 1995. *Asian Popular Culture.* Boulder: Westview Press.

Leong Mo-ling, ed. 1985. *Hong Kong Cinema '84.* Ninth Hong Kong International Film Festival. Hong Kong: Urban Council.

————. 1987. *New Hong Kong Films '86–'87.* Eleventh Hong Kong International Film Festival. Hong Kong: Urban Council.

————. 1988. *New Hong Kong Films '87–'88.* Twelfth Hong Kong International Film Festival. Hong Kong: Urban Council.

————. 1990. *New Hong Kong Films '89–'90.* Thirteenth Hong Kong International Film Festival. Hong Kong: Urban Council.

Leung, Benjamin K. P. 1996. *Perspectives on Hong Kong Society.* Hong Kong: Oxford University Press.

Leung, Noong-kong. 1982. "Towards a New Wave in Hong Kong Cinema." In *Hong Kong Cinema '79.* Hong Kong: Urban Council.

————. 2000. "Hong Kong Cinema: China and 1997." In *World Cinema: Critical Approaches,* ed. John Hill and Pamela Gibson. New York: Oxford University Press.

Leung, Ping-kwan. 1994. "Minzu Dianying yu Xianggang Wenhua Shenfen: cong Bawang Bieji, Qiwang, Ruan Lingyu kan wenhua dingwei" ["National Film and Hong Kong Cultural Identity"]. *Today [Jintian]* 27, no. 3: 193–204.

————. 1995a. *Hong Kong Culture.* Hong Kong: Hong Kong Arts Centre.

————. 1995b. *Xianggang Wenhua Zhuanji* [special issue on Hong Kong culture]. *Today [Jintian]* 28, no. 1.

————. 1997. "From Cities in Hong Kong Cinema to Hong Kong Films on Cities." In *Hong Kong Cinema Retrospective: Fifty Years of Electric Shadows,* ed. Law Kar. Twenty-first Hong Kong International Film Festival. Hong Kong: Urban Council.

————. 2000. "Urban Cinema and the Cultural Identity of Hong Kong." In *The Cinema of Hong Kong: History, Arts, Identity,* ed. Poshek Fu and David Desser, 227–51. Cambridge and New York: Cambridge University Press.

Li, Cheuk-to. 1988. "Cinema in Hong Kong: Contemporary Currents," *Cinemaya* 1 (autumn): 4–9.

————. 1989. "A Review of Hong Kong Cinema, 1988–1989." In *The Ninth Hawaii International Film Festival Viewers Guide,* 36–39. Honolulu: East-West Center.

————. 1990. *Bashi Niandai Xianggang Dianying Biji [Notes on Hong Kong Cinema of the 1980s]*. 2 vols. Hong Kong: Chuangjian chuban gongsi.

————. 1993a. *Guan Ni Ji [Collections of Viewings against the Grain]*. 2 vols. Hong Kong: Ci Wenhua Tang.

————. 1993b. "Tsui Hark and Western Interest in Hong Kong Cinema." *Cinemaya* 21 (autumn): 50–51.

————. 1994. "The Return of the Father: Hong Kong New Wave and Its Chinese Context in the 1980s." In *New Chinese Cinemas: Forms, Identities, Politics*, ed. Nick Browne et al., 160–79. New York: Cambridge University Press.

————. 1996a. *Linli Yingxiang Guan [Thorough Moving-Image Archive]*. 2 vols. Hong Kong: Ci Wenhua Tang.

————. 1996b. "Popular Cinema in Hong Kong." In *The Oxford History of World Cinema*, ed. Geoffrey Nowell-Smith. Oxford: Oxford University Press.

Li, Cheuk-to, ed. 1984. *A Study of Hong Kong Cinema in the Seventies*. Eighth Hong Kong International Film Festival. Hong Kong: Urban Council.

————. 1985. *The Traditions of Hong Kong Comedy*. Ninth Hong Kong International Film Festival. Hong Kong: Urban Council.

————. 1986. *Cantonese Melodrama (1950–1969)*. Tenth Hong Kong International Film Festival. Hong Kong: Urban Council.

————. 1987. *Cantonese Opera Film Retrospective*. Eleventh Hong Kong International Film Festival. Hong Kong: Urban Council.

————. 1988. *Changes in Hong Kong Society through Cinema*. Twelfth Hong Kong International Film Festival. Hong Kong: Urban Council.

————. 1989. *Phantoms of the Hong Kong Cinema*. Thirteenth Hong Kong International Film Festival. Hong Kong: Urban Council.

————. 1990. *The China Factor in Hong Kong Cinema*. Fourteenth Hong Kong International Film Festival. Hong Kong: Urban Council.

Lin, Nien-tung, ed. 1978. *Hong Kong Cinema Survey, 1946–68*. Third Hong Kong International Film Festival. Hong Kong: Urban Council.

Lippe, Richard. 1997. "Gay Movies, West and East." *CineAction* 45: 58.

Lo, Che-ying. 1992. *A Selective Collection of Hong Kong Movie Posters, 1950's–1990's*. Hong Kong: Joint Publishing.

Lo, Kwai-cheung. 1993. "Once Upon a Time in China: Technology Comes to China." *Modern Chinese Literature* 7: 79–96.

————. 1999. "Muscles and Subjectivity: A Short History of the Masculine Body in Hong Kong Popular Culture." *Camera Obscura* 39 (1996): 105–25.

Logan, Bey. 1995. *Hong Kong Action Cinema*. London: Titan Books.

Lok, Feng. 1995. *Shijimo Chengshi [Fin-de-siècle City]*. Hong Kong: Oxford University Press.

Lu, Sheldon Hsiao-peng. 2000. "Filming Diaspora and Identity: Hong Kong and 1997." In *The Cinema of Hong Kong: History, Arts, Identity*, ed. Poshek Fu and David Desser, 273–88. Cambridge and New York: Cambridge University Press.

————, ed. 1997. *Transnational Chinese Cinema: Identity, Nationhood, Gender*. Honolulu: University of Hawaii Press.

Marchetti, Gina. 1987. "Hong Kong Independent Filmmaking: An Interview with Roger Garcia." *Afterimage* 14, no. 10 (May): 16–17.

———. 1998. "Transnational Cinema, Hybrid Identities, and the Films of Evans Chan." *Postmodern Culture* 8, no. 2. At http://jefferson.village.virginia.edu/pmc/.

———. 2000. "Buying American, Consuming Hong Kong: Cultural Commerce, Fantasies of Identity, and the Cinema." In *The Cinema of Hong Kong: History, Arts, Identity,* ed. Poshek Fu and David Desser, 289–313. Cambridge and New York: Cambridge University Press.

McDonagh, Maitland. 1993. "Things I Felt Were Being Lost." *Film Comment* 29, no. 5 (September–October): 50–52.

Meyers, Richard, Amy Harlib, Bill Palmer, and Karen Palmer. 1991. *From Bruce Lee to the Ninjas: Martial Arts Movies.* Secaucus, N.J.: Citadel Press.

Mintz, Marilyn D. 1978. *The Martial Arts Film.* South Brunswick: Barnes.

———. 1983. *The Martial Arts Films.* Rutland, Vt.: C. E. Tuttle.

Ng, Ho. 1993. *Xianggang Dianying Minzu Xue [Ethnographic Study of Hong Kong Film].* Hong Kong: Ci Wenhua Tang.

Ng, Sylvia S. Y., ed. 1996. *The Metropolis: Visual Research into Contemporary Hong Kong, 1990–1996.* Hong Kong: Photo Pictorial Publishers and Hong Kong Arts Center.

Powers, John. 1988. "Glimpse Eastward." *Film Comment* 24, no. 3 (June): 34–56.

Redi, Craig D. 1995. "Interview with Tsui Hark." *Film Quarterly* 48, no. 3: 34–41.

Reynaud, Bérénice. 1996. "Hong Kong." *Cinemaya* 33 (summer): 53–54.

———. 1997. "High Noon in Hong Kong." *Film Comment* 33, no. 4 (July–August): 20–24.

Rayns, Tony. 1995. "Poet of Time." *Sight and Sound* 5, no. 9 (September): 12–14.

———. 1998. "Laying Foundations: Dragon Gate Inn." *Cinemaya* (winter/spring): 80–83.

Richie, Donald. 1995. *"The Day the Sun Turned Cold:* Some Aspects of Yim Ho's Film." *Cinemaya* 31 (winter): 16–18.

Rodriguez, Hector. 1997. "Hong Kong Popular Culture as an Interpretive Arena: The Huang Feihong Film Series." *Screen* 38, no. 1: 1–24.

———. 1999. "Organizational Hegemony in the Hong Kong Cinema." *Post Script* 19, no. 1 (fall): 107–19.

Ryan, Barbara. 1995. "Blood, Brothers, and Hong Kong Gangster Movies: Pop Culture Commentary on 'One China'." In *Asian Popular Culture,* ed. John A. Lent. Boulder: Westview Press.

Sandell, Jillian. 1994. "A Better Tomorrow? American Machismo and the Hong Kong Film." *Bright Lights* 13: 40–45, 50.

———. 1996. "Reinventing Masculinity: The Spectacle of Male Intimacy in the Films of John Woo." *Film Quarterly* 49, no. 4: 23–34.

Sek, Kei. 1997. "Hong Kong Cinema from June 4 to 1997." In *Fifty Years of Electric Shadows,* ed. Law Kar, 120–25. Twenty-first Hong Kong International Film Festival. Hong Kong: Urban Council.

Server, Lee. 1999. *Asian Pop Cinema: Bombay to Tokyo.* San Francisco: Chronicle Books.

Shen, Shiao-ying. 1995. "Where Has All the Capital Gone? The State of Taiwan's Film Investment." *Cinemaya* 30 (autumn): 4–12.

Shih, Shu-mei. 1999. "Gender and a Geopolitical Desire: The Seduction of Main-land Women in Taiwan and Hong Kong Media." In *Spaces of Their Own: Women's Public Sphere in Transnational China*, ed. Mayfair Mei Hui Yang, 278–307. Minneapolis: University of Minnesota Press.

Shu, Kei, ed. 1982. *Cantonese Cinema Retrospective, 1960–69*. Sixth International Film Festival. Hong Kong: Urban Council.

———. 1983. *A Comparative Study of Post-War Mandarin and Cantonese Cinema*. Seventh International Film Festival. Hong Kong: Urban Council.

———. 1996. 1994 *Xianggang Dianying Huigu* [1994 *Retrospective of Hong Kong Films*]. Hong Kong: Hong Kong Critics Society.

———. 1997. 1995 *Xianggang Dianying Huigu* [1995 *Retrospective of Hong Kong Films*]. Hong Kong: Hong Kong Critics Society.

Singer, Michael. 1988. "Chow Must Go On." *Film Comment* 24, no. 3 (June): 46–47.

———. 1998. "John Woo." In *A Cut Above: Fifty Film Directors Talk about Their Craft*, ed. Michael Singer and Leonard Maltin, 321–27. Los Angeles: Lon Eagle.

Sinn, Elizabeth, ed. 1995. *Culture and Society in Hong Kong*. Hong Kong: University of Hong Kong Press.

Smith, R. J. 1995. "The Coolest Actor in the World." *Los Angeles Times Magazine*, 25 March, 10–32.

Stephens, Chuck. 1996. "Time Pieces: Wong Kar-wai and the Persistence of Memory." *Film Comment* 32, no. 1 (January–February): 12–18.

Stockbridge, Sally. 1994. "Sexual Violence and Hong Kong Films: Regulation and Cultural Difference." *Media Information Australia* 74: 86–92.

Stokes, Lisa Odham, and Michael Hoover. 1999a. *City on Fire: Hong Kong Cinema*. London and New York: Verso.

———. 1999b. "Hong Kong to Hollywood." *Cinemaya* 46 (autumn): 37–38.

Stringer, Julian. 1994. "Hong Kong Cinema: Double Marginalization and Cultural Resistance." *Southeast Asian Journal of Social Sciences* 22: 53–71.

———. 1996–97. "Problems with the Treatment of Hong Kong Cinema as Camp." *Asian Cinema* 8, no. 2: 44–65.

———. 1997a. "Reconstructing the Bio-Pic." *CineAction* 42: 28–39.

———. 1997b. "Your Tender Smiles Give Me Strength: Paradigms of Masculinity in John Woo's *A Better Tomorrow* and *The Killer*." *Screen* 38: 25–41.

———. 1998a. "Category 3: Sex and Violence in Postmodern Hong Kong." In *Mythologies of Violence in Postmodern Media*, ed. Christopher Sharret, 361–79. Detroit: Wayne State University Press.

———. 1998b. "Cultural Identity and Diaspora in Contemporary Hong Kong Cinema." In *Asian American Screen Cultures*, ed. Darrell Hamamoto and Sandra Liu, 298–312. Philadelphia: Temple University Press.

Tam, Kwok-kan, and Wimal Dissanayake. 1998. "Stanley Kwan: Narratives of Feminine Anguish." In *New Chinese Cinema*, ed. Tam Kwok-kan and Wimal Dissanayake, 72–82. Oxford: Oxford University Press.

Tan, See Kam. 1993. "The Hongkong Cantonese Vernacular as Cultural Resistance." *Cineyama* 20 (summer): 12–15.

———. 1994. "Hong Kong Cinema: Double Marginalization and Cultural Resistance." *Southeast Asian Journal of Social Sciences* 22: 53–71.

Tateishi, Ramie. 1998. "Jackie Chan and the Reinvention of Tradition." *Asian Cinema* 10, no. 1: 78–84.

Teng, Sue-Feng. 1996. "From Bruce Lee to Jackie Chan: The Kungfu Film Carries On." *Sinorama* (June): 28–35.

Teo, Stephen. 1990. "Hong Kong Cinema: Hearing Asian Voices." In *1990 Hawaii International Film Festival Viewer's Guide*. Honolulu: East-West Center.

———. 1994. "The Hong Kong New Wave: Before and After." *Cinemaya* 23 (spring): 28–32.

———. 1997. *Hong Kong Cinema: The Extra Dimensions*. London: British Film Institute.

———. 2000a. "Hong Kong Cinema: Discovery and Prediscovery." In *World Cinema: Critical Approaches*, ed. John Hill and Pamela Gibson. New York: Oxford University Press.

———. 2000b. "The 1970s: Movement and Transition." In *The Cinema of Hong Kong: History, Arts, Identity*, ed. Poshek Fu and David Desser, 90–110. Cambridge and New York: Cambridge University Press.

Tobias, Mel. 1979. *Flashbacks: Hong Kong Cinema after Bruce Lee*. Hong Kong: Gulliver Books.

———. 1982. *Memoirs of an Asian Moviegoer*. Quarry Bay, Hong Kong: South China Morning Post Limited.

Tsui, Curtis K. 1995. "Subjective Culture and History: The Ethnographic Cinema of Wong Kar-wai." *Asian Cinema* 7, no. 2: 93–124.

Weinraub, Bernard. 1996. "On Location with John Woo: Ballets With Bullets." *New York Times*, 22 February.

Weisser, Thomas. 1994. *Asian Trash Cinema: The Book*. Houston, Tex.: Asian Trash Cinema/European Trash Cinema Publications.

———. 1995. *Asian Trash Cinema: The Book (Part 2)*. Miami, Fla.: Vital Sounds/Asian Trash Cinema Publications.

———. 1997. *Asian Cult Cinema*. New York: Boulevard Books.

Weitzman, Elizabeth. 1998. "Wong Kar-wai: The Director Who Knows All about Falling for the Wrong People." *Interview* 28, no. 2: 46.

Whitmore, Stuart. 1998. "Images of Change." *Asiaweek*, 17 April, 34.

Williams, Tony. 1995. "To Live and Die in Hong Kong: The Crisis Cinema of John Woo." *CineAction* 36: 42–52.

———. 1997a. "John Woo and His Discontents." *CineAction* 42: 42–46.

———. 1997b. "Space, Place and Spectacle: The Crisis Cinema of John Woo." *Cinema Journal* 36, no. 2 (winter): 67–84.

———. 1998a. "Border-Crossing Melodrama: *Song of the Exile* (Ann Hui, 1990)." *Jump Cut* 42: 94–100.

———. 1998b. "Kwan Tak-hing and the New Generation." *Asian Cinema* 10, no. 1: 71–77.

———. 2000. "Hong Kong Cinema, the *Boat People*, and *To Liv(e)*." *Asian Cinema* 11, no. 1: 131–43.

Wong, Cindy Hing-yuk. 1999. "Cities, Cultures and Cassettes: Hong Kong Cinema and Transnational Audiences." *Post Script* 19, no. 1 (fall): 87–106.

Wong, Edward. 1997. "Hong Kong's Final Cut?" *Los Angeles Times*, 15 June.

Wong, Jacob, ed. 1999. *Hong Kong Panorama 98–99*. Twenty-third Hong Kong International Film Festival. Hong Kong: Provisional Urban Council.

———. 2000. *Hong Kong Panorama, 1999–2000*. Twenty-fourth Hong Kong International Film Festival. Hong Kong: Leisure and Cultural Services Department.

Wong, Kar-wai. 1995. "Wong Kar-wai on *Chungking Express*." *Sight and Sound* (September): 14–16.

Wong, Tak-wai, ed. 1996. *Evans Chan's "To Liv(e)": Screenplay and Essays*. Hong Kong: University of Hong Kong, Department of Comparative Literature.

Wood, Miles. 1998. *Cine East: Hong Kong Cinema through the Looking Glass*. Guildford: FAB.

Yau, Esther C. M. 1994. "Border-Crossing: Mainland China's Presence in Hong Kong Cinema." In *New Chinese Cinemas: Forms, Identities, Politics*, ed. Nick Browne et al., 180–201. Cambridge and New York: Cambridge University Press.

———. 1997. "Ecology and Late Colonial Hong Kong Cinema: Imaginations in Time." In *Fifty Years of Electric Shadows*, ed. Law Kar, 100–113. Twenty-first Hong Kong International Film Festival. Hong Kong: Urban Council.

Yeh, Yueh-yu. 1999. "A Life of Its Own: Musical Discourses in Wong Kar-wai's Films." *Post Script* 19, no. 1 (fall): 120–36.

Yeh, Yueh-yu, Cheuk Pak-tong, and Ng Ho. 1999. *Romance of Three Cities: Studies on Chinese Cinemas*. Taipei: National Film Archive.

Yoke, Kong Kam. 1999. "Ann Hui for the Underdogs." *Cinemaya* 45 (summer): 17–19.

Yue, Audrey. 2000. "Preposterous Hong Kong Horror: *Rouge*'s (Be)hindsight and a (Sodomitical) *Chinese Ghost Story*." In *The Horror Reader*, ed. Ken Gelber, 364–73. New York: Routledge.

Zhang, Zhen. 1998. "The 'Shanghai Factor' in Hong Kong Cinema: A Tale of Two Cities in Historical Perspective." *Asian Cinema* 10, no. 1: 146–59.

Zhou, Juanita Huan. 1998. "*Ashes of Time*: The Tragedy and Salvation of the Chinese Intelligentsia." *Asian Cinema* 10, no. 1: 62–70.

Zuni, Icosahedron. 1995. *Xunzhao Xianggang Dianying Zhengce [In Search of Hong Kong Film Policy]*. Hong Kong: Zuni Icosahedron and Hong Kong Arts Development Council (sponsor).

Guides and References

Charles, John. 2000. *The Hong Kong Filmography: A Complete Reference to 1,100 Films Produced by British Hong Kong Studios, 1977 through 1997*. Jefferson, N.C.: McFarland.

Cheng, Ping, ed. 1995. *Zhongguo dianying tuzhi [Illustrated Record of Chinese Film]*. Zhuhai: Zhuhai chubanshe.

Dannen, Fredric, and Barry Long. 1997. *Hong Kong Babylon: An Insider's Guide to the Hollywood of the East*. New York: Hyperion, 1997.

Fu, Winnie. 2000. *Hong Kong Filmography*. Vol. 3, 1950–52. Hong Kong: Hong Kong Film Archive.

———, ed. 1998. *Hong Kong Filmography*. Vol. 2, 1942–1949. Hong Kong: Hong Kong Film Archive and Provisional Urban Council.

Hammond, Stefan, and Mike Wilkins. 1996. *Sex and Zen and a Bullet in the Head: The Essential Guide to Hong Kong's Mind-Bending Films*. New York: Fireside Books.

Julius, Marshall. 1996. *Action!: The Action Movie A–Z*. Bloomington: Indiana University Press.

Lapham, Sijo Art. 1999. *Art Lapham's Official Martial Arts Magazine Reference and Price Guide: 1999 Edition*. Somerset, Mass.: Darkwing.

The Making of Martial Arts Films as Told by Filmmakers and Stars. 1999. Hong Kong: Provisional Urban Council.

Monographs of Hong Kong Film Veterans: Hong Kong Here I Come. 2000. Hong Kong Film Archive Oral History Project. Hong Kong: Hong Kong Film Archive.

Palmer, Bill, Karen Palmer, and Ric Meyers. 1995. *The Encyclopedia of Martial Arts Movies*. Metuchen, N.J.: Scarecrow Press.

Tilston, Lisa, ed. 1994. *The Essential Guide to Hong Kong Movies*. Vol. 1. From materials compiled by Rick Baker and Toby Russell. London: Eastern Heroes.

———. 1995. *The Essential Guide to the Best of Eastern Heroes*. From materials compiled by Rick Baker and Toby Russell. London: Eastern Heroes.

Wong, Mary, ed. 1997. *Hong Kong Filmography, 1913–1941*. Hong Kong: Hong Kong Film Archive and Hong Kong Urban Council.

Zhang, Junxiang, and Cheng Jihua. 1995. *Zhongguo dianying da cidian*. [*Encyclopedia of Chinese Film*]. Shanghai: Shanghai cishu.

Zhang, Yingjin, and Zhiwei Xiao, eds. 1998. *Encyclopedia of Chinese Film*. London and New York: Routledge.

Zhongguo dabaike quanshu: dianying [*The Complete Encyclopedia of China: Film*]. 1991. Beijing: Zhongguo dabaike quanshu.

Zhongguo dianying dadian [*Encyclopedia of Chinese Film*]. 1996–98. 4 vols. Beijing: Zhongguo dianying.

Contributors

JINSOO AN is a doctoral candidate of film critical studies at the School of Theater, Film, and Television at the University of California, Los Angeles. He has contributed articles to Korean journals and is completing his dissertation on Korean melodramatic films of the 1950s and 1960s.

DAVID BORDWELL is Jacques Ledoux Professor of Film Studies in the Department of Communication Arts at the University of Wisconsin, Madison. His books include *Narration in the Fiction Film*, *Ozu and the Poetics of Cinema*, *Making Meaning: Inference and Rhetoric in the Interpretation of Cinema*, and *The Cinema of Eisenstein*.

REY CHOW, a native of Hong Kong, is currently Andrew W. Mellon Professor of the Humanities at Brown University. She is the author of a number of books, including *Primitive Passions: Visuality, Sexuality, Ethnography, and Contemporary Chinese Cinema*, which received the James Russell Lowell Prize from the Modern Language Association. Her more recent work on Chinese and Hong Kong films can be found in journals such as *South Atlantic Quarterly*, *Narrative*, and *Camera Obscura*.

STEVE FORE is associate professor at the School of Creative Media at the City University of Hong Kong. He has published essays on Hong Kong film in the anthology *Transnational Chinese Cinemas* (edited by Sheldon Hsiao-peng Lu), *Velvet Light Trap*, *Journal of Film and Video*, and *Post Script*.

ELAINE YEE-LIN HO is associate professor of English at the University of Hong Kong. She has published articles on Renaissance literature, postcolonial writing, and Hong Kong fiction, and is currently writing a book on the writer Timothy Mo.

LINDA (CHIU-HAN) LAI is assistant professor at the School of Creative Media at the City University of Hong Kong, teaching media and film history and cultural studies. She is also a doctoral candidate in cinema studies, New York University, now working on her dissertation. Her recent essay on Hong Kong cinema in the 1930s was published in the electronic journal *Screening the Past*.

LAW KAR (LAU YIU-KUEN) has been working with the Hong Kong International Film Festival since 1990. He is the programmer of the festival's Hong Kong Cinema Retrospective section and editor of its Hong Kong Cinema Retrospective catalogs. An active researcher in the history of Hong Kong film, he has published five books, including three volumes on Cantonese and Mandarin stars. He is now working on *Hong Kong Cinema, 1897–1997: A Cross-Cultural View*.

KWAI-CHEUNG LO received his Ph.D. in comparative literature at Stanford University. His critical essays on Hong Kong cinema and popular culture have been published in *Polygraph, Modern Chinese Literature, American Journal of Semiotics, Public Culture,* and *Camera Obscura*. Also a writer of poetry and fiction, he has taught literature studies at the University of California, Santa Cruz, and is assistant professor at Hong Kong Baptist University.

GINA MARCHETTI is associate professor in the Department of Cinema and Photography in the Roy H. Park School of Communications at Ithaca College. She is the author of *Romance and the "Yellow Peril": Race, Sex, and Discursive Strategies in Hollywood Fiction*. She has been a senior fellow at the School of Communication Studies at Singapore's Nanyang Technological University.

HECTOR RODRIGUEZ is assistant professor at City University of Hong Kong. He is the author of *Black Rain: A Critical Analysis,* a study of Imamura Shohei's film of the atomic bomb. He has also written various essays and reviews on Asian cinema and film theory.

BHASKAR SARKAR is assistant professor at the University of California, Santa Barbara. He is presently completing his dissertation on the representation of the 1947 partition of India in Indian cinema and on television. He has written essays for *Quarterly Review of Film and Video, Visual Anthropology, Film Criticism,* and *Journal of Postcolonial Studies*.

MARC SIEGEL is a doctoral candidate in critical studies at the Department of Film and Television at the University of California, Los Angeles. He has published essays and reviews about queer theory and experimental film in journals such as *Afterimage*, *CineAction*, and *Jump Cut*, as well as in the anthology *Between the Sheets, In the Streets: Queer, Lesbian, Gay Documentary* (edited by Chris Holmlund and Cynthia Fuchs; Minnesota, 1997).

STEPHEN TEO was born in Malaysia and has worked as a critic and filmmaker in Hong Kong. He is the English editor of the Hong Kong International Film Festival and also of the Hong Kong International Film Festival's Hong Kong Cinema Retrospectives catalogs. He has contributed numerous articles about Hong Kong cinema to regional publications, including *Cinemaya* (India). He is the author of *Hong Kong Cinema: The Extra Dimension*.

ESTHER C. M. YAU is associate professor of film studies at Occidental College. She is coeditor of *New Chinese Cinemas: Forms, Identities, Politics*. Her critical essays on mainland Chinese films have been published in *Film Quarterly*, *Wide Angle Discourse*, *The Oxford History of World Cinema*, *Film Quarterly: Forty Years—A Section*, and *Quarterly Review of Film and Video*.

Index